Corporate Risk Management

2nd Edition

Corporate Risk Management

2nd Edition

Tony Merna and Faisal Al-Thani

John Wiley & Sons, Ltd

Other Wiley Editorial Offices

John Wiley & Sons Inc., 111 River Street, Hoboken, NJ 07030, USA

Jossey-Bass, 989 Market Street, San Francisco, CA 94103-1741, USA

Wiley-VCH Verlag GmbH, Boschstr. 12, D-69469 Weinheim, Germany

John Wiley & Sons Australia Ltd, 42 McDougall Street, Milton, Queensland 4064, Australia

John Wiley & Sons (Asia) Pte Ltd, 2 Clementi Loop #02-01, Jin Xing Distripark, Singapore 129809

John Wiley & Sons Canada Ltd, 6045 Freemont Blvd, Mississauga, ONT, L5R 4J3, Canada

Wiley also publishes its books in a variety of electronic formats. Some content that appears
in print may not be available in electronic books.

A catalogue record for this book is available from the British Library

Library of Congress Cataloging-in-Publication Data

Merna, Tony.
  Corporate risk management / Tony Merna and Faisal Al-Thani. – 2nd ed.
    p. cm.
  Includes bibliographical references and index.
  ISBN 978-0-470-51833-5 (cloth : alk. paper)
  1. Risk management. 2. Corporations—Finance—Management.
  3. Industrial management.
  I. Al-Thani, Faisal F. II. Title.
  HD61.M463 2008
  658.15'5—dc22
                                                            2008004969

Typeset in 11/13pt Times by Aptara Inc., New Delhi, India
Printed and bound in Great Britain by TJ International Ltd, Padstow, Cornwall, UK

Tony Merna – to my loving mother; an inspiration

Faisal Al-Thani – to my family

Contents

1
Introduction

1.1 INTRODUCTION

If you can't manage risk, you can't control it. And if you can't control it you can't manage it. That means you're just gambling and hoping to get lucky.
(J. Hooten, Managing Partner, Arthur Andersen & Co., 2000)

The increasing pace of change, customer demands and market globalisation all put risk management high on the agenda for forward-thinking companies. It is necessary to have a comprehensive risk management strategy to survive in today's market place. In addition, the Cadbury Committee's Report on Corporate Governance (1992) states that having a process in place to identify major business risks as one of the key procedures of an effective control system is paramount. This has since been extended in the Guide for Directors on the Combined Code, published by the Institute of Chartered Accountants (1999). This guide is referred to as the 'Turnbull Report' (1999) for the purposes of this book.

The management of risk is one of the most important issues facing organisations today. High-profile cases such as Barings and Railtrack in the UK, Enron, Adelphia and Worldcom in the USA, and recently Parmalat, demonstrate the consequences of not managing risk properly. For example, organisations which do not fully understand the risks of implementing their strategies are likely to decline. Marconi decided to move into a high-growth area in the telecom sector but failed in two distinct respects. Firstly, growth was by acquisition and Marconi paid premium prices for organisations because of the competitive consolidation within the sector. Secondly, the market values in the telecom sector slumped because the sector was overexposed owing to debt caused by slower growth in sales than expected.

1.2 WHY MANAGING RISK IS IMPORTANT

The Cadbury Report on Corporate Governance Committee Working Party (1992) on how to implement the Cadbury Code requirement for directors to report on the effectiveness of their system of internal control lists the following criteria for assessing effectiveness on the identification and evaluation of risks and control objectives:

- identification of key business risks in a timely manner
- consideration of the likelihood of risks crystallising and the significance of the consequent financial impact on the business
- establishment of priorities for the allocation of resources available for control and the setting and communicating of clear control objectives.

The London Stock Exchange requires every listed company to include a statement in its annual report confirming that it is complying with this code, or by providing details of any areas of non-compliance. This has since been re-enforced and extended by the Turnbull Report (1999). The Sarbanes-Oxley Act (2002) is similar to the Turnbull Report. This Act introduced highly significant legislative changes to financial practice and corporate governance regulation in the USA. The Act requires chief executive officers (CEOs) and group financial directors (GFDs) of foreign private registrants to make specific certifications in annual reports.

In today's climate of rapid change people are less likely to recognise the unusual, the decision-making time frame is often smaller, and scarce resources often aggravate the effect of unmanaged risk. The pace of change also means that the risks facing an organisation change constantly (time related). Therefore the management of risk is not a static process but a dynamic process of identification and mitigation that should be regularly reviewed.

1.3   GENERAL DEFINITION OF RISK MANAGEMENT

The art of risk management is to identify risks specific to an organisation and to respond to them in an appropriate way. Risk management is a formal process that enables the identification, assessment, planning and management of risks.

All levels of an organisation need to be included in the management of risk in order for it to be effective. These levels are usually termed corporate (policy setting), strategic business (the lines of business) and project. Risk management needs to take into consideration the interaction of these levels and reflect the processes that permit these levels to communicate and learn from each other.

The aim of risk management is therefore threefold. It must identify risk, undertake an objective analysis of risks specific to the organisation, and respond to the risks in an appropriate and effective manner. These stages include being able to assess the prevailing environment (both internal and external) and to assess how any changes to that prevailing environment would impact on a project in hand or on a portfolio of projects.

1.4   BACKGROUND AND STRUCTURE

This book provides background knowledge about risk management and its functions at each level within an organisation, namely the corporate, strategic business and project levels.

Figure 1.1 illustrates a typical organisational structure which allows risk management to be focused at different levels. By classifying and categorising risk within these levels it is possible to drill down and roll up to any level of the organisational structure. This should establish which risks a project is most sensitive to so that appropriate risk response strategies may be implemented to benefit all stakeholders.

Figure 1.1 illustrates the corporate, strategic business and project levels which provide the foundation for this book. Risk management is seen to be integral to each level although the flow of information from level to level is not necessarily on a top-down or bottom-up basis. Merna and Merna (2004) believe risks identified at each level are dependent on the information available at the time of the assessment, with each risk being assessed in more detail as more information becomes available. In effect, the impact of risk is time related.

Figure 1.2 illustrates the possible outcomes of risk. The word 'risk' is often perceived in a negative way. However, managed in the correct way, prevailing risks can often have a positive impact.

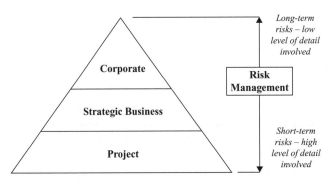

Figure 1.1   Levels within a corporate organisation (Merna 2003)

Figure 1.2   Relationship of risk to possible losses and gains

Risk management should consider not only the threats (possible losses) but also the opportunities (possible gains). It is important to note that losses or gains can be made at each level of an organisation.

1.5   AIM

The aim of this book is to analyse, compare and contrast tools and techniques used in risk management at corporate, strategic business and project levels and develop a risk management mechanism for the sequencing of risk assessment through corporate, strategic business and project stages of an investment.

Typical risks affecting organisations are discussed and risk modelling through computer simulation is explained.

The book also examines portfolio risk management and cash flow management.

1.6   SCOPE OF THE BOOK

Chapter 2 discusses the concept of risk and uncertainty in terms of projects and investments. It then outlines the sources and types of risk that can affect each level of an organisation.

Chapter 3 is a general introduction to the topic of risk management. It summarises the history of risk management and provides definitions of risk and uncertainty. It also describes the risk process, in terms of identification, analysis and response. It then goes on to identify the tasks and benefits of risk management, the risk management plan and the typical stakeholders involved in an investment or project.

Chapter 4 is concerned with the tools and techniques used within risk management. It prioritises the techniques into two categories, namely qualitative and quantitative techniques, and describes how such techniques are implemented. It also provides the elements for carrying out a country risk analysis and briefly describes the risks associated with investing in different countries.

Chapter 5 outlines the risks involved in financing projects and the different ways of managing them. The advantages and disadvantages of risk modelling are discussed, and different types of risk software described.

Chapter 6 is concerned with portfolios and the strategies involved in portfolio selection. Bundling projects is examined and cash flows specific to portfolios are analysed. Various methods of cash flow analyses are discussed.

Chapter 7 is specific to the corporate level within an organisation. It is concerned with the history of the corporation, corporate structure, corporate management and the legal obligations of the board of directors, corporate strategy and, primarily, corporate risk.

Chapter 8 is specific to the strategic business level within an organisation. It discusses business formation, and defines the strategic business unit (SBU). It is primarily concerned with strategic management functions, strategic planning and models used within this level. Risks specific to this level are also identified.

Chapter 9 is specific to the project level within an organisation. It outlines the history of project management, its functions, project strategy and risks specific to the project level.

Chapter 10 provides a generic mechanism for the sequence and flow of risk assessment in terms of identification, analysis and response to risk at corporate, strategic business and project levels.

Chapter 11 describes a number of corporate governance codes and how they address the need for risk management.

Chapter 12 introduces the Basel II framework and discusses, in particular, how probability default (PD) and loss given default (LGD) are addressed and other operational management issues.

Chapter 13 describes how quality management can be used to manage many of the risks inherent in organisations and how quality related risks can affect the profitability of an investment.

Chapter 14 provides Case Study 1 which investigates the pharmaceutical industry and illustrates the typical risks in a drug development process (DDP) and how many of these risks can be mitigated.

Chapter 15 provides Case Study 2 which shows the risks associated with the procurement of crude oil and the sale of refined products. This case study also addresses the risks in the supply and offtake contracts and utilises Crystal Ball as the simulation software for modelling and assessment of risks.

Chapter 16 provides Case Study 3 which describes the development of risk registers at corporate, strategic business unit and project levels and the development of a risk statement for a specific project.

The final chapter, Chapter 17, provides Case Study 4 which describes how the major risks at each level of a corporation can be identified and quantitatively analysed and then summarised to develop a risk statement for shareholders.

2

The Concept of Risk and Uncertainty and the Sources and Types of Risk

Man plans, God smiles

(Hebrew proverb)

Fortune favours the prepared

(Louis Pasteur)

2.1 INTRODUCTION

Risk affects every aspect of human life; we live with it every day and learn to manage its influence on our lives. In most cases this is done as an unstructured activity, based on common sense, relevant knowledge, experience and instinct.

This chapter outlines the basic concept of risk and uncertainty and provides a number of definitions of them. It also discusses the dimensions of risk and the perception of risk throughout an organisation. Different sources and types of risk are also discussed.

2.2 BACKGROUND

Uncertainty affects all investments. However, uncertainty can often be considered in terms of probability provided sufficient information is known about the uncertainty. Probability is based on the occurrence of any event and thus must have an effect on the outcome of that event. The effect can be determined on the basis of the cause and description of an occurrence. For example, the cause, description and effect can be illustrated by the following:

'Crossing the road without looking' will most likely result in *'injury'*.

Figure 2.1 illustrates the concept of risk in terms of uncertainty, probability, effect and outcome.

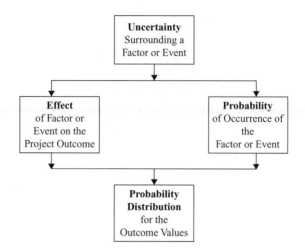

Figure 2.1   The concept of risk (Merna and Smith 1996) (Reproduced by permission of A. Merna)

Once the probability, cause and effect of an occurrence can be determined then a probability distribution can be computed. From this probability distribution, over a range of possibilities, the chances of risk occurring can be determined, thus reducing the uncertainty associated with this event.

The authors suggest that uncertainty can often be interpreted as prophecy, since a prophecy is not based on data or experience. A prediction, however, is normally based on data or past experience and thus offers a basis for potential risk.

2.3   RISK AND UNCERTAINTY: BASIC CONCEPTS AND GENERAL PRINCIPLES

According to Chapman and Ward (1997):

All projects involve risk – the zero risk project is not worth pursuing. Organisations which better understand the nature of these risks and can manage them more effectively can not only avoid unforeseen disasters but can work with tighter margins and less contingency, freeing resources for other endeavours, and seizing opportunities for advantageous investment which might otherwise be rejected as too risky.

Risk and uncertainty are distinguished by both Bussey (1978) and Merrett and Sykes (1983) as:

A decision is said to be subject to risk when there is a range of possible outcomes and when known probabilities can be attached to the outcome.

Uncertainty exists when there is more than one possible outcome to a course of action but the probability of each outcome is not known.

In today's business, nearly all decisions are taken purely on a financial consequences basis. Business leaders need to understand and know whether the returns on a project justify taking risks, and the extent of these consequences (losses) if the risks do materialise. Investors, on the other hand, need some indication of whether the returns on an investment meet their minimum returns if the investment is fully exposed to the risks identified. (Merna 2002) suggests:

we are at a unique point in the market where players are starting to recognise that risks need to be quantified and that information about these projects needs to be made available to all participants in the transaction.

Therefore identifying risks and quantifying them in relation to the returns of a project is important. By knowing the full extent of their gains and/or losses, business leaders and investors can then decide whether to sanction or cancel an investment or project.

2.4 THE ORIGIN OF RISK

The origin of the word 'risk' is thought to be either the Arabic word *risq* or the Latin word *riscum* (Kedar 1970). The Arabic *risq* signifies 'anything that has been given to you [by God] and from which you draw profit' and has connotations of a fortuitous and favourable outcome. The Latin *riscum,* however, originally referred to the challenge that a barrier reef presents to a sailor and clearly has connotations of an equally fortuitous but unfavourable event.

A Greek derivative of the Arabic word *risq* which was used in the twelfth century would appear to relate to chance of outcomes in general and have neither positive nor negative implications (Kedar 1970). The modern French word *risqué* has mainly negative but occasionally positive connotations, as for example in *'qui de risque rien n'a rien'* or 'nothing ventured nothing gained', whilst in common English usage the word 'risk' has very definite negative associations as in 'run the risk' or 'at risk', meaning exposed to danger.

The word 'risk' entered the English language in the mid seventeenth century, derived from the word 'risque'. In the second quarter of the eighteenth century the anglicised spelling began to appear in insurance transactions (Flanagan and Norman 1993). Over time and in common usage the meaning of the word has changed from one of simply describing any unintended or unexpected outcome, good or bad, of a decision or course of action to one which relates to undesirable outcomes and the chance of their occurrence (Wharton 1992). In the more scientific and specialised literature on the subject, the word 'risk' is used to imply a measurement of the chance of an outcome, the size of the outcome or a combination of both. There have been several attempts to incorporate the idea of both size and chance of an outcome in the one definition. To many organisations risk is a four-letter word that they try insulate themselves from.

Rowe (1977) defines risk as 'The potential for unwanted negative consequences of an event or activity' whilst many authors define risk as 'A measure of the probability and the severity of adverse effects'. Rescher (1983) explains that 'Risk is the chancing of a negative outcome. To measure risk we must accordingly measure both its defining components, and the chance of negativity'. The way in which these measurements must be combined is described by Gratt (1987) as 'estimation of risk is usually based on the expected result of the conditional probability of the event occurring times the consequences of the event given that it has occurred'.

It follows then that in the context of, for example, a potential disaster, the word 'risk' might be used either as a measure of the magnitude of the unintended outcome, say, 2000 deaths, or as the probability of its occurrence, say, 1 in 1000 or even the product of the two – a statistical expectation of two deaths (Wharton 1992). Over time a number of different, sometimes conflicting and more recently rather complex meanings have been attributed to the word 'risk'. It is unfortunate that a simple definition closely relating to the medieval Greek interpretation has not prevailed – one which avoids any connotation of a favourable or unfavourable outcome or the probability or size of the event.

The model shown in Figure 2.2 suggests that risk is composed of four essential parameters: probability of occurrence, severity of impact, susceptibility to change and degree of interdependency with other factors of risks. Without any of these the situation or event cannot truly be considered a risk. This model can be used to describe risk situations or events in the modelling of any investments for risk analysis.

The use of a risk model helps reduce reliance upon raw judgement and intuition. The inputs to the model are provided by humans, but the brain is given a system on which to operate (Flanagan and Norman 1993).

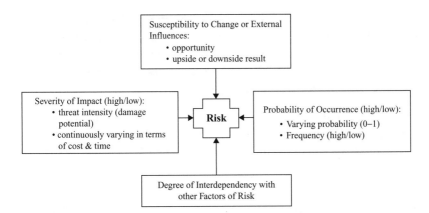

Figure 2.2 Typical risk parameters (Adapted from Allen 1995)

Models provide a backup for our unreliable intuition. A model can be thought of as having two roles:

1. It produces an answer.
2. It acts as a vehicle for communication, bringing out factors that might not be otherwise considered.

Models provide a mechanism by which risks can be communicated through the system. A risk management system is a model, it provides a means for identification, classification and analysis and then a response to risk.

2.4.1 Dimensions of Risk

A common definition of risk – the likelihood of something undesirable happening in a given time – is conceptually simple but difficult to apply. It provides no clues to the overall context and how risks might be perceived. Most people think of risk in terms of three components: something bad happening, the chances of it happening, and the consequences if it does happen. These three components of risk can be used as the basis of a structure for risk assessment. Kaplan and Gerrick (1981) proposed a triplet for recording risks which includes a set of scenarios or similar occurrences (something bad happens), the probabilities that the occurrences take place (the chances something bad happens), and the consequence measures associated with the occurrences.

In some ways, this structure begs the question of definition because it is still left to the risk assessors to determine what 'bad' actually means, what the scenarios or occurrences are that can lead to something bad, and how to measure the severity of the results. The steps involved in defining and measuring risk include:

1. Defining 'bad' by identifying the objectives of an organisation and the resources that are threatened.
2. Identifying scenarios whose occurrence can threaten the resources of value.
3. Measure the severity or magnitude of impacts.

The severity or magnitude of consequences is measured by a value function that provides the common denominator. The severity can be measured in common units across all the dimensions of risk by translating the impact into a common unit of value. This can be a dimensionless unit such as the utility functions used in economics and decision analysis or some common economic term (Kolluru *et al.* 1996).

The issue here is selecting an appropriate metric for measuring impacts and then determining the form of the effects function. This form has to be capable of representing risk for diverse stakeholders and of expressing the impacts to health, safety and the environment as well as other assets.

One response, still surprisingly common, is to shy away from risk and hope for the best. Another is to apply expert judgement, experience and gut feel to the problem. In spite of this, substantial investments are decided on the basis of judgement alone, with little or nothing to back them up.

2.5   UNCERTAINTIES

Risk and uncertainty as distinguished by both Bussey (1978) and Merrett and Sykes (1973) were discussed earlier in this chapter. The authors Vernon (1981) and Diekmann *et al.* (1988), however, consider that the terms risk and uncertainty may be used interchangeably but have somewhat different meanings, where risk refers to statistically predictable occurrences and uncertainty to an unknown of generally unpredictable variability.

Lifson and Shaifer (1982) combine the two terms by defining risk as:

The uncertainty associated with estimates of outcomes.

Uncertainty is used to describe the situation when it is not possible to attach a probability to the likelihood of occurrence of an event. Uncertainty causes a rift between good decision and good outcome. The distinguishing factor between risk and uncertainty is that risk is taken to have quantifiable attributes, and a place in the calculus of probabilities, whereas uncertainty does not (Finkel 1990).

Hetland (2003) believes the following assertions clarify uncertainty:

- Risk is an implication of a phenomenon being uncertain.
- Implications of a phenomenon being uncertain may be wanted or unwanted.
- Uncertainties and their implications need to be understood to be managed properly.

Smith *et al.* (2006) suggest that risks fall in to three categories: known risks, known unknowns and unknown unknowns.

Known risks include minor variations in productivity and swings in materials costs and inevitably occur in construction and manufacturing projects. These are usually covered by contingency sums to cover for additional work or delay, often in the form of a percentage addition to the estimated cost.

Known unknowns are the risk events whose occurrence is predictable or foreseeable with either their probability of occurrence or likely effect known. A novel example of this is as follows. An automobile breaker's yard in a borough of New York has the following sign on its gate.

These premises are protected by teams of Rottweiler and Doberman pinscher three nights a week. You guess the nights.

A potential felon can deduce from this sign that there is a 3/7 chance of being confronted by the dogs, and possibly being mauleds and a 4/7 chance of success. Therefore there is a better chance of not being caught than being caught, however, without any data regarding the respective nights – you guess the nights.

Unknown unknowns are those events whose probabilities of occurrence and effect are not foreseeable by even the most experienced practitioners. These are often considered as force majeure events. An example of unknown unknowns is common in the pharmaceuticals industry. In the first stage of a drug development process the side effects and their probabilities are unknown although it is known that all drugs have side effects.

Uncertainty is said to exist in situations where decision-makers lack complete knowledge, information or understanding concerning the proposed decision and its possible consequences. There are two types of uncertainties: uncertainty arising from a situation of pure chance, which is known as 'aleatory uncertainty'; and uncertainty arising from a problem situation where the resolution will depend upon the exercise of judgement, which is known as 'epistemic uncertainty'.

An example of aleatory risk is the discovery of the drug Viagra. Although this drug was initially being developed as a treatment for angina it was found during clinical trials that the drug had side effects which could help prevent sexual dysfunctional syndrome in males.

The situations of uncertainty often encountered during the earlier stages of a project are 'epistemic'. The phenomenon of epistemic uncertainty can be brought about by a number of factors, such as:

- lack of clarity in structuring the problem
- inability to identify alternative solutions to the situation
- the amount and quality of the information available
- futuristic nature of decision making
- objectives to be satisfied within decision making
- level of confidence concerning the post-decision stage of implementation
- the amount of time available
- personal qualities of the decision-maker.

Many of the above factors have been encountered in private finance initiative (PFI) types of investments where risk assessments are required to consider events over long operation periods once a project has been commissioned, in some cases 25 years or more. Rowe (1977) distinguished uncertainty within the decision-making process as descriptive uncertainty and measurement uncertainty. Descriptive uncertainties represent an absence of information and this prevents the full identification of the variables that explicitly define a system. As a result, the decision-maker is unable to describe fully the degrees of freedom of a system, for example problem identification and structuring, solution identification, degree of clarity in the specification of objectives and constraints.

Measurement uncertainties also represent the absence of information; however, these relate to the specifications of the values to be assigned to each variable in a system. As a result the decision-maker is unable to measure or assign specific values to the variables comprising a system,

Table 2.1   Risk–uncertainty continuum (Adapted from Rafferty 1994)

RISK		UNCERTAINTY
Quantifiable	→	Non-quantifiable
Statistical Assessment	→	Subjective Probability
Hard Data	→	Informed Opinion

for example the factors of information quality, the futurity of decisions, the likely effectiveness of implementation.

The need to manage uncertainty is inherent in most projects which require formal project management. Chapman and Ward (1997) consider the following illustrative definition of such a project:

> *An endeavour in which human, material and financial resources are organised in a novel way, to undertake a unique scope of work of given specification, within constraints of cost and time, so as to achieve unitary, beneficial change, through the delivery of quantified and qualitative objectives.*

This definition highlights the one-off, change-inducing nature of projects, the need to organise a variety of resources under significant constraints, and the central role of objectives in project definition. It also suggests inherent uncertainty which requires attention as part of an effective project management process.

The roots of this uncertainty are worth clarification. Careful attention to formal risk management processes is usually motivated by the large-scale use of new and untried technology while executing major projects, and other obvious sources of significant risk.

A broad definition of project risk is 'the implications of the existence of significant uncertainty about the level of project performance achievable' (Chapman and Ward 1997).

Uncertainty attached to a high-risk impact event represents a greater unknown than a quantified risk attached to the same event. Rafferty (1994) developed a 'risk–uncertainty continuum' as given in Table 2.1.

2.6   SOURCES OF RISK

There are many sources of risk that an organisation must take into account before a decision is made. It is therefore important that these sources of risk are available, thus allowing the necessary identification, analysis and response to take place. Many of the sources of risk summarised in Table 2.2 occur at different times over an investment. Risks may be specific to the corporate level, such as political, financial and

Table 2.2   Typical sources of risk to business from projects (Merna and Smith 1996)

Heading	Change and uncertainty in or due to:
Political	Government policy, public opinion, change in ideology, dogma, legislation, disorder (war, terrorism, riots)
Environmental	Contaminated land or pollution liability, nuisance (e.g., noise), permissions, public opinion, internal/corporate policy, environmental law or regulations or practice or 'impact' requirements
Planning	Permission requirements, policy and practice, land use, socio-economic impacts, public opinion
Market	Demand (forecasts), competition, obsolescence, customer satisfaction, fashion
Economic	Treasury policy, taxation, cost inflation, interest rates, exchange rates
Financial	Bankruptcy, margins, insurance, risk share
Natural	Unforeseen ground conditions, weather, earthquake, fire or explosion, archaeological discovery
Project	Definition, procurement strategy, performance requirements, standards, leadership, organisation (maturity, commitment, competence and experience), planning and quality control, programme, labour and resources, communications and culture
Technical	Design adequacy, operational efficiency, reliability
Regulatory	Changes by regulator
Human	Error, incompetence, ignorance, tiredness, communication ability, culture, work in the dark or at night
Criminal	Lack of security, vandalism, theft, fraud, corruption
Safety	Regulations (e.g., CDM, Health and Safety at Work), hazardous substances (COSSH), collisions, collapse, flooding, fire and explosion
Legal	Those associated with changes in legislation, both in the UK and from EU directives
The above list is extensive but not complete	

Reproduced by permission of A. Merna

legal risks. At the strategic business level, economic, natural and market risks may need to be assessed before a project is sanctioned. Project risks may be specific to a project, such as technical, health and safety, operational and quality risks. At the project level, however, the project manager should be confident that risks associated with corporate and strategic business functions are fully assessed and managed. In many business cases risks assessed initially at corporate and strategic business levels have to be reassessed as the project progresses, since the risks may affect the ongoing project.

A source of risk is any factor that can affect project or business performance, and risk arises when this effect is both uncertain and significant in its impact on project or business performance. It follows that the definition of project objectives and performance criteria has a fundamental influence on the level of project risk. Setting tight cost or time targets with insufficient resources makes a project more cost and time risky by definition, since achievement of targets is more uncertain if targets are 'tight'. Conversely, setting slack time or quality requirements implies low time or quality risk.

However, inappropriate targets are themselves a source of risk, and the failure to acknowledge the need for a minimum level of performance against certain criteria automatically generates risk on those dimensions. If, for example, a corporate entity sets unachievable targets to an SBU then it is highly likely that the projects undertaken by the SBU will suffer owing to the risk associated with meeting such targets.

Morris and Hough (1987) argue for the importance of setting clear objectives and performance criteria which reflect the requirements of various parties, including stakeholders who are not always recognised as players (regulatory authorities, for example). The different project objectives held by interested parties and stakeholders and the interdependencies between different objectives need to be appreciated. Strategies for managing risk cannot be divorced from strategies for managing or accomplishing project objectives.

Whatever the underlying performance objectives, the focus on project success and uncertainty about achieving it leads to risk being defined in terms of a 'threat to success'. If success for a project, and in turn the SBU, is measured solely in terms of realised cost relative to some target or commitment, then risk might be defined in terms of the threat to success posed by a given plan in terms of the size of possible cost overruns and their likelihood. This might be termed 'threat intensity' (Chapman and Ward 1997).

From this perspective it is a natural step to regard risk management as essentially about removing or reducing the possibility of underperformance. This is unfortunate, since it results in a very limited appreciation of project risk. Often it can be just as important to appreciate the positive side of uncertainty, which may present opportunities rather than threats.

On occasion opportunities may also be very important from the point of view of morale. High morale is as central to good risk management as it is to the management of teams in general. If a project team becomes immersed in nothing but threats, the ensuing doom and gloom can destroy the project. Systematic searches for opportunities, and a management willing to respond to opportunities identified by those working for them at all levels (which may have implications well beyond the remit of the discoverer), can provide the basis for systematic building of morale.

More generally, it is important to appreciate that project risk by its nature is a very complex beast with important behavioural implications. Simplistic definitions such as 'risk is the probability of a downside risk event multiplied by its impact' may have their value in special circumstances, but it is important to face the complexity of what project risk management is really about if real achievement is to be attained when attempting to manage that risk at any level in the organisation.

2.7 TYPICAL RISKS

2.7.1 Project Risks

The requirement is not only to manage the physical risks of the project, but also to make sure that other parties in the project manage their own risks. For example, the International Finance Corporation (IFC) division of the World Bank has a project team which travels round the locations in which the IFC has an interest and ensures not only that risks are controlled effectively, but that responsibilities are allocated and risks transferred by contract or insurance as appropriate. In this example the IFC would be similar to the corporate entity checking on its various projects undertaken by SBUs.

Risk and uncertainty are inherent to all projects and investors in projects or commercial assets are exposed to risks throughout the life of the project. The risk exposure of an engineering project, for example, is proportional to the magnitude of both the existing and the proposed investment. Generally, the post-sanction period up to the completion of construction is associated with rapid and intensive expenditure (cash burn) for the investor(s), usually under conditions of uncertainty, and consequently this stage of the process is particularly sensitive to risks. The subsequent operational phase is subject to risks associated with revenue generation and operational costs. Hence the two phases that are most susceptible to risk are:

1. the implementation stage (pre-completion) – relative to construction risks
2. the operational phase (post-completion) – relative to operational risks, the first few years of operation having the highest degree of susceptibility.

The most severe risks affecting projects are summarised by Thompson and Perry (1992) in project management terms as:

- failure to keep within cost estimate
- failure to achieve the required completion date
- failure to achieve the required quality and operational requirements.

Many project management practitioners suggest the following influence the risk associated with projects:

- project size
- technology maturity (the incorporation of novel methods, techniques, materials)
- project structural complexity.

In effect the larger the project the greater the risk. Increase in size usually means an increase in complexity, including the complexity of administration, management, communication amongst participants and so on; for example, inaccurate forecasts, late deliveries (supply chain), equipment break downs and the like.

Figure 2.3 illustrates the financial risk timeline. The maximum point of financial risk is when the project is near completion when debt service is at its highest. As the project moves through its life cycle and starts to generate regular revenues, the financial exposure is reduced considerably.

The risks which influence projects can also be categorised as global and elemental risks.

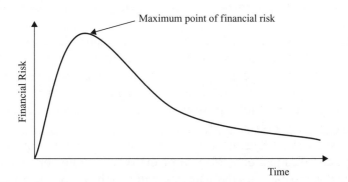

Figure 2.3   Financial risk timeline

2.7.2   Global Risks

Global risks originate from sources external to the project environment and although they are usually predictable their effect on the outcome may not always be controllable within the elements of the project. The four major global risks are political, legal, commercial and environmental risks (Merna and Smith 1996). These types of risk are often referred to as uncontrollable risks since the corporate entity cannot control such risks even though there is a high probability of occurrence. Normally these risks are dealt with at corporate level and often determine whether a project will be sanctioned.

2.7.3   Elemental Risks

Elemental risks originate from sources within the project environment and are usually controllable within the elements of the project. The four main elemental risks are construction/manufacture, operational, financial and revenue risks (Merna and Smith 1996). These types of risk are usually considered as controllable risks and are often related to the different phases of a project and mainly assessed at SBU and project levels.

2.7.4   Holistic Risk

Many organisations have developed risk management mechanisms to deal with the overt and insurable risks associated with projects. In most cases risk identification, analysis and response are seen to be the most important elements to satisfy clients and other project stake-holders.

There are, however, risks associated with intangible assets such as market share, reputation, value, technology, intellectual property (usually data, patents and copyrights), changes in strategy/methods, shareholder perception, company safety and quality of product. These are extremely important for organisations operating a portfolio of projects or business assets (Davies 2000).

Holistic risk management is the process by which an organisation firstly identifies and quantifies all of the threats to its objectives, and having done so manages those threats within, or by adapting, its existing management structure. Holistic risk management addresses many of the elements identified in the Turnbull Report (1999), and attempts to alleviate many of the concerns of shareholders.

2.7.5 Static Risk

This relates only to potential losses where people are concerned with minimising losses by risk aversion (Flanagan and Norman 1993). A typical example would be the risk of losing markets for a particular product or brand of goods by not risking the introduction of new products or goods onto the same market. Many established organisations have tried to mitigate this risk by entering into joint ventures with more dynamic companies, often from booming economies.

2.7.6 Dynamic Risk

This is concerned with maximising opportunities. Dynamic risk means that there will be potential gains as well as potential losses. For example, Marconi tried to gain by changing from a well-established market in the defence industry to new uncertain markets in the telecom industry. Dynamic risk is risking the loss of something certain for the gain of something uncertain. Every management decision has the element of dynamic risk governed only by the practical rules of risk taking. During a project, losses and gains resulting from risk can be plotted against each other and compared (Flanagan and Norman 1993).

2.7.7 Inherent Risk

The way in which risk is handled depends on the nature of the business and the way that business is organised internally. For example, energy companies are engaged in an inherently risky business – the threat of fire and explosion is always present, as is the risk of environmental impairment. Financial institutions on the other hand have an inherently lower risk of fire and explosion than an oil company, but they are exposed to different sorts of risk. However, the level of attention given to managing risk in an industry is as important as the actual risk inherent in the operations which necessarily must be performed in that industry activity. For example, until very recently repetitive strain injury (RSI) was not considered to be a problem, but it is now affecting employers' liability insurance (*International Journal of Project and Business Risk Management* 1998).

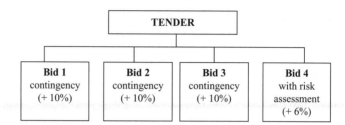

Figure 2.4   The effective bid process

2.7.8   Contingent Risk

This occurs when an organisation is affected directly by an event in an area beyond its direct control but on which it has a dependency, such as weak suppliers (*International Journal of Project and Business Risk Management* 1998). Normally a percentage of the overall project value is put aside to cover costs of meeting such risks should they occur.

The problem with assigning a contingency sum arises when such a sum is assigned to every supplier, irrespective of whether supply is considered as a risk.

Figure 2.4 illustrates how organisations bidding for a tender simply apply a 10% risk contingency. However, organisations may lose out to competitors assessing supplier risk for each individual supplier. In the example above it is no surprise to find that Bid 4 won the tender.

Hussain (2005) proposes that all bids should be accompanied by a risk envelope so that clients can assess the risks identified by each bidder to determine potential additional costs or savings. The risk envelope is developed on the basis of:

- analysis of each risk based on its probability of occurring
- analysis of each risk for its impact on the project should it actually occur
- a priority rating of the overall importance of each risk
- a set of preventive actions to reduce the likelihood of the risks occurring
- a set of contingent actions to reduce the impact should the risk eventuate.

The risk envelope can be used by clients to identify worst case scenarios and help in realising a realistic budget. The cost of managing each risk identified by bidders can be compared by the client in a similar way to that for other items identified in the bid such as the cost of concrete, falsework, excavation and the like. Hussain (2005) suggests that the risk envelope should form an essential part of the bid award process.

2.7.9 Customer Risk

Dependency on one client creates vulnerability because that client can take its business away, or be taken over by a rival. The risk can be managed by creating a larger customer base (*International Journal of Project and Business Risk Management* 1998).

2.7.10 Fiscal/Regulatory Risk

Only by keeping abreast of potential changes in the environment can a business expect to manage these risks. Recent examples in the UK include awards to women for discrimination in the armed forces, RSI and windfall profits tax in exceptional years (*International Journal of Project Business Risk Management* 1998). In October 2001, Railtrack Plc, a company listed on the London Stock Exchange, was put into administration by the UK Transport Secretary without any consultation with its lenders or shareholders. Shareholders taking the usual risks of rises and falls in stock market value were quickly made aware of this risk.

2.7.11 Purchasing Risk

Purchasing risk is a vital part of modern commercial reality but recently the subject has gained prominence in the work of leading academics and management theoreticians. Many businesses are designing and implementing new performance measurement systems and finding a particular challenge in developing measures for some key elements of purchasing contribution which are now regarded as strategic but which have not been historically analysed and measured in any serious way. The area of commercial risk is a prominent example of such a challenge. In the past, effective risk management has been cited as one of the key contributions that effective purchasing can make to a business, but its treatment has been largely a negative one; the emphasis has been on ensuring minimum standards from suppliers to ensure a contract would not be frustrated. The issues now being addressed by leading-edge practitioners in the risk area are much broader and are perhaps more correctly identified using terminology such as management of uncertainty (*International Journal of Project Business Risk Management* 1998).

2.7.12   Reputation/Damage Risk

This is not a risk in its own right but rather the consequence of another risk, such as fraud, a building destroyed, failure to attend to complaints, lack of respect for others. It is the absence of control which causes much of the damage rather than the event itself. In a post-disaster situation a company can come out positively if the media are well handled (*International Journal of Project Business Risk Management* 1998).

2.7.13   Organisational Risk

A poor infrastructure can result in weak controls and poor communications with a variety of impacts on the business. Good commu-nication links will lead to effective risk management. This can only be performed if members of teams and departments are fully aware of their responsibilities and reporting hierarchy, especially between different organisational levels.

2.7.14   Interpretation Risk

This occurs where management and staff in the same organisation cannot communicate effectively because of their own professional language (jargon). Engineers, academics, chemists and bankers all have their own terms, and insurers are probably the worst culprits, using words with common meanings but in a specialised way. Even the same words in the same profession can have different meanings in the UK and the USA.

2.7.15   IT Risk

The IT industry is one of the fastest growing industries at present. Huge amounts of money continue to be invested in the IT industry. Owing to pressures to maintain a competitive edge in a dynamic environment, an organisation's success depends on effectively developing and adopting IT. IT projects, however, still suffer high failure rates (Ellis *et al.* 2002).

IS (information software) development is a key factor which must be considered. Smith (1999) identifies a number of software risks. These include personal shortfalls, unachievable schedules and budget, developing the wrong functions, wrong user interface, a continuing stream of changes in requirements, shortfalls in externally furnished components, shortfalls in externally performed tasks, performance shortfalls and strained technical capabilities. In addition, Jiang and Klein (2001) cite the dimension of project risk based on project size, experience in the technology, technical application and complexity.

Software risks which are regularly identified include:

- project size
- unclear misunderstood objectives
- lack of senior management commitment
- failure to gain user involvement
- unrealistic schedule
- inadequate knowledge/skills
- misunderstood requirements
- wrong software functions
- software introduction
- failure to manage end user expectation.

2.7.16   The OPEC Risk

OPEC was founded at the Baghdad Conference on September 1960, by Iran, Iraq, Kuwait, Saudi Arabia and Venezuela. The five founding members were later joined by nine other members: Qatar, Indonesia, Socialist Peoples Libyan Arab Jamahiriya, United Arab Emirates, Algeria, Nigeria, Ecuador, Gabon and Angola. OPEC's member countries hold about two-thirds of the world's oil reserves. In 2005, OPEC accounted for c. 41.75% of the world's oil production, compared with 23.8% by Organisation for Economic Co-operation and Development (OECD) members and 14.8% by the former Soviet Union. OPEC member countries have, on a number of occasions, tried to adjust their crude oil supplies to improve the balance between supply and demand. OPEC's mission is to coordinate and unify the petroleum policies of member countries and ensure stabilisation of oil prices. OPEC has, however, had mixed success at controlling prices.

OPEC first sent shock waves throughout the world economy in 1973 by announcing a 70% rise in oil prices and by cutting production. The effects were immediate, resulting in fuel shortages and high inflation in many parts of the world. This brief example illustrates that risks associated with the oil price cannot be dismissed at any time when assessing the economic viability of an investment (Merna and Njiru 2002).

From 1982 to 1985 OPEC attempted to set production quotas low enough to stabilise prices. These attempts met with repeated failures as various members of OPEC produced beyond their quotas. During most of this period Saudi Arabia acted as the swing producer cutting its production to stem free falling prices. In August of 1985, the Saudis tired of this role. They linked their prices to the spot market for crude and by early 1986 increased production from 2 million barrels per day (MMBPD) to 5 MMBPD. Crude oil prices plummeted below $10 per barrel by mid-1986.

During the Gulf War, the United Nations announced a trade embargo against Iraq. The squeeze on the market strengthened OPEC's position. In 1997, OPEC raised production by 10% without taking account of the Asian crisis. As a result, prices fell by 40%, to $10 per barrel. OPEC reacted to the global economic crisis, which had caused the price of oil to fall below $20 per barrel, by reducing production for six months in the hope of forcing it up in 2002. Increasing oil demand in the US, China and India sent the price soaring to a historic high of more than $50 per barrel. It reached $70 in April 2006.

At the time of writing this book, oil prices have risen to approximately $93 per barrel (Brent Crude), a consequence not only of the current situation in the Middle East, but of uncertainty in other oil-producing countries. Although 'buying forward' is a common response to this risk, the large fluctuations in oil price make this technique a very risky option.

Other commodities such as steel, aluminium, timber and cement, common materials used in the construction industry, have also increased in cost as a result of greater demand by booming economies. Many construction companies are now 'buying forward' such materials to mitigate the risk associated with price and availability.

2.7.17   Process Risk

This arises from the project management process itself. Process risks arise when the fundamental requirements for running a project are established. The management and decision-making process for operating the project, including the communication methods and documentation standards to be adopted, will also be areas of risk.

The early stages of concept and planning are when project objectives are at their most flexible. The formation of a project's scope and the iterations of its requirements through feasibility studies provide the greatest opportunity for managing risks. This is the case because the early stages of a project have the option of 'maybe' alternatives through to the 'go/no go' decision, an option which is less available after a contract has been signed. When risks arise at a later stage in the project life cycle, the impact may generally be greater.

It is also important to note that there is an inherent risk in moving through the project life cycle, for example moving on to the design and planning phase before the basic concept has generally been evaluated.

Chapman and Ward (1997) believe that a thorough risk analysis should be part of the project process. For example, a review at the design stage may initiate consideration of the implications for the design further in the project life cycle. A change in design may reduce the risks associated with the manufacturing process/phase. Similarly decisions made at the corporate level may have implications at SBU and project levels.

2.7.18 Heuristics

Regardless of the industry, type of organisation or style of management, the control of risks associated with human factors will affect project and portfolio success. The human contribution to project success, or failure, encompasses the actions of all those involved in the planning, design and implementation of a project. Obviously there is potential for human failure at each stage of the project life cycle. Managing the risks associated with human failure remains a challenge for successful project management.

There has been a considerable amount of work done in the area of heuristics to identify the unconscious rules used when making a decision under conditions of uncertainty. Hillson (1998) argues that if risk management is to retain its credibility, this aspect must be addressed and made a routine part of the risk management process. A reliable means of measuring risk attitudes needs to be developed, which can be administered routinely as part of a risk assessment in order to identify potential bias among participants.

A number of studies have been undertaken to identify the benefits which can be expected by those implementing a structured approach to risk management (Newland 1997). These include both 'hard' and 'soft' benefits. Hard benefits include:

- better formed and achievable project plans, schedules and budgets
- increased likelihood of the project meeting targets
- proper risk allocation
- better allocation of contingency to reflect the risk
- ability to avoid taking on unsound projects
- identification of the best risk owner.

Soft benefits include:

- improved communication
- development of common understanding of project objectives
- enhancement of team spirit
- focus of management attention on genuine threats
- facilitation of appropriate risk taking
- demonstrated professional approach towards customers.

2.7.19   Decommissioning Risk

The purpose of decommissioning is often to return a former operational plant back to brown- or greenfield site status. Over the course of operations, many industries (mining, quarrying, chemical industries, nuclear) have to plan for the end of lifetime costs for their plants, whether dismantling or reconditioning the sites. These characteristics of the project have financial consequences in regard to cost estimating and financing, for which there does not exist one single answer to date, and thus by definition creates risk. In today's economic climate it is essential that these risks are taken into account before a project is sanctioned.

2.7.20   Institutional Risks

The term 'institutional' is used to summarise risks caused by organisational structure and behaviour. These risks occur in organisations and state bodies and affect projects both large and small (Kahkonen and Artto 1997). Typically dogma, beauracracy, culture and poor practice can lead to increased risks, usually pure risks.

2.7.21   Subjective Risk and Acceptable Risk

The extent to which a person feels threatened by a particular risk, regardless of the probability of the risk occurring, is subjective risk. Subjective risk may, amongst other things, be affected by an individual's personal level of risk aversion or risk preference. The severity of the consequences of the individual should the risk occur, the psychological factors and familiarity of the risk will all contribute to subjective risk.

Acceptable risk is the amount of subjective risk an individual or organisation is prepared to accept. In most cases acceptable risk is treated by organisations in such a way that should it occur the existence of the organisation is not threatened.

2.7.22 Pure Risks and Speculative Risks

Pure risks are those risks which only offer the probability of loss and not profit. Pure risks only present the possibility of undesirable consequences. The majority of pure risks, but not all pure risks, can be insured against.

In contrast to pure risks, speculative risks produce either a profit or a loss and can be expected to offer either favourable or unfavourable consequences. Business risks which are voluntarily and deliberately undertaken fall into the category of speculative risks.

2.7.23 Fundamental Risks and Particular Risks

Fundamental risks are risks such as natural disasters that affect whole or significant proportions of society which organisations and individuals have little or no control over. Management of these risks often only permits reducing the effects of such risks.

Particular risks are those risks that can be controlled in order to make a wider range of risk management options available, as they are particular to an organisation or individual.

2.7.24 Iatrogenic Risks

These are actions taken that may themselves generate further risks. An example would be increasing car security systems for unoccupied cars which may result in car jacking as a consequence of mitigating the risk of theft. Basically the consequences of managing a risk can lead to further risks that may have a greater impact than the initial risk.

2.7.25 Destructive Technology Risk

The authors define destructive technology as the possibility of new advanced technology completely taking over the old technology, which would make the old technology become prematurely obsolete. There are now more 'destructive technologies' around than at anytime in the past 10 years, especially in industries associated with IT and electronic development. The authors believe that destructive technologies present great threats to established businesses but can also create rewarding new opportunities.

2.7.26 Perceived and Virtual Risks

1. Perceived through science: cholera, for example, needs a microscope to see it and scientific training to understand it.
2. Perceived directly: climbing a tree, riding a bike or driving a car are all risks apparent by the actions and consequences.
3. Virtual risk: these are risks scientists do not fully understand or cannot agree on their impact. Examples include BSE vs CJD, global warming, low level radiation, pesticide residues, HRT, mobile phones, passive smoking, and eye laser treatment. These can be products of the imagination upon the imagination.

2.7.27 Force Majeure

A contract may provide liability to be excluded for any disruption to business continuity because something abnormal and unforeseeable by the parties to the contract is beyond their control. This is known as force majeure.

Force majeure (French for greater force) is a common clause in contracts which essentially frees one or both parties from liability or obligation when an extraordinary event or circumstance beyond the control of the parties such as war, strike, riot, act of God (flood, earthquake, volcano) prevents one or both parties from fulfilling their obligations under the contract. However, force majeure is not intended to excuse negligence or other malfeasance of a party of external forces such as predicted rain stops in an outdoor event or where the intervening circumstances are specifically contemplated.

Time critical and other sensitive contracts may be drafted to limit the shield of this clause where a party does not take reasonable steps (or specific precautions) to prevent or limit the effects of the outside interference, either when they become likely or when they actually occur.

Force majeure may also work to excuse all or part of the obligations of one or both parties. For example, a strike may prevent the delivery of goods, but not timely payment for the portion delivered. Similarly a widespread power outage would not be a force majeure excuse if the contract requires the provision of backup power or other contingency plans for continuity.

The importance of the force majeure clause in a contract, particularly one of any length of time, cannot be understated as it relieves a party from an obligation under the contract (or suspends that obligation). What is permitted to be a force majeure event or circumstance can be a source of much controversy in the negotiation of a contract and a party should generally resist any attempt by the other party to include something that should fundamentally be at the risk of that other party. For example, in a coal supply agreement, the mining company may seek to have 'geological risk' included as a force majeure event; however, the mining company should be doing extensive exploration and analysis of its geological reserves and should not even be negotiating a coal supply agreement if it cannot take the risk that there may be a geological limit to its coal supply from time to time. The outcome of that negotiation, of course, depends on the relative bargaining power of the parties and there will be cases where force majeure clauses can be used by a party effectively to escape liability for bad performance.

It should be noted that under international law force majeure refers to an irresistible force or unseen event beyond the control of a state making it materially impossible to fulfil an international obligation.

2.7.27.1   Typical Force Majeure Clause

No party shall be liable for any failure to perform its obligations where such failure is as a result of acts of nature (including flood, fire, earthquake, storm, hurricane or other natural disaster), war, invasion, act of foreign enemies, hostilities (whether war is declared or not), civil war, rebellion, revolution, insurrection, military or usurped power or confiscation, terrorist activities, nationalisation, government sanction, blockage, embargo, labour dispute, strike, lockout or interruption or failure of electricity or telephone service and no other party will have the right to terminate this agreement under a certain termination clause.

Any party asserting force majeure as an excuse shall have the burden of proving that reasonable steps were taken (under the circumstances) to minimise delay or damages caused by foreseeable events, that non-excused obligations were substantially fulfilled and that the other party was timely notified of the likelihood or actual occurrence which would justify such an assertion, so that other prudent precautions could be contemplated.

2.7.27.2   Events of Force Majeure

Events of force majeure shall mean and be limited to the circumstances set forth in Contract article relating to events of force majeure but only if and to the extent that:

1. such circumstance is not within the reasonable control of the party affected
2. such circumstance despite the exercise of reasonable diligence cannot be prevented, avoided or removed by such party
3. such event materially adversely affects the contractor to construct or operate the facility
4. the contractor has taken all reasonable precautions in order to avoid the effect of such event on the contractor's ability to construct or operate the facility
5. such event is not the direct or indirect result of failure by the contractor to perform any of his obligations under any of the project documents, and
6. such party has given the other party prompt notice describing such event, the effect thereof and the actions being taken in order to comply with this paragraph.

2.7.27.3   Instances of Force Majeure

Subject to the provisions of contract article relating to events of force majeure shall mean the following:

1. acts of war or the public enemy whether war be declared or not
2. public disorders, insurrections, rebellion, sabotage, riots, violent demonstrations or vandalism
3. explosions, fires, earthquakes, avalanche or other natural calamities
4. strikes, lockouts, or other industrial action of workers or employees
5. ionising radiations or contamination by radio activity from any nuclear fuel or nuclear waste
6. any order, legislation, enactment, judgement, ruling or decision made or taken by Government or judicial authority
7. unforeseeable unfavourable climatic or unforeseeable unsuitable ground conditions or sub-surfaces or latent physical conditions at the site which differ materially from those indicated in the Site Investigation Report or previously unknown physical conditions at the site of an unusual nature which differ materially for those ordinarily

encountered and generally recognised as inherent in work of the character provided for in an agreement
8. delays in obtaining Governmental authorisations
9. any other event which is not within reasonable control of the party affected.

2.8   PERCEPTIONS OF RISK

According to MacCrimmon and Wehrung (1986), different people will respond to seemingly similar risky situations in very different ways. Furthermore they state that there is no reason to believe that a person who takes risks in one specific situation will necessarily take risks in all situations: a trapeze performer (characterised as a risk taker) might not be cautious in financial matters, whereas a commodity broker (also characterised as a risk taker) might not be physically cautious. Although there is no standard way to assess a person's willingness to take risks, the general classification of managers into categories such as risk taking, risk neutral and risk averse can often be made.

Empirical evidence concerning individual risk response is often ignored in the risk analysis process. Experience, subjectivity and the way risk is framed all play a major role in decision making (Tversky and Kahneman 1974, Sitkin and Pablo 1992). Risk perception has a crucial influence on risk-taking behaviour. The perceived importance attached to decisions influences team behaviour and the consequent implementation methods (Sitkin and Pablo 1992). The level of perceived importance will also influence individual or group behaviour and link to the consequences of such behaviour (Ziegler *et al.* 1996).

Subjectivity is a key factor in assessing risk. Whether a problem is perceived in terms of potential gains or losses will not be assessed as a simple mathematical calculation of the problem, but as a subjective fear, often linked to the consequences of outcomes. There might be a tendency to overestimate 'fabulous' risk and to confuse probability with consequence; therefore there might be a temptation to focus on low-probability events or situations which would have a high impact if they were to occur, rather than high-probability risks with a much lower potential for consequential loss. There is also considerable variance in the estimation of risk, so the same set of circumstances might be evaluated differently by individuals. Basically, people are poor assessors of risk. Evidence suggests that individuals do not understand, trust or accurately interpret probability estimates (Slovic 1967, Fischhoff *et al.* 1983, March and Shapira 1987).

Risks are perceived by different stakeholders at different business levels. For example, the corporate level may concern itself with risks associated with political, legal, regulatory, reputation and financial factors affecting both the corporation and SBUs. These risks are usually assessed using qualitative methods. Enron, an American energy corporation, and Allied Irish Bank (AIB) have recently had their reputations damaged as a result of fraudulent activities within their organisations. SBUs may consider the above risks in greater detail in respect to their own businesses and consider risks associated with the business, projects, environment, market, safety and planning. At the project level a more detailed risk assessment, often quantitative, will concern the particular project. These risks may include the programme, planning, construction, manufacturing, production, quality, operation and maintenance, technical and specific risks associated with a project.

2.9   STAKEHOLDERS IN AN INVESTMENT

All investments have stakeholders, whether internal or external to an investment. It is important that all stakeholders are aware of the potential risks that could occur over an investment's life. Shareholders, for example, who provide funds in the form of equity should be made aware of the risks a corporation is taking on their behalf.

Although shareholders assume risk by 'default' they either retain or sell their shares. However, should a corporate entity make a decision regarding a particular investment, unknown to shareholders, this could result in a dramatic fall in the value of their shares.

Johnson and Scholes (1999) define stakeholders as:

Those individuals or groups who depend on the organisation to fulfil their own goals and on whom, in turn, the organisation depends.

It is therefore important to include external stakeholders who often have an adverse impact on a project, for example environmentalist groups and conservationists.

Mills and Turner (1995) suggest political, economic, social and technological (PEST) analysis to investigate stakeholders' position in a project. This approach focuses on analysing each stakeholder's influence on the political, economic, social and technological aspects of the project. The correct position of each stakeholder can be inferred from

Table 2.3 Internal and external stakeholders (Adapted from Winch 2002)

Internal stakeholders		External stakeholders	
Demand side	Supply side	Private	Public
Client	Architect	Local residents	Regulatory agencies
Financiers	Engineers	Local land owners	
Client's employees	Principal contractors	Environmentalists	Local government
Client's customers	Trade contractors	Conservationists	National government
Client's tenants	Materials suppliers	Archaeologists	
Client's suppliers			

the stakeholder's specific roles at corporate, business and project levels proportionally.

Winch (2002) states that it is useful to categorise the different types of stakeholders in order to aid the analysis, and hence managements of the problem. A first-order classification places them in two categories –internal stakeholders which are in legal contract with the client, and external stakeholders which also have a direct interest in the project. Internal stakeholders can be broken down into those clustered around the client on the demand side, and those on the supply side. External stakeholders can be broken down into private and public sectors. This categorisation, with some examples, is shown in Table 2.3.

It is important that managers focus on those individuals or groups who are interested and able actually to prevent them delivering a successful outcome for the project. This reflects the fact that the vested interest of stakeholders may not always be a positive one.

2.9.1 Stakeholder Identification

At the individual level, identification of the people or groups who influence an investment or project process or its outcome is crucial. It begins the process of eliciting information about the potential contribution to the business risks during and beyond the investment's life cycle and is the first step in dealing with human factors in risk management. Key information will be gained concerning stakeholders' abilities, perceptions, values and motivation. However, even in today's risk business environment project managers are only aware of a minority of stakeholders within a project and dismiss many of those which are external as unimportant and beyond their control. Therefore, many 'contributors' to the project and the risks they import may not be covered by the risk analysis process.

2.9.2   Stakeholder Perspectives

The stakeholders' perspectives are of particular importance to risk management as they concern the way each stakeholder 'sees' and interprets, for example, the project, its objectives, other stakeholders, potential gains and losses, and the relationship with the investment or project. Diverse perspectives and perceptions of the stakeholders concerning their tasks, roles and objectives have been recognised as important factors in risk (Sawacha and Langford 1984, Pidgion *et al.* 1992, Pinkley and Northcroft 1994).

Establishing stakeholders' perspectives or mental models concerning the business or project will identify, amongst other risks, potential areas of conflict, varying approaches to roles and responsibilities, and widely differing attitudes to risk and risk management. Identifying stakeholders' perspectives enables the development of appropriate intervention strategies to reduce risk and uncertainty through project risk management.

2.9.3   Stakeholder Perceptions

How risk is defined determines the response of an individual stakeholder to risk. Risk is often conceptualised as a hazard, a breakdown, or a failure to deliver to time and budget, rather than in wider terms of uncertainty about precise outcomes of planned actions and project processes (March and Shapira 1992). As with other stakeholders, what managers consider as risk depends, amongst other factors, on their perceptions, which may be based on flawed notions of control. Many key risk elements may be excluded from the risk management plan if they are not viewed as risks but as routine tasks for management. Areas of ambiguity cause psychological discomfort for project managers and encourage them to avoid in-depth exploration of the problem, preferring instead to focus on more tangible areas of management tasks. Cultural factors also contribute to misconceptions and misunderstanding (Hugenholtz 1992). Individual stakeholder perspectives can be regarded as 'lenses' through which issues are assessed (Pinkley and Northcroft 1994). Perceptions of stakeholders are largely social and subjective processes, which cannot be easily reduced to elements of mathematical models of risk (Pidgion *et al.* 1992). The stress placed on quantification processes, such as quantitative risk analysis, often fails to prompt a manager to take account of other areas that are more difficult or impossible to quantify. Thus a large element of potential risk is excluded and may even go unrecognised.

2.10 SUMMARY

Risk is an unavoidable feature of human existence and over time humans have developed procedures for survival in a constantly changing environment. The same philosophy is seen to form modern risk management practices.

One of the reasons for the development of risk management has been the failure of projects to meet their budgets, completion dates, quality and performance or generate sufficient revenues to service the principal and interest payments. The lessons to be learned from each failed project serve as a useful introduction to the need for better performance in risk management.

Clearly all risks need to be assessed at all levels. Corporate risks can affect the corporation in terms of reputation or the ability to raise finance, SBUs need to consider the risks associated with a portfolio of projects. The project manager should be confident about managing the risks associated with a project and that those risks outside his or her remit have been assessed at corporate and SBU levels. Management at all levels should be aware that risk can provide benefits and should not be considered purely on a negative basis.

This chapter has described the concept of risk and uncertainty, and their sources, the origin of risk and the dimensions of risk. Different types of risk have been outlined and different perceptions of risk discussed. Stakeholders involved in projects or investments were also discussed.

3

The Evolution of Risk Management and the Risk Management Process

3.1 INTRODUCTION

This chapter briefly describes the evolution of risk management. It illustrates the major stages of the risk management process, namely identification, analysis and response. The beneficiaries of risk management are outlined along with how risk management can be embedded into an organisation. A generic risk management plan (RMP) which forms the basis for all risk management actions and further risk activities for corporate, strategic business and project levels is discussed.

3.2 THE EVOLUTION OF RISK MANAGEMENT

Archibald and Lichtenberg (1992) state that risk is now openly acknowledged as part of real management life. Risk management is now considered to be one of the more exciting and important parts of planning and managing investments, assets and liabilities at corporate, strategic business and project levels, and is a function to be taken seriously.

3.2.1 The Birth of Risk Management

The idea of chance and fortune has existed in the most primitive of cultures. Playing games involving dice can be traced back at least 2000 years.

Probably the first insurance against misfortune was within a policy to cover the loss of cargo by shipwreck that had its origin in the Hummurabi Code. In the framework of that code the ship owner could obtain a loan to finance the freight, but it was not necessary to pay back the loan if the ship was wrecked.

The eighteenth century saw the rise of insurance companies as we currently know them. In 1752 Benjamin Franklin founded, in the USA, a fire insurance company called First American. The Society of Lloyd's in London was established in 1771 when several English businessmen combined their resources to insure potential losses of their clients involved in sea transportation, now known as marine insurance.

The twentieth century witnessed the development of probability in 'management science' and the birth of formal risk management. This method was further developed by Chapman (1998) and applied by Chapman and others (Jia and Jobbling 1998).

3.2.2   Risk Management in the 1970s – Early Beginnings

Until the advent of project risk management in the 1970s, risk was something that was little discussed and its effects on businesses and projects were either ignored, because they were not recognised, or possibly concealed if they were. Before and shortly after this advent both risk and uncertainty were treated as a necessary evil that should be avoided (Archibald and Lichtenberg 1992).

Project risk management developed rapidly throughout the 1970s, firstly in relation to quantitative assessment and then to methodologies and processes. At the end of the decade project management academics and professionals saw the need for a project management function devoted to risk analysis and management, and several authors published papers on the subject.

3.2.3   Risk Management in the 1980s – Quantitative Analysis Predominates

In the early 1980s risk management was commonly acknowledged as a specific topic in the project management literature (Artto 1997). The scope of risk identification, estimation and response was generally well known (Lifson and Shaifer 1982, Chapman 1998). Discussions on risk management emphasised quantitative analysis, some of which referred to the PERT (Programme Evaluation and Review Technique) type of triple estimates, and optimistic, mean, pessimistic and other more advanced new concepts.

The main project risk management applications were essentially focused on time and cost objectives, and also on project evaluation (feasibility). Software using probability distributions to analyse cost and time risk was frequently used on large projects. Significant use of risk analysis and management was made on large process plant projects.

Companies like BP and Norwegian Petroleum Consultants pioneered project risk management methods in that decade, in both the development and application of risk management methodology and of risk analysis techniques. BP developed the CATRAP (Cost and Time Risk Analysis Program) software for internal use. It allowed risk modelling with several subjective probability distributions and was used on offshore oil platform projects in the North Sea. Norwegian Petroleum Consultants developed NPC for the same types of project. NPC, like CATRAP, allowed risk quantification and modelling using subjective probability distributions. It also had the capacity to calculate objective distributions from real-life cost and time data and included the ability to combine subjective and objective distributions. NPC was also able to integrate cost and time risk in its modelling. In the late 1980s CASPAR (Computer-Aided Software for Project Risk Appraisal) was further developed at UMIST to provide risk analysis outputs for businesses as well as projects (Jia and Jobbling 1998).

The use of methods based on risk and response diagrams began in the 1980s. These methods are based on the notion that it is not possible to model a risk situation realistically without taking into account the possible responses. There are four reasons why risk response should be considered as part of risk analysis:

1. Estimation of the remaining risk is normally different in different response scenarios.
2. Responses need time and money; hence readjustments to the corresponding schedule and cost estimates are required.
3. A correct quantitative risk analysis model needs to include both risks and responses because without these elements the view of the situation may be distorted.
4. A specific response to a risk may bring secondary risks that will not exist in other cases.

Thus to make the best choice between several alternative responses, if they exist, to a risk situation, both the responses and their effects must be included in the model. Quantifying the results obtained will provide information which can be a valuable aid to the analysis.

The end of the 1980s was also the starting point for the use of influence diagrams combined with probability theory and for the first applications of systems dynamics. These techniques have been developed to a higher level and today there is commercial software available for both methods.

3.2.4   Risk Management in the 1990s – Emphasis on Methodology and Processes

Most of the risk management methodologies used today are based on methods developed in the 1980s. However, the use of questionnaires and checklists was greatly developed in the 1990s, and further development has led to the concept of knowledge-based systems.

Some important principles established in the 1980s in relation to the contractual allocation of risk have continued in the 1990s. The foundations of partnering and 'alliancing' strategies have been laid to avoid traditional contractual rivalry and promote a risk and reward sharing approach, particularly in the case of capital projects.

It is important to note that there has been a shift from a concentration on quantitative risk analysis to the current emphasis on understanding and improving risk management processes. Whereas in the 1980s project risk management software was used as an analysis tool, today the trend is to use risk quantification and modelling as a tool to promote communication and response planning teamwork rather than simply for analysis (capture and response). Currently risk quantification and modelling techniques are seen as a way to increase both insight and knowledge about a project and as a way to communicate that information to the project team members and interested parties (stakeholders).

The period since 1990 has seen a variety of proposals for risk management processes, all of which include a prescriptive approach, such as:

- the simple generic risk management process – identification, assessment, response and documentation
- the five-phase generic process – process scope, team, analysis and quantification, successive breakdown and quantification, and results.

Risk management is undoubtedly an important part of prudent project and business management, but may not always be easy to justify. The benefits which it generates are often unseen, while the costs are all too visible. To sell it successfully, it is important to focus on the benefits it will bring, quoting from real life where possible, and satisfying a genuine need within the organisation (Wightman 1998).

Historically, many organisations have looked at risk management in a somewhat fragmented way. However, for a growing number of organisations, this no longer makes sense and they are adopting a much more holistic approach. For example, organisations at the forefront of risk management now have risk committees, which are often chaired by a main board member or a risk facilitator and which have overall responsibility for risk management across their organisation. The point

is that a fragmented approach no longer works. In addition, risk management has clearly moved up the agenda for the board or management committee.
Risk management continues to evolve in many ways:

- 'Threat' focus becomes 'opportunity' focus with a view to taking more risk to improve profit expectations and to support the organisation.
- Multiple pass process emphasis leads to the development of simple first pass approaches to size risk prior to deciding whether or not further action is required.
- Separation of projects/investments from associated corporate/SBU strategy is increasingly seen as unhelpful.
- Building proactive risk management into capital investment appraisal, bidding and contract design is increasingly seen as fundamental.
- Good risk management cannot be achieved by simply adopting any simple off-the-shelf techniques. It needs careful thought, effort and recognition of key issues in each individual case.
- Non-monetary appraisals are now seen to be an important part of risk management, and include:
  o Environmental – a key element in most large projects considering impacts and mitigations measures on the environment during implementation or operation. An example is the control of pollution from process and waste plants.
  o Health and safety – general responsibilities under statute such as Hands at Work Act and under contract law construction, design and management (CDM) regulations place restrictions on designers to ensure safe methods of construction.
  o Ethical – as international and multi-cultural working become more common the need for ethical awareness is increasing. Contractors are often selected because they are not involved with arms trade, child labour, tobacco or drugs.
  o People – unmotivated staff, poor teaming, organisational structure, responsibility for decision making, distribution of work and workloads.
  o Cost – labour overruns, material overruns, supply overruns, monetary penalties.
  o Schedule – missed deliverables, missed market window, missed critical path activities, unrealistic schedules or programmes.
  o Quality – poor workmanship, unfinished details, legal infractions, untested technology, operation and maintenance of products or projects.

3.3   RISK MANAGEMENT

Risk management can be defined as any set of actions taken by individuals or corporations in an effort to alter the risk arising from their business (Merna and Smith 1996).

Meulbroek (2002) identifies that the goal of risk management is to:

Maximise shareholder value.

Handy (1999) summarises risk management as:

Risk management is not a separate activity from management, it is management. . . predicting and planning allow prevention. . . reaction is a symptom of poor management.

Risk management deals both with insurable as well as uninsurable risks and is an approach which involves a formal orderly process for systematically identifying, analysing and responding to risk events throughout the life of a project to obtain the optimum or acceptable degree of risk elimination or control.

Smith (1995) states that risk management is an essential part of the project and business planning cycle which:

- requires acceptance that uncertainty exists
- generates a structured response to risk in terms of alternative plans, solutions and contingencies
- is a thinking process requiring imagination and ingenuity
- generates a realistic attitude in an investment for staff by preparing them for risk events rather than being taken by surprise when they arrive.

At its most fundamental level, risk management involves identifying risks, predicting how probable they are and how serious they might become, deciding what to do about them and implementing these decisions.

3.4   THE RISK MANAGEMENT PROCESS – IDENTIFICATION, ANALYSIS AND RESPONSE

In the project management literature, a rather more prescriptive interpretation of risk management is expounded. To develop the concept as a management tool, authors have tended to describe the processes by which risk management is undertaken.

According to Smith (1995), the process of risk management involves:

- identification of risks/uncertainties
- analysis of implications
- response to minimise risk
- allocation of appropriate contingencies.

Risk management is a continuous loop rather than a linear process so that, as an investment or project progresses, a cycle of identification, analysis, control and reporting of risks is continuously undertaken.

Risk analysis and risk management have been carried out in many fields for a number of decades and are being increasingly used as integral parts of the overall business management approach and on most major projects; in some cases they have become a mandatory requirement for financial planning and regulatory approval. Many client organisations now require contractors to identify potential risks in an investment and to state how these risks would be managed should they occur.

Despite risk analysis being a growing element of major projects, there is no standard to which reference may be made for techniques, factors and approaches. To overcome this a number of organisations and research authorities have identified ways to describe the risk management process. Typically there are a number of phases associated with this process. Merna (2002) took three processes, namely risk identification, analysis and response, and implemented a 15-step sequence to account for risk management. However, four processes had been identified by Boswick's 1987 paper (PMBOK 1996), Eloff *et al.* (1995) and the British Standard BS 8444 (BSI, 1996). The Project Management Institute's (PMIs) *Guide to the Project Management Body of Knowledge* (PMBOK 1996) also identifies four processes associated with project risk management.

Chapman and Ward (1997) believe that there are eight phases in the risk management process. Each phase is associated with broadly defined deliverables (may be targets not achieved initially), and each deliverable is discussed in terms of its purpose and the tasks required to produce it. Below is a summary of these phases and deliverable structures:

- *Define.* The purpose of this phase is to consolidate any relevant existing information about the project, and to fill in any gaps uncovered in the consolidation process.
- *Focus.* The purpose of this phase is to look for and develop a strategic plan for the risk management process, and to plan the risk management process at an operational level. A clear, unambiguous, shared

understanding of all relevant aspects of the risk management process, documented, verified and reported should result from this.

- *Identify*. The purpose of this phase is to identify where risk may arise, to identify what might be done about the risk in proactive and reactive terms, and to identify what might go wrong with the responses. Here, all key risks and responses should be identified, with threats and opportunities classified, characterised, documented, verified and reported.
- *Structure*. The purpose of this phase is to test the simplified assumptions, and to provide a more complex structure when appropriate. Benefits here include a clear understanding of the implications of any important simplifying assumptions about relationships between risks, responses and base plan activities.
- *Ownership*. At this phase client/contractor allocation of ownership and management of risk and responses occur, such as the allocation of client risks to named individuals, and the approval of contractor allocations. Here, clear ownership and allocations arise; the allocations are effectively and efficiently defined and legally enforceable in practice where appropriate.
- *Estimate*. This phase identifies areas of clear significant uncertainty and areas of possible significant uncertainty. This acts as a basis for understanding which risks and responses are important.
- *Evaluate*. At this stage synthesis and evaluation of the results of the estimation phase occurs. At this stage, diagnosis of all important difficulties and comparative analysis of the implications of responses to these difficulties should take place, together with specific deliverables like a prioritised list of risks or a comparison of the base plan and contingency plans with possible difficulties and revised plans.
- *Plan*. At this phase the project plan is ready for implementation. Deliverables here include:
  - Base plans in activity terms at the detailed level required for implementation, with timing, precedence, ownership and associated resource usage/contractual terms where appropriate clearly specified, including milestones initiating payments, other events or processes defining expenditure and an associated base plan expenditure profile.
  - Risk assessment in terms of threats and opportunities. Risks are assessed in terms of impact given no response, along with assessment of alternative potential reactive and proactive responses.

o Recommended proactive and reactive contingency plans in activity terms, with timing, precedence, ownership and associated resource usage/contractual terms where appropriate clearly specified, including trigger points initiating reactive contingency responses and impact assessment.

o A management phase that includes monitoring, controlling and developing plans for immediate implementation. This stage allows revisiting earlier plans and the initiation of further planning where appropriate. Also exceptions (change) can be reported after significant events and associated further planning.

Corporate and strategic business elements should also be included in the process outlined by Chapman and Ward, since risks identified at these levels need to be addressed before a project is sanctioned.

For the purpose of outlining the risk management process, the PMBOK (1996) system has been used to give a brief description of the necessary processes, namely:

- risk identification
- risk quantification and analysis
- risk response.

PMBOK (1996) states that project risk management includes the processes concerned with identifying, analysing and responding to project risk. It also includes maximising the results of positive events and minimising the consequences of adverse events. The main processes involved in project risk management are discussed below.

3.4.1   Risk Identification

Risk identification consists of determining which risks are likely to affect the project and documenting the characteristics of each one. Risk identification should address both the internal and the external risks. The primary sources of risk which have the potential to cause a major effect on the project should also be determined and classified according to their impact on project cost, time schedules and project objectives.

The identification of risks using both historical and current information is a necessary step in the early stage of project appraisal and should occur before detailed analysis and allocation of risks can take place. It is also essential for risk analysis to be performed on a regular basis throughout all stages of the project. Risk identification should be carried out in a similar manner at both corporate and strategic business levels.

3.4.1.1 Inputs and Outputs of the Risk Identification Process

In order to investigate what the risk identification process entails, consideration should be given to its input requirements and the outputs or deliverables expected from it. Risk identification consists of determining which risks are likely to affect the project and documenting the characteristics of each one. Inputs to risk identification are given as:

- product or service description
- other planning outputs, for example work breakdown structure, cost and time estimates, specification requirements
- historical information.

Outputs are:

- sources of risk
- potential risk events
- risk symptoms
- inputs to other processes.

After identification:

- risks should be 'validated' – for instance, the information on which they are based and the accuracy of the description of their characteristics should be checked.
- risk response options should be considered.

The purpose of risk identification is:

- to identify and capture the most significant participants (stakeholders) in risk management and to provide the basis for subsequent management
- to stabilise the groundwork by providing all the necessary information to conduct risk analysis
- to identify the project or service components
- to identify the inherent risks in the project or service.

3.4.1.2 Participants in the Risk Management Process

Developing the above points further, before risk identification can commence the responsibility for undertaking the risk management process must be assigned. Whatever the organisational structure within which the risk management process is undertaken, it must be supported or 'championed' by the highest levels of management or it will not have access to the requisite information, neither will the organisation be likely to benefit from the implementation of its recommendations. This is often addressed in a similar way to the value management process by appointing a strong experienced facilitator to chair meetings where potential risks are identified and addressed. Participants in the identification will normally include individuals responsible for carrying out the project and those having a firm grasp of the business and technical aspects of the project and the risks confronting it from within and outside the organisation.

3.4.1.3   Information Gathering and Project Definition

The risk identification process is dependent on information, which may or may not be readily available. This may take the form of processed historical data, often risk registers from previous projects and operations or information from external sources. The better the informational foundation of the risk management process, the more accurate its results. Therefore determination of what information is required, where and how it may be collected and when it is needed is central to risk identification. This involves:

- gathering existing information about the project including its scope, objectives and strategy
- filling in gaps in the existing information to achieve a clear, unambiguous, shared understanding of the project.

3.4.1.4   Risk Identification Process Outputs

Primarily, a register of risks likely to affect the project should result from the process. A full and validated description of each risk as well as initial response options to each risk should be developed. The key deliverable is a clear common understanding of threats and opportunities facing the project.

Figure 3.1 illustrates the risk identification process with its outputs leading to the inputs in Figure 3.2 for risk analysis. The outputs of Figure 3.2 are then input into Figure 3.3 for risk response.

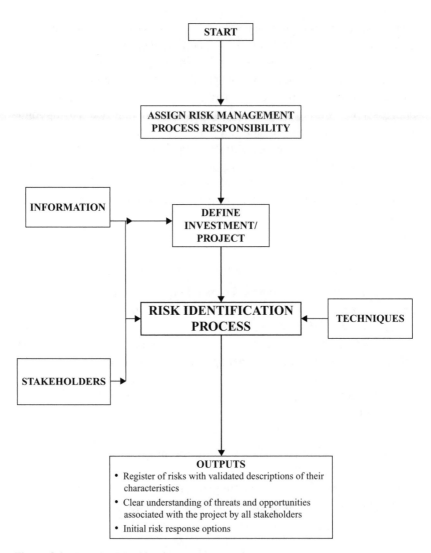

Figure 3.1   The risk identification process

3.4.2   Risk Quantification and Analysis

Risk quantification and analysis involves evaluating risks and risk interactions to assess the range of possible outcomes. It is primarily concerned with determining which risk events warrant a response. A number of tools and techniques are available for the use of risk analysis/quantification and the analysis process. These are explained in Chapter 4.

The major output from risk quantification and analysis is a list of opportunities that should be pursued and threats that require attention. The risk quantification and analysis process should also document the sources of risk and risk events that the management team has consciously decided to accept or ignore, as well as the individual who made the decision to do so.

Dawson *et al.* (1995) believe that objectives in risk management are an important part of risk analysis. The purpose of risk management is to determine the balance which exists between risk and opportunities in order to assist management responses to tilt the balance in favour of the opportunities and away from risks. These risks and opportunities might appear different when viewed from a company perspective as opposed to the more usual 'project' perspective. The identification of risks and opportunities for a project should be based on the objectives for undertaking the venture, and for a company should be based on the objectives of the company. These two sets of objectives are different but inextricably linked; the objectives of a company might include, in the short term, more experience in a particular type of work, whilst the risks to a project enabling this to happen might be seen to affect the profitability of the project and the esteem in which the manager is held. Hence, in order to perform risk management the objectives must be clearly defined at each level of an organisation.

There are mainly two types of methods used in the risk quantification and analysis process. These are qualitative risk analysis and quantitative risk analysis.

Qualitative risk analysis consists of compiling a list of risks and a description of their likely outcomes. Qualitative risk analysis involves evaluations that do not result in a numerical value. Instead, this analysis describes the nature of the risk and helps to improve the understanding of the risk. In this way, analysts are able to concentrate their time and efforts on areas that are most sensitive to the risk.

Quantitative risk analysis often involves the use of computer models employing statistical data to conduct risk analysis. Qualitative and quantitative techniques are discussed in Chapter 4.

Figure 3.2 illustrates the risk quantification and analysis process.

3.4.3   Risk Response

Risk response involves defining enhancement steps for opportunities and responses to threats. Responses to threats generally fall into one of the following categories.

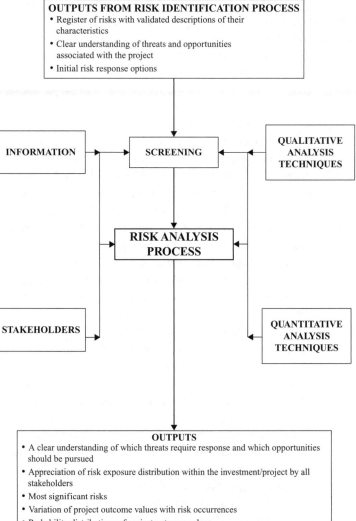

OUTPUTS FROM RISK IDENTIFICATION PROCESS
* Register of risks with validated descriptions of their characteristics
* Clear understanding of threats and opportunities associated with the project
* Initial risk response options

INFORMATION

SCREENING

QUALITATIVE ANALYSIS TECHNIQUES

RISK ANALYSIS PROCESS

STAKEHOLDERS

QUANTITATIVE ANALYSIS TECHNIQUES

OUTPUTS
* A clear understanding of which threats require response and which opportunities should be pursued
* Appreciation of risk exposure distribution within the investment/project by all stakeholders
* Most significant risks
* Variation of project outcome values with risk occurrences
* Probability distributions of project outcome values

Figure 3.2   The risk quantification and analysis process

3.4.3.1   Risk Avoidance

Risk avoidance involves the removal of a particular threat. This may be either by eliminating the source of the risk within a project or by avoiding projects or business entities which have exposure to the risk.

Al-Bahar and Crandell (1990) illustrate the latter avoidance option with the example of a contractor wishing to avoid the potential liability losses associated with asbestos, and so never acquiring any project that involves operations with this material. The same scenario, but this time considered from the client's perspective, also lends itself as an example of eliminating a source of risk within a project if the risk is avoided by redesigning the facility so that it uses an alternative material to asbestos.

3.4.3.2 Risk Reduction

Since the significance of a risk is related to both its probability of occurrence and its effect on the project outcome if it does occur, risk reduction may involve either lowering its probability or lessening its impact (or both). The severity of injuries from falling objects on a building site, for example, may be reduced by the compulsory wearing of hard hats, while the adoption of safer working practices can lessen the likelihood of objects falling.

3.4.3.3 Risk Transfer

Projects may be seen as investment packages with associated risks and returns. Since a typical project or business involves numerous stakeholders, it follows that each should 'own' a proportion of the risk available in order to elicit a return. For instance, if a project involves the construction of a facility, some risks associated with that construction should be transferred from the client organisation to the contractor undertaking the work; for example, the project is completed within a specified time frame. In consideration of this risk, the contractor will expect a reward. Contractual risk allocation will not be dealt with in detail here but the fundamental considerations are the same for all risk transfers regardless of the vehicle by which transfers are facilitated.

The example of the time frame in a construction contract can illustrate this. The party with the greatest control over the completion date is the contractor and, as such, is in the best position to manage this risk. The client stands to lose revenue if the facility is not built by a certain date and, to mitigate any such loss, includes a liquidated damages clause in the contract so that, if construction overruns this date, the contractor compensates the client for the loss. The contractor will consider this risk in its tender and can expect that the contract price will be higher than it would be in the absence of the clause; that is, the transferee imposes a premium on accepting the risk. However, if the revenue loss is likely to be too great for the contractor to compensate for, there is little sense in transferring the risk in this way.

Insurance is a popular technique for risk transfer in which only the potential financial consequences of a risk are transferred and not the responsibility for managing the risk.

Financial markets provide numerous instruments for risk transfer in the form of 'hedging'. This is best illustrated by way of example: the fluctuation in the price of an input may be 'hedged' through the purchase of futures options so that in the event of a future price rise, the (lower than current market value) options soften the effect. Consequently, the benefits of a price decrease are lessened by the cost of the futures options. Options, futures, futures options, swaps, caps, collars and floors are only some of the instruments available to cover such risk.

Basically, risk transfer is the process of transferring risk to another participant in the project. Transferring risk does not eliminate or reduce the criticality of the risk, but merely leaves it for others to bear the risk. Flanagan and Norman (1993) state:

> Transferring risk does not reduce the criticality of the source of the risk, it just removes it to another party. In some cases, transfer can significantly increase risk because the party to whom it is being transferred may not be aware of the risk they are being asked to absorb.

Therefore, several factors have to be considered when making the decision to transfer risks. Who can best handle the risks if they materialise? What is the cost/benefit of transferring risk as opposed to managing the risk internally?

3.4.3.4   Risk Retention

Risks may be retained intentionally or unintentionally. The latter occurs as a result of failure of either or both of the first two phases of the risk management process, these being risk identification and risk analysis. If a risk is not identified or if its potential consequences are underestimated, then the organisation is unlikely to avoid or reduce it consciously or transfer it adequately.

In the case of planned risk retention, this involves the complete or partial assumption of the potential impact of a risk. As suggested above, a relationship between risk and return exists such that, with no risk exposure, an enterprise cannot expect reward. Ideally, retained risk should be that with which the organisation's core value-adding activities are associated (risk which the organisation is most able to manage) as well as those risks which may be dealt with more costeffectively by the organisation than external entities (since risk transfer and avoidance must necessarily come at a premium). Finally, risk reduction may only be cost effective up to a point, thereafter becoming more costly than beneficial.

3.4.4 Selection of Risk Response Options

At this stage of the risk management process, alternative risk response options will have been explored for the more significant risks. Either risk finance provisions or risk control measures (or both) for each risk now require consideration and implementation.

3.4.5 Outputs from the Risk Response Process

Each significant risk should be considered in terms of which project party should 'own' it and which risk response options are suitable for dealing with it. The most appropriate response option or options in accordance with the corporate risk management policy and, consequently, the response strategy or strategies must then be selected. Figure 3.3 illustrates the risk response process.

3.4.6 Risk Management within the Project Life Cycle

Risk management is not a discrete single activity but a dynamic process, which becomes continuously more refined through its repetition during a project's life cycle. PMBOK (1996) suggests that each of the major processes of risk management will occur at least once in every phase of the project. (Projects are divided into several phases which are collectively referred to as the project life cycle.) Thompson and Perry (1992) and Simon *et al.* (1997) support the continuous application of risk management throughout the project life cycle, though the former observe that it is 'most valuable early in a project proposal, while there is still the flexibility in design and planning to consider how the serious risks may be avoided'.

Chapman (1998) also addresses the issue of the application of a risk management process earlier or later in the project life cycle. He suggests that while earlier implementation will yield greater benefits, the lack of a project definition at this stage will make implementing a risk management process more difficult, less quantitative, less formal, less tactical

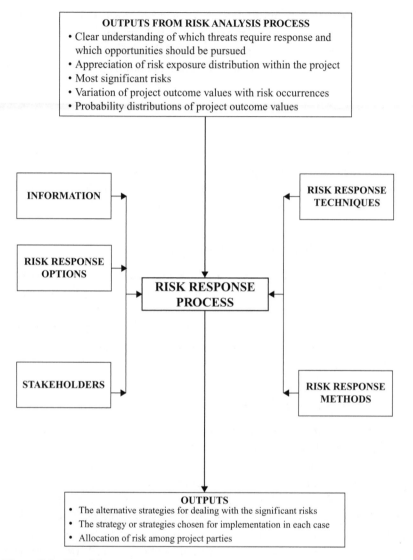

Figure 3.3 The risk response process

and more strategic. Conversely, at a stage of more accurate project definition, where implementation is easier, it is less beneficial.

In light of the above, this initial implementation of the risk management process should not only facilitate appraisal decision making, but also be seen as the first cycle of the risk management process within the project life cycle.

3.4.7   The Tasks and Benefits of Risk Management

The task of risk management is not to create a project or business that is totally free of risks (no undertaking regardless of size and complexity is without risk), but to make the stakeholders aware of the risks, both negative and positive, help them to take well-calculated risks and to manage risks efficiently. As this is necessary in every project phase from identification to implementation and operation, risk management should be used in each of these phases.

Chapman and Ward (1997) believe risk management has the following benefits:

- The risks associated with the project or business are defined clearly and in advance of the start.
- Management decisions are supported by thorough analysis of the data available. Estimates can be made with greater confidence.
- Improvement of project or business planning by answering 'what if' questions with imaginative scenarios.
- The definition and structure of the project or business are continually and objectively monitored.
- Provision of alternative plans and appropriate contingencies and consideration concerning their management as part of a risk response.
- The generation of imaginative responses to risks.
- The building up of a statistical profile of historical risk which allows improved modelling for future projects.

The benefits of risk management can also be expressed as follows:

- Project or business issues are clarified, understood and allowed from the start of a project.
- Decisions are supported by thorough analysis of the data available.
- The structure and definition of the project or business are continually and objectively monitored.
- Contingency planning allows prompt, controlled and previously evaluated responses to risks that may materialise.
- Clearer definitions of specific risks are associated with a project or business.
- Building up a statistical profile of historical risk to allow better modelling for future projects and investments.

Risk management requires the acceptance that uncertainty exists, a thinking process with ingenuity and imagination, and also a realistic attitude of the management in the evaluation of possible risks. As risk analysis is part of risk management it helps the project or commercial manager to anticipate and thus control future events (with risk response) and not be taken by surprise by the occurrence of already identified risks. It must be stressed that realistic base data (realistic assumptions) concerning cost, revenue, duration and quality are an essential prerequisite for risk analysis. If the risk analysis is based on unrealistic base data (often the base data in feasibility studies are too optimistic) the results are not only unrealistic economic parameters but also can mislead investors and both project and commercial managers by giving the (unrealistic) base data a sort of scientific approval.

3.4.8   The Beneficiaries of Risk Management

In 1991 the Association for Project Management (APM) set up a special interest group (SIG) on risk management to conduct a survey of practitioners to identify the beneficiaries of implementing risk management. The results were published in its mini-guide on PRAM (Project Risk Analysis and Management) in March 1992. The beneficiaries are:

- an organisation (corporate and SBU) and its senior management for whom a knowledge of the risks attached to proposed projects is important when considering the sanction of capital expenditure and capital budgets
- clients, both internal and external, as they are more likely to get what they want, when they want it and for the cost they can afford
- project managers who want to improve the quality of their work, such as bring their projects within cost, on time and to the required performance.

The beneficiaries of risk management would be not only at the project level, but also at corporate and strategic business levels, as well as the stakeholders.

The potential benefits of implementing risk management can be categorised into two types:

1. 'hard benefits' – contingencies, decisions, control, statistics and the like
2. 'soft benefits' – people issues.

Table 3.1   The hard and soft benefits of risk management (Adapted from Newland 1992, Simister 1994)

Hard benefits

Enables better informed and more believable plans, schedules and budgets
Increases the likelihood of a project adhering to its plans
Leads to the use of the most suitable type of contract
Allows a more meaningful assessment of contingencies
Discourages the acceptance of financially unsound projects
Contributes to the build up of statistical information to assist in better management
    of future projects
Enables a more objective comparison of alternatives
Identifies, and allocates responsibility to, the best risk owner

Soft benefits

Improves corporate experience and general communication
Leads to a common understanding and improved team spirit
Assists in the distinction between good luck/good management and bad
    luck/bad management.
Helps develop the ability of staff to assess risks
Focuses project management attention on the real and most important issues
Facilitates greater risk taking thus increasing the benefits gained
Demonstrates a responsible approach to customers
Provides a fresh view of the personnel issues in a project

These are listed in Table 3.1.

Table 3.2 illustrates the differing views of academics and practising managers with respect to risk and risk management. Typically risk has been considered as a threat to industry whereas the academic view is that risk can have both threats and opportunities and should be considered in greater detail from which strategies can be developed and risk management constantly applied.

Any organisation that is complacent about managing the significant risks it faces will surely fail. The Turnbull Report (1999) is a reminder of this and is also an opportunity to review what an organisation has in place and to make the appropriate changes. Risk management can be considered as the sustainability of a business within its particular environment. In the past large corporate failures have occurred because risk assessment has been wrong or never even considered. Reichmann (1999) states:

One of the most important lessons I have ever learnt, and I didn't learn it early enough, is that risk management is probably the most important part of business leadership.

Table 3.2 The views of academics and practitioners regarding risk and risk management

Academic view	View of practising managers
• Risk is defined in terms of possible outcomes and variability	• Risk defined as the downside potential of a course of action
• Risk can be calculated and factored in the expected outcome of a course of action	• Experience and intuition are more highly regarded than mathematical models and 'expected outcomes'
• Risk is a key element of strategic management	• Not adequately considered generally in management practice
• Risk management assumed to be consistently applied	• Different risk strategies applied in business areas depending on strategic importance
• Risk is an objective measure	• Risk factors are subject to interpretation and gut feeling. The eventual outcome is likely to determine the quality of a decision; a bad outcome was a mistake in the first place

However, organisations do need to be pragmatic. Risk is needed in order to gain reward. This is clearly addressed in the Turnbull Report (1999) which states that 'risk management is about mitigating, not eliminating risk'. By endorsing the Turnbull Report and complying with the Companies Act the board of directors of an SBU have overall responsibility and ownership of risks.

To manage risk effectively organisations need to have prevention and response strategies in place. Prevention strategies are there to help organisations understand the significant risks that they may face and to manage these risks down to acceptable levels. Response strategies need to be developed to enable organisations to respond, despite their efforts, to any risks that do crystallise, so as to reduce their impact as far as possible.

3.5 EMBEDDING RISK MANAGEMENT INTO YOUR ORGANISATION

Risk management cannot simply be introduced to an organisation overnight. The Turnbull Report (1999) lists the following series of events that need to take place to embed risk management into the culture of an organisation:

- *Risk identification.* Identify on a regular basis the risks that face an organisation. This may be done through workshops, interviews or questionnaires. The method is not important, but actually carrying out this stage is critical.
- *Risk assessment/measurement.* Once risks have been identified it is important to gain an understanding of their size. This is often done on a semi-quantitative basis. Again, the method is not important, but organisations should measure the likelihood of occurrence and the impact in terms of both image and reputation and financial impact.
- *Understand how the risks are currently being managed.* It is important to profile how the risks are currently being managed and to determine whether or not this meets an organisation's risk management strategy.
- *Report the risks.* Setting up reporting protocols and ensuring that people adhere to such protocols are critical to the process.
- *Monitor the risks.* Risks should be monitored to ensure that the critical ones are managed in the most effective way and the less critical ones do not become critical.
- *Maintain the risk profile.* It is necessary to maintain an up-to-date profile in an organisation to ensure that decisions are made on the basis of complete information.

3.6   RISK MANAGEMENT PLAN

A risk management plan (RMP) forms the basis of all risk management actions and further risk activities for corporate, strategic business and project levels. Based on the findings reported in a recent questionnaire (Merna 2002) the contents of such a plan might be:

- assignment of risk management responsibility
- the corporate risk management policy
- risk identification documentation – risk register, initial response options
- risk analysis outputs – risk exposure distribution within the project, most significant risks, variation of project outcome values with risk occurrences, probability distributions of project outcome values
- selected risk response options – risk allocation among project parties, provisions, procurement and contractual arrangements concerning risk, contingency plans, insurance and other transfer arrangements

- monitoring and controlling – comparison of actual with anticipated risk occurrences, control of the project with regard to the RMP
- maintenance of the risk management system – measures to update and maintain the RMP continuously and refine it
- evaluation – recording risk information for further RMP cycles within the project and for future projects.

Fraser (2003) highlights some key recommendations that are fundamental for the development of a successful risk management system (RMS):

- Executive level sponsorship and leadership for the programme is required.
- An RMS requires cultural and behavioural change.
- The operating management and business owners must take ownership of and be committed to the programme.
- There must be a formal structure and framework in place – the approach has to be transparent and when risks are identified and prioritised, information has to be shared across the board.

3.7   EXECUTIVE RESPONSIBILITY AND RISK

Risk management itself is fraught with risk. Any company that adopts an inappropriate approach to risk runs the danger of seriously damaging its business. It is important that companies understand that risk management is not an add-on but an integral part of the business. Often risk management forms part of an integrated management system along with quality management, planning, health and safety management, and change management. In a competitive economy, profits are the result of successful risk taking. If you are not taking much risk, you're not going to get much reward. Against this background, the Turnbull Report (1999) on companies' internal control and risk management, endorsed by the London Stock Exchange in the same year, strives not to be a burden on the corporate sector, but rather to reflect good business practice. The present authors suggest that by accepting 'best practice' at each organisational level many of the risks emanating from poor practice will be alleviated. Companies should implement any necessary changes in a way that reflects the needs of their business and takes account of their market. As and when companies make those changes, they should discover that they are improving their risk management and, consequently, get a benefit that justifies any cost.

The Turnbull Report is not just about avoidance of risk. It is about effective risk management: determining the appropriate level of risk, being conscious of the risks you are taking and then deciding how you need to manage them. Risk is both positive and negative in nature. Effective risk management is as much about looking to make sure that you are not missing opportunities as it is about ensuring that you are not taking inappropriate risks. Some companies will seek to be more risk averse than others. However, all should be seeking to achieve a balance between encouraging entrepreneurialism within their business and managing risks effectively.

In order for a company to be able to identify what risks it is taking and those it is not prepared to take, it must first identify its long-term objectives. Some companies have been much better than others in identifying in a concise but operational way what their business is about. Having identified their objectives, companies should not seek to identify, say, 1001 risks. Boards of directors at both corporate and strategic business levels should focus on what they believe to be their main business risks. The authors believe a reasonable number to manage and concern yourself about is 15–25. These risks will depend on the industry and the particular circumstances of the company and its projects at any given time.

When assessing the risks an organisation faces it is important to have the full support of the relevant board and that they appreciate the importance and understand the benefits of risk management. The board should receive regular reports from management so that they are fully conversant with the risks identified and those which appear as more information becomes more apparent. There is a danger that if risk is not addressed in a holistic manner by the board, larger risks which are hard to define, such as corporate reputation, will not be properly addressed. They may be partially considered in each of the organisation's decisions, but gaps will be left, or they may not be addressed at all. Recent evidence (Merna 2002) shows that in the past some companies viewed risk management in too narrow a way. Then risk management simply meant 'insurance'. However, companies should stop and ask themselves:

- Have we got an integrated approach to risk management?
- How are the risks covered – by insurance, by internal audit, or simply at a loose end?

As with any process, the output is only as good as the input. Unless organisations have effective systems for identifying and prioritising risks, there is a danger that they will build their controls on very shaky foundations. Having an effective system means that people at all levels, in different parts of the organisation, are involved in determining its main risks. Unless this is done, the danger arises that the organisation's RMS will be no more than a bottom-up process where lots of people work independently, resulting in aggregated ideas adding very little input. At the other end of the scale, the opposite may occur. If the identification and prioritisation of risk is done at the top by one person, or by a group of people, they could miss some very important strategic business, project and operational risks. Ultimately it should not be about choosing a bottom-up or top-down approach. There needs to be a mixture of both.

The authors suggest that there are a number of benefits to project professionals of building a simple decision-making support package and integrating risk assessment into the frameworks or standards they need to adhere to in their respective industries, which include:

- provides an easy and flexible structure to manage data and associated software
- promotes earlier management buy-in to a project
- prompts users to challenge and validate that data used are suitable, thus reducing risk
- provides a simple yet effective framework for decision making (as risk management is part of the decision-making process) and data storage
- provides a basis for identification and interrogation of subjective decisions and their associated risks
- decisions can be structured on the basis of confidence to proceed to the next decision
- reduction of risk associated with incorrect or out-of-date data
- provides quality assurance by allowing users to validate or challenge decisions
- all data, players and decision logic can be revisited
- decisions can be made in parallel and retraced
- decisions can be deferred due to insufficient data, unsuitable software or non-availability of decision-makers
- ensures that all stakeholders with input are involved in decision making
- decisions can be made in advance, if beneficial to do so, in the knowledge that all necessary data are available
- the system can be continually updated to accommodate new data and software

- can be accessed by any project team member at any stage of the project life cycle
- can be easily integrated into a project organisation.

3.8 SUMMARY

Risk management involves identifying risks, predicting how probable they are and how serious they might become, deciding what to do about them, and implementing these decisions. Despite the apparent widespread uptake of risk management, the extent to which risk processes are actually applied is somewhat variable. Many organisations adopt a minimalist approach, doing only what is necessary to meet mandatory requirements, or going through the motions of a risk process with no commitment to using the results to influence current or future strategy.

This chapter has discussed risk management, not only at the project level but at corporate and SBU levels. To ensure that risks are assessed effectively at all these levels it is paramount that a risk management process is developed so that all stakeholders are made aware of the risks associated with an investment.

4
Risk Management Tools and Techniques

4.1 INTRODUCTION

The management of risk is currently one of the main areas of interest for researchers and practitioners working in a wide range of projects because of the benefits of the process. Risk management is one of the key project management processes. Numerous techniques are available to support the various levels of the risk management process.

Risk management is a tool which is increasingly used in organisations and by public bodies to increase safety and reliability and to minimise losses. It involves the identification, evaluation and control of risks. Implicit in the process is the need for sound decision making on the nature of the potential socio-technical systems and their predicted reliability. The need for safety measures and guidance as to where they should be displayed are, in theory, the natural products of combined probabilistic risk assessment/human reliability analysis (PRA/HRA) studies. In an ideal world, good assessment should always drive effective error reduction.

This chapter describes the tools and techniques used in the assessment of risk, both qualitative and quantitative, and country risks which are often considered a major factor in risk assessment. The tools and techniques described can be used at corporate, strategic business and project levels.

4.2 DEFINITIONS

French and Saward (1983) describe a tool as any device or instrument, either manual or mechanical, which is used to perform work.

Distinguishing between a tool and technique is difficult. For the purpose of this book the present authors define tools as:

The methodology which employs numerous techniques to achieve its aim.

For example, risk management (tool) employs numerous techniques such as sensitivity analysis, probability analysis and decision trees. Value management (tool) employs such techniques as functional analysis, optioneering and criteria weighting.

4.3   RISK ANALYSIS TECHNIQUES

There are two main categories of risk analysis techniques: qualitative and quantitative. Qualitative methods seek to compare the relative significance of risks facing a project in terms of the effect of their occurrence on the project outcome. Simon *et al.* (1997) suggest that the information obtained from qualitative analysis is nearly always more valuable than that from quantitative analysis and that the latter is not always necessary. Thompson and Perry (1992) recommend qualitative analysis for developing an initial risk assessment.

Quantitative techniques attempt to determine absolute value ranges together with probability distributions for the business or project outcome and, consequently, involve more sophisticated analysis, often aided by the use of computers. According to Simon *et al.* (1997), to achieve this, a model is created of the project under consideration. It is then modified to quantify the impacts of specific risks determined by an initial assessment using qualitative techniques. The model will include all the elements which are relevant to the risk analysis and, against these elements, uncertain variables can be entered (rather than fixed values) to reflect areas of significant uncertainty.

4.3.1   Choice of Technique(s)

According to Norris (1992) and Simon *et al.* (1997) in determining which of the available analysis techniques is most suitable for application to a particular investment, management should consider:

- the availability of resources for analysis – human, computational and time
- the experience of the analysts with the different techniques
- the size and complexity of the project
- the project phase in which the analysis takes place
- the available information
- the purpose of the analysis.

In any analysis or assessment where data are required then the data should be considered as follows:

- Accuracy: are data accurate?
- Adequacy: are they adequate for the purpose of project?
- Relevancy: are they relevant to the subject?
- Coherence: has the information been classified in an orderly and meaningful way?
- Impartiality: has the analyst remained unbiased?
- Direction: does the analytical procedure lead to conclusions/ decisions?
- Logicality: is the reasoning sound?
- Validity: are comparisons, interpretations and implications valid?

The following provides a brief overview of some of the analysis techniques in use.

4.4   QUALITATIVE TECHNIQUES IN RISK MANAGEMENT

4.4.1   Brainstorming

Originating in Madison Avenue in the 1950s, brainstorming was long considered the preserve of those wild and wacky folk in advertising. In more recent years, however, it has spread into the mainstream and is now used by businesses of all kinds, not to mention civil servants, engineers, project managers and scientists or, indeed, anyone with a problem to solve.

The optimum size for a brainstorming session is 12 people and the ideal length of time is between 15 and 45 minutes, though sessions can last all day (*Sunday Times* 2001). The basic rules can be summarised as:

- imposition of a time limit
- a clear statement of the problem at hand
- a method of capturing the ideas, such as a flipchart
- somewhere visible to leave the ideas and let them incubate
- adoption of the principle that no idea is a bad idea
- suspension of judgement
- encouragement of participants to let go of their normal inhibitions and let themselves dream and drift around the problem
- encouraging quantity rather than quality (evaluation can come later)
- cross-fertilisation by picking up group ideas and developing them.

Chapman (1998) states that 'the brainstorming process, borrowed from business management and not specifically created for risk management, involves redefining the problem, generating ideas, finding possible solutions, developing selected feasible solutions and conducting evaluation'. However, Bowman and Ash (1987) believe there is a tendency for groups to make riskier decisions than individuals because of factors such as dispersed responsibility, where influential members of the groups have more extreme views and moderate members remain silent.

4.4.2   Assumptions Analysis

Assumptions analysis is an intuitive technique and is where assumptions typically made in project planning are identified. They are then assessed as to what impact their proving false will have on the project outcome. Assumptions to which the outcome is seen to be sensitive and which have a likelihood of proving false will form the basis of a list of risks (Simon *et al.* 1997). However, there is a danger that not all assumptions will be identified since a large number of them will be implicit.

4.4.3   Delphi

This is a technique for predicting a future event or outcome, in which a group of experts are asked to make their forecasts, initially independently, and subsequently by consensus in order to discard any extreme views. In some circumstances subjective probabilities can be assigned to the possible future outcomes in order to arrive at a conclusion.

Delphi is an intuitive technique and was developed at the RAND Corporation for technical forecasting. Merna (2002) stated that the technique involves obtaining group consensus by the following process:

- Respondents are asked to give their opinion on the risks pertaining to a project or investment.
- A chairperson then collates the information and issues a summary of the findings to the respondents requesting that they revise their opinion in light of the group's collective opinion.
- These steps are then repeated until either consensus is reached or the chairperson feels that no benefit will result from further repetitions.

The respondents are isolated from one another to avoid conflict and interact only with the chairperson. The Delphi process tends to take place through either the postal service or electronic interactive media.

Chapman (1998) cites that benefits from the Delphi Technique include that participants are free from group pressures and pressures of conformity, personality characteristics, and compatibility are avoided.

4.4.4 Interviews

This intuitive technique is used where information requirements need to be more detailed than a group can provide, or where group work is impractical. Interviews provide a means of soliciting information from individuals. Often corporate-level personnel will request interviews with project personnel to elicit information regarding potential risks at the project level which may affect the commercial viability of the project and thus affect the financial stability of the SBU undertaking it.

4.4.5 Hazard and Operability Studies (HAZOP)

'HAZOP' is an inductive technique and was developed by Imperial Chemicals Ltd for risk identification in chemical process plants. It is a type of structured brainstorming whereby a group systematically examine the elements of a process and define the intention of each (Ansell and Wharton 1995). Frosdick (1997) cites guidewords such as 'not', 'more' and 'less' to be used to identify possible deviations from the intention. Such deviations can then be investigated to eliminate their causes as far as possible and minimise the impact of their consequences.

The HAZOP approach is flexible and can be used to identify potential hazards in facilities of all kinds at all stages of their design and development. Alternatively, a review of contingency plans at an existing facility could be more comprehensively informed by a HAZOP exercise, which could identify hazards not previously planned for.

4.4.6 Failure Modes and Effects Criticality Analysis (FMECA)

FMECA is an inductive technique and undertaken by a single analyst with a thorough knowledge of the system under investigation. This technique may focus either on the hardware involved, with a concentration on potential equipment failures, or on events, with an emphasis on their outputs and the effect of their failure on the system. Every component of the system is considered and each mode of failure identified. The effects of such failure on the overall system are then determined (Frosdick 1997, Ansell and Wharton 1995). This technique uses a type of weighted score to identify areas of a project most at risk of failure. In a routine situation

FMECA is generally used at strategic business and project levels, it highlights areas of concern and it effectively points resources towards the perceived problem areas. The technique is often used for auditing company hardware (computer) and equipment.

4.4.7 Checklists

Checklists are deductive techniques derived from the risks encountered previously and provide a convenient means for management to rapidly identify possible risks. They take the form of either a series of questions or a list of topics to be considered. Organisations may generate checklists for themselves or make use of standard checklists available for their particular industry or sector.

4.4.8 Prompt Lists

These are deductive techniques and classify risks into type or area groups, for example financial, technical and environmental, or the task groups with which they are associated, for example design, construction and commissioning. They may be general, industry or project specific.

4.4.9 Risk Registers

A risk register is a document or database which records each risk pertaining to a project or particular investment or asset. As an identification aid, risk registers from previous, similar projects may be used in much the same way as checklists.

The risk register enables the data collected during the risk management identification process to be captured and saved, for review and as a data container for information on the choice of risk software. There are a number of 'prerequisite' data items necessary within the risk register, as follows:

- The title of the project. This should briefly describe the project.
- The project ID. This allows identification of specific projects where multiple projects are being developed.
- The activity ID.
- The activity acronym.
- The team leader's name, and the names of the individual teams. This information is necessary should any further investigation be needed or any queries in regard to the original risk assessment be raised.

Priority	Description	Probability	Impact	Owner	Key Dates	Current Actions	Review Date
1							
2							
3							
x^n							

Figure 4.1   Typical summary of a risk register output

- Activities. This column is a list of activity descriptions, preferably in order of sequence. The register may be used for network or spreadsheet models.
- Procedure. This is important for network-based risk software packages. It identifies the linkage between the activities from start to finish.
- Most likely. Estimated by the expert for the activities, this is a value used in the risk software package around which the optimistic and pessimistic values operate. This is commonly referred to as a three-point estimate.

Figure 4.1 illustrates a template for the summary of a risk register output that can be used at corporate, strategic business or project levels.

Risk measure charts can be developed from the risk register. The goal of a risk measure chart is not to solve the risks, but to assign tasks to the responsible party. For example:

- scenario – change in government
- action – foster political neutrality; predict scope or contract changes by new officials.

From these tasks, the responsible party can in turn perform risk analyses in further detail.

4.4.10   Risk Mapping

This involves the graphical representation of risks on a two-dimensional graph where one axis relates to the potential severity of a risk eventuating and the other to the probability of it doing so (Figure 4.2). Risks are considered in turn and plotted on the graph. Iso-risk curves drawn on the graph connecting equivalent risk with differing probability/severity serve to guide the analysts in determining the relative importance of the risks which they plot (Al-Bahar and Crandell 1990).

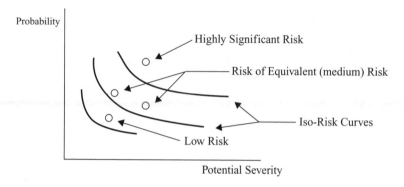

Figure 4.2   Risk mapping concept

4.4.11   Probability-Impact Tables

Probability–Impact (P–I) tables are used to assess the relative importance of risks. As with risk mapping, the probability of occurrence and the potential impact of a risk is determined by selecting from a range of low/medium/high, for example. The numerical meaning of each of the scale points should be predetermined for the project and investment.

P–I scores are then derived for each risk by multiplying their probability scores by their impact scores, allowing direct comparison of the risks – the higher the P–I score, the greater the severity of the risk (Simon *et al.* 1997). An example of P–I tables is shown in Figure 4.3. Probability impact grids will be discussed later in this chapter.

4.4.12   Risk Matrix Chart

The risk matrix chart is often used to segregate high-impact risks from low-impact risks. Figure 4.4 illustrates how the risk matrix chart partly qualifies the probability and impact of a risk, and is often used in risk management workshops where risks are identified and then assessed in terms of their impact and probability. For example, the risk of employees being late for work would be classed as a kitten since little attention is needed because employees finish their work in their own time. Rain in Manchester is highly probable but has little impact on construction work since operatives are trained to take specific measures to deal with such events. This would be classed as a puppy. Flooding of business premises could have a low probability due to its location but should flooding occur

| Scale | Probability | Probability Score | Impact on Probability | | Impact Score |
			Cost Increase	Time Increase	
V. Low	<10%	0.1	<5%	<1 month	0.05
Low	10–30%	0.3	5–10%	1–2 month	0.1
Medium	30–50%	0.5	10–15%	3–4 month	0.2
High	50–70%	0.7	15–30%	5–6 month	0.4
V. High	>70%	0.9	>30%	>6 month	0.8

| | | Probability | | | | |
		V. Low 0.1	Low 0.3	Medium 0.5	High 0.7	V. High 0.9
Impact	V. Low 0.05	0.005	0.015	0.025	0.035	0.045
	Low 0.1	0.01	0.03	0.05	0.07	0.09
	Medium 0.2	0.02	0.06	0.10	0.14	0.18
	High 0.2	0.04	0.12	0.20	0.28	0.36
	V. High 0.8	0.08	0.24	0.40	0.56	0.72

Figure 4.3   Probability–impact tables (Adapted from Allen 1995)

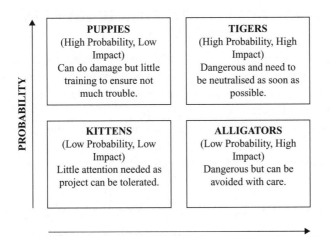

PUPPIES
(High Probability, Low Impact)
Can do damage but little training to ensure not much trouble.

TIGERS
(High Probability, High Impact)
Dangerous and need to be neutralised as soon as possible.

KITTENS
(Low Probability, Low Impact)
Little attention needed as project can be tolerated.

ALLIGATORS
(Low Probability, High Impact)
Dangerous but can be avoided with care.

PROBABILITY

IMPACT

Figure 4.4   Risk matrix chart

it would have a major impact on the businesse's profits. This alligator is managed by ensuring that flood protection is in place or by storing finished goods in a water tight structure. In the drug development phase of a pharmaceutical product the side effects of 'first in man' tests are highly probable and may have a high impact. This tiger is often mitigated by keeping the tests down to a small sample and by ensuring volunteers are insured against long-term effects.

Typically the tigers and alligators are mitigated before the puppies and kittens.

4.4.13   Project Risk Management Road Mapping

Table 4. illustrates the overall processes and applications that may be considered in the choice of a risk management system.

Each category of the road map in the table presents, firstly, the simplest techniques, followed by gradually increasing levels of work and complexity. It is important to focus on the added value which is provided by the subsequent level when you are trying to identify the appropriate level for a particular situation.

Many of such qualitative analysis methods are used at corporate and SBU levels in the early stage of project definition when little detailed information is available.

4.5   QUANTITATIVE TECHNIQUES IN RISK MANAGEMENT

Quantitative techniques are used when the likelihood of the investment or project achieving its objectives within time and budget is required – typically for budget authorisation or presentation of the project's status to the board of directors.

It should be borne in mind that the output from quantitative analysis is only as good as the input information, so adequate time should be allowed for its collection and validation.

4.5.1   Decision Trees

Management are often faced with multiple choices, which in turn are faced with many options. In many cases management only have the

Table 4.1 Risk management (RM) road map

1 Organisation and scope	2 Risk identification	3 Risk analysis
1.1 No need to focus on RM	2.1 Experience and intuitive awareness	3.1 Project risk list
1.2 Personal task for project manager	2.2 Interviewing	3.2 Verbal risk description
1.3 RM workshops	2.3 Generic checklist – broad headings	3.3 Project risk list and additional data – causes, timing, responsibility
1.4 Facilitators' involvement needed	2.4 Generic checklist – hierarchical list including more detailed risk drivers	3.4 Quantification and charting – impacts of risks on project outcome
1.5 Project – systematic procedures for continuous RM	2.5 Generic checklist – generic headings + problems/earlier projects	3.5 Charting – dependencies between individual risk
1.6 Company – systematic procedures for continuous RM	2.6 Use of checklist + decision conferencing techniques	3.6 Quantification and charting – scenario analysis
1.7 Company – integration of management procedures		3.7 Quantification and charting – simulation model

4 Decision on risk strategy	5 Planning and decisions on responses	6 Continuous control and feedback
4.1 Modify project objectives	5.1 Response list	6.1 Responsibility control
4.2 Risk avoidance	5.2 Response list and additional data – costs of responses and timing	6.2 Advanced reporting practice
4.3 Risk prevention	5.3 Quantification and charting – effects of planned responses	6.3 Regularly updated experiential checklist (hierarchical)
4.4 Risk mitigation	5.4 Quantification and charting – trade-off analysis	6.4 Project risk knowledge base – problems encountered, close events
4.5 Develop contingency plans		
4.6 Keep options open		
4.7 Monitor simulation		
4.8 Accept risk without any actions		

resources to opt for one, which presents management with the problem of opportunity cost. However, deciding to adopt an option can be difficult and a useful technique to assess options is the decision tree. This technique explores various investment options available to the decision-maker under risk and uncertainty which are graphically represented in the form of sequential decisions and probability events (Merrett and Sykes 1983).

PMBOK (1996) describes decision trees as diagrams that depict key interactions between decisions and associated chance events as they are understood by the decision-maker. Decision trees show a sequence of interrelated decisions and the expected outcomes under each possible set of circumstances. Where probabilities and values of potential outcomes are known, they are used as a method of quantification which aids the decision-making process.

The aim of the decision tree is to produce an expected value for each option which is the sum of the probabilities and their weighted values. The diagram begins with a decision node at the top of the sheet and consequential chance events and decisions are drawn sequentially as the decision-making process proceeds from top to bottom. Decisions are depicted as square nodes. These are linked by labelled straight lines or 'branches' which denote either decision actions if they stem from decision nodes or alternative outcomes if they stem from chance event nodes (Hertz and Thomas 1983, 1984, Gregory 1997).

Figure 4.5 illustrates a typical decision tree. The example forecasts possible outcomes from opening or not opening a new factory. The example takes account of competitor reaction and the state of the economy, and the decision of whether to go ahead or not is expressed statistically as return on capital employed (ROCE).

According to Thompson and Perry (1992), this technique can help clarify and communicate a sequence of choices and decisions. The technique has been used in industry to decide methods of construction, contractual problems and investment decisions. In theory the technique could be used in any situation where there is an option, or opportunity cost, and a decision is needed.

4.5.2   Controlled Interval and Memory Technique

The controlled interval and memory (CIM) model provides a mathematical means of combining probability distributions for individual risks.

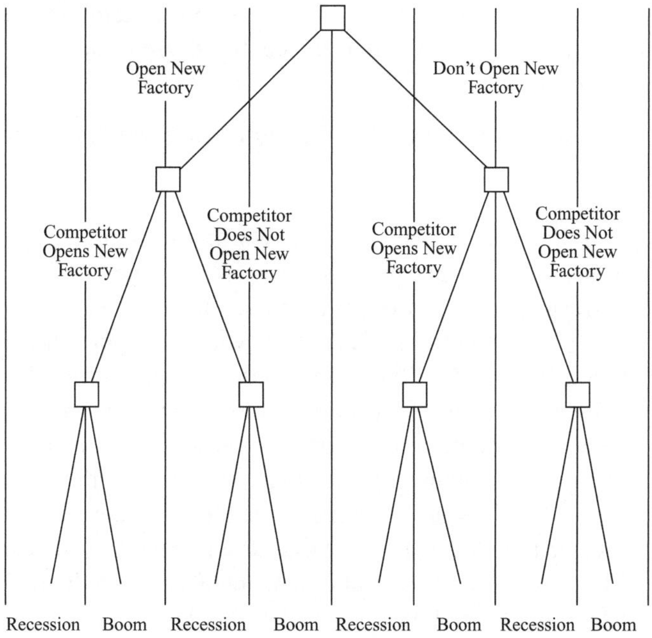

Sales	100	150	120	300	60	100	100	125
Return on Sales	5	10	5	20	0	3	5	6
Operating Profit	5	15	6	40	0	3	5	705
Capital Employed	90	90	90	90	50	50	50	50
ROCE (%)	6	17	7	44	0	6	10	15
Probability	0.1	0.1	0.4	0.4	0.25	0.25	0.25	0.25

Expected value of ROCE

$=0.1(6) + 0.1(17) + 0.4(7) + 0.4(44)$

$=22.2\%$

Expected value of ROCE

$=0.25(0) + 0.25(6) + 0.25(10) + 0.25(15)$

$=7.8\%$

Figure 4.5   Typical decision tree (Adapted from Marshell 2000)

According to Simon *et al.* (1997) this technique has largely been super-seded by simulation techniques and is not widely used.

4.5.3   Monte Carlo Simulation

This technique derives its name from its association with chance or uncertain situations and its use of random numbers to simulate their consequences. Simulation is an art and science of designing a model which behaves in the same way as a real system. The model is used to determine how the system reacts to different inputs. Four important steps are required as follows:

1. Assign a probability distribution to each variable which affects the IRR/NPV (see below).
2. Assign the range of variation for each variable.
3. Select a value for each variable within its specific range. This is done in such a way that the frequency with which any value is selected corresponds to its probability in the distribution.
4. Carry out a deterministic analysis with the input values selected from their specified distributions in random combinations. Each time a new value is generated for each variable, a new combination is obtained – hence a new deterministic analysis is done. This is repeated a number of times to obtain a result. The number of combinations of probability distributions required is usually between 200 and 1000. The greater number of iterations used will result in increased accuracy. The diagrammatic output of a Monte Carlo simulation in the form of a cumulative probability distribution diagram is shown in Figure 4.7. A brief assessment of the strengths and weaknesses of Monte Carlo simulations is shown in Table 4.2.

Table 4.2   Monte Carlo simulation strengths and weaknesses

Strength	Weakness
Stochastic – easier to compute for multiple inputs	Probability distributions are assumed based in part on previous experience
Allows a probability distribution to be used avoiding single point estimations	Risk profiles are often underestimated, due to excluding the tails of the distributions
Provides a more representative prediction of risk, provided initial assumptions are reasonable	Most Monte Carlo packages, with the exception of the high end ones, do not allow for interdependence of input variables
Relatively fast with modern computing technology, brute force approach to calculation	Use of historical data can propagate previous erroneous assumptions
	Subjective judgement is typically used to come up with starting points
	Can become too complex and unwieldy

4.5.4   Sensitivity Analysis

In any project or investment, the data used at the planning stage are bound to vary and are therefore subject to risk. Sensitivity analysis is used to produce more realistic values, supported by a range of possible alternatives that reflect any uncertainty and provide some means of validity of the assumptions. Sensitivity analysis is carried out to identify the most sensitive variables affecting the project's estimated worth, usually in terms of net present value (NPV) or internal rate of return (IRR) (Norris 1992).

Sensitivity analysis is used to determine the effect on the whole project of changing one of its risk variables. The technique aims to identify the risks which have a potentially high impact on the cost or timescale of the project.

A major advantage of sensitivity analysis is that it shows the robustness and ranking of alternative projects. It identifies the point at which a given variation in the expected value of a cost parameter changes a decision. Then, the range of change for each variable is defined and a picture of the possible range of minimum and maximum effects on the project's outcome is gradually determined as each of the important risks is investigated. The weakness of the method is that risks are considered independently and without their probability of occurrence.

There are several ways in which the results of a sensitivity analysis can be presented. Most practitioners tend to present the data in either a tabular or diagrammatic form. However, if several variables are changed, a graphical representation of the results is most useful; this quickly illustrates the most sensitive or critical variables. Norris (1992) and Skoulaxenou (1994) state that a 'spider diagram' of percentage change in variables versus percentage change in outcome value is the most popular means of expressing the results.

Sensitivity analysis is usually adequate and effective for projects during the appraisal process when comparing options and for preliminary approval, where only a limited number of identified risks are assessed.

Figure 4.6 illustrates the sensitivity analysis of a project's economic parameters; these are cash lock-up (CLU), payback (PB) and net present value (NPV) in relation to the internal rate of return (IRR). Although Figure 4.6 is generated on the basis of economic data, sensitivity diagrams can also be used at both corporate and SBU levels. For example, a sensitivity diagram may be used at the corporate level to show the

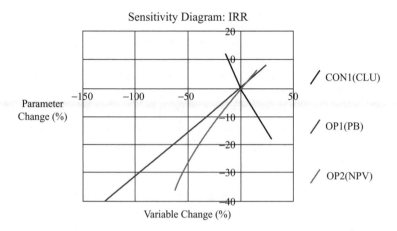

Figure 4.6   Typical sensitivity analysis diagram

sensitivity of a number of SBUs when considered against specific risks occurring, such as demand and market changes.

Similarly SBUs can use a spider diagram to show the effects of risk, say delay, to a number of projects in its portfolio. Sensitivity is normally considered in terms of change to IRR, NPV and time.

Figure 4.7 represents the uncertainty in a project in terms of IRR. In this example the project has a 40% chance of the IRR being less than 7.5% and a 60% chance of it being greater than 7.5%. Similarly the

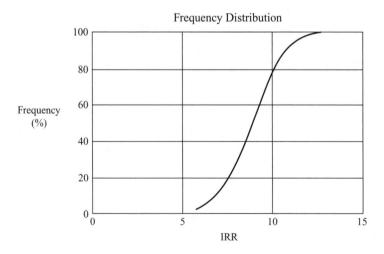

Figure 4.7   Cumulative probability distribution

project has an 80% chance of the IRR being less than 10% and a 20% chance of it being greater than 10%, with a 50% chance of it being less than or greater than 8%.

As with sensitivity analysis, cumulative distribution curves can be used to illustrate the probability of both SBUs and a portfolio of projects. It is important to note that the steeper the curve, the less the uncertainty in the investment, since the range of possibilities for values of IIR, in this case, is more certain.

4.5.5 Probability–Impact Grid Analysis

When the impact parameters for a risk (cost, programme, performance) have been established, a broad-band rating system may be used to rank the risk based on the probability–impact grid (PIG) method (Kolluru *et al.* 1996). The ranges of the impact bands are often determined at SBU and project levels and defined in the risk management plan (RMP).

The 'most likely values' for cost and programme gathered during the identification phase are applied to the band ranges in determining the level of impact, for instance low, medium and high. An example of a weighted factor can be seen in Table 4.3. The weighting of the impact scale serves to focus the risk response on high-impact risks with less weighting being given to probability. The P–I score can be determined by multiplying the impact scores (Table 4.3) and the probability scores (see Figure 4.8).

A threshold for the P–I score may be set in a resulting matrix as shown in Figure 4.8. In this case a 5 by 5 matrix is shown. A 3 by 3 matrix is, however, more commonly used.

The cost and programme impacts may fall into different levels of severity for any particular risk. In this event the worst case result is used for overall ranking.

Table 4.3 Impact weighting factors for PIG analysis

Impact score	PIG factor (weighted)
Very low	0.05
Low	0.1
Medium	0.2
High	0.4
Very high	0.8

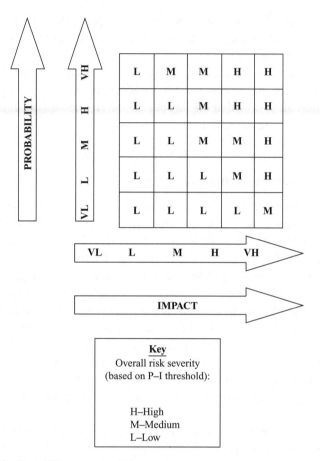

Figure 4.8   Probability–impact grid

The result of this assessment is a ranking order for all risks within the project register. They may be ranked in terms of cost, schedule and/or performance, for example answering the question of what are the top 10 risks. It will also indicate which risks should be prioritised when generating the risk response plans or allocating project resources.

4.6   QUANTITATIVE AND QUALITATIVE RISK ASSESSMENTS

Figure 4.9 illustrates a typical cumulative cash flow curve for a project. The usage of qualitative and quantitative techniques is also illustrated.

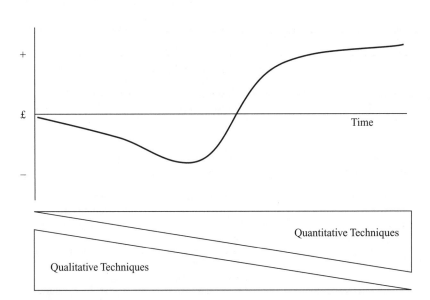

Figure 4.9 Typical project cumulative cash flow and the types of risk management techniques used throughout the life cycle of a project

At the start of a project the risk management techniques tend to be more qualitative. However, as the project moves through its life cycle the risk management techniques tend to become quantitative the more project information and detail there are available.

4.7 VALUE MANAGEMENT

Over the past decade, there has been a trend towards applying value management techniques at ever earlier stages in a project or investment life cycle. Ganas (1997) states that value management has become a blanket that covers all value techniques whether they entail value planning, value engineering or value analysis. However, there is no universally accepted definition of value management, and a number of different definitions have arisen to describe the same approach of application.

The ICE design and practice guide (1996) states that:

Value Management addresses the value processes during the concept, definition, implementation and operation phases of a project. It encompasses a set of systematic, logical procedures and techniques to enhance project value throughout the life of the facility/project.

Table 4.2   Typical qualitative and quantitative risk assessment techniques (Burnside 2007)

Risk analysis techniques		
Qualitative — Assessment based on experience, description and scales	**Semi-Quantitative** — Qualitative scales are given values	**Quantitative** — Analysis based on mathematical formulas
None mathematical subjective determination	— Deterministic (non-random)	Probabilistic
— Brainstorming — Interview — Intuition	— Sensitivity analysis — dependency — Spider diagrams/plots	Random: — Monte Carlo — Latin hyper cube
— Questionnaire	— Confidence envelope (probability contours)	— Artificial neural networks
— Assumptions analysis	— Decision tree analysis	Stochastic (dynamic)
— Hierarchical Holographic modelling — Nominal group Technique	— Non-dependency — Tornado diagrams	— Markovian logic — Network scheduling
— Soft system Methodology	— Network scheduling — Programme Evaluation and Review Technique (PERT) Controlled Conversion Matrix (CCM)	Conditional probability — Baye's theorem
— Risk matrix chart	— Critical Path Method (CPM)	— Bayesian networks (risk maps)
— Probability- impact Tables — Risk mapping — Risk registers — Prompt lists — Checklists — Failure modes and Effects Criticality — Analysis (FMECA) — Hazard and operability studies (HAZOP) — Interviews		

Connaughton and Green (1996) define value management as:

A structured approach to define what value means to a client in meeting a perceived need by establishing a clear consensus about the project objectives and how they can be achieved.

Although the definitions are similar and contain the key elements of structure and achieving value, there does seem to be some ambiguity surrounding the understanding of the cited terms. Ganas (1997) identified this and introduced the following definitions to clear any ambiguities:

> *Value is the level of importance that is placed on a function, item or solution. The four traits of value are speed, quality, flexibility and cost.*

> a) *speed – how quickly a firm can deliver a product to the customer or design and produce a product*
> b) *quality – how well a product meets a customer's expectations*
> c) *flexibility – how easily the firm can change a product to closely meet the customer's expectations/wants*
> d) *costs – elements to be included in a life cycle costing are – capital, finance, operating, maintenance, replacement, alteration, expansion and innovation costs, and residual values*

Value management (VM) is the title given to the full range of available techniques. It is a high-order title and linked to a particular project stage at which value techniques may be applied. It is a systematic, multidisciplinary, effort directed towards analysing the functions of projects for the purpose of achieving the best value at the lowest overall life cycle project cost (Norton and McElligott 1995).

Value planning (VP) is the title given to value techniques applied during the concept or 'planning' phases of a project. VP is used during the development of the 'brief' to ensure that value is planned into the whole project from its inception. This is done by addressing the function and ranking of the stakeholders' requirements in order of importance for guidance. This term can be further subdivided to include strategic VP, which is a technique that can be applied during and prior to the feasibility stage when alternatives to a built solution will be considered.

Value engineering (VE) is the title given to value techniques applied during the design phases of a project and, as required, in the implementation processes also. VE investigates, analyses, compares and selects amongst the various options to produce the required function and the shareholders' project requirements. VE produces a range of 'how' design options for the whole project or for defined parts of it. These are tested against the stakeholders' value objectives and criteria to remove unnecessary cost without sacrificing function, reliability, quality or required aesthetics.

Value analysis (VA) is the title given to value techniques applied retrospectively to completed projects to 'analyse' or to audit a project's performance, and to compare a completed project against predetermined expectations.

Risk management and VM are all part of a single management structure. It is important, however, to differentiate between them so that the right techniques are introduced at the right time. Risk management is mainly concerned with events that might affect the 'achievement' of investment objectives. It requires objectives to be well defined – you cannot assess whether investment objectives will be adversely affected unless there is a prior statement of what they are. Risk management (and, in particular, risk identification and analysis) therefore has a vital role to play in identifying and choosing between competing technical solutions, which is the subject of VE.

Risk management is also an important part of VM, even though it may seem unhelpful to try to identify and manage risks until there is agreement about what the objectives are. In fact, a strategic diagnosis of the risks may well influence how the objectives are set. A consideration of investment risks is likely to feature in outline design proposals during investment feasibility (Connaugton and Green 1996).

4.7.1   Value Management Techniques

4.7.1.1   Concurrent Studies

These are structured reviews of detailed proposals, undertaken by the project team in parallel with the design work, and led by the value manager.

4.7.1.2   Contractor's Change Proposals

These concern tender and post-tender design and/or construction changes suggested by the contractor and are intended primarily to reduce costs or improve buildability. These changes are usually linked to an incentive scheme which rewards the contractor for savings achieved.

4.7.1.3   Criteria Weighting

This is the assignment of arithmetic weights to different project criteria to reflect their relative importance.

4.7.1.4   Functional Analysis

This is a technique designed to help in the appraisal of value by careful analysis of function; for instance, the fundamental reason why the project element or component exists or is being designed.

4.7.1.5   Functional Analysis System Technique (FAST)

FAST is a form of functional analysis expressed in diagrammatic form to show the relationship between functions and the means of achieving them.

4.7.1.6   Job Plan

This is a logical and sequential approach to problem solving, which involves the identification and appraisal of a range of options, broken down into their constituent steps and used as the basis of the VM approach.

4.7.1.7   Matrix Analysis (Optioneering)

This is a technique for the evaluation of options where scores are awarded for each option against key criteria. These scores are then multiplied by the appropriate criteria weights and the total weighted scores for each option are examined to identify which offers the best value for money.

The optioneering technique is most valuable when assessing risks. Each option will have its own risks and these risks should be taken into account before an option is agreed. For example, option A may be seen to have very little engineering risk compared with option B. If, however, option A has a shorter operating life than option B then the risk associated with option A is reduced revenue generation. If the prime objective of the investment is NPV then option A is presumed to be too risky to meet such an objective. Figure 4.10 illustrates the VM stages.

4.7.1.8   Objectives Hierarchy

This is a breakdown of the primary objective into successively lower levels of sub-objectives until all the project objectives have been accounted for. Subobjectives may be ranked and weighted as for criteria weighting.

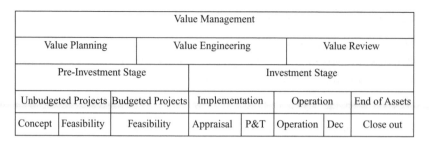

Value Management						
Value Planning		Value Engineering			Value Review	
Pre-Investment Stage			Investment Stage			
Unbudgeted Projects	Budgeted Projects	Implementation		Operation		End of Assets
Concept	Feasibility	Feasibility	Appraisal	P&T	Operation	Dec	Close out

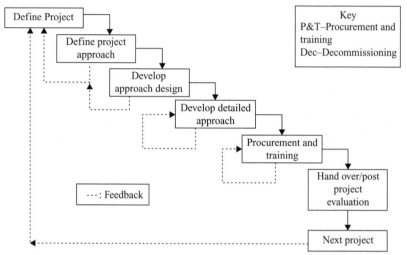

Figure 4.10   The value management stages. (More emphasis at corporate level is made at the pre-investment stage with detailed SBU and project level involvement during the investment phase)

4.8   OTHER RISK MANAGEMENT TECHNIQUES

4.8.1   Soft Systems Methodology (SSM)

SSM is a qualitative technique and was developed in the late 1970s and early 1980s. Its purpose was to overcome the inability of traditional decision theory to solve adequately all but the most structured of problems. A particular strength of SSM is that it can begin with the simple desire to 'make things better'.

Smith (1999) states that SSM is typically employed in a cycle of seven stages, as indicated in Figure 4.11.

The first two stages involve finding out about the situation considered as problematic, such as investigating the environment and culture in which the problem exists, the specific problems considered, the reasons

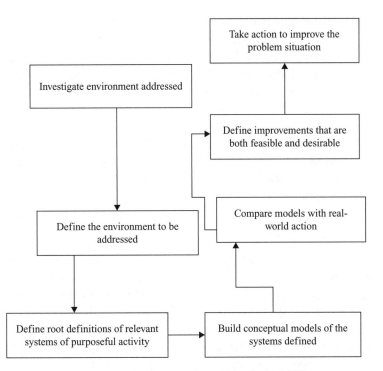

Figure 4.11   Soft systems methodology (Adapted from Smith 1999)

why the situation is considered problematic, and the improvements that are sought in the third stage of SSM. A view of the problem is selected which provides an insight into how improvements can be achieved. This is undertaken through the use of root definitions: that is, neutral definitions of the activities or tasks to be undertaken which provide insight into the problem.

The fourth stage involves the building of conceptual models that are logical expansions of the root definitions generated in the previous stage. The models developed are those of systems which can adapt to and survive changes through their processes of communication and control.

The fifth stage of SSM requires that the models developed are compared with reality. This provides a means of instigating debate into how benefits in the systems can be attained. This process directs attention onto assumptions made, highlights alternatives, and provides an opportunity for rethinking many aspects of real-world activity.

The purpose of the sixth stage of SSM is to define changes that will bring about mediation benefits. Such changes have to meet criteria of systematic durability and cultural feasibility. Systematic desirability will include factors such as mechanisms to determine effectiveness and ensuring that logical dependencies are reflected in real-world sequential actions. Cultural feasibility will make allowances for illogical human actions, and the political environment in which decisions are taken.

The final stage of SSM is the implementation of the changes proposed. Undertaking these changes alters the perceptions of the initial problem situation. If required, further cycles of SSM can be employed to seek additional improvements. This process will have been made considerably more straightforward through the structuring of the problem undertaken in the first application of SSM (Smith 1999).

4.8.2   Utility Theory

Modern utility theory, developed from the work of Von Neumann and Morgenstern, is concerned with anticipating consumer behaviour under conditions of uncertainty and suggests that an individual will seek to maximise expected utility. To accommodate the notion that consumers are risk averse, for instance, successively smaller increments of utility are derived from each additional unit of wealth accumulated; it is generally assumed that they possess quadratic utility functions.

Indifference curves, such as those labelled D1, D2, D3 in Figure 4.12, are used to explain what combination of goods a consumer will choose.

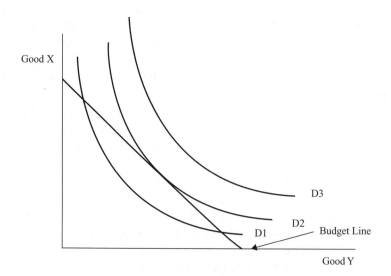

Figure 4.12   Typical indifference map (Adapted from Coyle 2001)

The optimum point is where the consumer's budget line is tangent to an indifference curve on the indifference map. Thus a consumer will show no preference between combinations of goods X and Y that lie on the same indifference curve, but in seeking maximum expected utility, the consumer will prefer a higher indifference curve to a lower one, that is D3 rather than D2. The point of tangency between the budget line and an indifference curve indicates the consumer will be in equilibrium, maximising utility where relative prices are equal to the marginal rates of substitution.

The concept of utility theory could be applied to the central problem of decision making under uncertainty – the attitude of decision-makers to risk; however, in most industries utility theory tends to be regarded as a theoretical technique, not easily applied. Hertz and Thomas (1983) describe efforts to turn theoretical utility theory into a practical tool. They conclude that, for the present, it is important to alert managers to the possibility of bias in decision making.

4.8.3   Risk Attitude and Utility Theory

With a rudimentary knowledge of probability, it is possible to calculate the expected monetary value (EMV) for decision outcomes (Rafferty 1994). Using this one can pursue the maximisation of EMV as a decision criterion when dealing with decisions under risk. However, it is frequently seen in practice that rational consumers will prefer an alternative to the option that offers the highest expected value.

Utility theory offers a model for understanding this behaviour. Personal attitudes to risk are measured by understanding and studying individual trade-offs between gambles and certain pay-offs. From this we can place individuals into three, self-explanatory categories:

- risk neutral
- risk seeking
- risk averse.

The comparisons are usually made from the use of the 'Basic Reference Lottery Ticket' (BRLT). For example, suppose an individual owns a lottery ticket which has an even chance of winning £10 000 or nothing at all. The EMV for the ticket is given in the following expression:

$$EMV = (£10\,000 \times 0.5) + (£0.00 \times 0.5) = £5000$$

Now if you were to ask the three different groups of individuals what price they would be willing to pay for the ticket, their responses will vary as follows:

- *Risk neutral.* This group would, in theory, be willing to sell the ticket for a minimum price of £5000, which is the EMV. The seller would be indifferent between the two outcomes; for instance, for this group, the certainty equivalent of the gamble is £5000.
- *Risk seeking.* This group would want to retain the ticket for the thrill of the gamble and may not be willing to part with the ticket until the prospective purchaser was willing to pay well over its EMV. This seems mathematically irrational.
- *Risk averse.* Here the group may decide that it is worth selling the ticket, which has a 50% chance of winning nothing, for a sum less than the mathematical EMV.

Figure 4.13 shows how, but not why, rational people sometimes prefer outcomes which do not have the highest monetary value. Utility theory suggests that instead of maximising EMV, people maximise their own utility. Utilities vary from person to person. The utility function of an individual is unlikely to be identical to the utility function of that individual's employing organisation.

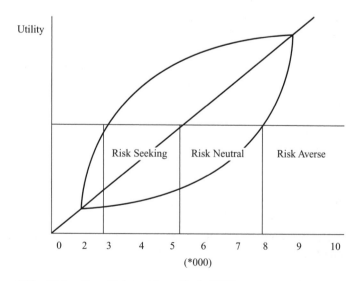

Figure 4.13   Risk options (Adapted from Coyle 2001)

4.8.4 Nominal Group Technique

Nominal group technique (NGT) is a variant of brainstorming. It is a method of generating ideas which has been developed in an attempt to overcome some of the perceived failures of brainstorming. In NGT, each group member records a number of risks and these risks are presented to the group for discussion. During the presentation, members of the group individually score each risk and the scores are ranked. The scores are then mathematically aggregated to yield a group decision (Frosdick 1997).

4.8.5 Stress Testing and Deterministic Analysis

A stress test is basically a deterministic model typically run in Microsoft Excel. The inputs are derived from factors such as cash flow magnitude, cash flow start and end points, production cost and an estimate of potential project cost escalation over and above the project contingency. Each project stakeholder is responsible for developing a range of possible outcomes, usually as a percentage and typically for their respective factors. For example, marketing is responsible for sales volume and pricing assumptions, manufacturing is responsible for the cost data and project engineering is responsible for project cost escalation assumptions. These factors are typically single point sensitivities. The financial model calculates IRR, NPV and payback period. After the model has been run for the base case, it is then run for a variety of sensitivity cases with each variable set independently for best and worst predicted outcome. The result is either a spider diagram or a tornado diagram showing the individual impact of each factor on project economic parameters such as NPV. Additionally these same impacts are then put into a project risk table that identifies the risk and its NPV impact on the project. The model is then run for the worst case scenario by setting all input variables to their worst anticipated outcomes thereby giving the worst project outcome. Conversely, each input is then set to the most optimistic case giving the best case scenario. Once these scenarios have been compiled, the assumptions are challenged by the various stakeholders in a brainstorming-type format. It is the stakeholders' responsibility to thoroughly challenge or 'stress test' each assumption. Only after the respective stakeholders agree with the project assumptions is the appropriation request sent forward for corporate approval.

Table 4.4   Stress test strengths and weaknesses

Strength	Weakness
Uses more than one analysis tools to evaluate risk	Uses relatively weak financial model in that only single point assumptions are used
Seeks to challenge assumptions by brainstorming methods	Relies on individual groups to come up with point assumptions
Reasonably simple to use with minimal inputs required to generate an output	Being simple to use, brings with it a lack of robustness that more advanced techniques possess
Full breadth of risks analysed even though outliers may not be overly realistic	Does not, typically, take into account interdependence of input variables
	As with Monte Carlo relies on historical subjective data for variances from base. Risks tend to be overestimated to ensure a high degree of comfort
	Does not output a formal document identifying risk owner or mitigating actions

The strengths and weaknesses of this methodology contains some strengths not found in Monte Carlo analysis due primarily to the fact that it contains not one but a variety of different risk management tools all rolled into one. Despite this fact, the methodology has inherent weaknesses that the authors feel are better addressed by Monte Carlo techniques. Table 4.4 contrasts these perceived strengths and weaknesses.

The stress test methodology, while outputting a variety of sensitivities and having many similarities to established practices, cannot be pigeonholed into any one category. The methodology outputs do identify the risks and magnitude, but do a relatively weak job of tying down respective probabilities. The tendency is to overestimate the risks and put enough cushion in the appropriation to ensure a viable project.

In contrast, the concept of Monte Carlo simulation, in principle, is fairly simple. Project risk inputs are given probability distributions and run through a mathematical model to generate a resultant risk probability curve. However, depending on the application these models can be highly complex and give misleading results to the inexperienced user. If the user disregards the tails on a distribution, this can eliminate up to 30% of the cumulative probabilities. As with any analysis tool the user needs to fully understand the mechanism, its advantages and weaknesses when applying it. Monte Carlo analysis has proven itself a valuable risk analysis tool if used correctly. Conversely, if used incorrectly it can raise as many questions as answers.

4.8.6   Tornado Diagram

The Tornado diagram is derived from the sensitivity analysis technique. Activities within a project can be subjected to percentage increases or decreases based on the uncertainty at the time of analysis.

Initially those activities, for example those shown in Figure 4.14, are considered to have various outcomes. The effect of risk is expressed quantitatively on each of the items which are then illustrated on a Tornado diagram. The best case scenario is the one that shows a positive saving and the worst case scenario shows the potential losses on each of the activities. The best and worst case scenarios are the outer lines in Figure 4.14. The inner line represents the savings and losses after risk mitigation. For example, before risk mitigation, metal prices have a range of minus $400 and plus $600. This is identified as the most sensitive activity. Insurance, on the other hand, is seen as less sensitive, having a range of plus $250 and minus $150. The risk associated with these activities can then be mitigated by buying forward in the former case and changing insurers in the latter case. Similarly the other activities are mitigated and the inner line can now be drawn to show the worst and best cases for each activity. The smaller the area between the worst case and best case line the less the uncertainty in the scheduled activities.

4.9   COUNTRY RISK ANALYSIS

Country risk assessment was considered to be a new discipline at a premature stage with unclear boundaries and terminology (Leavy 1984). In order to support this argument, a comparison with 'sovereign risk' and 'political risk' assessment was put forward. 'Sovereign risk assessment' is the term normally used in the banking world to refer to the risks related to the provision of loans to foreign governments, while 'political risk assessment' is the technique used to predict the political stability and the non-business risk in conducting operations in the different socio-political environment. Notable research has been carried out in the area of political risk, resulting in commercially produced inventory checklists, specialised publications and quantitative approaches, which are

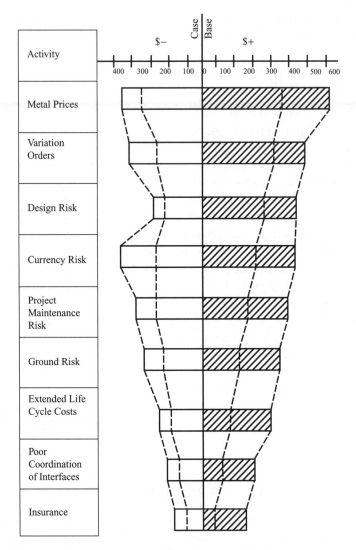

Figure 4.14 Typical Tornado diagram for project schedule elements

based mainly on decision-tree analysis, systematic Delphi techniques and other multivariate statistical analyses used to assess political risk factors, particularly in less developed countries (Desta 1985).

Leavy (1984) stated that 'country risk assessment' aims at the evaluation encapsulating the total risk, non-business (alpha risk) and business (beta risk) borne by a country, which may influence foreign investment.

Techniques and frameworks to serve this purpose have been actively developed, with researchers seeking the most suitable system to extract and evaluate information. Blank (1980) reported that the primary analytical methods used by companies in a formalised country risk assessment process are standardised checklists, scenario development, structured quantitative formats, statistical analysis, computerised investment models and Delphi techniques. Many of these methods are also used by corporations investing in their countries of origin, and are thus not specific to overseas investment.

4.9.1   Country Risk Sources – the Checklist

The country risk appraisal aims to identify all the external factors affecting an organisation, resulting in a thorough assessment of the project's viability. The prevailing country risk assessment methods generally classify the risk components into three categories – political, financial and economic risks (Sealy 2001). Leavy (1984) mentioned the necessity to consider the intricacies arising from socio-cultural differences when operating in a foreign country.

Nagy (1979) stated that in order to carry out the country risk assessment, it is imperative to have a good knowledge of the country's political, economic and social structure, including the individual and collective character of the ruling government. The legislative, institutional and regulatory framework is equally crucial. This may be ameliorated by familiarity with the facts and figures about past and current political trends that can be used in a logical and systematic manner to assess the possibility of events occurring in the future.

4.9.2   Political Risk

Categorised under political risk are political events that may affect the prospects for the profitability of a given investment (Haendel 1979). In the view of Gutmann (1980) this area is of major interest to companies in their investment decisions. This is confirmed by the fall of the Shah of Iran, which signified the dramatic impact of political events on all financial transactions. Many internationally founded projects were expropriated by the new regime, invoices went unsettled and the local currency was devalued.

The elements of political risk drawn from IBC USA's international country risk guide in the order of their criticality as quoted by Sealy (2001), combined with various other sources of the literature, are:

- government stability
- socio-economic conditions
- investment climate
- internal conflict and military intervention in politics
- external conflict
- corruption
- religious and/or ethnic tensions
- policy system and management of economy
- law and order
- democratic accountability and quality of the bureaucracy.

4.9.2.1   Government Stability

Government stability reflects both the government's ability to carry out its declared programme and its ability to stay in office (Sealy 2001). It is comprised of the government's unity, intergovernment relations, its legislative strength and the level of support from the people. This includes the possibility of change in the regime under which the country operates, rebellion for political power and coups (Thunell 1977).

The probability of a take-over by an extremist government is considered to be high when the present government is incompetent or weak, when either the democratically elected government is based on a small majority or an authoritarian government has a shaky power base, or when there exists a well-organised extremist group (Nagy 1979).

4.9.2.2   Socio-economic Conditions

Sealy (2001) cites that the presence of socio-economic pressures in society, including high levels of unemployment and poverty, could restrain government action or fuel social dissatisfaction. A government of a country with a low per capita income may be forced to delay debt repayments when it requires a reduction in the standard of living because of a restrained budget in other expenditures. Gutmann (1980) mentioned that unfavourable social conditions, such as extremes of wealth due to unequal income distribution between social classes or regions, may lead to discontent in the society and riots.

Leavy (1984) has carried out a more in-depth study of the socio-cultural factors of a country, including the type of economy, ideology (capitalist, social democratic, democratic or communist), demographic pattern, level of education, social norms/values/beliefs, social mobility and structure and culture.

A government's incapability to resolve structural problems such as excessively rapid population growth, disparities in income distribution, substandard labour relations and illiteracy contributes to heightening socio-economic problems (Nagy 1979). A project is prone to the risk of a strike, particularly in a country that has a history of widespread labour unrest, where strikes are legal, the government is weak in imposing strike bans, wages are low, labour unions are strong and the labour market is tight.

4.9.2.3 Investment Climate

The risk associated with the investment profile may be a standalone factor or a result of other components of political, economic and financial risks. Thunell (1977) and Haendel (1979) quote the variables of the investment climate: namely, the constitutional support for foreign ownership, discrimination and control over foreign business activity, capital repatriation, stability of the local currency and domestic prices, political stability, willingness to grant tariff protection and availability of local capital. Sealy (2001) identified the risks surrounding an investment in a project: namely, contract viability or expropriation probability, repatriation of profits and payment delays.

4.9.2.4 Internal Conflict and Military Intervention in Politics

In assessing the risk of internal conflict, Sealy (2001) pointed out the need to evaluate the extent of political turbulence in the country and its impact on the government. Countries whose government has no armed opposition and does not indulge in arbitrary violence against the civilian population are favoured by investors. On the other hand, the risk of internal conflict is considered to be high in a country that experiences frequent demonstrations and guerrilla activities or is embroiled in an ongoing civil war, terrorism/political violence and civil disorder.

Strong involvement of military forces in politics diminishes the democratic accountability of a country, indicating that the government is incapable of functioning effectively, which poses an obstruction for foreign businesses to carry out their operations efficiently. Moreover, it raises the possibility for the formation of an armed opposition, which brings about the danger of a military take-over in an extreme case.

4.9.2.5   External Conflict

Pressure from foreign action can affect the ruling government, in the form of non-violent influences such as diplomatic pressure, withholding aid, trade restrictions, territorial disputes and sanctions and violent influences ranging from cross-border conflicts to all-out war. The way such external conflict may adversely affect foreign business is cited by Sealy (2001): namely, the possibility of restricting operations, trade and investment sanctions, distortion in the allocation of economic sources and forced change in the societal structure.

4.9.2.6   Corruption

Corruption within the political system is regarded as a threat to foreign investment because it may disrupt the economic and financial environment, reduce the efficiency of government and business by the appointment of incapable personnel under unfair patronage and cause instability in the political system (Sealy 2001). Evidence of corruption can be found in actual or potential situations of excessive patronage, nepotism, job reservation, 'favours for favours', misallocation of public funds and secret party funding. The damaging effect of corruption can be strong enough to cause the fall or overthrow of the government, the restructuring of the country's political institutions or a breakdown in law and order.

In practice, corruption is commonly found in the financial process in the forms of bribery for import and export licences, exchange controls, tax assessments, grant of permission, tender and bid procedures, police protection or loans. Corruptive practices impede a country's development in various ways: they reduce growth, drive away foreign investors and deprive the country of development funds.

4.9.2.7   Religious and/or Ethnic Tensions

The degree of risk is pronounced by the extent of tension within a country attributable to religious, racial, nationality or language differences that undermine the country's stability (Gutmann 1980).

The supremacy of a single religious group in the society or government suppresses the religious freedom of the minority and may even lead to the introduction of religious law to replace the civil law and the division of a country in the worst cases, particularly when the group is vocal, strongly backed, well organised, well armed and under the influence of a fanatical, impulsive and irresponsible leader (Nagy 1979). A country with intolerant and openly conflicting, opposing religious and ethnic groups is clearly considered to be risky under this classification.

There is a high probability of riots, disorder and civil war arising when there is deep-seated or bitter antagonism between segments of the population due to ethnic, tribal, religious or ideological differences, coupled with the government's inability to control the situation through structured reforms. In the case of riots, civil disorder or revolution, the debt-servicing ability of the country will decline, since these incidents will possibly result in a drain on the country's resources, production paralysis, decrease of productive capacity, capital flight, loss of entrepreneurial, managerial and technical expertise, and, of course, impairment of the country's ability to borrow abroad.

4.9.2.8 Policy System and Management of Economy

The policy factors cited by Goodman (1978) are concerned with the quality of a country's economic and financial management in relation to the country's political leadership. Poor quality or mismanagement of the economy may result in adverse economic developments.

4.9.2.9 Law and Order

Sealy (2001) mentioned the importance of evaluating the strength and impartiality of the legal system in place, including the level of adherence to it in practice.

4.9.2.10 Democratic Accountability and Quality of the Bureaucracy

Democratic accountability is measured by assessing whether or not the incumbent government is employing a proactive approach towards the people (Sealy 2001). It ranges from a high degree of democracy to autocracy in extreme cases. A favourable, highly democratic country is signified by freedom and fairness in the election of the government, the existence of active political parties, the transparent control and monitoring of the government's executive, legislative and judicial actions, the evidence of justice and constitutional or legal guarantees of individual liberty. Democratic accountability is often indicated by the non-dominating, alternating attainment of authority. On the other hand, autocracy refers to the unrelenting leadership of the state by a single group or person either by means of military force or by inherited right.

4.9.2.11   Economic Risk

Appraisal of the economic risk is an exercise that aims to produce a review of a country's economic strengths and weaknesses. It reveals the condition of the current balance of payments and serves as a means of projecting the long-term growth prospects of the country under scrutiny– provided that correct interpretation is used (Nagy 1979).

In an economic appraisal, the indicators used by IBC USA's international country risk guide as quoted by Sealy (2001) are:

- gross national or domestic product (GNP or GDP) per head
- real GNP or GDP growth
- annual inflation rate
- budget balance as a percentage of GNP or GDP
- current account as a percentage of GNP or GDP.

An overview of a country's current level of development can be obtained from the total GNP, the balance of payments and the current account. It is generally acceptable that a country with a larger economy, that is one with a high value of these three indicators, offers greater opportunity, diversity and stability for investment (Goodman 1978).

In a review of a country's economic situation, Ariani (2001) raised several supplementary considerations, namely level of unemployment as an element of economic development stage, assessment of the economic development plan and its feasibility, including main bottlenecks, and the resource base, the condition of natural and human resources and their availability.

Gutmann (1980) pointed out the importance of the country's supply of energy associated with the distribution of world energy resources. The disparity between producing and consuming countries is underlined by the sharp rises in the price of oil imposed by OPEC since 1973, which still continues today. The extent to which a country is dependent upon imported energy, particularly oil, and the level of utilisation of indigenous energy resources, should be taken into account when assessing the country's long-term economic prospects. A country that relies on imported oil for a large proportion of its energy supplies is considered vulnerable under this criterion.

Cyclical recession occurs and spreads as part of the economic process, and its effects are particularly damaging to a country that is economically vulnerable to external shocks (Nagy 1979). Severe deterioration of the general economic condition, including overheating of the economy, a tight labour market, a decline in the current account or balance of payments, high and ever-increasing interest rates, steep price rises and a decline in the country's business, may result in an economic recession.

4.9.3   Financial Risk

According to Sealy (2001) the essence of financial risk is concerned with the country's ability to 'pay its way', which includes the official, commercial and trade debt obligations. In practice, this covers a wide area, incorporating all of the existing financial support systems and frameworks available to a particular country. The financial risk components are:

* foreign debt as a percentage of GDP
* foreign debt service as a percentage of exports of goods and services
* current account as a percentage of exports of goods and services
* net international liquidity as months of import cover
* exchange rate stability.

According to Goodman (1978), the financial risks are directly or indirectly associated with the net international liquidity of a country. A favourable condition is achieved when the foreign assets and liability decrease while the maturity increases. The measure of assets is obtained from the value of international reserves to imports and the measure of liability is drawn from the debt–service burden of the country under question.

While Gutmann (1980) argued that among these financial indicators, the ones related to a country's external debt, particularly the debt–service ratio that depicts the current debt burden, serve as the most relevant guide, an assessor should bear in mind the fact that the available information often excludes unguaranteed private debt, recently signed debt and the due liability of debt repayments of the current contract.

As a refinement of the financial analysis of a country, Gutmann (1980) stated that the quality of its financial institutions is an essential matter. A country having a fundamentally strong financial establishment – comprising an efficient central bank and a sound institutional framework – is considered to be proficient in its debt management and international financial relations. Institutional support is valuable in providing stability for the financial performance, in the event of political or social disturbances.

The political, economic and financial risks of a country discussed above are the major areas that are closely related to and considered to have substantial effects on foreign investment. A systematic procedure to provide an early warning of risks should be developed to facilitate a thorough appraisal, especially in view of the volatile international business environment.

4.9.4   Organisational Usage of Risk Management Techniques

The following points summarise the results from a recent survey in terms of the risk management techniques used at each level of an organisation (Merna 2003).

The risk management techniques used at the risk identification stage are as follows:

- Brainstorming is a very popular technique which is used at corporate and strategic business levels.
- Checklists are very popular at the project level, with over 70% of targeted organisations using them.
- Prompt lists or risk measures are a popular technique at the project level.
- Risk registers are used throughout organisations. Over 70% of targeted organisations use this technique at strategic business and project levels.
- Very little value management is exercised at corporate and strategic business levels. Value management is primarily seen as a project-level tool; however, the business case stage of the value management process is normally undertaken at the corporate level.

The risk management techniques used at the risk analysis stage are as follows:

- Interviews are very popular techniques used at the corporate level.
- Value management is a more project-oriented tool and not used at the corporate level.
- Probability impact tables are more commonly used at strategic business and project levels.
- Decision trees are seen to be a project-level technique, with over 60% of targeted organisations using them.

- Monte Carlo simulation and sensitivity analysis are seen more as project-level-oriented techniques.
- The majority of risk analysis occurs at the project level, followed by the strategic business level and then the corporate level.
- The mathematics-oriented techniques are primarily carried out at the project level.

4.10 SUMMARY

The choice of risk management technique and application is extremely important in the assessment of project and business investments. Contingency sums should not be added to a project or business without a thorough assessment.

Risk management techniques are generic to all risk assessment. The tools and techniques chosen by an organisation will be based on the type of investment or project to be undertaken. It is important to note there is no 'specific' technique to analyse a particular risk. The use of a particular risk management technique is at the discretion of the practitioner.

This chapter has described the choices of tools and techniques, both qualitative and quantitative, used in the risk management process that can be applied at corporate, strategic business and project levels. The key features of the value management process and its application have also been described.

5
Financing Projects, Their Risks and Risk Modelling

5.1 INTRODUCTION

It is important to understand the difference between corporate and project finance. Corporate finance is traditional finance where payment of loans comes from the organisation, backed by the organisation's entire balance sheet, not from the revenues of projects. Lenders look at the overall financial strength or balance sheet of an organisation as a prerequisite for lending for a project (Merna and Njiru 2002). In project finance, projects are undertaken by a special project vehicle (SPV), owing to the fact that the project is an off-balance-sheet transaction. Lenders have no recourse to the main organisation's assets.

In this chapter the main sources of finance are discussed. It then briefly describes the major stages of risk faced during the management process, namely identification, analysis and response. The risks affecting financial options are outlined along with how these risks can be managed. The chapter also outlines the uses and benefits of risk management software and modelling.

5.2 CORPORATE FINANCE

Corporate finance is the specific area dealing with the financial decisions corporations make and the tools and techniques used to make the decisions. The discipline as a whole may be divided between long-term capital investment decisions and short-term working capital management.

Figure 5.1 summarises the corporate finance process and illustrates the three categories of corporate financial decision making. These categories include:

- *Objectives – investment decisions.* Management must allocate limited resources between competing opportunities. Corporate-level

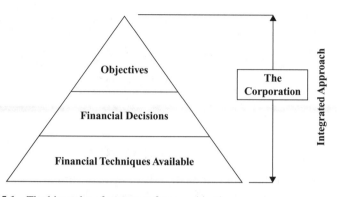

Figure 5.1   The hierarchy of corporate finance objectives

management face these decisions on a regular basis and develop expertise and specific industry knowledge which aids the decision-making process.

• *Financial decisions.* Any corporate investment must be financed appropriately. The financing mix can impact the valuation of an organisation (and hence the level of risk an organisation faces will be affected). Management must therefore identify the 'optimal mix' of financing – the capital structure that results in maximum value (Damodran 1997).

• *Financial techniques available – dividend decisions.* Management must decide whether to invest in additional projects, reinvest in existing operations, or return free cash as dividends to shareholders. The dividend is calculated mainly on the basis of the organisation's unappropriated profit and its business prospects for the coming year. If there are no NPV positive opportunities then management must return excess cash to investors. Techniques which can be applied to this decision-making process include (Damodran 1997):
  o present value
  o financial statement analyses
  o risk and return
  o option pricing.

Most corporations are financed through a mixture of debt and equity. The gearing of a corporation is determined by the ratio of debt to equity. A highly geared corporation will have high debt borrowing and a low geared corporation a high equity stake. Many corporations seek to identify the weighted cost of capital. Table 5.1 shows an example of the weighted cost of capital.

Table 5.1 The weighted cost of capital

Gearing	Percentage	Cost %	Weighted cost
Debt	£40 million	6.5	2.6
Equity	£60 million	11	6.6

The risks to corporations regarding the debt–equity ratio are twofold.

1. A high debt–equity ratio requires debt to be serviced as per the terms of the loan often at the expense of shareholders through low dividend payments.
2. A high proportion of equity can result in the risk of the corporation losing control of the entity to shareholders.

5.3   PROJECT FINANCE

The concept of project finance is widely used in business and finance in developed countries, although there is currently no precise legal definition of 'project finance'.

The term project finance is used to refer to a wide range of financing structures. However, these structures have one feature in common – the financing is not primarily dependent on the credit support of the sponsors or the value of the physical assets involved. In project financing, those providing the senior debt place a substantial degree of reliance on the performance of the project itself (Tinsley 2000).

Merna and Owen (1998) have described the concept of project finance in the following way:

> *Each project is supported by its own financial package and secured solely on that project or facility. Projects are viewed as being their own discreet entities and legally separate from their founding sponsors. As each project exists in its own right, SPV's are formulated. Banks lend to SPV's on a non or limited recourse basis, which means that loans are fully dependent on the revenue streams generated by the SPV, and that the assets of the SPV are used as collateral. Hence, although there may be a number of sponsors forming the SPV, the lenders have no claim to any of the assets other than the project itself.*

Project financing refers to the long-term financing of infrastructure, industrial projects and public services based upon non-recourse or limited recourse financial structures where project debt, mezzanine finance (usually in the form of bonds) and equity are used to finance the project and paid back from the cash generated by the project (International Project

Finance Association in 2003). Private sector organisations use project finance as a means of funding major concession projects off balance sheet. The essence of project finance is to create a robust financing structure for the private enterprises in which risks are contained within the project itself, leaving no recourse to the project's sponsors.

Esty (2004) concurs with the definitions of project finance given above, but states that the following should not be considered as project finance: secured debt, vendor-financed debt, subsidiary debt, lease, joint ventures or asset-backed securities, since all these infer recourse to assets.

5.3.1   Basic Features of Project Finance

Within project finance there are features which form an integral part of the finance tool (Nevitt 1983). Below is a brief description of each of these features.

5.3.2   Special Project Vehicle (SPV)

An SPV is a separate company from the promoter's organisation and operates under a concession, normally granted by government. Usually, the seed equity capital for the SPV is provided by the sponsors of the project company (Spackman 2002). An SPV is usually highly geared, through a high debt to equity ratio.

5.3.3   Non-recourse or Limited Recourse Funding

In non-recourse funding the lenders to the project have no recourse to the general funds or assets of the sponsors of the project. However, in limited recourse, access to the sponsor's general assets and funds is provided if the sponsors provide a guarantee of repayment for certain identified risks.

Advantages are as follows. Lenders will have more confidence because the project is not burdened with losses or liabilities from activities unrelated to the project. Non-recourse lending also helps to protect the security interests of the lenders in the project company with a right to replace the project management team in the event of poor performance of the project or even to foreclose and sell the project (step-in clauses) to recover their interests in the project to the maximum possible extent.

A disadvantage could be that investors are left with a partially completed facility that has little or no residual value. Lenders therefore have to act very cautiously and completely satisfy themselves that the project facility will be able fully to meet its debt, bonds and equity liabilities, and on top of that earn a reasonable margin of profit for the sponsors to retain their interest (Merna and Dubey 1998).

5.3.4 Off-balance-sheet Transaction

The non-recourse nature of project finance provides a unique tool to project sponsors to fund the project outside their balance sheet. This structure enables funding of a variety of projects which might not otherwise have been funded, particularly when the sponsors:

- either are unwilling to expose their general assets to liabilities to be incurred in connection with the project (or are seeking to limit their exposure in this regard)
- or do not enjoy sufficient financial standing to borrow funds on the basis of their general assets (Benoit 1996, Heald 2003).

5.3.5 Sound Income Stream of the Project as the Predominant Basis for Financing

The future income stream of the project is the most critical element in any project financing. The entire financing of the project is dependent on an assured income stream from the project since lenders and investors have recourse to no funds other than the income streams generated by the project, once it is completed, and assets of the project that may or may not have any residual value (Spackman 2002). The project sponsors, therefore, have to demonstrate evidence of future income through various means such as a power sales contract for a power plant, a concession agreement for a toll road project allowing the collection of tolls, or tenant leases for a commercial real estate project (Tinsley 2000). Modelling projects through computer software can be an effective way of securing finance. Expected costs and revenues can be input into a simulation model and decisions can be made as to whether the project should be sanctioned.

5.3.6 Projects and Their Cash Flows

Broadly speaking, a project may be said to pass through three major phases:

1. project appraisal
2. project implementation
3. project operation.

Cash flow is defined by the sum of cash inflows and cash outflows through the project stages in a particular time period. The cash flow of a project is the only source of income for the promoter. After servicing the debt, paying the dividends on equity, paying the coupon rate on bonds, spending for general operation and maintenance, and tax to the government, the promoter is left with either a surplus or a deficit. The amount of surplus or deficit depends on the terms of repayment, the revenue generation capacity of the SPV and the risks involved in the project. A project can still be considered a risk until it crosses the break-even point. During the appraisal phase, the projected cash flows of a project would be the basis on which various contractual agreements with the parties involved are shaped and a decision whether to sanction the project or not is made.

Cumulative cash flows, also known as net cash flows, are defined as the sum of cash flows in each fiscal year of the project. The cumulative flow for a particular year in the life cycle of the project is calculated by adding the net cash inflows to the net cash outflows (Turner 1994). Cumulative cash flows can be used to determine surpluses or deficits within each time period.

A typical cumulative cash flow curve for a project is illustrated in Figure 5.2.

The precise shape of the cumulative cash flow curve for a particular project depends on variables such as:

- the time taken in setting up the project's objective
- obtaining statutory approvals
- design finalisation
- finalisation of the contracts
- finalisation of the financing arrangement
- the rate and amount of construction
- operation speed.

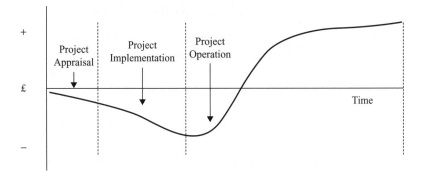

Figure 5.2   Typical cumulative cash flow stages of a project

Negative cash flow, until a project breaks even, clearly indicates that a typical project needs financing from outside until it breaks even. The shape of the curve also reveals that in the initial phase of the project relatively less financing is required. As the project moves on to the implementation phase there is a steady increase in the finance requirement, which peaks at the completion stage. This point is defined as the cash lock-up (CLU) in the project. The rate of spending is also depicted by the steepness of the curve. The rate of spending is often termed the 'cash burn', which is the rate at which cash is spent over a specified period of time. The steeper the curve, the greater the need for finance to be available. Once the project is commissioned and starts to yield revenues the requirement of financing from outside the project becomes less. Finally, the project starts to generate sufficient resources for the operation and maintenance and also a surplus of cash. However, even after the break-even point, the project may require financing for short periods, to meet the mismatch between receipts and payments (Merna and Njiru 2002).

In project financing, it is this future cash flow forecast that becomes the basis for raising resources for investing in the project. It is the job of the finance manager of the project to package this cash flow in such a way that it meets the needs of the project and at the same time is attractive to potential agencies and individuals willing to provide resources to the project for investment. In order to achieve this objective effectively, a thorough knowledge of the financial instruments and the financial markets in which they are traded is essential (Khu 2002).

Cash flows and their relationship to portfolios are discussed in Chapter 6.

5.4 FINANCIAL INSTRUMENTS

Organisations procuring projects need to raise cash to finance their investment activities. In most cases capital is raised through issuing or selling securities. These securities, known as financial instruments, are in the form of a claim on the future cash flow of the project. At the same time, these instruments have a contingent claim on the assets of the project, which acts as a security in the event of future cash flows not materialising as expected. The nature and seniority of the claim on the cash flow and assets of the project vary with the financial instrument used.

The authors describe financial instruments as the tools used by an organisation/promoter to raise finance for a project.

Traditionally, financial instruments were in the form of either debt or equity. However, developments in the financial markets and financial innovations have led to the development of various other kinds of financial instruments which share the characteristics of both debt and equity. These instruments are normally described as mezzanine finance instruments, particularly bonds. Debt is senior to all other claims on the project cash flow and assets (Merna and Njiru 2002).

Ordinary equity refers to the ownership interest of common stockholders in the project. On the balance sheet, equity equals total assets less all liabilities. It has the lowest rank and therefore the last claim on the assets and cash flow of the project. Equity is best described as 'risk finance'.

Mezzanine finance occupies an intermediate position between the senior debt and the common equity. Mezzanine finance typically takes the form of subordinated debt, junior subordinated debt and preferred stock, or some combination of each.

Besides debt, equity and mezzanine finance a project may also utilise certain other types of instruments such as leasing, venture capital and aid.

5.5 DEBT

Debt instruments refer to the raising of term loans from banks or other financial institutions which include commercial, merchant and investment banks, development agencies, pension funds and insurance companies, debentures and export credits.

5.5.1   Term Loans

Term loans are negotiated between the borrower and financial institutions. For large projects a group of banks and financial institutions pool their resources to provide the loans to the project. This is known as syndicated lending. Banks and financial institutions set their own internal exposure limits to particular types of project. This helps in spreading the risk. Generally an investment bank or a merchant bank acts as the agent or lead bank to manage the debt issue. Many banks specialise in lending to certain types of infrastructure projects of which they have both technical and financial experience. For example, development banks in transitional and developing countries.

The terms and conditions of loans vary between different lenders and borrowers. There can be a fixed interest rate or floating interest rate. Repayment of the loan could be between 7 and 10 years for an oil sector project to 16 and 18 years for a power project (Merna and Owen 1998). One reason for variance is the 'gestation lag' of the project. The type of loan is determined by the project's characteristics and availability of the instruments.

According to Merna and Smith (1996) the cost of raising debt capital includes certain fees besides the interest. These are:

- *Management fee.* A percentage of the loan facility for managing the debt issue, normally to be paid up front.
- *Commitment fee.* Calculated on the undrawn portion of the loan to be paid when the loan is fully drawn.
- *Agency fee.* Normally an annual fee to be paid to the lead bank for acting as the agent to the issues after the loan has been raised.
- *Underwriting fee.* Paid up front as a percentage of the loan facility to the bank or financial institution which guarantees to contribute to the loan issue if it is not fully subscribed.
- *Success fee.* Paid up front as a percentage of the total loan once all loans have been secured.
- *Guarantee fee.* Paid annually on the outstanding loan amount if it is guaranteed against default.

All, none or some of these may be present in a specific loan proposal. In certain cases the lenders submerge all the fees in the interest rate they offer. A careful analysis of the cost of loans offered from different sources is therefore required. Still the overall cost of raising a term loan is less compared with any other mode of large-scale financing because the project has to negotiate and deal with only a small number of lenders of money through a lead manager of the issue. Also, in the event of default it is easier to renegotiate a term loan compared with any other instrument of financing (Tinsley 2000).

5.5.2   Standby Loans

An organisation/promoter may arrange standby loans with the lenders. Standby loans are more expensive than term loans, since they are used to meet draw-down in excess of term loans, which are often due to lower than expected revenues in the early phase of the operation (Merna and Njiru 2002).

5.5.3   Senior and Subordinate Debt

Senior debt ranks the highest among the financial instruments in terms of claims on the assets of a corporation/project. This means that in the event of default, the lenders of senior debt have the right to claim on the assets of the projects first (Khu 2002). Lenders take into account the debt service coverage ratio (DSCR), defined by Merna and Smith (1996) as the annual cash flow available for debt service divided by the loan balance outstanding. In the UK lenders seek a typical DSCR of 1.2 based on the economic parameters of the worst case scenario. In developing markets the DSCR can be as high as 2.8, basically this is a contingency required by lenders (Lamb and Merna 2004b). Each industry sector tends to have a target DSCR ratio based on the characteristics of the industry. Tinsley (2000) claims that the risk adjustment is made in project financing and the project financier has to adjust a specific project financing structure to generate its corresponding target DSCR. Typically, power sector projects have a lower DSCR than infrastructure projects whereas infrastructure projects tend to be lower than mining, oil and gas and telecoms projects.

Subordinate debt is subordinate to senior debt and generally has only second claim to the collateral of the project company. This means that in the event of default by the promoter, all senior debt claims must be met before any claim can be made by subordinate debt lenders. As it is second to senior debt in terms of claims on assets, lenders seek higher returns on subordinate debt. The interest rate on it is usually higher than the interest rate on senior debt (Khu 2002). For example, the interest rate on senior debt may be London interbank offered rate (LIBOR) plus 200 basis points, but the interest rate on subordinate debt could be LIBOR plus 400 basis points. Subordinate debt is often used for refinancing needs or for the restructuring of the finance package of a project.

5.6   MEZZANINE FINANCE INSTRUMENTS

There are many financial instruments in this category. They are senior with respect to an equity issue and lower than debt. Some of them are close to a debt issue and some of them share features of an equity issue.

Higgins (1995) defines bonds as a fixed income security. The holder receives a specified annual interest income and a specified amount at maturity (unless the organisation goes bankrupt). The difference between bonds and other forms of indebtedness such as term loans and secured debenture is that bonds are a subordinate form of debt compared with term loans and secured debentures. Similar to debentures, these are issued by the borrowing entity in small increments, usually $1000 per bond in the USA. After issue, the bond can be traded by investors on organised security exchanges.

Khu (2002) identifies the variables which characterise a bond, namely:

- par value
- coupon rate
- maturity date
- bond yield
- yield to maturity.

In a sinking fund arrangement, bonds can be either repaid entirely at maturity or repaid before maturity. The repayment takes place through a sinking fund. A sinking fund is an account maintained by the bond trustee for the repayment of bonds. Typically the borrower makes an annual payment to the trustee. Depending on the indenture agreement, the trustee can either purchase bonds from the market or select bonds randomly using a lottery and purchase them, generally at face value. A sinking fund has two opposing effects on the bondholders: it acts like an early warning system, for the lenders, when the borrower is in financial difficulties and unable to meet the sinking fund requirements; and it is beneficial to the borrowers both when the price of the bond is high as well as when it is low. In the event of lower market bond price the borrower buys back the bonds at the lower market price and in the event of higher market bond price the borrower still buys the bonds at the lower face value (Tinsley 2000).

5.6.1   Bond Ratings

The success of a bond issue, *inter alia,* depends upon its credit quality. There are many companies which analyse the investment qualities of publicly traded bonds. The findings are published in the form of bond ratings. The ratings are determined by using various financial parameters of the borrowing agency, general market conditions in which the borrower operates, the political situation of the country in which the project is located, and other sources of finance which have been tied up by the project. The ratings are based, in varying degree, on the following considerations:

- the likelihood of default by the bond issuer on its timely payment of interest and repayment of principal
- the nature of the bond
- provisions of the obligations.

The ratings are normally depicted in letters such as A, B or C or a combination of letters and numbers such as in certain financial markets; public issue of bonds is not permitted if the bonds have not been rated, such as the US bond market. Rating is also important because bonds with lower ratings tend to have higher interest costs. The rating agencies keep reviewing the financial performance of the borrower, the general market situation and the political situation in the country of the borrower. Depending upon the emerging situations the ratings are revised upwards or downwards.

An organisation's ability to honour interest payments and principal payment on schedule is important to bondholders. Some organisations are financially stronger than others and this affects their ability to honour the debt. An organisation's ability to pay off its debt is rated. Bond ratings are a reflection of the creditworthiness of an organisation and are based on:

- the likelihood an organisation will default on its interest repayment
- the likelihood an organisation will default on its principal repayment
- the creditors' protection in the event of a default.

The two leading bond-rating organisations are Standard and Poor's (S&P) and Moody's. Table 5.2 explains the ratings and the definitions of the types of bonds available.

Table 5.2   Bond ratings (Adapted from Khu 2002, Merna 2002)

Bond ratings		Comments
S&P	Moody's	
		High-grade bonds
AAA	Aaa	Capacity to pay interest and principal is very strong
AA	Aa	
		Medium-grade bonds
A	A	Strong capacity to pay interest and repay principal, although it
BBB	B	is somewhat more susceptible to the adverse effects of
		changes in circumstances and economic conditions. Both
		high-grade and medium-grade bonds are investment-quality
		bonds
		Low-grade bonds
BB	Ba	Adequate capacity to pay interest and principal, although
B	B	adverse economic conditions or changing circumstances are
CCC	Caa	more likely to lead to a weakened capacity to pay interest
CC	Ca	and principal. These are regarded as mainly speculative
		bonds, with CC and Ca being the bonds with the highest
		degree of speculation
		Very low-grade bonds
C	C	This rating is reserved for income bonds on which no interest
		is being paid
D	D	This rating is in default, and payment of interest and/or
		repayment of principal is in arrears

5.6.2   Types of Bonds

5.6.2.1   Plain Vanilla Bonds

A plain vanilla or fixed rate bond is a bond for which the coupon rate is fixed at the time of issuing the bond. The disadvantage of a fixed rate bond is that the bondholder will be at a loss if inflation rises and interest rates move up during the maturity period. On the other hand, the bondholder will be in profit if interest rates fall, as the bondholder will be getting coupons at the previously agreed rate.

5.6.2.2   Floating Rate Bonds

These are bonds for which the coupon rate is adjusted periodically according to a predetermined formula. The coupon rate is tied to some short-term interest rate such as the six-month LIBOR. In this case, when the inflation and interest rates fluctuate during the maturity period, the coupon rate will be adjusted accordingly following the predetermined formula. Generally floating rate bonds sell at or near par.

5.6.2.3 Zero Coupon Bonds

These are also known as a deep discount or pure discount bonds, or original issue discount bonds or zeros. Zero coupon bonds do not pay interest through the life of the bonds. Instead, investors buy zero coupon bonds at a deep discount from their par value, which is the amount the bond will be worth when it matures or comes due. When a zero coupon bond matures, the investor will receive one lump sum equal to the initial investment plus the interest that it has accrued. These long-term maturity dates allow an investor to plan for a long-range goal, such as paying for a child's college education. With the deep discount, an investor can put up a small amount of money that can grow over many years.

5.6.2.4 Junk Bonds

These are also known as high-yield bonds or low-grade bonds and with a rating of BB or Ba or lower generally pay interest above the return of more highly rated bonds. Junk bonds are considered for high-risk projects. For example, a casino, which is considered as a high risk, can be funded through junk bonds (now referred to as high-risk bonds). A casino could also be funded by a revenue bond, whereby investors' income is directly related to the project's income/revenue.

5.6.2.5 Municipal Bonds

These are bonds issued by the state or local government unit. The advantage of such bonds is that they are exempt from government tax. They may also be exempt from state and local taxes.

5.6.2.6 Income Bonds

These are bonds similar to revenue bonds, which are linked directly to the borrower's income. They are similar to conventional bonds except that the coupon payment is made only when the project's income is sufficient. For example, income bonds used to finance a casino would only pay coupons related to the profits made by the casino which cannot be accurately forecasted at the time of sale.

5.6.2.7 Wrapped and Unwrapped Bonds

Wrapped bonds are guaranteed by a monoline insurer, which makes them very creditworthy. Monoline insurance companies provide guarantees to issuers often in the form of wraps that enhance the credit of the issuer. Issuers will often go to the monoline company either to boost the rating of one of their debt issues or to ensure that a debt issue does not become downgraded. As a result of the guarantee the bonds are rated AAA/Aaa, therefore reducing the cost of borrowing. Unwrapped bonds have no guarantor and the bond is rated on the project itself. The bond pricing will, in turn, be driven by the project's rating.

The use of bond finance, through private placement, usually depends on the size of the finance required. The Office of Government Commerce (2002) suggests that in the UK bond finance tends to be used in projects requiring in excess of £90 million. For projects between £60 and £70 million, bond finance needs to be assessed in greater detail by monoline insurers to determine whether such finance can be cost effective owing to the costs associated with raising bond finance. Monoline insurers, for example, seek a return of 1% to 2% of the total bond finance raised to cover identified risks.

Table 5.3 illustrates the characteristics of bank and bond financing.

At the time of writing the first edition of this book in 2005 interest rates have tended to increase worldwide. In 2005 interest rates in the UK, USA and EU were 4.75%, 1.25% and 2.0% respectively. At the time of writing this edition of the book the UK base rate is 5.75%, the USA base rate is 4.75% and the EU base rate 3.0%.

These low interest rates have meant that investors have sought debt rather than bonds to finance projects. Many authors also suggest that the sharp decline in the use of bonds since 2002 in the USA is due to the Enron scandal. Debt is the cheapest form of lending and the most flexible, and as such has seen greater demand than bond financing over the last three years.

5.7   EQUITY

5.7.1   Ordinary Equity and Preference Shares

Merna and Owen (1998) define equity capital as pure equity for the provision of risk capital by investors to an investment opportunity and usually results in the issue of shares to those investors.

Rutterford and Carter (1988) define a share as an intangible bundle of rights in an organisation, which both indicates proprietorship and defines the contract between the shareholders. The terms of the contract, that is

Table 5.3   Characteristics of bond and bank financing (Adapted from Office of Government Commerce 2002)

Financial characteristic	Bank financing	Bond financing
Source of funds	Direct from bank(s)	Bond investors
Arrangement of funds	Negotiations between bank and lender	Via bond arranger
Certainty of funds	After agreement: certain	Less certainty: Only know if funding is forthcoming when the bond goes on sale
Maturity repayments	Up to 30 years	Up to 38 years
Flexibility	High: Early payments can be made, and refinancing is possible	Very little. No room for negotiation on interest and capital repayment
Receipt of funds	Staged: Works on a draw-down process	Whole: After the bond is sold
Assessment of project risk	Banks assess risks	Bond arranger assesses risks
Costs	Interest of the funds borrowed, and a commitment fee for funds yet to be drawn down	Interest to the bond investors, a fee to the bond arranger and an insurance fee (optional)
Ongoing project scrutiny	Significant. Possible step in clauses	Very little. Bond investors have little influence on the project once it is funded
Optimum size	No optimum size	Approximately £100–400 million
Opportunities for refinancing	Yes, if project risks become less than those assumed in the initial financing	Unlikely. Bond terms tend to be fixed for the life of the project

the particular rights attaching to a class of shares, are contained in the article of association of the company (Merna 2002).

Equity is the residual value of a company's assets after all outside liabilities (other than to shareholders) have been allowed for. Equity is also known as risk capital, because these funds are usually not secured and have no registered claim on any assets of the business, thus freeing these assets to be used as collateral for the loans (debt financing). Equity, however, shares in the profits of the project and any appreciation in the value of the enterprise, without limitation. Equity holders are paid dividends on the performance of the organisation (dividends are the amount of profits paid to shareholders). No dividends are paid if the business does not make a profit. Dividends to the shareholders can be paid only after debt claims have been met. The return on the equity, therefore, is the first to be affected in case of financial difficulties faced by the project entity. This means that equity investors, in the worst case scenario, may be left with nothing if the project fails and hence they demand greater return on their capital in order to bear a greater risk. This explains the general rule that high-risk projects use more equity while low-risk projects use more debt.

A high proportion of equity means low financial leverage and high proportion of debt equals high leverage. Leverage is measured by the ratio of long-term debt to long-term debt plus equity. Leverage is also called gearing or explained in terms of the debt–equity ratio. High financial leverage means that relatively more debt capital has been used in the project, signifying more debt service and fewer funds being available for distribution as dividend payments to the equity holders. However, once the project breaks even and profits start to accrue, shareholders receive a higher dividend. The seed capital provided by the sponsors of the project, which is normally a very small amount compared with the total finances raised for the project, is also known as founders or deferred shares. These are lower in status compared with ordinary and preference shares in the event of winding up.

In non-recourse financing the debt–equity ratio may be higher if the interest rate is high, provided lenders are satisfied with the risk structure of the project. If, however, a project is considered innovative then more equity will be demanded by lenders and the equity will be drawn down before debt becomes available to the project (Khu 2002).

Ordinary share capital is raised from the general public. Holding these shares entitles dividends, provides the right of one vote per share held, and the right to a pro rata proportion of the project's winding up. The right to participate in the assets of the project provides the opportunity for highest return on the capital invested (Merna 2002).

Preference shares are the shares that possess priority rights over ordinary shares. These shares give the holder a preferential right over lower ranked ordinary shares in terms of both dividend and return on capital in the event of liquidation. Normally the preference shareholders have the right to a fixed annual dividend, the right to receive repayment of any amount paid up on the preference shares on a winding up, and restricted voting rights. The board of directors of the issuing organisation may decide not to pay the dividend on preferred shares and this decision may have nothing to do with the current income of the issuer organisation

(Merna 2002). The dividends payable on the preference shares are either cumulative or non-cumulative. If cumulative dividends are not paid in a particular year they are carried forward. Usually both the cumulative preferred dividend and the current preferred dividend must be paid before ordinary shareholders can receive anything. Unpaid dividends are not treated as debt. The issuer organisation may decide to defer the payment of dividend on preferred shares indefinitely. However, if it does so the ordinary shareholders also do not receive anything. It is argued that preferred shares are in fact debt in disguise. The preferred shareholders receive only a stated dividend, and a stated value in the event of liquidation of the issuing organisation. However, unlike interest on debt, dividend on preferred shares is not deductible before determining the taxable income of the borrower (Merna 2002).

Other forms of financial instruments, such as depository receipts, lease finance and venture capital, are discussed by Merna and Njiru (2002).

5.8   FINANCIAL RISKS

The following financial risks are thought to have the most impact on the financial viability of an organisation/project. These risks all have an effect on the shape of the cumulative cash flow curve. Their effects on projects are identified by Merna and Njiru (2002):

- construction delay
- currency risk
- interest rate risk
- equity risk
- corporate bond risk
- liquidity risk
- counter-party risk
- maintenance risk
- taxation risk
- reinvestment risk
- country risk.

5.8.1   Construction Delay

This is the risk that the construction will not be completed on time or to specification. An uncompleted project is unlikely to generate any revenue and therefore the lenders will not be repaid. Long delays could also increase the cost of the project and therefore reduce its commercial viability, specifically its ability to generate revenues. There are many factors affecting project delay: the more usual ones include design flaws, government regulations, finance problems and sponsor management. All the above risks would have an adverse effect on a portfolio's economic parameters (Leiringer 2003).

5.8.2 Currency Risk

This arises when there is a cross-border flow of funds. With the collapse of fixed parities in the early 1970s, exchange rates of currencies are free to fluctuate according to the supply and demand for different currencies. The operation of speculators in the money market has added to the volatility of the exchange rates. Foreign exchange transactions involving any currency are therefore subject to currency risk (Merna 2002). In some cases, however, if an entity has a foreign currency payment and can match this payment with currency receivable, then the net exposure is zero. A convertible currency is one which can be freely exchanged for other currencies or gold without special authorisation from the appropriate central bank. The introduction of the euro to most EU countries has reduced currency risk for companies trading within these economies (Merna 2002).

5.8.3 Interest Rate Risk

Interest rate risk directly affects both the borrowing and the investing entity. The exposure depends on the maturity of the funds raised and developments in the financial market from where the funds have been raised.

Interest rate risk can broadly be classified in two categories. Firstly, risk on securities or financial instruments which are used for raising short-term finance. These facilities mature during a short period. Interest rate risks on these facilities largely depend on developments in the money market. Secondly, financial instruments which have a longer maturity, but where the longer period is split into smaller periods (Tinsley 2000).

5.8.4 Equity Risk

Equity risk is derived from the rise and fall of share prices which affect the entity holding the instrument. They also, however, affect company shares which are publicly quoted. Such companies may find it difficult to raise finance if the market price of their shares significantly falls in value (Logan 2003).

5.8.5 Corporate Bond Risk

Corporate bonds which are junior to debt and senior to equity in terms of call on the business assets are issued by corporate bodies to raise funds for investment; the funds raised may be used to inject capital into a project or portfolio. Bonds are credit rated by S&P and Moody's. For example, if they award an AAA rating it means the bond is almost as safe as a government stock; these would be classed as high-grade bonds. Medium-grade bonds would be rated A, speculative grade bonds would be rated B and high-risk bonds, often referred to as junk bonds, rated E. The rating of a bond is determined by the risk associated with the organisation and the business to be funded by the bond. Clearly, corporate bodies must know the risks associated with an investment, as must the rating agencies. Project risk and business risk must therefore be addressed before bonds are rated and issued (Merna and Dubey 1998, Khu 2002).

5.8.6 Liquidity Risk

Liquidity risk is an outcome of commercial risk. If a project or portfolio is not able to generate sufficient resources to meet its liabilities it enters into liquidity risk. Liquidity risk is the potential risk arising when an entity cannot meet payments when they fall due. It may involve borrowing at excessive rates of interest, or selling assets, in some cases projects within a portfolio, at below market prices. Liquidity risk is extremely important because most of the borrowing, whether loan or bond, has a 'cross-default' clause. This means that if the organisation has defaulted on any of its obligations then a debt with a 'cross-default' clause may be called back by lenders for immediate repayment. If this provision is triggered then the organisation may face even more liquidity problems and may be forced to declare bankruptcy. Liquidity risk is generally described as a cash flow problem (Khu 2002).

5.8.7 Counter-party Risk

Any financial transaction involves two or more parties, and the parties run the potential risk of default by the other parties. This is known as counter-party risk. For example, if an organisation has a tied line of credit from a bank or a financial institution then it runs the risk of the lender not being able to meet its commitments in providing the funds at the right time. On the other hand, after the loan has been dispersed the lender runs the risk of default in repayment and interest payment by the borrower. The magnitude of the counter-party risk depends on the size of all outstanding positions with a particular counter-party and whether or not any netting arrangement is in force (Galitz 1995, Smithson 1998).

Fraser *et al.* (1995) also covers risks identified by Merna and Njiru (1998), but defines the following risks specific to the banking sector:

- *Credit risk.* The risk that the bank will not get its money back (or payment will be delayed) from a loan or an investment. This has been the cause of most major bank failures over the years.
- *Operational risk.* The risk that operating expenses, especially non-interest expenses such as salaries and wages, might be higher than expected. Banks that lack the ability to control their expenses are more likely to have unpleasant earning surprises. Over an extended
- time in a competitive market environment, banks with excessively high operating costs will have difficulty surviving.
- *Capital risk.* The risk of having inadequate equity capital to continue to operate. This may be viewed either from an economic perspective so that inadequate equity capital occurs when customers refuse to leave their funds with the bank (causing a liquidity crisis), or from a regulatory perspective (where the bank regulatory authorities close the bank because capital is below regulatory minima).
- *Fraud risk.* The risk that officers, employees or outsiders will steal from the bank by falsifying records, self-dealing or other devices. Fraud risk is associated with unsound banking processes that could result in bank failure.

5.8.8   Maintenance Risk

Maintenance risk arises when the completed project does not function efficiently. Operating risks include the operator's experience and resources, supply of skilled labour, and other party risk (Khu 2002).

5.8.9   Taxation Risk

Profits made within a country are subjected to tax. Promoters will most probably include the cost of paying these taxes in their model. However, the models often do not take into account tax increases, and if they do occur they could seriously compromise the project (Merna and Njiru 1998).

5.8.10 Reinvestment Risk

Reinvestment risk results from the fact that interest or dividends earned from an investment may not be able to be reinvested in such a way that they will earn the same rate of return as the invested funds which generated them. For example, falling interest rates may prevent bond coupon payments from earning the same rate of return as the original bond (Fabozzi 2002).

5.8.11 Country Risk

A large number of projects are undertaken by corporate and strategic businesses in overseas countries (Ariani 2001). Hefferman (1986) defines country risk as 'the risk associated with publicly guaranteed loans or loans made directly to a foreign government'; however, this is a very narrow definition. The identification of country risks is discussed in Chapter 4.

5.9   NON-FINANCIAL RISKS AFFECTING PROJECT FINANCE

These risks also affect the shape of the cumulative cash flow and therefore the commercial viability of a project or portfolio. The risks include:

- dynamic risk
- inherent risk
- contingent risk
- customer risk
- regulatory risk
- reputation/damage risk
- organisational risk
- interpretation risk.

5.9.1 Dynamic Risk

Dynamic risk is concerned with maximising opportunities. Dynamic risk means that there will be potential gains as well as potential losses: that is, risking the loss of something certain for the gain of something uncertain. Every management decision has the element of dynamic risk governed only by practical rules of risk taking. During a project, losses and gains resulting from risk can be plotted against each other (Flanagan and Norman 1993, Merna 2002).

5.9.2 Inherent Risk

The way in which risk is handled depends on the nature of the business and the way that business is organised internally. For example, energy companies are engaged in an inherently risky business – the threat of fire and explosion is always present, as is the risk of environmental impairment. Financial institutions on the other hand have an inherently lower risk of fire and explosion than an energy company, but they are exposed to different sorts of risk. However, the level of attention given to managing risk in an industry is as important as the actual risk inherent in the operations which necessarily must be performed in that industry activity. For example, until very recently repetitive strain injury (RSI) was not considered to be a problem; however, it is now affecting employers' liability insurance (*International Journal of Project Business Risk Management* 1998). Another example is Gulf War syndrome.

5.9.3 Contingent Risk

Contingent risk occurs when an organisation is directly affected by an event in an area beyond its direct control but on which it has a dependency, such as weak suppliers (*International Journal of Project Business Risk Management* 1998). Normally a percentage of the overall project value is put aside to cover the costs of meeting such risks should they occur.

5.9.4 Customer Risk

Dependency on one client creates vulnerability because that client can take its business away, or be taken over by a rival. The risk can be managed by creating a larger customer base (*International Journal of Project Business Risk Management* 1998).

5.9.5 Regulatory Risk

Only by keeping abreast of potential changes in the environment can a business expect to manage these risks. Recent examples in the UK include awards to women for discrimination in the armed forces, RSI and windfall profits tax in exceptional years (*International Journal of Project Business Risk Management* 1998, Merna 2002). In October 2001, Railtrack Plc, a company listed on the London Stock Exchange, was put into administration by the UK Transport Secretary without any consultation with its lenders or shareholders. Shareholders taking the usual risks of rises and falls in stock market value were quickly made aware of a new type of risk (Merna 2002).

5.9.6   Reputation/Damage Risk

This is not a risk in its own right but rather the consequence of another risk, such as fraud, a building destroyed, failure to attend to complaints, lack of respect for others. It is the absence of control which causes much of the damage rather than the event itself. In a post-disaster situation an organisation can come out positively if the media are well handled (Leiringer 2003).

5.9.7   Organisational Risk

A poor infrastructure can result in weak controls and poor communications with a variety of impacts on the business. Good communication links will lead to effective risk management (Borge 2001).

5.9.8   Interpretation Risk

This occurs where management and staff in the same organisation cannot communicate effectively because of their own professional language (jargon). Engineers, academics, chemists and bankers all have their own terms, and insurers are probably the worst culprits, using words with common meanings but in a specialised way. Even the same words in the same profession have different meanings in the UK and the USA.

5.10   MANAGING FINANCIAL RISKS

There are various methods of managing risks. The following number of risks associated with financial options, and possible means of mitigation, are discussed below:

- construction delay
- currency risk

- interest rate risk
- equity risk
- corporate bond risk
- liquidity risk
- counter-party risk
- maintenance risk
- taxation risk
- reinvestment risk
- country risk.

5.10.1 Construction Delay

A promoter can edge construction risk by using fixed price contracts, typically lump sum turnkey contracts, and impose liquidated damages on the contractors if they fail to complete a project on time. However, if performance is better than expected the contractors could be awarded bonuses. In most circumstances liquidated damages cover additional interest repayments arising through delay, and compensate equity investors for lost income and fixed costs incurred. However, Ruster (1996) states that liquidated damages are always capped at a certain percentage of the contract price (usually 10–15%).

The sponsor can also include contingency funds in the construction budgets to cover unexpected cost increases. In some cases the promoter will arrange for a standby loan to cover additional costs that may arise in construction or early operation of the project. Standby loans are expensive to arrange and service and should be avoided if cheaper loans are available to cover such costs (Merna and Smith 1996).

Insurance is another way of managing construction risk. Insurance cover ranges from employee liability to acts of God.

5.10.2 Currency Risk

Fluctuations in exchange rates can cause problems if the revenue generated from a project is in local currency and the loan repayment is in a foreign currency. If the value of the local currency depreciates against the value of the foreign currency then the promoter would have to exchange more local currency in order to service the debt, therefore eating into the profits of the project and affecting its commercial viability (Ariani 2001). There are several financial engineering techniques a promoter can use to manage currency risk (Khu 2002) as follows.

5.10.2.1   Currency Forward Exchange

This eliminates risk by fixing the exchange rate at which future trade will take place. A forward contract is made which states the exchange rate for several future payments at the current rate. The contract provides an edge against future fluctuations in the currencies the project is dealing with.

5.10.2.2   Currency Swaps

These are another way of managing risk. The promoter borrows in a hard currency and finances the project in the local currency. The promoter can enter into an agreement whereby the hard currency is swapped for the local currency, allowing hard currency financing.

5.10.2.3   Currency Options

This method of risk reduction is to fix the exchange but give the promoter an option to buy from the open market if the rates are favourable to the company.

5.10.2.4   Use Local Currency

The use of local currency in developing countries to finance projects can be an advantage because it reduces the project's reliance on foreign currency.

5.10.3   Interest Rate Risk

Volatility in interest rates can have significant consequences for an organisation/promoter. However, financial engineering techniques have been developed in the derivatives market to compensate for this problem. These techniques include the following.

5.10.3.1   Interest Rate Forward Agreement (FRA)

These agreements are similar to futures contracts, although, according to Glen (1993), they do have other advantages. These are that FRAs are customised so that the maturity and amount can be written to correspond more to the risk exposure, and FRAs are agreed with the local bank, which means creditworthiness is easier to prove. Consider as an example of an FRA a promoter who wants to borrow £5 million in six months' time when the current loan has been paid, but the promoter expects the rate of interest to rise. This expected rise in interest rates can be compensated for by arranging the FRA now, for the loan it will buy in six months' time.

5.10.3.2   Interest Rate Swap

An interest rate swap is an agreement between two parties to pay each other a series of cash flows, based on fixed or floating interest rates, in the same currency, over a given period of time.

Suppose that a company has assets which produce a fixed stream of income unrelated to fluctuations in interest rates. To finance its activities, the company borrows funds at a floating rate. This creates a mismatch between its income (which is constant) and its outgoings (which fluctuate with changes in interest rates).

To protect against this mismatch risk, the company can enter into an interest rate swap. It will pay the swap counter-party a fixed rate and receive from the swap counter-party a payment which fluctuates with floating rates, which it can then use to service its floating rate borrowings. The principal amounts are not usually exchanged and are expressed to be notional. The parties typically agree to settle the payments on a net basis, with the party owing the larger amount paying the excess to the other.

5.10.3.3   RPI Swaps

An inflation-linked or Retail Price Index-linked (RPI) swap allows parties to manage the risk of inflation being higher or lower than expected.

Suppose a company is in receipt of a series of fixed equal cash flows. While the investor is certain of the magnitude of the flows, the investor is concerned that the purchasing power of the flows will erode through inflation. To hedge this risk he enters into an RPI swap in which he pays the swap counter-party the fixed flows and receives in return another flow linked to RPI. With this swap, the investor has given up his certain cash flow for a cash flow that will have the same purchasing power through time.

One of the most popular types of RPI swap is the real rate swap. This is similar to an interest rate swap, except that it uses 'real' interest rates, that is net of inflation, rather than nominal interest rates (the ordinary percentage figure). With this type of swap, a party, such as a pension fund, can invest in a portfolio of fixed-rate bonds and swap the fixed cash flows from the bonds for cash flows that match the timing and inflation characteristics of its pension outgoings.

5.10.3.4   Caps and Floors

These can reduce risk. For example, the promoter agrees a term loan with a bank of LIBOR + 2%. The promoter also buys a cap for 7% and sells a floor for 5%, creating a collar. Under this agreement the promoter can pay no higher than 7% if interest rates rise. However, if the interest rate falls below 5% the promoter would have to pay the difference (Khu 2002).

5.10.4   Equity Risk

Equity risk can be managed either through reinsurance, or through hedging. For the issuer of the equity the risk of changes in the price of equity is not direct but indirect. The market price of the equity is a rough barometer of the health of the organisation. If the organisation has been performing well or has a good potential for better performance then the market price of the equity of such an organisation will be high. More and more investors will like to own the shares of such a organisation. It will provide good potential to raise additional funds either through the issue of more equities or through debt instruments. Whereas the investors in the equity can use the financial engineering instruments to manage their risk, the issuers of the equity are not permitted to deal in their own shares because they have internal information about the organisation which may tempt them to indulge in undue speculation at the cost of the owners of the equity, who do not have access to such information. However, sometimes organisations in need of funds when their equity price is falling resort to issuing bonus shares to the existing equity owners at below market price to retain the interest of these investors in the organisation and also to raise resources. In the long run the organisation must show good results if it wants its equity to perform well (Cornell 1999).

5.10.5   Corporate Bond Risk

A convertible bond gives the holder of the bond the right to exchange it for a given number of shares before the bond matures. Changing the instrument from debt to equity will change the gearing of the company. When the company is not doing well it will prefer a low gearing ratio. However, in an ideal world the holders of convertible bonds would like to retain the bond and not change it to equity because it could reduce their investment (Merna and Dubey 1998).

5.10.6   Liquidity Risk

Successful management of the liquidity risk hinges on successful cash management of the project. Delays in construction and commissioning, problems with the operation of the project and problems of input supplies and off-take of the produce may lead to unmatched cash inflows and cash outflows and hence liquidity risk.

The problem of liquidity due to cost overruns can be managed by arranging a standby loan. Although standby loan facilities are expensive compared with the normal type of loan, they provide a safety net in the case of cost overruns.

Another method of managing liquidity risk is debt–equity swap. If the liquidity problem is for a short period and the project has a good potential of success then the providers of debt capital may agree to convert their debt into equity. This gives them an opportunity to share in the profits of the company in the future. Conversion of debt to shares totally changes the nature of liability of the company. With shares, the company needs to pay the shareholders only when a dividend is declared. This helps manage the liquidity of the company but at the cost of reduced gearing. Debt for equity swaps have been considered for the Channel Tunnel (Merna and Smith 1996).

Liquidity management is governed by eight key principles:

1. Developing a structure for managing liquidity.
2. Measuring and monitoring net funding requirements.
3. Managing market access.
4. Contingency planning.
5. Foreign currency liquidity management.
6. Internal controls for liquidity risk management.
7. The role of public disclosure for improving liquidity.
8. Supervision.

5.10.7   Counter-party Risk

Controlling counter-party risk is done through both parties involved in the project by monitoring their credit risks and only releasing funds on completion of the other party's obligations (Smithson 1998, Galitz 1995).

5.10.8 Maintenance Risk

Operation of the project by a reputable and financially sound operator whose performance is guaranteed should minimise maintenance risk. However, other ways of hedging operation risks include agreements with equipment and input suppliers, business interruption insurance, and loss of profit insurance in the early years of operation (Tinsley 2000).

5.10.9 Taxation Risk

Taxation is an external influence which is beyond the control of the promoter. Tax regimes greatly influence the commercial viability of a project. However, governments can attract foreign promoters by offering exemption from corporate tax for concessional periods (tax holidays), and fixed tax structures for the concessional period (Merna and Njiru 1998).

5.10.10 Reinvestment Risk

The present authors suggest that when investing returns from a project or portfolio a careful analysis must be made to ensure that future investments will generate higher returns than they would from being reinvested in the original project or portfolio. Surplus cash generated from a portfolio of projects can be used for cross-collateralisation or invested in other commercially viable ventures.

5.10.11 Country Risk

The risks associated with investing in different countries can only be managed through a complete country risk assessment before the project is sanctioned. This will allow possible risks to be identified and analysed. Contingencies can then be put in place in the event of the risk transpiring. However, the risk analysis could highlight the fact that the project carries too many risks and therefore would not be sanctioned (Merna 2002, Ariani 2001).

To eliminate country risk it is important that the government takes prime responsibility to provide security through the duration of the project (Nagy 1979).

5.11   RISK MODELLING

Alabastro *et al.* (1995) define a model as a simplified representation of a complex reality. Modelling is the act of developing an accurate description of a system (Jong 1995). A model means to understand.

Computers are fast and efficient tools for evaluating data but it is important that the users should not lose sight of the assumptions on which software packages are based. The output from a computer model is determined by the information input, which means that accurate data are essential. The idea that if the computer has produced something then it must be right is a belief held by too many people and is certainly not true.

It is essential that the software should fit the project rather than the modeller attempt to fit the project to the software. Software tools should be matched to the kind of project work that is undertaken by an organisation and the way that the organisation manages its projects. The choice of software, for use in project modelling, is very important and requires careful consideration.

It is difficult to find 'off-the-shelf' risk management programs that match the project or portfolio characteristics and the project manager's needs. The majority of programs that are available off the shelf for commercial use are designed to meet the needs of many different types of businesses. Although these programs are user-friendly they tend to lack the modelling flexibility that is required.

There are many advantages in using a computer to model a project or a portfolio. Listed below are some of the more significant ones (Smith 1999):

- *Flexibility.* Computers are very flexible in the way in which they can accept information, enabling most projects to be modelled using a computer. The programs used to model projects can be either off-the-shelf packages or tailored to the needs of the user (bespoke).
- *Speed and accuracy.* When the complexity of a model is such that no manual analytical technique can be used, computers often provide the only means available for modelling. A computer can carry out many complex calculations very quickly, compared with humans, and

reliance can be placed on the accuracy of the calculations. This combination of accuracy and speed is essential for most of the probabilistic risk analysis techniques.

- *Additional reality.* Computer simulation enables real-life complications, such as exchange rates, inflation rates and interest rates, to be included in the project model, and to calculate their effect on the project's economic parameters.
- *Assistance in the decision-making process.* The project model enables a number of 'what if' questions and possible scenarios to be simulated, and shows the effects in terms of the outcome of the project. This simulation process shows the way in which the project is expected to react to certain events or changes and allows contingency plans to be drawn up that can be used in the event that any of the scenarios occur.
- *Scenario analysis.* Often there are no historical data available, from a similar project or portfolio, that relate to the project/portfolio scenarios drawn up by the project organisers, so computer simulation is the only way to see how the project or portfolio might react to particular scenarios.
- *Reduced dependence on raw judgement.* Few people have a reliable intuitive understanding of business risk, and risk modelling removes the reliance on this intuition. A model provides a structure for the project and outputs, which, although based on subjective inputs, gives a basis for decision making.

There are a number of limitations to using a computer to model a project or portfolio. Listed below are some of the more significant ones:

- Poor data lead to an inaccurate model. A model of a project is only as good as the data that are input, so if these data are inaccurate then the model will not accurately reflect the project.
- The model is not representative of the actual project. Even if the data are accurate, it is possible for an inexperienced modeller to create a model that is not representative of the actual project. It is necessary for the project modeller to have a thorough understanding of the particular project to be modelled in order to create a representative model.
- It is too easy to create inaccurate models. Project modelling programs are designed to be user-friendly, which increases the dangers associated with the inexperienced/novice modeller.
- There is a heavy reliance on subjective judgement. The data may not always be available when the project is being modelled, and some subjective assumptions may have to be made in order to complete

the model. So as a result of the data requirement, a heavy reliance is placed on subjective assumptions and personal judgement. This is particularly the case when modelling the project variables or risks.

- Inability fully to reflect real-life complications. The model produced is only a mathematical representation of real life and, therefore, does not necessarily accurately reflect the reaction of the actual project or portfolio to real-life complications. It is impossible to be sure that the model will react in exactly the same way as the real project, because the project does not yet exist and everything is based on what is expected to happen (unless the project being modelled is identical to a previous project or portfolio).

- Reliance on computer output. Too much reliance is placed on the output from computers and often there is insufficient checking of the model or the program used to create the model. It is difficult to tell whether a project model is an accurate representation of reality or not. If the model is very inaccurate it will be easily detected, but if it is nearly accurate then this is much more difficult to detect. It is in situations where the model is almost, but not exactly, accurate that problems arise, because the model does not react to real-life complications in the same way that the actual project would (Ould 1995).

5.12   TYPES OF RISK SOFTWARE

Many of the risk management software packages available that have the capabilities to perform quantitative probability analysis generally use a random number generator based on either the Monte Carlo or the Latin Hypercube systems. Network packages also employ Markovian logic so that the interdependence of project activities on the identified risks may be simulated.

The types of risk software are described below.

5.12.1   Management Data Software Packages

These tend to be large software systems based around database material. Essentially they are designed to process data and are therefore concerned predominantly with the automating of administrative work. They may be tailored for a specific application or be general in nature, depending upon the users' requirement. These software packages are expensive to purchase. They are suitable if there is an adequate database from which information can be fed to the system; however, generally at the present time the majority of companies do not have the necessary database to make these programs economically and practically viable.

5.12.2   Spreadsheet-based Risk Assessment Software

This group of programs are used in the evaluation of risk in models which are designed to carry out analysis for specific analytical requirements. These programs are generally add-in programs, that is programs that are normally macro programs which are specifically designed to combine with commercially marketed, proprietary software packages; they import risk assessment analysis capabilities within the receiving program.

5.12.3   Project Network-based Risk Assessment Software

This group of programs are also used in the evaluation of risk in models which are designed to carry out analysis for specific analytical requirements. These programs may be add-in or stand-alone programs. Add-in programs are normally macro programs specifically designed to combine with commercial software and import risk assessment analysis capabilities within it.

5.12.4   Standalone Project Network-based Risk Assessment Software

This type of software is intended to be self-contained in terms of the construction of the risk model, the parameters and the variables that are input. These programs also produce the required output of the risk analysis results and can generate comprehensive reports contained within the program or they may be exported to other software packages if necessary.

5.13   SUMMARY

Raising finance for projects is an important issue. Without finance the project cannot go ahead. Therefore organisations/promoters need to determine the sources of finance available.

Debt (Senior)

↓

Mezzanine/Bonds

↓

Equity (Junior)

Figure 5.3   Seniority of financial instruments

This chapter briefly described both corporate and project finance. It also discussed the types of financial instruments that are used as a source of finance. The seniority of these instruments, in terms of their claims on project assets in the event of default, are illustrated in Figure 5.3.

Debt is the most used instrument to fund projects. With debt there is an interest charge on the loan. Bond issues are becoming popular amongst promoters to raise project finance. Projects worldwide have been funded partly by bonds. Equity is considered as risk capital because investors bear a higher degree of risk than other lenders. Equity ranks the lowest in terms of its claim on the assets of the project.

The debt–equity ratio assigned to a project investment is a measure of the risk in that project investment. The greater the equity issue, the greater the perceived risk.

Risk management involves identifying risks, predicting how probable they are and how serious they might become, deciding what to do about them and implementing these decisions.

Major risks associated with finance include construction risk, currency risk, interest rate risk, equity risk, liquidity risk, counter-party risk, maintenance risk and taxation risk. There are different ways to manage these risks, for example financial engineering techniques prove to be an excellent way to manage currency and interest rate risks.

Modelling risk is an important element of the risk analysis process and should only be performed with data that reflect the investment in terms of cost and time. The choice of risk management software is paramount to a successful risk assessment. Risk management software is readily available and numerous programs have been developed to assess project risk. The key is finding the right software for the project in hand.

6
Portfolio Analysis and Cash Flows

6.1 INTRODUCTION

This chapter briefly defines portfolio analysis and outlines portfolio construction, strategy and the concept of bundling projects. Models used in financial markets are then examined. Cash flows and cash flow principles are also outlined and an example of portfolio modelling and its benefits is discussed.

6.2 SELECTING A PORTFOLIO STRATEGY

Ghasemzadeh and Archer (2000) define portfolio selection as the periodic activity involved in selecting a portfolio of projects which meets an organisation's stated objectives without exceeding the available resources or violating other constraints. The present authors suggest that a corporate body can consider its SBU as part of a portfolio of businesses and similarly an SBU can consider its projects as a portfolio of investments.

Given the investment objectives and the investment policy, the investor must develop a 'portfolio strategy'. Portfolio strategies can be classified as either a passive or active portfolio.

An active portfolio strategy uses available information and forecasting techniques to seek a better performance than if the portfolio was simply diversified broadly. Essential to all active strategies are expectations about the factors that influence the performance of the class of assets. For example, equity forecasts may include earnings, dividends or price–earnings ratios (Fabozzi 2002).

A passive portfolio involves a minimum expectational input and instead relies on diversification to match the performance of some index. In effect a passive strategy assumes that the marketplace will reflect all available information in the price paid for securities.

Whether an active or passive strategy is chosen depends on the investors' view as to how 'price efficient' the market is and the investors' risk tolerance.

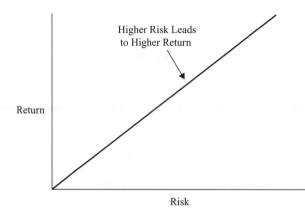

Figure 6.1   Typical risk/return profile

In today's volatile business environment, it is essential to have an understanding of individual project risk. The notion of 'no risk, no return' is widely accepted in the business world. All projects have risk – the zero risk project is not worth pursuing. It is commonly acknowledged that investment projects/programmes that are likely to yield the greatest returns on capital employed are fundamentally likely to be more risky as shown in Figure 6.1.

Therefore achieving the goal of maximising return on capital employed (ROCE) requires an element of risk taking in an environment where risk/return outcomes are increasingly more uncertain. Therefore, successful businesses, portfolios are likely to have effective risk management processes and practices in place that ensure an optimal balance between risk and return as shown in Figure 6.2.

A company in Zone 1 is not taking sufficient risk, and its capital is being underutilised. The company would be advised to increase risk through growth or acquisition or to bring capital down by increasing dividends. In Zone 3, the company is taking too much risk. The level is above and beyond its risk absorption capability in terms of capital and/or risk management capability. In Zone 2, the company has found its optimal portfolio – the 'sweet spot' that optimises risk and ROCE.

6.3   CONSTRUCTING THE PORTFOLIO

An efficient portfolio is one that provides the greatest expected return for a given level of risk, or, equivalently, the lowest risk for a given expected return (Fabozzi and Markowitz 2002).

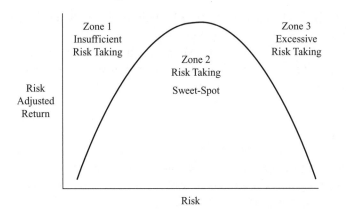

Figure 6.2   Risk adjusted return/risk profile (Pressinger 2005)

Indexing projects is a popular passive strategy. A portfolio is assembled that attempts to match the performance of an index. The amount a particular project is worth should be equal to the index it is being compared with.

Cash flow modelling is also a popular method to assess portfolio strategy. Discounting cash flow models begins by projecting cash flows of a project or security over their expected concessional period or life. Then the discounted value (or present value) of each cash flow is obtained by using the appropriate discount rate. The sum of all expected cash flows is the theoretical value of the project or security. It is the theoretical value, or aggregate, that is then compared with the market price or expected value. It can then be decided whether securities are fairly priced or not. In the case of projects the NPV or IRR can be analysed before and during the project's life to determine the commercial viability of the project or portfolio.

Discounted cash flows can be used to calculate the expected value rather than the theoretical value. This is done by starting with the market price and the expected cash flows. The expected return is then based on the interest rate that will make the present value of the expected cash flow equal to the market price. A more commonly used name for the expected return is IRR. The procedure for computing the IRR involves reiterating different interest rates until one is found that makes the present value of the expected cash flows equal to the market price.

Many organisations have difficulty in assessing the strategic performance of each of their business units and allocating their resources selectively. De Wit and Meyer (1994) believe diversified industries need a formal tool such as portfolio planning.

The following data from the Meta Group's research (2002) show that a very small proportion of organisations practise effective portfolio risk management:

- 89% of organisations are flying blind with virtually no metrics in place except for finance
- 84% of organisations do not carry out business cases for any of their projects or do them on a 'select only' principle (key projects)
- 84% of organisations are unable to adjust and align their budgets with business needs more than twice a year.

6.4   PORTFOLIO OF CASH FLOWS

Projects in general and more specifically construction projects have a cash flow ranging over a period of time from 5 to 25 years. This is known as the life cycle.

Establishing and attaching risks cannot be carried out using modern portfolio techniques. A project is deemed long term relative to securities and future costs and revenues are forecast on the basis of the current economic climate and demand. Project time and cost data can be modelled and future cash flows simulated. Current risk management software packages can attach risks through probabilities or ranges. Such software is widely available; however, the choice of software depends on the economic inputs and outputs used to assess the commercial viability of the project. Cooper *et al.* (1998) suggest that financial analysis in terms of portfolios is widely undeveloped.

In order to assess a portfolio of projects, specifically through the project's cash flows, the present authors suggest that a software package capable of assessing the worst, base and best case scenarios is required. It is of paramount importance that the same software is used to assess individual projects as a combination of individual project cash flows.

Software can be used to generate the worst, base and best case cash flows for individual projects. By assigning risks to each project a combination of all the cash flows can be computed as a portfolio cumulative cash flow through the application of a spreadsheet. There is no limit to how many projects the analyst can add to a portfolio. Outputs can include a portfolio cash flow with the identified risks attached for the base, worst and best case scenarios. Economic parameters such as the IRR, NPV,

CLU and PB period can be generated. The result is a flexible package which can take into account various changes in the micro- and macro-economic climate. An example of this is shown later in this chapter.

6.5 THE BOSTON MATRIX

The Boston matrix is a management tool developed to assist in portfolio planning. It has two controlling aspects, namely market share (meaning relative to the competition) and the rate of market growth. Each individual product or project in a portfolio is placed into the matrix to determine relative market share. This is simplistic in many ways and the matrix has some understandable problems, but the authors consider that the balanced mix described by Johnson and Scholes (1999) below can be assessed within a portfolio:

- A star is a project where costs are reducing over time.
- The question mark (or problem child) is a project where cost reductions are unlikely.
- The cash cow is a project which is a cash provider.
- The dog may be a project that is a drain on company finances and resources.

In many cases, only projects with robust revenue streams are likely to be financed through the private sector. However, investors with high-earning/low-risk infrastructure stock may be willing to accept less attractive stock (piggybacking) which may offer rewards in the long term (Merna and Smith 1999).

6.6 SCENARIO ANALYSIS

Scenario analysis is a derivative of sensitivity analysis, which tests alternative scenarios as options. When undertaking a scenario analysis the key variables are identified together with their values (Flanagan and Norman 1993). The present authors suggest that a financial engineer may wish to assess a number of different financial instruments in a portfolio of projects. If the instrument of choice is debt then the scenarios will be based on the most likely, optimistic and pessimistic forecasts of three possible interest rates. The results will represent the range of possible outcomes. The effects of these changes in one project can then be assessed with changes in the portfolio of projects.

6.7   DIVERSIFICATION

Pollio (1999) states that diversification is used to minimise the risk of the overall loan portfolio and thus stabilise interest income. Diversification is the key to the management of portfolio risk because it allows investors to lower portfolio risk significantly without adversely effecting return.

The authors believe both the above statements to be relevant when defining diversification.

Depending on an organisation's current financial position and future needs, the organisation would most probably hold money in a number of investments, which together form a portfolio. Some funds would go into low-risk, fixed interest, easily liquidated savings accounts or securities, and the remainder might go into high-income capital growth securities according to need. The attraction of sinking all funds into one security is that it may realise a high return on the investment; however, there is also a danger that all the investment could be lost if the security is risky. Investing in more than one security, therefore, does not necessarily reduce the risk.

Correlation is the glue that allows investors to aggregate returns on individual assets into a return for the portfolio. This is the process of identifying how the risks in the portfolio are related to each other. If two risks behave similarly – they increase for the same reasons or by the same amount – they would be considered highly correlated. The greater the correlation of identified risks in the portfolio, the higher the risk. Correlation is a key concept in risk diversification. Correlation can range from -1.00 to 1.00. For example, a portfolio with a correlation of 1.00 means that its returns move in the same direction as the index, whereas a correlation of -1.00 means that it moves in totally the opposite direction to the index. Ideally, a company should look to select portfolios that have varying degrees of correlation amongst themselves.

If several investments are in the same related industry, and their cash flows react in a manner similar to changes in the general economy, the investments are said to be positively correlated. Figure 6.3 illustrates that changes in cash flow 'A' are reflected closely by cash flow 'B'. Clearly, there is no reduction in risk from combining such investments.

When the cash flows of two investments behave in exactly opposite ways within the same economic climate, the correlation between the two is said to be negative. Risk is reduced by this combination in a portfolio. Figure 6.4 illustrates that equivalent amounts are invested in 'A' and 'D'. The result is that rising and falling cash flows are combined to yield the smoothed-out return 'C' over time.

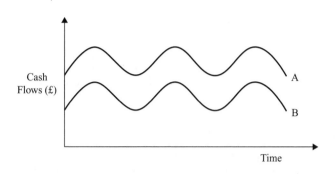

Figure 6.3   Positively correlated cash flows

Most securities and business projects are nearer to positive than negative correlation, although they are very rarely perfectly correlated. Therefore there will always be some benefit in combining projects of an unlike nature in terms of risk diversification.

6.7.1   Diversification of Risk

Portfolio managers need to be concerned with the different stages in maturity of the portfolio, which varies according to the sizes of the projects, the geographical location of the projects, the different stages each project is at within the portfolio, the operational track record of each project, and the experience and creditworthiness of sponsors and counterparts (Silk *et al.* 2002).

It is clear that the diversification of risk profiles between the projects within a portfolio allow sponsors to finance more economically. Projects with strong revenues may offset and diversify the risk on those that have

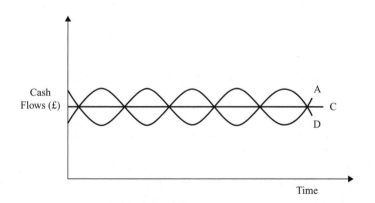

Figure 6.4   Negatively correlated cash flows

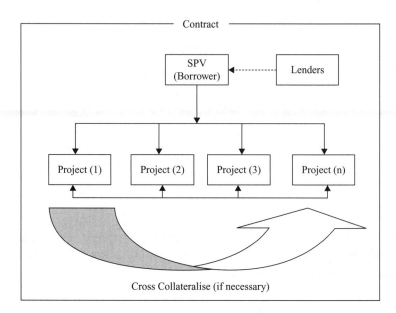

Figure 6.5   Interdependencies of projects within a portfolio

less robust cash flows. In terms of addressing individual risks of projects, lenders demand a higher level of interest to protect their investment. In some cases higher DSCRs are required and enhanced sponsor support, especially where construction risk is identified.

Figure 6.5 illustrates how a portfolio can, through cross-collaterali-sation, support a project in the event of a negative impact or a number of projects in the portfolio. Cross-collateralisation is discussed further in this chapter.

However, contracts binding the portfolios should contain clauses allowing projects to maintain some degree of independence, so in ex-treme cases external influences do not affect the whole portfolio.

6.8   PORTFOLIO RISK MANAGEMENT

There are two reasons for adopting portfolio risk management:

1. Risks inherent in projects cannot be separated from the aspects of general business management.
2. All projects are unique, therefore risk and uncertainty belong to a significant part of project business. Whether or not these risks are brought through to the portfolio is a different matter.

As far as the risk management associated with project portfolios is concerned, there may be several aspects in analysis and making strategic choices associated with the projects at the strategic business level. For example, for an organisation operating in international markets, country and area and specific local risk need to be taken into account. The country risks may not affect a project alone, but may affect the whole portfolio indirectly (Ariani 2001). Country risks are discussed in Chapter 4.

Particular geographical regions, customers, product types, lines of business and other important aspects can serve as criteria against which project portfolio risk should be considered, such as the local creditworthiness of different project portfolio areas of an organisation.

The process of portfolio risk management is very similar to project risk management. It consists of the following stages:

- risk identification
- risk classification
- risk analysis
- risk response.

Portfolio risk management can have the following benefits:

- Reduces the cost of capital by managing portfolio risk rather than individual project risks.
- Reduces the risk of projects from developing their own inertia and boundary definition.
- Increases the awareness of the critical risks by senior managers.
- Reduces project overrun and overspend.
- Identifies which risks exploit competitive advantage.
- Protects and enhances shareholder value.

The authors suggest that portfolio risk management should first consider the risks associated with the economic parameters of each project within the portfolio and project interdependencies before assessing the portfolio of projects as one entity.

6.8.1 Bundling Projects

Dybvig (1988) first used the term bundling to represent the particular consumption of a bundle of similar commodities, in this case electricity, purchased from different electricity generating organi-sations. The distribution price of the bundle is determined by setting a margin above the purchase price(s) and then developing an average sale price that the market will bear for sale to consumers. The word 'bundling' is used today throughout the business world and in particular in private finance initiative (PFI) projects.

Bundling is the grouping of projects or services within one project structure in a manner which enables the group to be financed as one project. Porter (1987) suggests that projects with similar characteristics and interdependencies can be aggregated as a bundle of projects rather than disaggregated stand-alone projects. The key benefits are that this allows small projects to be financed by increasing the overall debt within the bundle to an economic level and allows various projects to cross-collateralise each other. Key issues are that cash flows from the single project are robust (a single cash flow is often preferred) and the liabilities of each party, particularly those of the public sector partners, are adequately addressed in the event of, for example, partial or full termination (Frank and Merna 2003).

Many possibilities of bundling are being considered. Some initiatives involve the construction, refurbishment and operation of projects into manageable bundles; these are often described as batches (Public Private Partnership-Initiative NRW 2003). However, bundling can also involve bringing together pre-existing projects and refinancing/restructuring them by using financial resources more efficiently. Examples include providing lower interest rates than those currently in place and extending the term of original debt (Foster 2002).

In September 2004, the Irish-based bank Depfa bundled £394 million of PFI loans relating to 25 PFI schemes into a specially created financial entity. Floating rate notes will be issued against £31.75 million worth of this debt, while £358 million of it will be matched by a credit default swap, a financial derivative that provides what amounts to insurance cover for the credit risk. The floating rate notes will be issued in six trenches with preliminary ratings by credit rating agency S&P, ranging from AAA to BB (*Financial Times* 2004).

The private sector should be more willing to invest in schemes with greater than critical mass, as such schemes bring greater scope to offer innovation and deliver more cost-effective solutions in terms of finance, capital, life cycle and operational costs. Bid costs per project reduce as the number of projects increase (McDowall 2001, Lamb and Merna 2004*a*).

Projects can also be considered for refinancing. This is particularly true of projects where construction has been completed and certain risks have passed. A more favourable rate of financing can then be negotiated.

Loan refinancing, bond refinancing, leasing, and debt to equity swap are identified by Merna and Njiru (2002) as ways of finance restructuring. Refinancing is defined as repaying existing debt and entering into a new loan, typically to meet some corporate objective such as the lengthening of maturity or lowering the interest rate. In other words, refinancing involves paying off an existing loan with proceeds from a new loan, using the same property as collateral. Similarly, in some cases, corporate bonds with a long maturity and identifiable coupon payments can be issued to refinance short-term loans.

There are two situations where the project needs to be refinanced or restructured. First of all, if the current interest rate is lower than the rate on the debt, refinancing may be considered so that short loans can be rolled over into longer-term maturity loans. Secondly, if a project is having difficulties in generating sufficient revenues the promoter has to restructure its financing techniques to maintain its project financial viability. When the project is facing difficulties but has great potential for growth the debt to equity swap technique can be employed. The benefit of debt to equity swap is reducing the level of debt payment so the project can be given sufficient time to overcome such difficulties.

The authors believe, in the capital-incentive refinery industry for example, that when the final financial package has been determined, the borrower can look at the prospects of refinancing a particular facility after the completion of the project; similarly; the promoter also needs to consider the refinancing risk if the project risks such as delay or cost overrun occur. This can be assessed by the cash flow modelling which is discussed later.

Consideration could be given to bundling projects for refinancing to provide larger debt. This allows alternative methods of financing to be considered. Construction companies could refinance to provide them with an exit strategy once the project is up and running (PFI Fact Sheet 2003).

Although there are many advantages of bundling projects, if the projects are not managed properly costs will be a lot higher than expected because of the multiplier effect (Munro 2001). Paddington Hospital, the government's largest PFI hospital scheme which involved bundling three hospital schemes, was estimated to cost £360 million, but because of redesign, inflation and mismanagement, the costs are expected to exceed £1 billion (Leftly 2003).

Capital markets' funding will tend to concentrate on larger projects and is therefore not available as an option for smaller projects. The transaction costs on projects with a capital value of around £10 million can be disproportionately high and severely affect returns and value for money (VFM) (McDowall 2001, Spackman 2002).

Bundling projects can provide cash flows sufficient to produce a reasonable return after operating and debt service costs are addressed. It can also spread the risk for funders between different projects and locations. Smaller projects that would not be economically viable individually may be economically viable when in bundles (Frank and Merna 2003). The present authors suggest that bundling projects can allow ethical, non-commercially viable projects to be procured through cross-collateralisation of funds.

Benefits of bundling to the public sector include:

- single contract for construction
- simplified monitoring
- simplified payment.

Benefits of bundling to project management according to Frank and Merna (2003) and Lamb and Merna (2004a) are:

- effective use of resources, one project team, one set of advisers
- simplified chain of reporting/command
- improved VFM
- economies of scale
- replicability
- economies through innovative finance, such as the use of bond financing with larger deals
- spread procurement and transaction costs.

Bundling projects consolidates operational, financial and strategic activities into one package. This is an option governments are now considering in order to sanction smaller PFI projects. However, the task can be difficult. Public–private partnerships (PPPs) often involve the private sector partner providing a bundle of services such as the design, construction, operation and maintenance, and both soft and hard services. Bundling thus differs from traditional contracting out whereby separate contracts are let for each service. Bundling can provide VFM which cannot be obtained by contracting services separately. Integration of design, operation and maintenance over the life of an asset, within a single-project finance package, improves performance and reduces project life costs (McDowall 2001).

When considering bundling a group of projects the opportunity cost of capital should be taken into account. This is 'the highest price or rate of return an alternative course of action would provide'.

6.8.2 Considerations

Bringing projects together for financing, however, must consider the following issues (Frank and Merna 2003):

- *Different commencement times.* If projects have staggered commencement times the project company will not want to borrow until funding is needed. This could happen when planning permission is delayed on one of the sites of the project.
- *Partial completion.* If one part of the project is completed before the others then the project company will want services to start in that area first before the other areas are completed.
- *Partial termination.* The project may falter in one area. This does not necessarily mean the whole project is not viable – the viable parts could still go ahead. The project company would need to ensure that the funders were in agreement and that the financial viability of the overall project was not affected.
- *Variations.* Bundled projects may be more prone to variations or changes and additional debt may need to be raised to cover this.

Each of these complexities needs to be addressed in both the project and financial documentation.

6.8.3 Bundling Projects into a Portfolio

Figure 6.6 illustrates how a project or bundle of projects transpires from an idea by the principle through to the financing of the venture.

The bundle could be funded by one 'lead bank'. However, depending on the risks and the size of the bundle, the loan could be syndicated through a number of banks, therefore reducing the risk to the lead bank (Frank and Merna 2003).

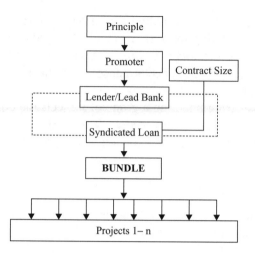

Figure 6.6   The lending ladder

Projects 1 − n must have cash outflows and generate revenue streams over defined concessional periods. Different financial instruments will be used depending on the project size and the prevailing economic climate (Frank and Merna 2003, Merna and Young 2005).

6.9   CROSS-COLLATERALISATION

Most projects are traditionally procured on a standalone or stranded basis, their commercial success being dependent on the revenues generated by the project's assets, although projects procured using corporate finance often receive financial assistance from the corporate body when they suffer short-term liquidity problems. In standalone projects it is prohibited to offset gains and losses from one project to another. When projects are bundled together in a portfolio, cross-collateralisation can take place by combining project cash flows over the length of the concession or by one project's revenues cross-collateralising with another project's over a specified duration before combining cumulative cash flow in a portfolio.

A typical definition of cross-collateralisation is when collateral for one loan also serves as collateral for other loans. For example, in real estate situations cross-collateralisation can occur when a person already owns a house, and wants to buy another one.

The authors define cross-collateralisation as:

The use of funds generated by one project with strong cash flows within a portfolio, to fund another project within the same portfolio, which may be experiencing cash flow difficulties and defaulting on debt repayments.

Cross-collateralisation is a relatively new expression. It is basically the use of collateral generated from one project to fund another project that may be experiencing cash flow deficiencies, and thus unable to service debt payments, in terms of principal and interest. These deficiencies may arise from the numerous risks a project is susceptible to over its life cycle.

6.10   CASH FLOWS

Cash flows are a measure of a project's health. They are simply cash receipts minus cash payments, over a given period of time. It is the cycle of cash inflows and outflows that determines business solvency (Turner 1994).

Cash flow management is the process of monitoring, analysing and adjusting business cash flows. The most important issue of cash flow management is to avoid extended cash shortages, specifically lack of liquidity at any given time over the project life cycle. To avoid these shortages cash flow management needs to be performed on a regular basis. Cash flow forecasting can be used to head off cash flow problems. Most project accounting programmes have built-in features to make forecasting quicker and easier. Cash flow management requires the development and use of strategies that will maintain adequate cash flow within a project (Hwee and Tiong 2001).

Cash flows are generated from a cycle of business cash inflows and outflows, with the purpose of maintaining adequate cash for a project, and to provide the basis for cash flow analysis. This involves examining the components of a business that affect cash flow, such as accounts receivable and payable (counter-party risk), credit terms and finance payments. By performing a cash flow analysis on these separate components, cash flows can be managed. Smith (2002) suggests that the success of a venture is largely dependent on the effort expended during the appraisal stage preceding sanction. The authors concur with Smith and suggest that cash flows and their associated risks are paramount to the appraisal stage.

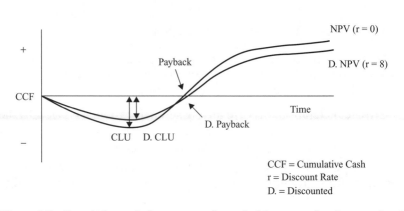

Figure 6.7   Cumulative cash flow curves of a typical base case for discounted and non-discounted inflows and outflows of cash

The authors describe a cash flow as a financial model of the project. In its simplest form a cumulative cash flow can provide vital information to a manager. It is concerned with the flow of money in and out of the account per unit of time. The net cash flow is the difference between cash in and cash out. In its cumulative form it is described as the net cumulative cash flow (Ye and Tiong 2000). A cumulative cash flow curve is a graphic presentation of the flows of money mentioned above. The cumulative net cash flow curve depicts net project cash outflows as a negative function and net project cash inflows as a positive function. This represents the true nature of project cash flow: an outflow results in a negative cash position and an inflow results in a positive cash position.

Figure 6.7 illustrates the cumulative cash flow of a typical base case for discounted and non-discounted inflows and outflows of cash from the following economic parameters which can be computed:

- NPV
- IRR
- PB
- maximum CLU
- discounted net return
- discounted PB period
- discounted CLU.

The base case cumulative cash flow is defined by Esty (2004) as the cash flow projection with variables measured at their expected values; that is, a cash flow that is not subjected to any risks over its life cycle.

6.10.1   Cash Flow Definition for Portfolios

The authors define a cash flow as an external flow of cash and/or securities (capital additions or withdrawals) that is client initiated. Transfers of assets between asset classes within a portfolio or manager-initiated flows must not be used to move portfolios out of composites on a temporary basis. The cash flow may be defined by the organisation as a single flow or an aggregate of a number of flows within a stated period of time. In cases of multiple cash flows over an extended period of time, organisations should refer to the discretion section of the guidance statement on the definition of composites and consider whether the portfolio should be classified as non-discretionary.

Figure 6.8 illustrates the effects of combining base case cumulative cash flows. Figure 6.8(c) illustrates the cumulative base case cash flow of combining the base case cash flows of Project 1 and Project 2 illustrated by Figures 6.8(a) and (b) respectively. New economic parameters can now be computed for the combined base case cumulative cash flows which can be described as a portfolio of two projects.

Many organisations use this method of combining base case cash flows to assess the economic parameters of a combination of project cash flows. This method does not, however, take into account risks associated with individual projects and only provides a basic approximation for decision making.

Currently many organisations use the red line method for assessing the commercial viability of the portfolio. This typically involves computing a worst case scenario for the portfolio cash flows by assuming a risk range, for example 10% negative risk, illustrated by a red line below the base case cumulative cash flow of the portfolio.

Figure 6.9 illustrates the base case cumulative cash flow of a portfolio and the red line case below it. The area between the two curves is deemed to be robust in terms of meeting a minimum acceptable rate of return. Should the base case cumulative cash flow fall below the red line, decisions can be made to reassess individual projects as part of the portfolio.

Dealing with large, external cash flows in a portfolio is a common struggle for most investment managers. These large flows, of cash and/or securities, can have a significant impact on investment strategy implementation and, thus, on a portfolio's and composite's performance.

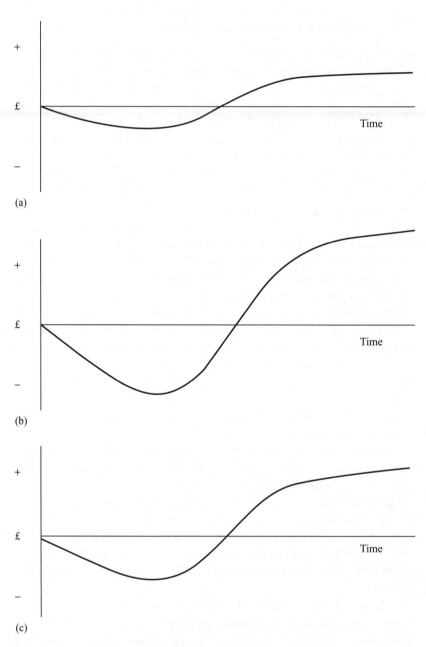

Figure 6.8   Cumulative combined base case cash flow for (a) Project 1, (b) Project 2 and (c) Projects 1 and 2

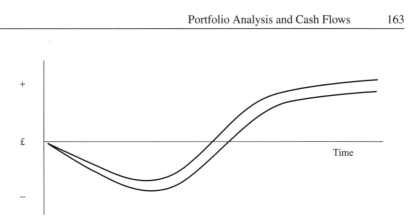

Figure 6.9   Comparison of the red line (lower curve) cumulative cash flow

6.10.2   Reasons for Choosing Cash Flow Curves

A project or portfolio is a commercial venture. All the important parties associated with a project, such as the promoter, the contractor and the providers of capital, invest in the project with the aim of achieving some desired benefits or returns. Normally the most important financial objective is always profitability and liquidity. Smith (1975) suggests that profitability implies making an adequate return on the capital and assets employed in the enterprise, whereas liquidity implies an adequacy of cash flows to enable the unit to pay its way and ensure continuation of the operation. Financial management in a business hinges on the management of cash flows. Whether or not a business survives is a matter of suitable cash flows, rather than profitability, which is realised at a later stage in any project. Profitability is dependent on the cash flow. Good management of a project is, therefore, not only dependent on achieving the triple constraints of specification, budget and schedule but is also dependent on being able to manage the liquidity (cash flow) of a project. Cash flow curves are highly sensitive to changes in project conditions and therefore can act as an early warning system, in case of problems, to help initiate proper rectification measures, for example, a change in the design of the project which increases or decreases the project cost, delays leading to cost overruns, fluctuations in the interest rate affecting the cost of capital used and fluctuations in the input and output costs can be easily depicted on a cash flow curve.

6.10.3   Projects Generating Multiple IRRs

Some project cash flows can generate NPV = 0 at two different discount rates (Brealey and Myers 2000). An investment project in which the

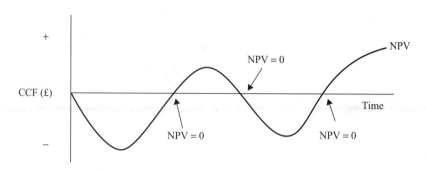

Figure 6.10   Cumulative cash flow-generating multiple IRRs

summary cash flow numbers are characterised by alternating cash inflows and outflows can have more than one, or multiple, IRRs. Projects can be denoted by $(- +, -)$ or $(+, - +)$ where the signs correspond to the sequence of the cash flows. There can be as many IRRs as there are reversals in the direction of cash flow (Werner and Stoner 2002). In projects procured by project finance an existing revenue, followed by a cash outflow and a further revenue, may form part of a concession contract (Merna and Smith 1996). Figure 6.10 illustrates the cumulative cash flow of such a project.

Typically a project generating two positive IRRs and a positive NPV is considered to be commercially viable.

6.10.4   Model Cash Flow

The following five stages to build a model cash flow curve are recommended by the present authors:

1. Compile the base case cash flow simply by adding the costs and revenue over the entire life cycle of the project or contract.
2. Refine the base case cash flow to take account of delays between incurring a commitment and paying or receiving the money.
3. Calculate the resulting cost and benefit together with the investment required.
4. Consider the risk and uncertainty.
5. If necessary, examine the implications of inflation.

The model cash flow curve depicts the forecasted pattern of money inflows and money outflows, in money terms or real terms, of the accounts of the project during its life. However, it is not realistic to expect a very

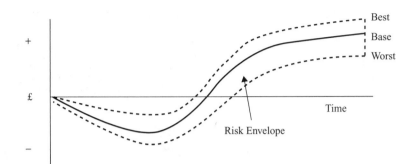

Figure 6.11   Risk envelope for project or portfolio

high degree of accuracy in any financial prediction based on this cash flow because it uses certain assumptions and estimates. In order to overcome this problem, normally a range of possible changes in the cash flow, both beneficial as well as adverse, as a result of risks and uncertainty, are built into the model. This provides a band around the model cash flow.

Cumulative cash flows can be developed to show the worst, base and best case cumulative cash flows of projects or portfolios. Figure 6.11 illustrates the envelope bound by the worst and best case cumulative cash flows. The closer the curves of these worst and best case cumulative cash flows, the less risk or uncertainty is assumed in the project or portfolio. A robust finance package is one that will service principal, interest, dividends and coupon payments for any economic outcome that may occur within the risk envelope.

6.11   AN EXAMPLE OF PORTFOLIO MODELLING

The following example uses a risk management software package based on Monte Carlo simulation to generate worst and best case scenarios from risks identified by the techniques discussed in Chapter 4.

Figure 6.12 illustrates the probability of a project's/portfolio's cash flow over a certain period of time.

The trend line of the cash flow can be produced as follows:

1. Set each year's cash flow as a forecast.
2. After completing a simulation of cash flow forecasts for each year a trend chart illustrating the certainty ranges of all the forecasts can be prepared as shown in Figure 6.12.

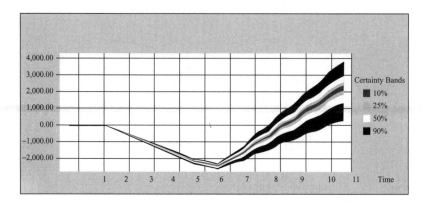

Figure 6.12   Trend chart of probabilities in terms of cumulative cash flow over time

3. The choice of certainty bands can be determined to suit requirements. Trend charts display certainty ranges for multiple forecasts in a series of bands. Each band represents the certainty ranges into which the actual values of forecasts fall. For example, the 50% band shows that the cash flow has a 50% chance of being in this range.

Analysing projects on a project-by-project basis is a relatively simple operation. Many software packages exist which can accommodate the financial appraisal in terms of economic parameters and carry out sensitivity and risk analysis, using Monte Carlo simulation. The financial analysis of these bundled projects can be considered as a portfolio of projects. Each individual project will have different cost and revenue implications and be subjected to different risk scenarios. When projects are considered individually some may be commercially viable as standalone projects and others may not be commercially viable on a standalone basis. However, when the projects are bundled together the overall portfolio of projects may meet a promoter's MARR (minimum acceptable rate of return) and be deemed commercially viable. These non-commercially viable projects can, however, be financed by cross-collateralisation of funds to make them viable as part of a portfolio of projects.

Traditionally the commercial viability of a portfolio of projects has been assessed on the correlations between returns when calculating the portfolio standard deviation (Cuthbertson and Nitzsche 2001) or on a project-by-project basis. The present authors, however, have developed a financial risk mechanism to provide economic parameters based on risk ranges for a portfolio of projects by combining an existing risk management program with spreadsheets. The outputs from the program and spreadsheets indicate the economic parameters of the base, worst and best case scenarios of the portfolio of projects in terms of economic parameters illustrated by cumulative cash flows as one project.

6.11.1 Financial Instruments

As discussed in Chapter 5, individual projects are typically financed by a combination of financial instruments that often include debt, mezzanine finance (bonds) and equity. Merna and Khu (2003) state that the types of financial instruments available for project financings have always been of concern to investors and promoters. In many infrastructure projects the debt–equity ratio is seen to be a measure of the risk in a project, the greater the risk the greater the equity contribution. In effect equity, particularly ordinary equity, can be described as risk capital in project financings.

The modelled portfolio of projects will identify the economic parameters based on individual project financing. The financing of individual projects can be reassessed by substituting debt for equity to determine the effect on the portfolio of projects. Economic parameters of the amended portfolio will reflect such changes in individual project financings. For example, an individual project may be deemed to be sufficiently risky to require equity in its financing, but when considered as part of a portfolio of projects cross-collateralisation can be used to service debt rather than a potentially more expensive equity contribution. Clearly the financial instruments used in individual projects can be reassessed once the economic parameters of the portfolio and associated risks have been identified.

6.11.2 Development of the Mechanism

The mechanism depends on the identification of the following outputs:

- CLU
- NPV
- IRR
- PB.

Each project P_1 to P_n is assessed on the basis of an individual project. Typically these are based on a network of project activities which are time and cost related. The software is used to assess the economic parameters of the base case without risks being considered. Ranges representing risks are then attached to activities in the network to determine the sensitivity of each activity to risk and a probability distribution is computed. Each project is assessed in a similar way (Merna and Khu 2003).

The outputs in terms of worst, best and base case can be combined to determine the overall economic parameters of the portfolio of projects. The economic parameters can then be assessed to determine the commercial viability of the portfolio rather than of the individual project.

6.11.3   Spreadsheets

6.11.3.1   Financial Modelling in Excel

With advances in technology and improvements in Excel itself, Excel has become the preferred tool for creating all but the largest and most computationally intensive financial models. The advantages of Excel for financial modelling are numerous and are discussed in Chapter 5. Excel's application for business management and analytical requirements has several benefits which are useful within a business environment, these include:

- *Familiarity* – Most business professionals are already familiar with the Microsoft Excel application. This translates into a faster acceptance and shorter learning curve to users presented with an Excel-based solution disseminated within an organisation.
- *Customisation* – The flexible nature of Excel makes applications developed with it relatively easy to customise to specific end user requirements. Such customisation may be accomplished within the applications themselves or, where application is protected or locked, through separate workbooks and modules that interact with the main application.
- *Scalability* – The abilities to link formulas and call compiled modules from separate workbooks in Excel make developed solutions scalable to meet growing demands of analytical (especially banking) requirements. As business needs evolve over time, additional functionality can be developed and integrated with the original application.
- *Interoperability* – With the proliferation of Microsoft Office as the choice of operating software for many organisations worldwide, Excel-based solutions can interoperate with other Office applications both within and between organisations.

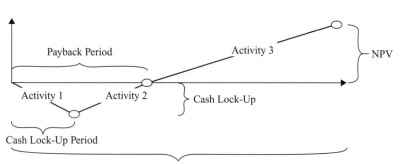

Figure 6.13   Straight-line interpolation of base case cumulative cash flow

However, despite its power, Excel has many limitations, and there are many financial models – some even relatively simple ones – that either cannot be created in Excel or will be overly complex or cumbersome to create in Excel. What's more, when you create a highly complex model in Excel, it can be difficult to understand, debug and maintain (Sengupta 2004).

In this case study portfolio the development of spreadsheets is based on an approximation of the cumulative cash flow curves. The risk simulation output data form the basis of the model. Through a straight-line interpolation between the four points – Start, CLU, PB period and NPV – each project is represented by three activities as illustrated in Figure 6.13. The cumulative cash flow for the worst, base and best cases are developed stochastically.

The outputs from a portfolio of projects can then be illustrated on a spreadsheet. The economic parameters for the base, worst and best case are then computed. The output shows the commercial viability of the portfolio rather than of individual projects. The envelope created within the best and worst case cash flows indicates the riskiness of the portfolio compared with the base case cash flow.

It is possible to create different scenarios by changing project start dates, or to assess interdependencies by reprogramming individual projects and adding or subtracting individual projects to determine the effect on the portfolio. The complexity of the spreadsheet is dependent on the risk practitioner's experience.

Figure 6.14 summarises the bundling mechanism stages.

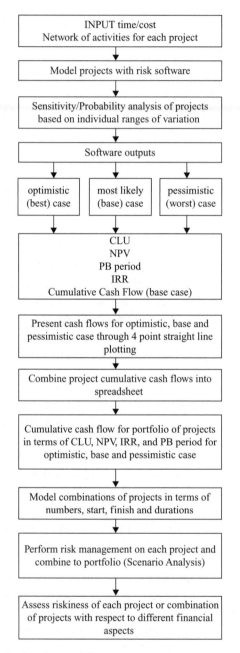

Figure 6.14   Mechanism for portfolio assessment

6.11.4   A Portfolio of Oil and Gas Projects

The example used involves the construction of seven new projects and the refurbishment and operation of eight existing facilities. The projects are to be procured using project finance. The cost of constructing seven new projects is estimated at £956 484 900 and the cost of the refurbishment of the eight existing facilities is estimated at £290 000 000.

Table 6.1 shows the individual and total construction, finance, operation costs and revenues ($£ \times 10$) of the 15 projects. The debt to equity ratio for all 15 projects in the portfolio is approximately 89:11. This would not be considered a risky portfolio due to the small equity, risk capital contribution. Projects 9, 11 and 15 are seen to have no equity contribution at all and thus perceived to have minimum risk. Projects 4 to 7 inclusive have a debt to equity ratio of 90:10, implying there is a small amount of risk in these projects. Projects 10, 12, 13 and 14 have debt to equity ratios of 80:20 meaning that they are perceived to be the riskiest projects in the portfolio. If these latter projects sought finance individually they may not be financed due to their individual risk. Under a portfolio, however, risk in these projects is diluted due to the strength of the less risky projects, particularly in their ability to generate revenues.

The 15 projects were individually modelled in a program based on Monte Carlo simulation to determine their economic parameters and associated upstream and downstream risks. The economic parameters are then assessed using the bundling mechanism developed by the authors.

Forecasting is an essential part of the preparation of any economic evaluation as it is based upon the best information available at any given time. It is often necessary to alter the forecast from time to time as information or conditions change. These changes can be simulated to determine the optimistic and pessimistic scenarios.

The authors developed two batches of projects, these being the seven new projects and the refurbishment and operation of eight existing facilities. Table 6.2 gives the economic parameters for the seven new projects procured as a batch.

The eight refurbished facilities were also developed as a batch. The economic parameters of this batch are given in Table 6.3.

The batch of new projects is commercially viable having worst and best case IRRs of 20.65% and 26.10% respectively as shown in Table 6.2.

In the refurbished batch of projects the IRRs of the worst and best cases, that is 5.82% and 11.73% respectively as shown in Table 6.3, are

Table 6.1 Individual and total project costs and revenues

Project no.	Sources of finance		Cost of finance			Cost of operation (£)	Revenue generation (£)
	Cost of construction (£)	Debt (£)	Equity (£)	Interest (£)	Dividend (£)		
1	5 999 998	5 399 989	599 999	1 618 553	179 839	5 770 800	20 791 296
2	18 770 052	16 893 047	1 877 005	3 995 395	443 933	59 649 876	122 349 948
3	6 878 450	6 190 605	687 845	8 247 186	916 354	1 379 800	41 088 360
4	14 000 000	12 600 000	1 400 000	5 040 000	2 760 000	32 200 000	161 000 000
5	10 000 000	9 000 000	1 000 000	3 240 000	2 300 000	27 600 000	138 000 000
6	18 000 000	16 200 000	1 800 000	7 360 000	3 740 000	37 400 000	198 000 000
7	22 000 000	19 800 000	2 200 000	8 640 000	4 400 000	44 000 000	220 000 000
8	4 000 000	3 200 000	800 000	1 200 000	1 440 000	18 000 000	36 000 000
9	7 000 000	7 000 000	0	2 500 000	0	7 700 000	18 600 000
10	6 000 000	4 800 000	1 200 000	1 740 000	1 200 000	6 000 000	18 000 000
11	4 000 000	4 000 000	0	360 000	0	4 900 000	10 900 000
12	1 000 000	800 000	200 000	240 000	380 000	1 900 000	3 800 000
13	1 000 000	800 000	200 000	240 000	200 000	800 000	3 000 000
14	3 000 000	2 400 000	600 000	1 050 000	720 000	360 000	9 600 000
15	3 000 000	3 000 000	0	2 000 000	0	4 500 000	10 500 000
New projects (£)	95 648 490	86 083 641	9 564 849	38 141 134	14 740 126	208 000 476	901 229 604
Refurbishment projects (£)	29 000 000	26 000 000	3 000 000	9 330 000	3 940 000	44 160 000	110 440 000
Total (£)	124 648 490	112 083 641	12 564 849	47 471 134	18 680 126	252 160 476	1 011 629 604

Table 6.2 Worst, base and best case economic parameters for a batch of seven new projects

	Economic parameters		
	Worst	Base	Best
NPV ($)	3 910 471 970	5 447 793 760	6 149 026 810
CLU ($)	−724 881 590	−712 709 240	−705 301 990
IRR	20.65%	24.54%	26.10%
PB period (years)	7.07	6.55	6.43
Duration (years)	29.00	29.00	29.00
Time of max. CLU	3.00	3.00	3.00

not commercially viable since a promoter would expect an MARR of at least 15% IRR.

However, by procuring the 15 projects in a portfolio as given in Table 6.4, the relative strengths of combining the batch of the seven new projects with the batch of eight refurbished projects, a commercially viable portfolio can be achieved.

By combining the two batches of projects into a portfolio it can be seen from Table 6.4 that the worst case IRR is 18.07% and the best case IRR is 23.28%. Clearly the combination of the batches results in a commercially viable portfolio in terms of meeting a higher MARR.

Figure 6.15 illustrates the cumulative cash flows of the portfolio. The cash burn rate of the base case is approximately £316.0 million/year and the PB period is 7.02 years. The steepness of the cumulative cash flow line from the 3-year CLU point to the 7.02-year PB point shows that there is very little chance of liquidity risk in this portfolio as revenue generation can meet operational costs and service debt.

Table 6.3 Worst, base and best case economic parameters for a batch of eight refurbished facilities

	Economic parameters		
	Worst	Base	Best
NPV ($)	127 720 000	240 400 000	380 200 000
CLU ($)	−246 008 960	−245 350 680	−244 975 450
IRR	5.82%	8.82%	11.73%
PB period (years)	10.10	9.46	8.88
Duration (years)	20.00	20.00	20.00
Time of max. CLU	3.00	3.00	3.00

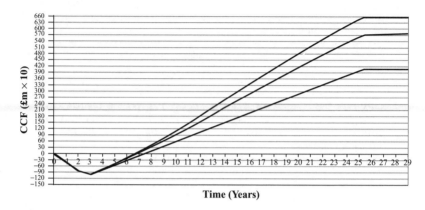

Figure 6.15 Cumulative cash flow for a portfolio of projects (worst, base, and best cases)

The portfolio can now be expressed in terms of a project of three activities, namely cash expenditure, revenue generated to PB, and PB to NPV as shown in Figure 6.11. Once the projects have been combined to make a portfolio they can be assessed using sensitivity and probability analyses. Figure 6.16 illustrates the sensitivity of the portfolio's economic parameters of PB, CLU and NPV in relation to the IRR. Figure 6.17 illustrates the portfolio 'S' curve in relation to the portfolio IRR. Sensitivities and probabilities can also be carried out in relation to the NPV, CLU and PB. In both cases the more inelastic (steeper) the curves, the less sensitive the variables are to perceived risks.

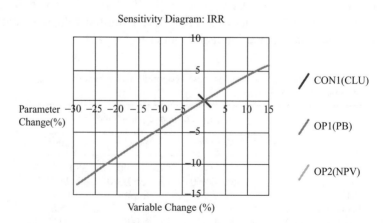

Figure 6.16 Sensitivity analyses for portfolio shown in Table 6.4 for economic parameters CLU, PB and NPV in relation to IRR

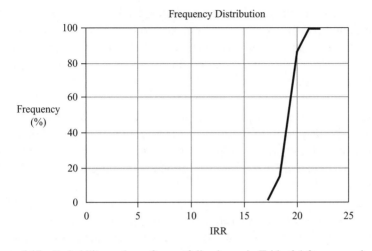

Figure 6.17   Probability analyses for portfolio shown in Table 6.4 for economic parameters for mean, best and worst cases in relation to IRR

Figure 6.17 illustrates an approximation of the risks associated with the outcome of the IRR. In this case the worst case gives an IRR of approximately 18% and a best case of 23% as given in Table 6.4.

The mechanism developed by the authors clearly illustrates the best, worst and base case economic parameters and cumulative cash flows of a portfolio of 15 small oil and gas projects. The authors have shown how the mechanism in conjunction with a risk management program combined with spreadsheets can be used to combine individual projects or batches of projects to produce a portfolio.

Table 6.4   Worst, base and best case economic parameters for a portfolio of 15 projects

	Economic parameters		
	Worst	Base	Best
NPV ($)	4 038 191 970	5 688 193 760	6 529 226 810
CLU ($)	−970 890 550	−958 059 920	−950 277 440
IRR	18.07%	21.65%	23.28%
PB period (years)	7.52	7.02	6.86
Duration (years)	29.00	29.00	29.00
Time of max. CLU	3.00	3.00	3.00

The eight refurbished facilities are considered unviable both in terms of individual projects and as a batch of projects. However, when combined with a commercially viable batch of projects, the overall viability of the portfolio is shown to be commercially viable as it exceeds the MARR desired.

The output mechanism depends solely on the NPV, CLU, PB period and relative start date of individual projects. The mechanism can be used by stakeholders such as lenders, insurers, constructors or promoters to assess their returns from the portfolio. Promoters and constructors will find the mechanism extremely useful when deciding whether to bid for a portfolio of projects.

The mechanism, in its simplest form, provides an effective method for assessing portfolios or programmes of projects that have a project period followed by a revenue generation period. The mechanism allows the user to add or subtract costs or revenues during any period over the portfolio project and thus provides a strategic project tool. The start date of any individual project or number of projects can be changed to determine the effect on the portfolio's economic parameters. If, for example, the start date of one individual project is moved forward by two years then the CLU may be reduced.

Sensitivity analysis can be used to identify the most sensitive projects or activities prior to probability analysis. It is also possible to consider a portfolio of projects with no financing element attached to any individual project and then assume financing the portfolio as one project and thus to determine the base, best and worst case scenarios based on this financial package.

6.12 SUMMARY

Within any portfolio the potential for uncertainty increases with the breadth of the portfolio and the range of the projects or investments. The level of interdependencies and interrelationships will also affect the potential for positive or negative risks.

Portfolio selection and strategy, scenario analysis and diversification, and portfolio risk management were discussed in this chapter.

Considerations of bundling projects and financing bundles were also examined. The benefits of cross-collateralising projects within portfolios were discussed and how cross-collateralisation can be used in portfolios of projects to improve economic parameters.

Cumulative cash flows, how they are developed and how economic parameters are computed were also discussed. A number of examples of how cumulative cash flows are combined to assess a portfolio's base case were discussed and suggestions for modelling portfolio cumulative cash flows presented.

Risk Management at Corporate Level

7.1 INTRODUCTION

There has been very little research carried out as to what risks are assessed at the corporate level, who carries out these risk assessments, and the general functions of the corporate body in relation to risk management.

This chapter briefly outlines the history of the corporation, the powers it has, those involved in decision making within the corporate body, the functions carried out at the corporate level and the risks deemed to affect the corporate body, SBUs and projects.

7.2 DEFINITIONS

French and Saward (1983) define a corporation as:

An association of persons that is itself regarded in law as a separate entity which may be put into legal relationships (such as the owner of a property, a party to a contract, or a party to legal proceedings) and which continues in existence until dissolved in accordance with the law.

The persons who are associated together in a corporation are called 'corporators' or 'members' of the corporation.

The *Dictionary of Management* (French and Saward 1983) states:

A corporation is a succession of persons or body of persons authorised by law to act as one person and having rights and liabilities distinct from the individuals forming the corporation. The artificial personality may be created by royal charter, statute, or common law.

The most important type is the registered company formed under the Companies Act. Corporations aggregate are composed of more than one individual, such as a limited company. Corporations can hold property, carry on business and bring legal actions, in their own name.

The authors agree with the above statements, but for the purpose of this book the authors suggest that corporations are profit-pursuing enterprises, whose goals include growth, efficiency and profit maximisation.

Chambers and Wallace (1993) define management as:

> *The members of the executive or administration of a business or organisation. They will not necessarily be the owners of the business, but will be selected by the owners to be responsible for the different functions of the organisation. Management may be motivated by different factors to owners, such as by market share or by success in sales, rather than profitability and dividends.*

Chambers and Wallace (1993) also define a management technique as:

> *A variety of approaches that have been introduced into decision making to help improve the quality of the final outcome. Some are based on taking a certain approach to decision making, such as management by objectives or human resource management. Other approaches are based on the use of models and statistical techniques, such as forecasting methods, operations research and ratio analysis. These techniques are used as aids to decision making and still require managers to weigh up the results in the light of other experience.*

For the purpose of this book corporate management is defined as:

> *The management of the activities carried out by the corporate body and those organisations forming part of the corporation which utilise tools and techniques to aid decision making processes.*

The London Stock Exchange (2002) defines itself as:

> *An organised market for securities formed in 1973 by the amalgamation of the London Stock Exchange and several other exchanges in different cities. The whole exchange is administered by a council. Members of the council are elected annually and can be listed under two categories.*

Members are of three types: individual persons, unlimited companies (members of which must be members of the London Stock Exchange) and limited companies (directors of which must be London Stock Exchange members). Only individual persons are entitled to elect council and unit committees but individuals are not allowed to transact business on their own behalf – all business must be transacted in the name of an unlimited company or limited company member or in the name of a partnership of individual members. All partnerships and company members must submit annual audited accounts to the council.

Transactions must only take place in securities listed by the council and government stocks. Each company trading as a jobber must provide a list of securities it will deal in. Brokers must normally deal only with jobbers and may not deal directly with each other unless no jobber deals in the particular security required. The FTSE index simply lists the companies that deal on the London Stock Exchange for the use of traders. The authors suggest that the main function of the stock market is to raise funds, through the sale of shares. The shareholders need to be aware of the risks taken by the corporate body on their behalf.

The FTSE illustrates the performance of corporations in 39 business sectors listed on the London Stock Exchange. The stock market reports information regarding a corporation's share price, increase in value from the previous day, 52-week high and low share value, volume of shares sold, yield from each share and the profits/earning (P/E) ratio. Share values are given, in most cases, in pence or pounds sterling although some share prices are denominated in euros, US dollars or yen.

Stock market investors assess current share price against predicted changes in a corporation's profit performance and share value when making decisions on buying and selling shares. The FTSE listings give investors a quick appraisal of how a sector or a specific corporation is performing.

Another function of the FTSE is to rate organisations in terms of their respective social and environmental record. Cole (2002) explains:

> For Good takes the top 300 companies and rates them according to their environmental and social record.

These listings also affect an organisation's share price.
Taylor and Hawkins (1972) believe:

> The corporate entity must clarify its own attitude towards shareholders, not for the day of reckoning but for every day. It must make the efforts to define corporate objectives: that set of principles which will pin point why the company is in business, and set out criteria for its conduct and measure its progress.

The present authors concur with this statement.

7.3   THE HISTORY OF THE CORPORATION

The corporation is an ingenious device for acquiring rights and shedding responsibilities. This was not, however, how the institution was conceived. The solicitor Daniel Bennett has written a brief history of corporate emancipation (Bennett 1999). He notes that the first corporations in Great Britain were charitable institutions, churches, schools and hospitals, which used incorporation to avoid the legal and financial problems – such as death duties – encountered by a body which outlived its founders. These organisations were licensed by the Crown, which determined what they could and could not do. Engaging in profitable commercial activities was forbidden.

As time moved on the monarch began to award 'charters of incorporation' to trade associations. The associations were granted royal monopoly in certain economic sectors, but did not buy and sell in their own right. Businesses had to join an association in order to trade. However, over time the system began to break down and transformed itself into a profit-making company of shareholders, jointly owning the stock which previously belonged to its member businesses. Other trade associations swiftly followed suit, and soon the Crown and Parliament began to license them as commercial corporations. Gradually they acquired many of the legal rights hitherto granted only to humans. Governments lost the ability to destroy them if they exceeded their powers.

Throughout the twentieth century companies learnt new ways of discarding their obligations: establishing subsidiaries, often based offshore and in possession of no significant assets, for example to handle contentious operations. In 1998, a leaked letter from the Lord Chancellor's office revealed that the government was planning to protect UK-based business from legal claims made against it by workers in the Third World. In 1999, the court of appeal forbade 3000 South Africans suffering asbestos poisoning from suing Cape plc, the corporation alleged to be responsible, in the UK courts, even though Cape is a UK company. While they seem to be able to exempt themselves from national law, multinational companies also remain immune from international human rights law, which applies only to states. At the same time, however, corporations in the UK are able to sue for libel, to call the police if their property is threatened, and to take out an injunction against protestors and workers. They may use the law as if they are human beings, in other words, but in key respects they are no longer subject to it (Monbiot 2000).

It is also true that many corporations are efficient and well managed. But they are, by definition, managed in interests at variance with those of the public. Their directors have a 'fiduciary duty' towards the shareholders: they must place their concerns above all others. The state, by contrast, has a duty towards all member states, and must strive to achieve a balance between their competing interests. Surprisingly,

Peter Mandelson, the minister regarded by many as the most amenable to corporate power, appears to recognise this conflict. 'It is not practical or desirable', he wrote in 1996, 'for company boards to represent different stakeholder interests. Boards should be accountable to their shareholders' (Mandelson and Liddle 1996). 'The government of an exclusive company of merchants', Adam Smith observed, 'is, perhaps, the worst of all governments for any country whatever.'

The directors of UK companies are individually responsible for keeping the price of their shares as high as possible. If they neglect this 'fiduciary duty', they can be prosecuted and imprisoned. If, on the other hand, they neglect to protect their workforce, with the result that an employee is killed, they remain, in practice, immune from prosecution. The company, if it is unlucky, will suffer an inconsequential fine, which will not touch the directors.

Around 360 people are killed at work every year in Great Britain. Research suggests that around 80 of those deaths should result in prosecution for corporate manslaughter, but only two companies, both of which are relatively small, have ever been prosecuted (Slapper 1999). The problem is that while corporations have acquired many of the rights of human beings, they have managed to shed many of the corresponding responsibilities. A company can be convicted of manslaughter only if a director or senior manager can be singled out as directly responsible for the death. If the responsibility is shared by the board as a whole, the firm is innocent of reckless or intentional killing.

The authors believe that the problem is compounded by the reluctance of the government's Health and Safety Executive (HSE) to prosecute anyone or anything. The Centre for Corporate Accountability calculates that of the 47 000 major injuries in the workplace reported between 1996 and 1998, only 11% were investigated by the HSE (Select Committee on Environment, Transport and Regional Affairs 1999).

In 1996, the Law Commission reported that the corporate killing laws were in urgent need of reform. In 1997, two weeks after the Southall rail crash, in which seven people died, the Home Secretary told the Labour Party that he would introduce 'laws which provide for conviction of directors of companies where it is claimed that due to a result of dreadful negligence by the company as a whole, people have lost their lives'. It took two and a half years for the Home Secretary to launch a consultation document on corporate killing. Even so, while the government proposes that companies could be convicted of corporate manslaughter whether or not an executive has been singled out for the blame, it suggests that the directors of grossly negligent companies should no longer be subject to no greater penalty than disqualification.

7.3.1   Equity Capital of a Corporation

The equity capital of a corporation is acquired through the sale of stock. The purchasers of the stock are part owners (stakeholders) of the corporation and its assets. In this manner, ownership may be spread throughout the world, and as a result an enormous amount of capital can be accumulated. Owing to the nature of shares, although the stockholders are owners of the corporation and entitled to dividends (sharing profits), they are not liable for debts of the corporation. Generally the life of a corporation is continuous, therefore long-term investments can be made and the future faced with some degree of certainty, which also makes debt capital easier to obtain.

There are many types of stock, but there are two of primary importance. These are common stock (ownership without special guarantees of return on an investment) and preferred stock (certain privileges and restrictions which are not available with common stock) (Sullivan *et al.* 2003).

7.4   CORPORATE STRUCTURE

Figure 7.1 depicts the multidivisional structure, cited by Johnson and Scholes (1999). The multidivisional structure is subdivided into units (divisions) on the basis of products, services, geographical areas or the processes of the organisation. These divisions then carry out the necessary functions.

However, for the purpose of this book the present authors have adapted Figure 7.1 as illustrated in Figure 7.2.

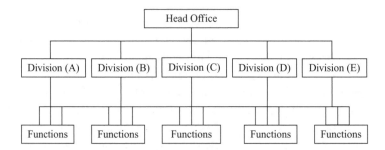

Figure 7.1   Multidivisional structure (Adapted from Johnson and Scholes 1999)

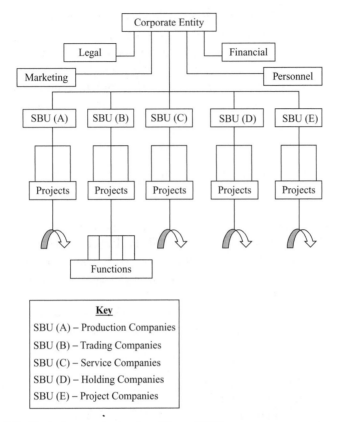

Figure 7.2   Typical corporate structure (Merna 2003)

At the top of the hierarchy in Figure 7.2 lies the corporate entity. This is the level under which the rest of the company trades. Here all the financial and acquisition decisions will be made. Second in the hierarchy is the SBU level. These SBUs are divided into separate strategic business operations, such as production companies, holding companies and service companies. At the bottom of the hierarchy lies the project level. Here projects are carried out under an SBU and with the necessary functions being carried out, usually by undertaking projects to generate revenues.

7.5   CORPORATE MANAGEMENT

Corporate management, often referred to as corporate strategy, is concerned with ensuring corporate survival and increasing its value not just in financial terms but also by variables such as market share, reputation and brand perception. Thus the scope of corporate risk management is wide ranging to support the corporate strategy.

A senior corporate manager owns the process and has the staff to resource the analysis and administrative activities. A board member champions the process ensuring access to information and resources.

A core group of corporate board members and strategic business unit executives can draw additional input from stakeholders such as:

- shareholder representatives
- representatives from major customers, partners and suppliers
- external experts.

The scope covers the current markets and project portfolios of the SBU and also looks for potential new markets. Results fed back from the SBU are assessed along with changes and trends in international markets (customers, suppliers and competitors), legislation, regulation, politics and social attitudes.

The authors believe that the information used often comes from a range of sources, sometimes more than one, which may include:

- internally generated information
- corporate strategy plan
- corporate financial reports
- business unit financial reports
- feedback from business unit risk monitoring
- information from the public domain
- competitor, customer, supplier and partner financial reports
- benchmarking and forecasts from professional bodies, such as the Confederation of British Industry (CBI)
- research papers
- information from pressure groups
- government-generated initiatives
- economic statistics and forecasts
- demographic and socio-economic trends
- White and Green Papers (UK government)
- consultation on proposed legislation
- information purchased from specialist organisations, such as independent research analysts
- consumer trends

- technology forecasts
- information from past and present projects.

At the corporate level a corporate strategy plan (CSP) is often produced. Johnson and Scholes (1999) believe the plan is produced within the following objectives:

- Create and maintain a strategy that achieves the corporate intent, corporate commitments and expectations of the customers, shareholders and other stakeholders.
- Incorporate and maintain the commitments and the requirements of business sectors, specifically SBUs and process owners that support the strategic direction.
- Communicate the strategic direction and relevant objectives and target to each SBU.
- Manage strategic change to maintain or gain competitive advantage.

The corporate strategy is a portfolio of integrated business strategies that will deliver the corporate intent and are consistent with the financial investments or constraints facing the group. The corporate strategy comprises the following self-contained, but integrated, sub-processes: analyse corporate strategic requirements, assemble corporate strategy portfolio, commit to corporate strategy, manage strategic change, and manage corporate risk.

However, with the ever-increasing diversification within corporations senior managers are faced with new problems:

- How to manage a wide spread of businesses? (Especially when firms have little knowledge in each individual business and they are in competition with firms which have core competencies in these individual areas.)
- How to organise the corporation?
- How much power should the organisation delegate?
- How is the scarce capital allocated between the diverse businesses?
- The risks associated with each business and its management.

The questions above could be summed up as 'what are the advantages to the shareholder of investing in this corporation?'

7.5.1   The Corporate Body

At the corporate level much of the responsibility for strategy often lies with the top executives. The degree of responsibility and accountability they face will depend on the degree of autonomy allowed, and the constraints imposed, by corporate governance. However, the ultimate responsibility for corporate management/strategy always rests with the corporate board.

7.5.2   The Legal Obligations of Directors

Loose (1990) states that a director of a firm is accountable, both individually and jointly with the other directors, for the company's viability and future success. Therefore a director's responsibility is fundamentally different from a manager's, because where a manager shares responsibility with others, the director is ultimately accountable for the whole company.

This accountability is to the company, not to the shareholders. If a majority of the shareholders disagree with the decisions of the board of directors, those shareholders are not normally free to change that decision directly. Therefore, when the annual general meeting (AGM) of a company is held and the directors are proposing the payment of a dividend, the shareholders have no powers there and then to raise the dividend. Similarly, the shareholders have no powers to order any specific action by the employees of the company. Shareholders' real power resides in their ability to remove the directors and replace them with others.

Parker (1978) suggests that a company's chance of success depends heavily on the quality of the board, senior management and the company's competitive position. The authors agree with the above, but also cite the general state of the economy, such as the rate of interest, inflation and exchange rate, and external environmental factors, such as those concerned with politics, economics, society and technology, as critical factors in determining the success of a corporation.

Unlike traditional shareholders, who often have a long-term vision for the business and prefer to take a back seat approach to its management, a new breed of shareholder activists are spurning the gentleman's agreement that complaints should be aired over coffee and biscuits. Hedge funds and speculators have found that a public campaign can often yield quicker results. Barclays is the latest firm to have the activists breathing down its neck.

At the time of writing Atticus Capital, which owns around 1% of the bank, valued at £47 billion is trying to halt the acquisition of ABN Amro. Atticus has stated that Barclays are not the best owner for ABN Amro's sprawling collection of assets and if Barclays proceed with the acquisition Atticus will vote against the deal and encourage other shareholders to do likewise. Atticus stated that continuing to pursue such a risky acquisition would harm management credibility and anger shareholders, ultimately making Barclays vulnerable to a bid.

A major risk to corporations comes more and more from private equity firms. Often these firms buy out established corporations and cash in on the best revenue generators and saleable assets, such as land. Corporations also need to consider the risks associated with take-overs from government backed organisations.

Of course corporations and private companies can also mitigate the risks associated with one or a number of strategic business units by selling them off. Ford has recently sold Aston Martin and now seeks to sell off Jaguar as this is seen as a loss maker.

7.5.3   The Board

According to Houlden (1990) the board's main roles are:

- to direct the company
- to appoint the managing director/chief executive
- to delegate the appropriate powers for running the company
- to monitor the performance of the company
- to take corrective action where necessary.

However, there are three characteristics of the board of directors that are of particular importance:

1. *Board structure.* Different countries have different board structures. Some countries, such as Germany and Finland, require a two-tier system, whereas other countries such as the UK and Japan require a single-tier board. In France and Switzerland companies are free to choose the system they prefer. In a two-tier system there is a formal division of power, with a management board made up of the top executives and a distinct supervisory board made up of non-executives, with the task of monitoring and steering the management board.

    In a one-tier (or unitary) board system, executives and non-executives (outside) sit on the board together.

2. *Board membership.* The composition of a board of directors can vary sharply from company to company. Differences occur such as the number, stature and independence of outside directors.
3. *Board tasks.* Tasks and authority of the board of directors also differ significantly between companies. In some cases boards meet infrequently and are merely asked to vote on proposals put in front of them. Such boards have little or no power to contradict the will of the chief executive officer (CEO). In other companies, boards meet regularly and play a more active role in corporate governance, by formulating proposals, proactively selecting new top managers, and determining objectives and incentives. Normally, non-executive directors' power depends to a large degree on how they define their own role.

It is important that corporate bodies note the importance of the CEO and that they consider, in terms of risk management for example, the following:

> *The effectiveness of risk management can be hugely enhanced or destroyed by the chairman – chairmen can be major destroyers or major value adders to the effectiveness of non execs.*

> (Pye 2001)

7.5.4 The Composition of the Board

Companies need good leadership. This should involve enthusiasm and drive balanced with wisdom and good judgement (Houlden 1990). Mintzberg (1984) states that in a broader view, the board of directors are only part of the governance system. For instance, regulation by local and regional authorities, as well as pressure from social groups, can function as checks and balances to limit top management's discretion.

7.6 CORPORATE FUNCTIONS

Every firm needs a corporate mission. This mission encompasses the basic points of departure that send the organisation in a particular direction. McCoy (1985) cites that the purpose of an organisation is the most important point of departure of strategy making, but also influential are the values embodied in an organisation's culture. Falsey (1989) believes that values shared by an organisation's members will shape what is seen as ethical behaviour and moral responsibilities, and therefore have an impact on strategic choices.

Other reasons directing the corporation include where the corporation wishes to focus its efforts, and the competitive ambitions or intentions as an important part of the mission (Abell 1980, Pearce 1982, Bartlett and Ghoshal 1994).

The corporate mission can be articulated by means of a mission statement, but in practice not everything that is called a mission statement meets the above criteria. However, the present authors believe that companies can have a mission, even if it has not been recorded on paper, although this will increase the risk of divergent interpretations throughout the corporate level (Pearce 1982, Collins and Porras 1996).

In general the corporate-level mission provides three important roles for an organisation. These roles are:

1. *Direction.* The corporate mission should point the organisation in a certain direction. This is done by defining boundaries, within which strategic choices and actions must take place. However, by specifying the fundamental principles on which strategy must be based, the corporate mission limits the scope of strategic options, therefore setting the organisation on a specific course.
2. *Legitimisation.* The corporate mission can convey to all stakeholders, on each level and outside the company, what the organisation is pursuing, and that these goals and objectives will add value to the company. By specifying the business philosophy that will guide the company, it is hoped stakeholders will accept, support and trust the corporate heads within the organisation, thereby generating support throughout corporate, strategic business and project levels.
3. *Motivation.* In some cases, the authors believe that the corporate mission can go one step further than the legitimisation, by actually inspiring individuals and different levels of the organisation to work together in a particular way. By specifying the fundamental principles driving an organisation, a 'corporate spirit' can evolve, generating a powerful capacity to motivate people over a prolonged period of time.

Within corporations a concept that is often confused with mission is vision. A corporate vision is a picture of how the corporation wants things in the future to be. While a corporate mission outlines the basic point of departure, a corporate vision outlines the desired future at which the company hopes to arrive. However, the above corporate themes are very important considerations and a great deal of time and effort must go into generating these at the corporate level (David 1989).

7.6.1   Corporate Governance

At the corporate level an area that requires attention is who determines the corporate mission and regulates the corporate activities, that is corporate governance: who deals with the issue of governing the strategic choices and actions of top management (Keasey *et al.* 1997)?

Corporate governance is concerned with building in checks and balances to ensure that top management pursue strategies that are in accordance with the corporate mission. Corporate governance encompasses all tasks and activities that are intended to supervise and steer the behaviour of top management. This is known as the corporate governance framework. It determines whom the organisation is there to serve and how the purposes and priorities of the organisation should be decided. It is concerned with both the functioning of the organisation and the distribution of power among different stakeholders. This is strongly culturally bound, resulting in different traditions and frameworks in different countries (Yoshimori 1995).

The Turnbull Report (1999) cites several principles of good corporate governance. Firstly, there are the directors. Factors controlled by directors include the board, the chairman and the CEO, board balance, supply of information, appointments to the board and re-election.

Every company listed on the London Stock Exchange should be headed by an effective board which should lead and control the company. There are two key aspects at the top of every public company, namely the running of the board, and the executive responsibility for running the company's business. There should be a clear division of responsibilities at the head of the company which will ensure a balance of power and authority, such that no one individual has unfettered powers of decision.

The board should include a balance of executive and non-executive directors (including independent non-executives) such that no individual or small group of individuals can dominate the board's decision taking. It should also be noted that there should be a formal and transparent procedure for the appointment of new directors to the board.

The purpose of the Turnbull Report (1999) is to guide UK businesses and help them focus on risk management. Key aspects of the report include the importance of internal control and risk management, maintenance of a sound system of internal control with the effectiveness being reviewed constantly, the board's view and statement on internal control, due diligence and the internal audit.

Tricked (1994) cites the common definition of corporate governance as 'addressing the issues facing board of directors'. Attention must, therefore, be paid to the roles and responsibilities of the stakeholders involved at the corporate level.

The authors believe there are three important functions to be addressed at the corporate level:

1. *Forming function.* The first function is to influence the forming of the corporate mission. The task here is to shape, articulate and communicate the fundamental principles that will drive the organisational activities. Determining the purpose of the organisation and setting priorities among claimants are part of the forming function. Yoshimori (1995) suggests that the board of directors can conduct this task by questioning the basis of strategic choices, influencing the business philosophy, and explicitly weighing the advantages and disadvantages of the firm's strategies for various constituents.

2. *Performance function.* This function contributes to the strategy process with the intention of improving the future performance of the corporation. The task here at the corporate level is to judge strategy initiatives brought forward by top management and to participate actively in strategy development. Zahra and Pearce (1989) believe the board of directors can conduct this task by engaging in strategy discussions, acting as a sounding board for top management, and networking to secure the support of vital stakeholders.

3. *Conformance function.* This function is necessary to ensure corporate conformance to the stated mission and strategy. The task of corporate governance is to monitor whether the organisation is undertaking activities as promised and whether performance is satisfactory. Where management is found lacking, it is a function of corporate governance to press for changes. Spencer (1983) believes that the board of directors can conduct this task by auditing the activities of the corporation, questioning and supervising top management, determining remuneration and incentive packages, and even appointing new managers.

Hussey (1991) categorised the objectives/functions of a company as primary, secondary and the corporate goals a firm wishes to achieve:

- *Primary objective.* Profit is the prime motivation for all companies, and many managers argue that achieving profit maximisation is their prime function. However, in some cases the above may be untrue because no company is willing to do anything for profit. For example, few companies would be willing to work their employees into a state of physical and mental exhaustion. When dealing with customers, most purchases or transactions are likely to be repeated in the future, therefore looking for a high one-off profit will have an adverse effect on long-term profit.

- *Secondary objective.* At the corporate level the secondary objective is a description of the nature of the company's business. At this corporate level the question should be asked, 'What is my business?' This can be answered at corporate appraisal. However, this is not an objective; to overcome this the question 'What should my business be?' can be asked. From this information the CEO and his or her immediate managers, such as marketing, production and finance, can decipher 'where', 'when' and 'why' the company chooses a particular direction.

    However, the authors believe that it must be recognised that every CEO has in mind 'where', 'what' and 'how' he or she wants the company to operate, regardless of company strategy.

- *Corporate goals.* Goals are quantifiable objectives that provide a unit of measurement, from which the CEO can confirm that his or her strategies have been carried out. They are, therefore, more difficult to formulate than profit goals because profit goals are directly related to the strategies put in place. Goals are the landmarks and milestones which mark the selected path the company takes to reach the reference point (Handy 1999).

The authors believe that these corporate landmarks and milestones should be quantifiable, allowing targets for each of the important company operations to be compared and in the long run achieved. There should be as many goals as it is practical to develop. There is little point in developing figures or targets that the company has no intention of addressing or that are of no relevance to the task.

The authors cite a number of practical goals to be carried out as a governing meter at the corporate level:

- employment figures
- ratios describing shares of defined market (percentage)
- accounting figures such as liquidity ratio or gearing
- minimum customer figures
- maximum figures for hours lost in industrial disputes
- return on capital employed
- absolute sales targets

- a value for operational profit improvement
- staff turnover rate (lower targets each year, i.e. continuously improve employees' situation by listening).

7.7   CORPORATE STRATEGY

Corporate strategy is the pattern of decisions in a company that determines and reveals its objectives, purposes and goals. It produces the principal policies and plans for achieving those goals and defines the range of business the company is to pursue (Andrews 1998).

Ellis and Williams (1995) cite corporate strategy as a means of adding value in respect of two equally important key areas of decision making:

1. the overall scope of the organisation's activities
2. corporate parenting.

Figure 7.3 illustrates the key components concerned with corporate strategy.

At the corporate level organisational activities and scope can be defined in terms of the business the organisation wants to be in. In making additions to and deletions from the range of industries and markets in which a firm competes, sources of additional corporate value added will accrue to the extent that corporate managers judge whether individual businesses are able to achieve acceptable rates of return. If they do not businesses should be divested from the company's portfolio.

The second task is that of corporate parenting. This is concerned with how corporate management should manage the various businesses within the organisation. Goold and Campbell (1989) have discerned a

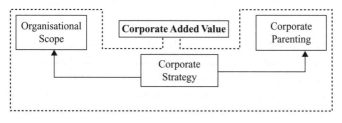

Figure 7.3   Key corporate strategy components

number of principles that exist with regard to corporate parenting, as described below:

- Parent companies add value to businesses in their portfolio either because the headquarters team has some special skill which can be used to help business, or because it can create synergy between businesses in the portfolio.
- A company should add a business to its portfolio if it believes it can create more parenting value in relation to the new business than other potential bidders.
- A company should divest a business in its portfolio when it believes the business will perform better as an independent company or as part of the portfolio of another company.

Strategic management can be differentiated through the use of two dimensions:

1. *Planning.* The influence and co-ordination of head office in formulating business strategy.
2. *Control.* The type of performance control imposed by head office.

From these dimensions three styles of corporate management can be identified:

1. *Strategic planning.* At the corporate level, there is a strong emphasis to influence the direction of the business through planning. Control of this is available through the use of both strategic and financial goals (Hussey 1991).
2. *Strategic control.* This is left to the management at the business level. The corporate level rarely gets involved here; however, the larger the project, the more likely is its involvement.
3. *Financial control.* With this method, Ellis and Williams (1995) identify the use of delegation from corporate headquarters. Budgets are set and become almost like a 'contract' between the corporate and business levels. It is then up to the business level to achieve these targets via strategy and the use of financial tools.

In the authors' opinion risks identified at the corporate level must be carried out with due diligence to alleviate such risks being absorbed by SBUs or the projects undertaken by SBUs. Pavyer (2005) suggests that the key to successful risk management is a formalised process of identifying, assessing and responding to and controlling risk. The demands of Sarbanes-Oxley (SOX), for example, in terms of accountability can be simply demonstrated with an effective risk management process that maintains accountability of all the participants in a business. Pavyer also states that to comply with SOX, businesses must be forthcoming to shareholders, the first step being a documented process. Armed with reliable and up-to-date information, management can ensure that material changes in financial condition or operation of the company's projects are communicated to shareholders in a timely manner.

Conklin and Tapp (2000) cite a movement away from the traditional hierarchical structure of a corporation. More common is the fact that organisations have decentralised decision-making units operating with some independence within the overall corporate structure. For such organisations, strengthening the creative web is an internal challenge. With the shift of responsibility from a hierarchical corporate structure to separate but related work groups, a central issue is the set of systems that can best foster 'intrapreneurship'.

7.8   RECOGNISING RISKS

For real-world companies in viciously competitively environments, it is not good enough simply to protect the physical and financial assets of the corporation through a combination of good housekeeping and shrewd insurance and derivative buying. The pressure on margins is too intense and the vulnerability to volatility simply too great for that to be an adequate strategy for most companies, even small ones. The focus must shift to the far greater and far less tangible world of expectations and reputation, and thereby sustaining investor value – hence the inexorable rise of risk management and its sudden popularity in the board room (Monbiot 2000).

Equity and credit analysts are increasingly focusing on risk and the quality of risk management within the companies they analyse, which is further sharpening focus in the board room. Analysts want to be able to tell current and potential investors that the corporate managers know what they are doing and that they are using the company's capital in the most effective manner possible, and that they are in control of the SBUs and consequently future profits.

Senior management are increasingly using company reports and press departments to boast about their latest risk management initiatives and policies, but learning the vocabulary associated with risk management and simply slipping the words into glossy brochures does not constitute risk management. Corporations that want to report the stable, secure, socially responsible and ever-increasing earnings that investors and other stakeholders demand must take risk management seriously and put such words into practice (Parkinson 1993).

In the corporate sector, more enlightened senior management have hired overall risk managers, more often than not promoted from the insurance management function. Here these individuals' core responsibility has normally been the identification, measurement and mitigation of risk, as well as arranging its funding when feasible and desirable. In many cases these individuals have attempted to co-ordinate the risk management activities of other departments and to promote a risk management culture throughout the organisation.

A recent survey of CEOs and risk managers in the UK, Europe and the USA has shown constantly that the main perceived issues today are: corporate governance; extortion, product tampering and terrorism; environmental liability; political risk; regulatory and legal risk; fraud; and a whole host of risks ushered in by modern technologies (Monbiot 2000). The causes of this shift in emphasis are of course many, varied and inextricably interrelated. But, essentially, corporate and financial risk has grown in scale and complexity in tandem with the globalisation of the world economy. The globalisation of trade and the removal of barriers at national and international levels have led to a massive process of consolidation in all sectors as essentially uneconomic organisations, which previously relied on a combination of customer ignorance, lack of external competition and government assistance, have been forced to adapt or die.

In this global, relatively and increasingly service-dominated economic environment, corporate success increasingly comes to rely on two key drivers – perception and knowledge. Risk management is an integral part of these and a thorough understanding of the concept will drive an organisation one step further to success. Companies must have the ability to source raw materials at a good price and turn them into a marketable product at a price that delivers a healthy margin. However, contingencies must be put in place, through the use of a complete, structured and up-to-date risk management system.

One major risk to corporations is from hostile bids. Corporations often increase their financial gearing to employ more debt than equity and thus make themselves less attractive to opportunistic take-overs. Shareholders, however, do not necessarily want too much debt, as debt service is senior to dividend payment and may result in poor or no dividends to shareholders.

The authors cite that companies in the UK are not legally classified as monopolies until they own 26% of the market in which they trade. If one assesses all the major sectors in which superstores trade, then Tesco, the largest, emerges with 17% (twice as high as two years ago), and Sainsbury's has 13%. If on the other hand you assess the sales of groceries, then Tesco emerges with 26% and Sainsbury with 20%.

Hopes that Internet shopping would provide opportunities for new companies to challenge the dominance of the big stores have also been banished. Tesco, the market leader in the grocery business, has already emerged as the biggest online grocer in the world. At the beginning of 2000 it boasted annual Internet sales of £126 million and claimed it would treble that number by the end of the year. In this example Tesco took the risk of developing a new market long before its competitors identified the benefits of Internet shopping.

Some analysts have argued that the UK's biggest chains collectively meet the legal definition of a monopoly. The five biggest supermarket chains sell 74.6% of all groceries sold in the UK. This could be the most concentrated market on earth and is seen by many as a cartel which sets the prices of groceries and thus reduces the risks of competition from smaller organisations in the grocery market. Their profits have long been higher than those of similar chains anywhere in continental Europe (Monbiot 2000).

The four large UK banks, Barclays, HSBC, Lloyds TSB and Royal Bank of Scotland, control approximately 86% of small-business banking. These banks are currently being investigated by the Competition Commission and face the risk of being fined for fixing charges to customers, thus reducing competition.

The authors believe that outsourcing is a major tool in which corporations and SBUs relieve risks. Many businesses transfer risk by outsourcing specific activities to other parties. A major supermarket chain, for example, often outsources the storage, quality checks, security and transport of its grocery items to the supplier as a method of transferring risks that are outside its control.

7.9   SPECIFIC RISKS AT CORPORATE LEVEL

For corporate manslaughter the current situation is that companies should be prosecuted and convicted for the same general offences as individuals and subject to the same general rules for the construction of criminal liability. The law should recognise and give effect to the widely held public perceptions that companies have an existence of their own and can commit crimes as entities distinct from the personnel comprising the company. The best method of assessing whether a company possesses the requisite degree of blameworthiness is through adoption of the corporate *mens rea* doctrine. While this inevitably will raise problems of how to assess policies and procedures to ascertain whether they reflect the requisite culpability, such a task is not impossible (Mokhiber and Weissman 2001).

The message is clear: there is now a momentum, fuelled by strong public opinion in the wake of recent disasters, for companies and their directors to be held accountable when death and serious injury occur owing to their perceived failures. In the wake of these events, corporations are subject to new risks and must therefore incorporate sufficient guidelines into their health and safety legislation.

In seeking to reduce risk, opportunities for privatisation are now more limited than in the mid 1980s because the more accessible possessions of the state have already been procured, and public resistance is greater for more ambitious schemes. Now many of the larger corporations have chosen a new route to growth – consolidation. By engineering a single harmonised global market, in which they can sell the same product under the same conditions anywhere in the world, corporations are looking to extract formidable economies of scale. They are seizing, in other words, those parts of the world that are still controlled by small and medium-sized businesses. The authors suggest that decisions associated with investments on a global basis must take into consideration the country risks described in Chapter 4.

Consolidation in the print and the broadcast media industries has also enabled a few well-placed conglomerates to exert a prodigious influence over public opinion. They have used it to campaign for increased freedom for business. Globalisation, moreover, has enabled companies to hold a gun to the governments' head. Governments refusing to meet corporate demands will be threatened with dis-investment, or shifting the whole operation to different countries, such as Thailand, resulting in wide-scale unemployment. The result is unprecedented widespread power for corporate bodies (Monbiot 2000).

Oil companies often suffer from cash flow risk when crude oil prices fall because the companies' cash flows are based on higher crude oil prices. The risk associated with crude oil prices is normally outside the control of the oil companies and can often result in projects being delayed or decreasing output (Energy Information Administration 2001).

7.10 THE CHIEF RISK OFFICER

The present authors suggest that the key to making the enterprise or integrated approach actually happen is through the appointment of one key individual who takes charge of the whole process and is given the power at board level to follow through all ideas. Often the person nominated is the chief risk officer (CRO). However, despite the success of firms using this method, many corporate activities do not have a designated risk officer. According to Blythe (1998) there were as little as 60 designated CROs worldwide, and there is little evidence to suggest that this number has increased in the last four years to more than 100. From all the text acknowledging the importance of risk management this growth rate in the number of CROs is nowhere near as fast as it should be.

There are, of course, those who argue that none of the so-called new risks identified are new at all and it is simply a last-ditch attempt for risk managers to be recognised. There are also those who believe that most business risks are simply those that come with any commercial enterprise and that if you attempt to take them away, you are removing a large portion of the value in any company.

7.11 HOW RISKS ARE ASSESSED AT CORPORATE LEVEL

Managing corporate risk is a continuous process in which the main principle in risk management is used as identified by Thompson and Perry (1992). This includes:

* identification of risks/uncertainties
* analysis of implications
* response to minimum risk
* allocation of appropriate contingencies.

The objective to managing the corporate risk is to understand the risk that is known to be associated with the corporate strategy plan. This corporate risk management plan will enable the communication of the risks and risk treatments to be passed down to the SBUs that may be impacted by the risk and maintenance of the corporate risk register. Harley (1999) states that:

Risk is now beginning to be consolidated as a fundamental threat that runs through an organisation's entire structure and a company's approach to risk is coming to be seen as just as important as its approach to operations, finance, or any other basic corporate function. The way a company engineers its risk structure is a fundamental part of corporate strategy.

Although risks are evaluated at the corporate level, the power they maintain over governments and consumers is phenomenal. A number of corporations respond to legislative and regulative risks by demanding tax breaks, threatening governments with relocation of SBUs and forming cartels to fix prices in certain industry sectors. The following quote from Monbiot (2000) further reinforces this:

While taxpayers' money is being given to corporations, corporations are required to contribute ever decreasing amounts of tax.

7.12   CORPORATE RISK STRATEGY

Corporate risk strategy often entails planned actions to respond to identified risks. A typical corporate risk strategy includes the following:

* Accountabilities for managing the corporate risk.
* A corporate risk register will be maintained as a record of the known risks to the corporate strategy plan; the types of mitigating actions can then be taken, and the likely results of the mitigating action recorded.
* Treatment plans are identified that form part of the corporate strategy and will be communicated to the SBUs, so they in turn may manage the risk which may affect them.

A first estimate of potential effects can be determined using assumption analysis, decision tree analysis and the range method. These models can then be used to evaluate the effectiveness of potential mitigating actions and hence select the optimum response. Chapman and Ward (1997) believe mitigating actions can be grouped into four categories and potential action includes:

1. Risk avoidance:
   * cancel a project
   * move out of a market
   * sell off part of the corporation.

2. Risk reduction:
   • acquisitions or mergers
   • move to the new market
   • develop a new product/technology in an existing market
   • business process re-engineering
   • corporate risk management policy.
3. Risk transfer:
   • partnership
   • corporate policy on insurance.
4. Risk retention:
   • a positive decision to accept the risk due to the potential gain it allows.

Many of the mitigating actions at the corporate level generate (or cancel) individual projects or entire programmes conducted at lower levels.

The authors suggest that risks affecting the corporate level may be mitigated through GAP analysis. GAP analysis involves identifying ways of closing the gap between the actual and the projected levels of performance. Methods include:

• Change the strategy.
• Add businesses to or delete them from the corporate portfolio.
• Change SBU political strategies.
• Change objectives.

7.12.1   Health and Safety and the Environment

The need for safety in construction and manufacture has always been evident, and one of the earliest written references to safety is from the Code of Hammurabi, around 1750 BC. His code stated that if a house was built and it fell down due to poor construction, killing the owner, then the builder himself would be put to death. Corporate entities need to accept that health and safety should be a major part of their risk management system

Safety is defined as the freedom from danger of risks. This applies to:

• danger of physical injury
• risk of damage to health over a period of time.

The word safety has been defined by Merna (2007) as:

The elimination of hazards, or their control to levels of acceptable tolerance as determined by law, institutional regulations, ethics, personal requirements, scientific and technological capability, experimental knowledge, economics and the interpretations of cultural and popular practices'.

Its interpretation is multi-faceted, and dependent on where in the world one is working.

Accident is defined as:

An unexpected, temporarily limited occurrence entailing danger to life and limb or property.

An accident is an unplanned process of events that leads to undesired injury, loss of life, and damage to the system or the environment.

The UK Health and Safety Executive (1993) define an accident as:

Any unplanned event that results in injury or ill health of people, or damage or loss to property, plant, materials or the environment, or loss of business opportunity.

Merna (2007) defines an incident as

An unexpected, temporarily limited occurrence within a technical system in which it cannot from the outset be excluded that a case of imperilment is occurring.

Accidents are unplanned and unintentional events that result in harm or loss to personnel, property, production, or nearly anything that has some inherent value. These losses increase an organisation's operating costs through higher production costs, decreased efficiency and long-term effects of decreased employee morale and unfavourable public opinion.

7.12.1.1 The Domino Effect

Accidents do not just happen, they are the result of a long process consisting of a number of steps which have to be completed before an accident can occur. If one of these steps is removed then the accident may be prevented, or its effects mitigated against. The process of removing one of the steps in the accident causation process is known as the 'domino effect'.

Events that lead to an accident are shown in Figure 7.4.

- Preliminary events – anything that influences the initiating event (long working hours, poor or incomplete maintenance)
- Initiating events – trigger event; it is the actual mechanism that causes the accident to occur.

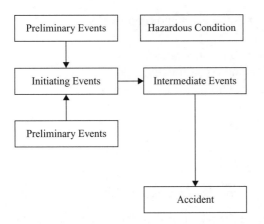

Figure 7.4   Events leading to accidents

- Intermediate events – these can have two effects, they can either propagate or ameliorate the accident. For example, defensive driving on a highway will help us to protect ourselves from other drivers, or it will ameliorate the effects of their bad driving.

7.12.1.2   Hazards and Risks

People often confuse hazards and risk since they are used interchangeably as if they have the same meaning.

Hazard is a condition that can cause injury, or death, damage or loss of equipment or property, environmental harm.

A hazard as also been defined by Merna (2007) as:

The source of energy and the physiological and behavioural factors which, when uncontrolled, lead to harmful occurrences.

Hazards in the construction industry include the following:

- Physical injury hazards, e.g.
  o excavations
  o scaffolding
  o falsework
  o structural framework
  o roof work
  o cranes

o transport, mobile plant and road works
o tunnelling
o sewers and confined spaces
o demolition and contaminated sites
o work over water.
• Health hazards, e.g.
o Chemical
o Physical
o Biological.

7.12.1.3   Relationship of Hazard and Risk

A hazard can be the result of a system or component failure but this is not always the case; a hazard can exist without anything failing. Hazard is concerned with the severity or the end result, whereas risk combines the concept of severity of the accident consequence and the likelihood of it occurring.

The most common safety human errors and their causes are as follows:

• Most common errors:
o misunderstanding of spoken or written instruction/information
o mistake in performing a simple familiar task
o failure to notice something is wrong
o forgetting completely or missing a step in a task
o mis-estimation of quantity of work and time to do it
o taking inappropriate action
o mistake in performing complex/unfamiliar tasks
o failure to comprehend the full implications of decisions
o mistakes involving passing information from one person to another
o difficult and unfamiliar tasks are reported less often and give rise to error.
• Causal factors:
o workload too high
o boredom
o emotional pressure
o time pressure
o interruptions
o environmental pressures
o feeling tired or unwell
o use of faulty informal/unapproved procedures
o faulty job and system designs

o objectives/instructions unclear
o absence of plan to deal with contingencies.

7.12.1.4   Environmental Management System (EMS) ISO 14001:2004

ISO 14001 is the generic name given to the family of standards around which an EMS can be implemented. The ISO Standard development committee TC 207 started to develop the ISO 14000 series including ISO 14001 in 1994 and this was published in September 1996.

The standard was revised in 2004 to become ISO 14001:2004.

There are other environmental standards and guidelines that have been developed, most relevant being:

* ISO 14004: EMS – General Guidelines on Principles, Systems and Supporting Techniques
* ISO 19011 – Guidelines for Quality and/or Environmental Systems Auditing

One of the most effective ways to minimise environmental risks, meet legislative requirements and demonstrate corporate governance is through the implementation of an environmental management system (EMS).

Certification to the internationally recognised EMS standard, ISO 14001 from an accredited and reputable provider is becoming a preferred choice for organisations looking to demonstrate their environmental credentials worldwide.

An effective EMS certified to ISO 14001 can help an organisation operate in a more efficient and environmentally responsible manner by managing its impacts, including those which can control and influence, while also complying with relevant environmental legislation and its own environmental policy.

The numerous benefits associated with a certified ISO 14001 management system include:

* compliance with legislative and other requirements by providing a systematic approach for meeting current and identifying future legislation
* helping you demonstrate conformance and that you are fulfilling policy commitments and making continual improvement against specific targets to meet overall objectives
* competitive edge over non-certified businesses when invited to tender

- improved management of environmental risk
- increased credibility that comes from independent assessment
- continual improvement which helps drive more efficient use of raw materials and enhanced performance leading to cost reductions
- shareing common management system principles with ISO 9000:2000 and OHSAS 18001 (Occupational Health and Safety Management Systems) enabling integration of your quality, environmental and occupational health and safety management systems.

7.13   CORPORATE RISK: AN OVERVIEW

Most failures are caused almost exclusively by human failure and by an absence of satisfactory risk management controls. For example, the recent terrorist attack on the twin towers in New York was an unforeseen event; however, the risk management team should have taken measures to evacuate personnel in the event of a terrorist attack based on the data held by US government agencies. The UK security services use a warning system to determine the current threat from potential terrorist attacks on the UK mainland. This system has five levels: low, moderate, substantial, severe and critical. The threat level can be accessed from a UK Government website. This helps businesses and individuals to plan (usually contingency planning) potential mitigation methods for each level of alert.

The worrying fact for senior managers of all types of companies is that the potential for corporate disaster on a large scale is growing at an alarming rate, and, worse still, the spectre of corporate Armageddon is growing at a faster rate than the ability of most organisations to cope. History shows that corporate vulnerability is mainly due to human error. Avoidance of these risks can be achieved by comparing old, painful risks with some new, excruciating ones. Only 16 years ago, the majority of risks faced by firms in the UK were related to day-to-day operations. The most obvious ones were physical, including standard property risks such as fire and theft of plant and machinery, and human, including standard liability, risks such as injury to the workforce or customers. These risks still exist today and have not diminished in significance, but many forward-thinking firms are now willing and able to retain a much higher level of mainly 'attritional' risks, which helps them focus attention on a whole host of new risks of an altogether more complex and unpleasant nature (Jacob 1997).

7.14   THE FUTURE OF CORPORATE RISK

In the 1970s ignorance was the best form of defence. Organisations simply believed that a disaster was far more likely to happen to someone else. Money invested in loyalty programmes had created customers for life, and it was firmly believed that customers would support rather than reject the business in a disaster.

In the 1980s, the rise of the auditor meant that businesses were more aware of the risks they faced, but in reality this simply meant higher levels of insurance. By the 1990s, attitudes had shifted again. Increasing evidence showed that disaster could happen to any business and a spate of terrorist activity compounded with emerging corporate governance caused an overnight change. Now, in the twenty-first century, organisations declare that it won't happen to them, because failure is no longer an option.

With this new emerging environment comes new risks and a new understanding of risk. The use of more technology will increase the threat of hacking, virus attack and cyberterrorism. It should also be noted that the manner in which business will view and subsequently protect itself from risk will also change. Where risk may once have been defined by its point of failure, the emphasis is moving towards the impact it has, usually financially, within the organisation (Jacob 1997).

Most importantly, when a corporation has proved to be a menace to society, the state must be empowered to destroy it. The authors believe that we should reintroduce the ancient safeguard against corporate governance: namely, the restrictive corporate charter. In 1720, after corporations had exceeded their powers in Great Britain, the government introduced an Act which provided all commercial undertakings 'tending to the common grievance, prejudice and inconvenience of His Majesty's subjects would be rendered void' (The Bubble Act, S 18, 1720, cited by March and Shapira (1992), the Creation and Development of English Commercial Corporations and the Abolition of Democratic Control over their Behaviour, Programme on Corporations, Law and Democracy). Corporations which broke the rules of their charters could be wound up. Big business, once again, must be forced to apply for a licence to trade, which would be revoked as soon as its terms were breached.

The Department of Trade and Industry's booklet *Protecting Business Information* (1996) advises executives to 'reduce the risk of damage to your companies' reputation' by protecting sensitive information. Staff should be gagged ('ensure a confidentiality agreement is signed') and all sensitive documents should be destroyed 'by approved cross-cut shredding, pulverising, burning or pulping'. Amongst those from whom material should be hidden are 'investigative journalists' seeking 'to obtain newsworthy information' (Department of Trade and Industry 1996).

However, the present authors believe that some government policies have been approved which displease corporations: the introduction of the minimum wage, for example, or energy taxes, limiting working hours and the recognition of trade unions.

7.15 SUMMARY

The corporate level is concerned with the type of business the organisation, as a whole, is in or should be in. It addresses such issues as the balance in the organisation's portfolio, and strategic criteria such as contribution to profits and growth in a specific industry. Questions concerning diversification and the structure of the organisation as a whole are corporate-level issues.

This chapter defined the corporation and its history, the functions of the FTSE, corporate structure, the board of directors – their functions, obligations and membership – corporate functions, corporate risk strategy and the future of corporate risk.

It also highlighted the power and control of the corporation, what it considers as risks, and the relationship with the rest of the company, namely the SBUs and the projects they carry out.

8
Risk Management at Strategic Business Level

8.1 INTRODUCTION

This chapter outlines business formation and the differences between private and public limited companies. It is primarily concerned with SBUs' functions, strategy and planning. Risks specific to the SBU level are also outlined.

The corporate body operates separate SBUs which are often managing many different projects, therefore portfolio theory is described along with a brief example using five different investments in separate markets and identifying their associated risks. Matrix systems and programme management are also discussed.

8.2 DEFINITIONS

French and Saward (1983) describe business as:

> *The activities of buying and selling goods, manufacturing goods or producing services in order to make a profit.*

French and Saward (1983) also define strategy as:

> *A general method or policy for achieving specified objectives.*

Collins English Dictionary (1995) defines a business as:

> *A commercial or industrial environment.*

The present authors believe strategy to be a set of rules which guide decision-makers about organisational behaviour and which go on to produce a common sense of direction. For the purposes of this book the authors believe strategic business management can basically be summarised as the management of SBUs.

8.3   BUSINESS FORMATION

The birth of a business is different to that of a corporation. A business often transforms into a corporation over time through acquisition and growth.

The authors believe there are three essential requirements for starting a business:

1. The financial resources needed to support a business.
2. A product or service that is wanted outside the business, and can be sold and exploited by it.
3. Sufficient people to operate the business.

When a business is formed the owners can choose from one of many legal forms; however, most businesses start off as a sole trader and grow accordingly. For the purposes of this book, the authors consider larger companies, specifically SBUs, and their relation to corporate bodies and the projects they undertake.

The law relating to incorporated companies is enshrined in the Companies Act. The most recent and important changes in the UK were made in 1985. Incorporated firms, or joint stock companies, are the most common form of business. Two types of limited company are found in the UK: private and public limited companies.

A limited company, private or public, is a legally separate body from its owners, the shareholders and its directors. The company can make contracts and agreements, and can be held responsible and sued in its own name. Under certain circumstances directors may also be sued, as in the case of negligence, but the important aspect here is that they are sued as well as the company.

Shareholders are not liable for the debts of the business beyond the value of their shares. In other words, the financial responsibility is limited. The value here is the original price, or the original investment, not the value based on the current price of the shares quoted on the stock market. The company has a life of its own and can exist beyond the life of its original owners.

Limited companies in the UK have to be registered with Companies House, and a strict procedure has to be followed if registration is to be granted. In particular, two key documents have to be prepared and lodged with the Registrar of Companies, namely:

1. Memorandum of Association
2. Articles of Association.

The Memorandum of Association describes generally the objectives of the company, and what the business is. It will contain the name of the organisation, its registered address, its objectives and its initial capital. It is a document relating to those outside the organisation, for external stakeholder use.

The Articles of Association describe the rules that govern the operation of the company. They are an internal document in many ways, and state how the business should be run. They must include a description of the rights of shareholders, election of directors, conduct of meetings, and details of keeping financial accounts (Birchall and Morris 1992).

On payment of the correct fee, the Registrar will issue a Certificate of Incorporation. After registration the company may sell shares and start to trade. Each year thereafter it will have to report to the Registrar by submitting as well as the directors' report, a set of accounts which will normally consist of a balance sheet, a profit and loss account, a cash flow statement, a set of detailed explanatory notes and a report from the company's auditors. However, this process does take time. Some businesses are registered in advance, and in suitably vague terms, so that they can be sold to people who want to register a company quickly. These are known as 'shell companies' (Birchall and Morris 1992).

The present authors also note that it is simpler to become a limited company than a public company. The answer as to whether an organisation will be a public or private company is: 'it all depends'.

There are specific rules governing the qualification of limited companies or plcs. Table 8.1 lists the differences between a private limited company and a public limited company.

Private limited companies tend to be regional, rather than national, firms and are often family businesses. Senior managers, directors and shareholders tend to be very close; sometimes they are one and the same. They tend not to be household names, unless they happen to be SBUs of plcs.

Public limited companies often find it easier to borrow money from banks, and tend to be much larger organisations than limited companies. They tend to inspire greater confidence, but there is no 'solid' reason why they should. Plcs seem to be the large companies in a country.

Table 8.1   Legal differences between private and public limited companies (Adapted from Birchall and Morris 1992)

	Private limited company	Public limited company
Memorandum of Association		Must state that company is a public company
Name	End with the word Ltd	Must end with word plc
Minimum authorised capital	None	£50 000
Minimum membership	2	2
Minimum number of directors	1	2
Retirement of directors	No set age	70 unless resolved
Issue of shares to public	Sale only by private agreement	May do on stock exchange by means of a prospectus
Company secretary	Anyone	Must be qualified as such
Accounts	Modified accounts	Must file B/S, P/L account, and auditors' and directors' report
Meetings	A proxy may address the meeting	A proxy cannot speak at a public meeting

Thus there are far more limited companies in the UK than plcs, but the majority of invested capital is in the latter.

8.4   STRATEGIC BUSINESS UNITS

Johnson and Scholes (1999) define an SBU as:

> *A part of the organisation for which there is a distinct external market for goods and services.*

Langford and Male (2001) define an SBU as follows:

> *Large firms will normally set up a strategic business unit. It will have the authority to make its own strategic decisions within corporate guidelines that will cover a particular product, market, client or geographic area.*

For the purposes of this book the present authors use the definition developed by Langford and Male (2001).

Within an SBU effective financial management must address risk as well as return. Objectives relating to growth, profitability and cash flow emphasise improving returns from investment. However, businesses should balance expected returns with the management and control of risk. Therefore, many businesses include an objective in their financial perspective which addresses the risk dimension of their strategy, for example diversification of revenues streams through globalisation. Risk management is an overlying or additional objective which should complement the strategy chosen by the particular business unit.

8.4.1   The Need for Strategic Linkages

The need for strategic linkages is essential for information transfer and can operate as a top-down or bottom-up process. Toffler (1985) states:

> *A corporation without strategy is like an aeroplane weaving through stormy skies, hurling up and down, slammed by the wind, and lost in the thunderheads. If lightning or crushing winds do not destroy it, it will simply run out of fuel.*

A major concern of both senior management and project participants is that projects seem to arise at will across the organisation. Confusion normally arises from:

- a lack of clarity as to how these projects align and link with the organisation's strategy
- the absence of a business process for selecting projects
- senior management's apparent lack of awareness of the number, scope and benefits of the projects being undertaken.

This results in many people feeling that they are working not only on many unnecessary projects but also at cross-purposes with other areas of the business.

Giving projects a strategic focus goes a long way to resolving these concerns. Combining a strategic focus with a business process for selecting and prioritising projects is an important step in creating an environment for successful projects. Some form of strategic planning is done at all levels of organisations. For clarity and simplicity, Verway and Comninos (2002) adopted the following terminology:

- Strategic planning at the organisational level results in a set of 'organisational imperatives'.
- The business managers convert these into business strategies.
- Business strategies are in turn carried out through projects whose strategy is the 'project approach or plan'.

8.4.2   The Wrappers Model

The wrappers model developed by Verway and Comninos (2002) is an overall approach which integrates the organisation's strategic business and project management levels. At the core of the model is the Business Focused Project Management (BFPM) protocol, which contains the Objective Directed Project Management (ODPM) process. Each level 'wraps' its functionality around the one within. The wrappers can be peeled off or added as required. Figure 8.1 illustrates the wrappers. The following subsections explain each wrapper layer in the model.

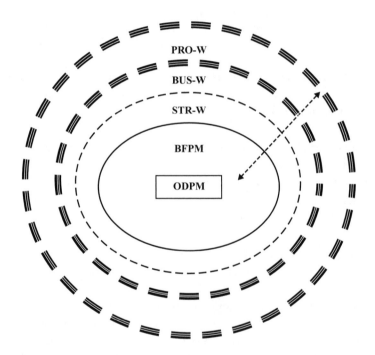

ODPM – Objective Directed Project Management

BFPM – Business Focused Project Management

STR-W – Strategic Wrapper

BUS-W – Business Wrapper

PRO-W – Project Wrapper

Figure 8.1   The wrappers model

8.4.2.1 The Strategic Wrapper

The inner wrapper is the strategic wrapper containing the organisation's vision, mission, goals and objectives. The executive level of the organisation, which is responsible for setting organisational strategy, primarily owns this wrapper.

An organisation's strategic planning develops vision, drives the mission and states which objectives/outcomes are necessary for success. Organisational strategy is converted into action through business strategies, which in turn enable the setting of goals and identification of a potential portfolio of projects.

The strategic wrapper further defines the relationship between the organisation and its environment, identifying the organisation's strengths, weaknesses, opportunities and threats (SWOT). The context includes social, technical, economic and environmental issues, political/public perceptions, and operational and legal aspects of the organisation's functions (STEEPOL). The SWOT and STEEPOL analyses form an integral part of the organisation's strategic planning.

In the absence of an organisation's strategic planning, projects will deliver results that are not aligned with desired business outcomes. Portfolio and project performance measures will exist in a vacuum created by the lack of strategic direction (Verway and Comninos 2002).

8.4.2.2 The Business Wrapper

The middle wrapper is the business wrapper and is owned by senior management. It receives project proposals from operations and functions and considers them in a prioritisation and selection process. These proposals are prepared in support of the organisation's imperatives and are generated by departments or at the executive level.

The result of the prioritisation and selection process is a portfolio of projects. The executive or board sanction the portfolio, thus committing organisation-wide resources. The CEO champions the complete portfolio, while an executive manager or senior management sponsor has the responsibility for ownership of individual projects. This ownership is of utmost importance to successful project delivery.

A portfolio council, comprising representatives of the executive and senior management, manages the project portfolio. Portfolio council members usually own the organisation-wide resources required to deliver the projects and therefore have a strong interest in ensuring that only well-scrutinised projects are approved (Verway and Comninos 2002).

8.4.2.3   The Project Wrapper

The outer wrapper is the project wrapper, representing the project management level. It is jointly owned by the project sponsors, project managers and participating functional managers. It is here that projects are initiated, planned, and executive and project results integrated into the business. The project manager and the core team member primarily manage this level. Subject to the functional managers' mandate, core team members represent their functional areas.

Authority to implement resources is given to the sponsor by the executive, and the sponsor is accountable to the executive for the results. The project manager's authority to manage the project is derived partly from the sponsor and partly from interpersonal influences.

An essential part of BFPM is a project planning process that focuses on measurable results and not on detailed planning, which is dealt with at team level. These results are objective or result directed and are addressed at ODPM level. They link to the performance measures and give direction to team-level planning. Project managers and team members expand these results to the next level – the task deliverables. Team members can now focus on the work required to achieve the deliverables.

Team members take on the responsibility for planning the work to achieve the deliverables. These deliverables lead to results, which in turn contribute to the intended business outcomes. From this planning will flow an understanding of what each individual contributes towards a deliverable and how its individual performance is measured (Verway and Comninos 2002).

Johnson and Scholes (1999) state:

> It has been shown that there needs to be a compatibility between corporate-level strategy and the strategy of the SBUs.

The relationship between the strategic business and corporate levels is often detached. The client enters into a contract with the SBU to carry out projects. The corporate body is merely a trading name listed on the stock exchange, so there is no contract between a client and the corporate entity. However, if a project does not go to plan, resulting in action by the client, the corporate body will often step in, although it is not obliged to. This is the case because the SBU, which is part of the corporation, does not want bad publicity, resulting in a damaged reputation.

8.4.3   The Business Management Team

Often the chairmen of SBUs are members of the corporation's board of directors and are duly responsible for ensuring that corporate policies are introduced into their respective SBUs.

A corporation is conceived of as a number of SBUs, with each SBU responsible for maintaining a viable position in the sale of products and services and maintaining its core competencies (Prahalad and Hamel 1998).

8.4.4   Strategic Business Management Functions

In general, the roles and responsibilities of strategic business managers are as follows:

- They are responsible for managing and co-ordinating various issues at strategic business level, and for ensuring coherency with and conformity to the corporate strategy implementation plan as well as the strategic business plan.
- They will be concerned with macro aspects of the business. These include:
  - o political and environmental issues
  - o finding a niche in the market and exploiting it
  - o business development
  - o sustainability or long-term goals of the strategy
  - o stakeholders' satisfaction
  - o long-term demands of customers or end users
  - o identifying and responding to strategic business risks.

In terms of legal focuses the strategic business manager will abide by planning regulations, environmental restrictions and British Standards. At the strategic business level the manager will look at a wider perspective, for example stakeholder arrangements (balancing equity, bonds, debt and contractual legal arrangements between partners). Business managers ensure that everything conforms with current legislation throughout the strategy. The use of an environmental impact assessment at strategy level provides a platform for the public to participate in mitigation decisions. This in turn fosters integrity and co-ordination and shows the stakeholders the benefits of the strategic business manager (Johnson and Scholes 1999).

In terms of risk management, the strategic business manager will need to address all possible risks, mitigate and review, documenting them as work in progress. The business manager will be concerned with a wider view of business risks, such as the interdependencies of the projects within the strategy, the overall financial risks of the projects, risks posed from delays in completion of tasks and sudden changes due to external influences.

In terms of schedule and cost, the strategic business manager will have to look at the whole picture, where comparisons can be made between different projects. The business manager will be concerned with predicting overall profit and loss within the business level and long-term profitability, as well as realising the benefits of the business strategy. Strategic business managers co-ordinate the interface of the projects within the strategy, the co-ordination logistics, both in design as well as in the implementation stages. They also consolidate and analyse changes with respect to the overall impact on the business strategy plan and cost.

8.4.5   Typical Risks Faced by Strategic Business Units

The typical risks faced by a SBUs include:

- Exposures of physical assets
- Exposures of financial assets
- Exposures of human assets
- Exposures to legal liability.

8.4.5.1   Exposures of Physical Assets

Physical asset or property exposure to risk can be classified in four ways: according to (1) the class of property affected, (2) the cause of gain or loss, (3) whether the outcome is direct, indirect or time element in nature and (4) the nature of the organisation's interest in the property. The causes of loss or gain might be divided into three classes: (1) physical, (2) social and (3) economic. Physical peril or causes include natural forces, such as fires, windstorms, and explosions, that damage or destroy property, or in the case of speculative risks – that in some sense enhance the value of the property. Social perils or causes are (a) deviations from expected individual conduct, such as theft, vandalism, embezzlement, or negligence, or (b) aberrations in group behaviour, such as strikes or riots. Economic perils or causes may be due to external or internal forces. For example, a debtor may be unable to pay off an account receivable because of an economic recession or a contractor may not complete a project on schedule because of management error. Two or more of these perils may be involved in one loss. For instance, a negligent act by an employee may lead to an explosion; an economic recession and a windstorm may together so severely cripple a debtor's organisation that the debtor cannot pay the amount owed to a supplier.

8.4.5.2   Exposures of Financial Assets

Today financial price risk can not only affect quarterly profits, it can also determine a business's very survival. Unpredictable movement in exchange rate, interest rates and commodity prices presents risks that cannot be ignored.

A financial asset is a legal instrument that conveys rights to the owner of the contract, although the right does not necessarily apply to a specific tangible object. When an organisation issues a financial asset, it appears as a liability on the issuer's balance sheet and an asset on the holder's balance sheet. An organisation can be exposed to risk from holding financial assets or as a result of issuing financial assets.

8.4.5.3   Types of Financial Assets

The variety of financial assets employed by individuals, business and governments is enormous and growing. Common stock, subordinated debentures, mortgage-backed securities, zero-coupon bonds, revenue bonds, futures, options, swaps and preferred stocks are but a few examples of the instruments used to finance private and public projects. Innovation continues to lead to the development of new financial assets to adapt to the ever-increasing complexity of financial markets. Embedded within this complex array of financial assets are a few attributes. Three elements are present in a typical financial asset, either singly or in combination:

- a promised payment or series of promised payments
- a right to another asset, which might be contingent or event - specific
- control rights, possibly through a voting privilege.

Uncertainty in the global financial environment has caused many economic problems and disruptions, but it has also provided the impetus for financial innovation. Through financial innovation, the financial intermediaries were soon able to offer their customers products to manage or even exploit the new risk. Through this same innovation, financial institutions became better able to evaluate and manage their own asset and liability position. The marketplace recognised early that the uncertainty about foreign exchange rates, interest rates, and commodity prices could not be eliminated by 'better forecasting'. This recognition induced firms to begin actively managing financial risk. The financial institutions – exchanges, commercial banks, and investment banks – have provided a range of new products to accomplish this risk management:

- In response to the increased foreign exchange risk, the market provided forward contracts on foreign exchange, foreign exchange futures (in 1972), currency swaps (in 1981), and options on foreign exchange (in 1982).
- For managing interest rate risk, futures contracts were the first to appear (in 1975), followed by interest rate swaps (in 1982), interest rate options (in 1982) and finally interest rate forwards – called 'forward rate agreements' (in 1983).

In addition to the existing forward contracts for metal and long-term contracts for petroleum, the onset of the increased price volatility in the late 1970s led to the appearance of futures contracts for commodities (for oil in 1978 and for metal in 1983). These were followed by commodity swaps (in 1986) and commodity options in 1986.

8.4.5.4 Exposures of Human Assets

The productive resources of an organisation include property (physical capital) and human resources (human capital); earlier, we discussed exposures due to ownership of physical and financial assets. The discussion now turns to assessing exposures related to the organisation's human asset. The main risks to personnel are:

- death
- poor health
- old age, and
- unemployment.

Individual employees and their families bear the direct consequences of these losses. In the absence of measures to mitigate the effect of these losses, individual employees' concerns about these exposures and their efforts to manage them can affect their productivity and contribution to the organisation's mission. Further, loss of human assets can have direct economic effects on an organisation. Hence risk managers have valid reasons for being interested in human resource exposure.

8.4.5.5   Exposure to Legal Liability – tort law

In general use the word 'tort' means a wrong, legally speaking; however, a tort is a civil wrong other than a breach of contract for which the court will provide a remedy in the form of money damages. There are three basic types of tort: intentional torts, involving conduct that may be by intention or design but not necessarily with the intention that the resulting consequences should occur; (2) unintentional tort, involving the failure to act or not act as a reasonable prudent person would have acted under similar circumstances; and (3) tort in which 'strict' or absolute liability applies. In summary these include:

- liability arising from ownership, use and possession of land
- liability arising from maintaining a public or private nuisance
- liability arising from the sale, manufacture, and distribution of products or services
- liability arising from fiduciary relationships
- professional liability
- agency and vicarious liability
- contract liability
- work related injury, and
- motor vehicle liability.

8.5   BUSINESS STRATEGY

Corporate strategy is concerned with the company as a whole and for large diversified firms it is concerned with balancing a portfolio of businesses, different diversification strategies, the overall structure of the company and the number of markets or market segments within which the company competes (Langford and Male 2001).

Business strategy, however, is concerned with competitiveness in particular markets, industries or products. Large firms will normally set up an SBU with the authority to make its own strategic decisions within corporate guidelines that will cover a particular product, market, client or geographic area. Finally, the operating or functional strategy is at a more detailed level and focuses on productivity within particular operating functions of the company and their contribution to the corporate whole within an SBU (Grundy 1998, 2000).

An organisation's competitive business strategy is the distinctive approach taken at business level when positioning itself to make the best use of its capabilities and stand out from competitors. From the work of Michael Porter (1970–2002), the authors have developed four key elements that determine the limits of competitive strategy at business level. These are divided into internal and external factors. Internal factors include the organisation's strengths and weaknesses, and the values of key implementers at the strategic business level. External factors include business opportunities, threats and technology advances, and expectations of the business environment within which the organisation operates.

Porter believes an organisation's strategy is normally defined by four components:

1. *Business scope.* The customers/end users served, their needs and how these are being met.
2. *Resource utilisation.* Resourcing properly the areas in which the organisation has well-developed technical skills or knowledge bases – its distinctive capabilities.
3. *Business synergy.* Attempting to maximise areas of interaction within the business such that the effect of the whole is greater than the sum of the parts.
4. *Competitive advantage.* Determine these sources.

At the corporate level of the organisation, senior managers will develop a corporate strategy that is concerned with balancing a portfolio of businesses. Corporate strategy is company wide and is concerned with creating competitive advantage within each of the SBUs. Business strategy is concerned with which markets the firm should be in and transferring the relevant information to corporate level. The division-alised structure, as part of the whole portfolio of businesses, will have different strategic time horizons for each division that has to be incorporated by the main board to produce an integrated corporate strategy (Bernes 1996).

8.6 STRATEGIC PLANNING

Strategic planning is essentially concerned with strategic problems associated with defining objectives in the overall interest of the organisation and then developing corresponding courses of action required to realise these objectives. It should be clearly differentiated from tactical planning, which is short term and chiefly concerned with functional planning and not with the setting of strategic goals. Tactical planning is carried out largely by functional management, whereas strategic planning, because of its very nature, must be the prerogative of top management. For effective strategic planning it is essential to get top management support and the active participation of both corporate and SBU management. The strategic plan must cover all aspects of the organisation's activities in an integrated manner.

The plan should be comprehensive enough to cover all the major aspects concerning corporate success. It should have a regular control and monitoring policy (Taylor and Hawkins 1972).

8.6.1   Strategic Plan

The present authors believe that for effective decision making the strategic plan should include the broad objectives for the corporation as a whole, and also for the individual SBUs and projects. These objectives should look at both quantitative and qualitative angles. Targets for each major activity will also be required. For example, for the marketing sector the objective should clearly indicate for each product or service target sales/volumes and the corresponding sales/price to be achieved over the plan period; and a study of the environmental factors such as marketing trends, political developments, technology and general economic factors which are likely to affect the business. The plan should include forecasts of these variables over the planned period. All environmental assumptions should be clearly justified. These forecasts and assumptions will form the essential basic ingredient of all those planning operations of the organisation and should embrace all those elements where top management believe detailed knowledge is essential. The more obvious elements would be:

- the rate of economic growth with the most likely social and political developments
- total industry demand for the products and services specific to the organisation
- breakdown of the total industry into sectorial demand
- availability and cost of alternative sources of raw material
- effects on the business of competition

- selling prices and quality of the goods manufactured
- capital investment requirements
- availability of funds, both internal and external
- identification of risks in each area from past experience, often in the form of a risk register.

The above merely indicate the types of environmental factors which need to be taken into account in building a strategic plan. These should be followed by:

- An audit of the organisation's existing resources to indicate its relative strengths and weaknesses.
- A systematic analysis of constraints within which the organisation has to operate. There must be a clear definition of objectives and constraints.
- Set strategies and action programmes to enable the organisation to meet its overall financial goals.

8.6.2   Strategy and Risk Management

Most organisations are concerned with the risk and variability of their returns. When it is strategically important, organisations will want to incorporate explicit risk management objectives into their financial perspective. Metro Bank, for example, chose a financial objective to increase the share of income arising from fee-based services not only for its fee-based potential but also to reduce its reliance on income from core deposit and transaction-based products. Such income varied widely with variations in interest rates. As the share of fee-based income increased, the bank believed that the year-to-year variability of its income stream would decrease. Therefore the objective to broaden revenue sources serves as both a growth and risk management objective (Kaplan and Norton 1996).

8.7   RECOGNISING RISKS

Bower and Merna (2002) describe how a business which is part of an American corporation, operating in the UK, optimises the contract strategies for a number of its projects. The risks identified by the authors led them to suggest that alliance contracts should be developed by the business and used on future projects as a means of transferring the risks identified. In this case the projects carried out by the business were similar and risks associated with each project were those relating to time, cost, quality and safety.

8.7.1   Specific Risks at Business Level

Many SBUs need to borrow money to finance projects. Lenders often require parent company guarantees from the corporation in case of default by the SBU. SBUs will, in some cases, use the corporation's profit and loss accounts as a means of illustrating their financial stability to clients rather than their own accounts, which are often not as financially sound.

8.7.2   Typical SBU Organisation

Figure 8.2 illustrates the relationship between the SBUs and the corporate and project levels. SBUs are seen to be subordinate to the corporate entity but senior to projects in diverse business sectors whilst remaining under the corporate umbrella.

An example of an organisation with two business levels is shown in Figure 8.3. Two examples of British corporations operating through four SBUs are BT in the telecoms sector and Rolls Royce in the engineering sector.

The sub-business units, often referred to as divisions, are responsible for the business risk assessment in conjunction with the SBU. In other cases sub-businesses are often managed on a regional basis as described by Langford and Male (2001).

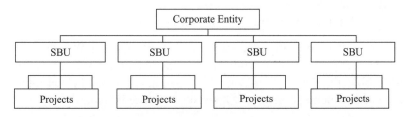

Figure 8.2   Typical SBU organisation (Adapted from Merna 2003)

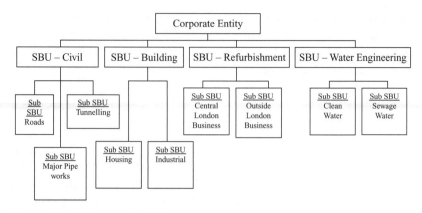

Figure 8.3   SBUs and sub-SBUs

Joint ventures (JVs) between similar SBUs (either within an organisation or with competitors) may also be formed. Wearne and Wright (1998) summarise the advantages of creating JVs as:

- to share costs and spread the risks of a project, contract or new market
- to share technical, managerial and financial resources
- to respond to a customer's wish to deal with a single organisation, or to demonstrate to a customer that the enterprises concerned are seriously committed to co-operating with each other in carrying out a project and accepting a proper share of the risks involved
- to gain entry into a new market or a potential customer list of approved bidders
- to share partners' licences, agencies, commercial or technical know-how
- to utilise international partners, credit advantages or lesson escalation risks
- to form more powerful bases for negotiations with customers, government, bankers, suppliers or others
- to develop interdisciplinary teams with new skills.

However, there are risks inherent with JVs. Wearne and Wright (1998) believe that partners may differ in their understanding or interpretation of the objectives, and this may not be apparent before the JV has entered into commitments to others. Other risks JVs face include:

- Divergence of interests between parties is greater if the JV is formed to share risks.

- Partners can vary in experience of JV projects and risks. Inexperienced partners may greatly underestimate risks.
- JV work is only part of the interests of each partner.
- Joint activities and risks may need management styles and systems different from those used by partners in their normal business.

JVs may be brought about by political necessity. For example, many Third World countries insist that foreign organisations have a domestic partner if they are to receive the necessary approval for the proposed activity. A domestic partner could help mitigate risks such as language and cultural barriers.

8.8   PORTFOLIO THEORY

According to the *Oxford English Dictionary* (1989), a portfolio is a:

Collection of securities held by an investing institution or individual.

Collins English Dictionary (1995) suggests that an investor's portfolio is the total investments held by that individual or organisation. For the purposes of this book both these definitions are too narrow: the first limits a portfolio to securities and the second to the complete set of investments. The authors propose that a portfolio is any subset of the investments held by an individual or organisation to avoid both limitations.

Investors spread risk by making numerous investments instead of 'putting all their eggs in one basket' with a single investment. This is the underlying principle of portfolio theory (Rahman 1997). By splitting the total investment into smaller packages which are subject to different risks, the level of exposure to any single risk event is reduced. *The Economist* (1998), with reference to the banking sector, explains the thinking behind portfolio theory thus:

If different assets are unlikely to take a beating simultaneously, or if price falls in some tend to be off-set by rises in others, the bank's overall risk may be low even if the potential loss on each individual class of asset is high.

The authors suggest that an SBU will be subjected to the same risk as the bank described above. Some projects will make profits, some break even and some lose. Providing the profit is greater than the loss, the SBU will be seen to be profitable.

8.8.1 Modern Portfolio Theory

Long before modern portfolio theory was developed Erasmus (1467–1536) stated:

Trust not all your goods to one ship.

In the analysis of financial markets, to a greater extent than in other areas of investment management, considerable study has been undertaken to quantify the reduction in risk resulting from diversification of portfolios and determine the optimal allocation of an investor's funds among available assets. The label applied to the mathematical models and their underlying assumptions and theories is modern portfolio theory (MPT). The essential differences between MPT and 'portfolio theory' are the former's emphasis on the quantification of the variables involved and its almost exclusive application to investments in financial markets.

In the 1950s, the American economist Harry Markowitz proposed that 'for any given level of risk, the rational investor would select the maximum expected return, and that for any given level of expected return, the rational investor would select the minimum risk'. This appears obvious but has certain implications, according to Dobins *et al.* (1994):

• the measurement of risk (which had previously been neglected) is central to investment decision making
• there exists a trade-off between risk and return.

Portfolio analysis comprises a set of techniques which are often used by strategic planners to integrate and manage strategically a number of subsidiaries, often operating in different industries, that comprise the corporate whole (Langford and Male 2001).

The larger the business, the more likely it is there will be a number of SBUs in existence which need to be integrated and managed strategically. The present authors believe that the main method of doing this is portfolio analysis. Its use is primarily discussed in terms of large, diversified organisations that have to consider many different businesses or SBUs, with different products or services on the market or under development. In order to provide a structure and subsequent guidance for decision making under these conditions, a number of different techniques have been developed, using the same form as matrix analysis.

According to McNamee (1985), portfolio management necessitates the three fundamental characteristics of a product's or SBU's strategic position:

1. its market growth rate
2. its relative market share in comparison with the market leader
3. the revenues generated from the product's sales of the SBU's activities.

In the construction industry, for example, portfolio management techniques can be applied at corporate level, for service products, end products and for the management of multi-project strategies. Scenario testing permits strategists to create alternative futures through economic forecasting, visioning or identifying branching points where discontinuities may occur. Cross-impact analysis can also assist scenario testing by looking at the strength of impacting events that may either be unrelated to a situation or enhance the occurrence of an event. To be worthwhile, however, scenario testing must be credible, useful and understandable by managers.

An example of portfolio analysis was carried out by Witt (1999). He analysed five investment scenarios and identified their major global risks. In the study the investment scenarios were:

- a toll road bridge under a concessional contract (construction)
- a supermarket (retail)
- a football team (leisure)
- commercial property (real estate)
- copper (commodity).

The information gathered was then processed within a framework of appraisal and a portfolio design mechanism (PDM). Table 8.2 shows the investment risks and the overall risk based on Witt's (1999) study.

8.8.2   Matrix Systems

To achieve leadership of each project and of each specialisation used by the projects, organisations and public authorities have evolved what are called matrix systems of management with separate roles for functional and project managers (Smith 1995).

Figure 8.4 shows an example where the resources of three departments are shared amongst three projects.

Matrix systems provide opportunities to employ leaders with different skills and knowledge in these two types of managerial role, but the project and specialist managers should theoretically influence decisions.

Table 8.2 Investments risks and descriptions (Adapted from Witt 1999)

Risk category	Risk description	Overall perceived risk
Road bridge		
Environmental	Pressure groups	
Political	Legislation affecting vehicle use	
Legal	Resolution of disputes	
Commercial	Changes in demand for facility	Medium
Commercial	Inflation	
Commercial	Competition from other facilities	
Commercial	Interest rates	
Retail		
Legal	Changes in regulation	
Legal	Standards and specialisation changes	
Commercial	Cost escalations	Medium
Commercial	Competition	
Commercial	Quality of services	
Football team		
Legal	Third-party liability	
Commercial	Competition/performance	
Commercial	Sponsorship/TV rights	
Other	Support	High
Other	Injuries	
Other	Management	
Commercial property		
Legal	Changes in legislation with regard to property	
Legal	Changes in standards and specifications	
Commercial	Competition in office space provision	
Commercial	Demand for office space	Medium
Commercial	Recession	
Commercial	Interest rates	
Commercial	Inflation	
Other	Location	
Copper		
Environmental	Environmental impacts of mining and processing	
Political	Political stability of producer countries	
Political	Production agreements between producer countries	
Commercial	Demand	
Commercial	(Global) Recession	High
Commercial	(Global) Interest rates	
Commercial	Exchange rates	
Commercial	Supply	

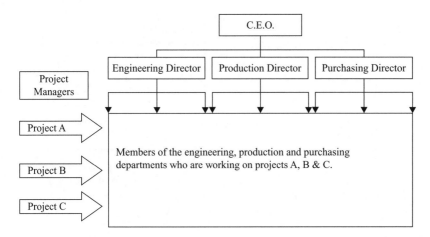

Figure 8.4   Matrix management of department resources (Adapted from Smith 1999)

Matrix systems can work to overall given, defined objectives and priorities for projects and with agreed amounts and quality of resources. They do not necessarily avoid conflict over these. Examples indicate that their success depends on:

- management's control of resources
- the personal skills and knowledge of the project manager
- joint planning and decisions on priorities.

8.9   PROGRAMME MANAGEMENT

The Central Computer and Telecommunication Agency (CCTA) (1994) defines programme management as:

> *Selection and planning of a portfolio of projects to achieve a set of business objectives; and the efficient execution of these projects within a controlled environment such that they realise maximum benefit for the resulting business operation.*

Reiss (2000) believes programme management is about implementing strategic change and realising benefit. He states that a precise definition would be:

> *The effective implementation of change through multiple projects to realise distinct and measurable benefits for an organisation.*

Figure 8.5 Key components of programme management (Adapted from Sandvold 1998)

Lockitt (2000) gives a more lengthy and thorough definition of programme management. He believes:

> *Programme management is that set of management activities and processes which facilitate the translation, conversion, prioritisation, balancing and integration of new strategic initiatives within the context of the current organisation and planned time and cost constraints, thereby minimising risk and maximising benefit to the organisation.*

For the purposes of this book, however, the authors believe that the CCTA definition is most appropriate. Nonetheless, the execution of the definition will be carried out through the use of management 'templates' (guidelines) to facilitate the use of the technique.

Programme management has a set of techniques and approaches to be used for managing complex change programmes in a business setting. The key components of effective programme management are those fundamental building blocks required to implement the discipline (Sandvold 1998).

Figure 8.5 illustrates the key components of programme management. These key components, according to Sandvold (1998), are as follows:

- *Organisational arrangements* – defining and maintaining the programme management environment.
- *Requirements management* – keeping track of the requirements and changes to the requirements.

- *Financial management* – the policies, procedures, practices, techniques and tools necessary to establish and maintain effective financial planning and reporting.
- *Resource management* – the direction and co-ordination of all resources throughout the programme's life cycle.
- *Risk management* – systematic identification of, analysis of and proactive response to risks, issues and problems, both real and anticipated, throughout the programme's life cycle.
- *Contract management* – the organisational, procedural and functional tasks, policies and practices for the day-to-day handling of comercial, legal, administrative and monetary considerations of the contracts between the programme and its suppliers.
- *Procurement management* – acquisition of purchased services and labour, goods, physical plant and equipment, operational equipment, raw material, component finished parts and equipment, and software for the programme.
- *Timeline management* – the guidelines, techniques, knowledge and tools required to develop and maintain appropriate allocations of time and effort throughout all phases of the programme's life cycle. Time planning, estimating standards and guidelines, supplier and third-party inputs, scheduling guidelines and control techniques ensure the rapid, high-quality delivery of programme goals and objectives that meet corporate requirements.
- *Quality management* – the composite of technical and managerial standards, procedures, processes and practices necessary to empower and provision each person fully to accomplish and exceed the mission, objectives, needs, requirements and expectations for which the programme was established.
- *Performance analysis and reporting* – disciplines, techniques, tools and systems necessary and adequate to establish and maintain programme performance analysis and reporting throughout the life cycle of the programme.

8.10   BUSINESS RISK STRATEGY

Each business unit must submit a summary of its proposed strategies and business plans to the corporate board. This is called the five-year commitment (FYC). The combined FYCs of all the businesses must achieve the corporate objectives. The FYC is a five-year business plan which is updated each year and moved forward by the year. The SBUs will update or add more issues and commitments and will include a business risk register covering similar points to that of the corporate risk strategy.

8.11 TOOLS AT STRATEGIC BUSINESS UNIT LEVEL

The tools and information used at the SBU level are similar to those at the corporate level. The business unit strategy, derived from the corporate strategy, is still concerned with survival and increasing value but is focused on its particular market area, normally a portfolio of similar projects.

Focusing on the difference, the owner comes from the SBU and the champion is a senior executive with regular contact with the corporate board. It is now more important that the core senior executives and project managers consider input from the customers, partners and suppliers as that interface is much closer. Major decisions must be ratified through regular contact with the corporate board.

The scope is focused on the market but extends beyond the current project portfolio looking for new opportunities. It now includes review and control of individual projects, as well as compliance with corporate strategy decisions.

Much of the same information is used when assessing SBUs; however, managers focus in greater detail on the particular market area. The same identification tools are appropriate, namely PEST and SWOT. In addition, health and safety management and environmental management systems will identify some risks that are generic to all projects in that market area, particularly those associated with production processes and methods, such as chromium plating, removal of toxic waste and working conditions

8.12 STRATEGIC BUSINESS RISK: AN OVERVIEW

Today's marketplace demands cost effectiveness, competitiveness and flexibility from a business if it is to survive and grow. Such demands necessitate effective business plans, both strategic in support of longer-term goals and tactical in support of ever-changing business needs and priorities and their associated risks.

A critical factor in this is the synergy required between business operations and associated information systems and technology architectures. A further key factor is understanding and dealing with the legislative, environmental, technological and other changes that impact on an organisation's business.

8.13 SUMMARY

The strategic business level is concerned with how an operating unit within the corporate body can compete in a specific market. SBUs are created at corporate level, and can be subsumed under it. The strategies of SBUs can be regarded as the parts which require and define the organisation as a whole.

The authors believe that SBUs should monitor all projects within their organisation. Risks occurring in one project may not occur in similar projects, but those risks could be of such a consequence that they impact on the financial stability of the SBU. It is paramount that all risks reported from projects, past and present, are made known at SBU level.

A risk management programme should be integrated within any organisation's overall business or financial strategy. Risk management should not be approached in an ad hoc manner or delegated to employees who are unfamiliar or uninvolved in formulating an organisation's overall strategy.

This chapter defined a business and an SBU. The chapter looked at strategic models such as the wrappers model, portfolio theory, matrix systems and programme management. Other areas considered were business strategy, the functions of business management teams, strategic planning and business risk.

9
Risk Management at Project Level

9.1 INTRODUCTION

Many businesses today depend on project-based activities for their growth and long-term well-being. Although ongoing operation is an important part of any business, it is the project elements that are usually at the cutting edge. This is why project management has emerged as an important and critical part of any going concern.

This chapter describes how project management has evolved, project management team functions and goals, and the concept of project risk management. The chapter also describes risks specific to projects.

9.2 THE HISTORY OF PROJECT MANAGEMENT

Project management, in its modern form, began to take root only a few decades ago. Starting in the early 1960s, businesses, especially SBUs and other organisations, began to see the benefit of organising work around projects and to understand the critical need to communicate and integrate work across multiple departments and professions.

9.2.1 The Early Years: Late Nineteenth Century

During the latter half of the nineteenth century the rising complexities of the business world led to further evolvement of principles within project management. Large-scale government projects were the impetus for making important decisions that became management decisions. Business leaders found themselves often faced with the daunting task of organising manual labour and the manufacturing and assembly of unprecedented quantities of raw material (Turner and Simister 2000).

9.2.2 Early Twentieth-century Efforts

At the turn of the last century, Frederick Taylor (1856–1915) began his detailed studies of work. He applied scientific reasoning to work by showing that people at work can be analysed and improved by focusing on its elementary parts. He applied his thinking to tasks found in steel mills, such as shovelling sand, lifting and moving parts. Before then, the only way to improve productivity was to demand harder and longer hours from workers. The inscription on Taylor's tomb in Philadelphia attests to his place in the history of management: 'the father of scientific management'.

Taylor's associate, Henry Gantt (1861–1919), studied in great detail the order of operations in work. His studies of management focused on naval ship construction during the First World War (1914–1918). His charts, complete with task bars and milestone markers, outline the sequence and duration of all tasks in a process. Gantt chart diagrams proved to be such a powerful analytical tool for managers that the charts remained virtually unchanged for nearly a hundred years. It was not until the early 1970s that link lines were added to these task bars, depicting more precise dependencies between tasks.

Taylor, Gantt and others helped evolve management into a distinct business function that requires study and discipline. In the decades leading up to the Second World War (1939–1945), marketing approaches, industrial psychology and human relations began to take hold as integral parts of business management.

9.2.3   Mid Twentieth-century Efforts

After the Second World War, the complexity of projects and a shrinking wartime labour supply demanded new organisational structures. Complex network diagrams called PERT (Programme Evaluation and Review Technique) charts and the critical path analysis method were introduced, giving managers greater control over massively engineered and extremely complex projects (such as military weapon systems with their huge variety of tasks, risks and numerous interactions at many points in time).

Soon these techniques spread to all types of industries as business leaders sought new management strategies, tools and techniques to handle their businesses' growth in a quickly changing and competitive world. In the early 1960s, general system theories of science began to be applied to business interactions.

9.2.4   Late Twentieth-century Efforts

This view of business as a human organism implies that in order for a business to survive and prosper, all of its functional parts must work in concert towards specific goals. In the following decades, this approach towards project management began to take root in its modern form. While various business models evolved during this period, they all shared a common underlying structure (especially for larger businesses): that is, the project is managed by a project manager, who puts together a team and ensures the integration and communication of the workflow horizontally across different departments.

Modern project management is a strategic, company-wide approach to the management of all change. Although it is underpinned by the traditional discipline of project management, it is broader in its application, concepts and methods. Central to the modern project management paradigm is the definition of a project according to Lane (1993) as:

> *a vehicle for tackling business-led change within the organisation.*

Using this definition modern project management is applicable to activities not traditionally regarded as project work, such as mission and strategy setting, education and training, and organisational restructuring.

9.3   DEFINITIONS

A project is a unique investment of resources to achieve specific objectives. Projects are realised to produce goods or services in order to make a profit or to provide a service for the community. The project itself is an irreversible change with a life cycle and defined start and completion dates. Any organisation has an ongoing line management of the organisation requiring management skills. According to PMBOK (1996):

> *Project Management is the planning, organisation, monitoring and control of all aspects of a project and the motivation of all involved to achieve project objectives safely and within defined time, cost and performance.*

Project management is needed to look ahead at the needs and risks, communicate the plans and priorities, anticipate problems, assess progress and trends, get quality and value for money, and change the plans if needed to achieve objectives (Smith 1995).

Project management includes creating the right conditions by organising and controlling resources to achieve specific objectives (Elbing 2000). Every project has fundamental characteristics that make it unique in some way. These characteristics include objectives, value, timing, scope, size, function, performance criteria, resources, materials, products, processes and other physical parameters that define the project.

Project management is a central point in the organisation's structure of a project where all information should be channelled. Clients of large projects often have no or less experience in project management than those involved in smaller repetitive projects. The main task is to lead the client through the life cycle and to realise the project on behalf of the client.

9.4   PROJECT MANAGEMENT FUNCTIONS

Turner (1994) presented quite a rosy future for project management, and recognised the changes for the years ahead. In this challenging and ever-changing environment, project management has emerged as a discipline that can provide the competitive edge necessary to succeed, given the right manager. The new breed of project manager is seen as a natural sales person who can establish harmonious customer relations and develop trusting relations with stakeholders. In addition to some of the obvious keys to project managers' success – personal commitment, energy and enthusiasm – it appears that, most of all, successful managers must manifest an obvious desire to see others succeed (Clarke 1993).

The project manager's responsibilities are broad and fall into three categories: responsibility to the parent organisation, responsibility to the project and the client, and responsibility to members of the project team. Responsibility to the SBU itself includes proper conservation of resources, timely and accurate communication and careful, competent management of the project. It is very important to keep senior management of the parent organisation fully informed about the project's status, cost, timing and prospects. The project manager should note the chances of being over budget or being late, as well as methods available to reduce the likelihood of these dreaded events. Reports must be accurate and timely if the project manager is to maintain credibility, protect both the corporate body and the SBU from high risk, and allow senior management to intercede where needed.

Communication is a key element for any project manager. Running a project requires constant selling, reselling and explaining the project to corporate and SBU levels, top management, functional departments, clients and all other parties with an interest in the project, as well as to members of the project team itself. The project manager is the project's liaison with the outside world, but the manager must also be available for problem solving, and for reducing interpersonal conflict between project team members. In effect the project manager is responsible to all stakeholders regarding the project to be managed.

The control of projects is always exercised through people. Senior managers in the organisation are governed by the CEO, who is directed by such groups as the executive committee and/or the board of directors. Senior managers in turn try to exercise control over project managers, and the project managers try to exert control over the project team. Because this is the case, there is a certain amount of ambiguity, and from time to time humans make mistakes. It is therefore important that there are effective communication controls and standards and procedures to follow.

According to Turner and Simister (2000), the roles and responsibilities for the project manager are as follows:

* The project manager is responsible for managing and co-ordinating various issues at project level, and for ensuring coherency and conformity to the project strategy implementation plan by working hand in hand with the strategic business manager.
* The project manager will be more project focused. For example, concerned with the micro aspects of each project in question, such as the mechanics of delivery of a single project to timescale, cost budgets and quality of deliverables.
* In terms of legal focuses, the project manager will abide by planning regulations, environmental restrictions and standards.
* Here the project manager will adopt the standard legal requirements specified at the business level but tailor these requirements to suit each project.
* In terms of risk management, the project manager will need to address all possible risks, mitigate and review, documenting as work progresses.
* The project manager will assess risks in the individual projects, but will report to the business manager on the next level if significant impact on the overall strategy and cost is foreseen.
* In terms of schedule and cost, the project manager will have to look at the individual project, and use the tools and techniques available to analyse it.
* The project manager will be concerned with the individual profitability.
* The project manager will co-ordinate the interface of the individual stages of the project.

- Work should be completed to cost, time and quality restraints.
- Cost plan and cost control must meet the allocated budget for each project.
- The project manager should monitor changes and report them to business level if necessary.

Figure 9.1 illustrates the typical project management functions carried out at project level by the project management team. The different functions are often dependent on the type of project undertaken and these are often monitored by the SBU as well as the project manager.

Figure 9.2 depicts the vertical hierarchy of a construction organisation's site project management team. All team members report through different routes to the project manager who in turn reports to the SBU.

9.4.1   The Project Team

The project team is made up of people from different organisational units. Their work together must be done in a spirit of tolerance and mutual understanding.

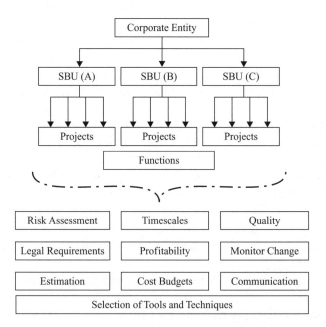

Figure 9.1   Typical project management functions (Merna 2003)

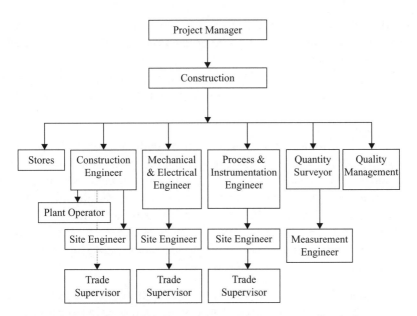

Figure 9.2   Typical organisation for a multi-disciplinary construction project

The relationships between the project manger and the line managers are important. Often heads of organisational units who are higher than the project manager in the existing hierarchical organisation do not want to co-operate as they should. They want the power to decide independently on things which are not within their competence. If they do not get what they want they hamper the project through passive or covert opposition. Members of the project team who are higher up the hierarchical ladder sometimes will not permit 'some project managers' to report on their work and report on it to an executive (Field and Keller 1999).

Below is a list of typical members of a project team with their usual duties:

- *Project engineer.* This engineer is in charge of product design and development and is responsible for functional analysis, specifications, drawings, cost estimates, quality/reliability, engineering changes and documentation.
- *Process manufacturing engineer.* This engineer's task is the efficient production of the product or process the project engineer has designed, including responsibility for manufacturing, engineering, design and production, production scheduling and other production tasks.

- *Commission field manager.* This person is responsible for the installation, testing and support of the product/process once it is delivered to the customer.
- *Contract administrator.* The administrator is in charge of all official paperwork, keeping track of customer changes, billings, questions, complaints, legal aspects, costs and other aspects related to the contract authorising the project.
- *Project controller.* The controller keeps daily accounts of budgets, cost variances, labour charges, project supplies and capital status. The controller also makes regular reports and keeps in touch with both the project manager and the company controller. If the administrator does not serve as a historian then the company controller will.
- *Support services manager.* This person is in charge of product support, subcontractors, data processing and general management support functions.

It is important to note that all these roles will not be required in all projects; however, most of these people will be required in large projects. Project managers in charge of smaller projects will often be responsible for nearly all the above roles and tasks.

9.4.2   Project Risk Assessment Teams

Project risk assessment teams can serve the organisation in a number of different ways. They can:

- conduct competent risk assessments for every project
- develop a process risk assessment including standards and procedures for the organisation
- serve a mentoring and consulting role for players in the organisation who need guidance on appropriate risk assessment practices
- offer risk management training, both formally and through the classroom
- select and maintain risk management tools and techniques
- serve as the central resource repository for the distribution of risk management resources to the organisation
- liaise with SBU managers or risk officers.

However, Hillson and Murray-Webster (2006) state that it is a fact that risk attitudes to a particular situation vary from person to person, team to team, organisation to organisation and, some would say, nation to nation. These authors suggest that risk attitude is a source of significant bias on decision making and the effectiveness of the risk management process. They suggest that to improve risk management more should be understood about risk attitude.

9.4.3 Project Goals

The most important task at the beginning of a project is to agree the project's objectives with the client. Without agreed objectives there is not enough support for the decisions and there is no measurement of success. With the agreed objectives the project management team must identify key indicators for control of the successful project realisation (Gorog 1998). It is also very important to determine at this stage the sharing of risk between the client and the contractor.

The question of project success can be answered on different levels or at different points of view. If one project participant, for example a contractor, architect or consultant, achieves a reasonable profit, the project is a success for this party. From a project management point of view, success is realising a project on time, within budget and to specifications. The project must satisfy the client (Fachtagung Projektmanagement 1998).

For investors their success can be measured in terms of return on their investment. However, there are other measures for success. If the project is a great service for the community it is also a success up to a certain level independent of the costs and completion date. Examples include the Thames Barrier and the Sydney Opera House (Morris and Hough 1987).

9.5 PROJECT STRATEGY ANALYSIS

In the world of project management, it has been common to deal with estimates of task durations and costs as if the information were known with certainty. On occasion, project task workers inflated times and costs and deflated specifications on the grounds that the project manager or SBU manager would arbitrarily cut the budget and duration and add to the specifications, thereby treating the problem as a decision under conflict with the management as an opponent.

In fact, a great majority of all decisions made in the course of managing a project are actually made under conditions of uncertainty. In general, many project managers adopt the view that is usually best to act as if decisions are made under conditions of risk. This will often result in estimates being made about the probability of various outcomes. If project managers use appropriate methods to do this, they can apply the knowledge and skills they have to solving project decision problems.

Project risk management is a process which enables the analysis and management of risks associated with a project. Properly undertaken it will increase the likelihood of successful completion of a project to cost, time and performance objectives. However, it must be noted that no two projects are the same, causing difficulties with analysis and troubleshooting. In most cases things go wrong that are unique to a particular project, industry or working environment. Dealing with project risks is therefore different from situations where there is sufficient data to adopt an actuarial approach (Gareis 1998).

The first step at project level is to recognise that risk exists as a consequence of uncertainty. In all projects there will be risks of various types:

- a technology is yet to be proven (innovation risk)
- lack of resources at the required level
- industrial relations problems
- ambiguity within financial management.

Project risk management is a process designed to remove or reduce the risks which threaten the achievement of the project's objectives. It is important that management regard it as an integral part of the whole process, and not just simply a set of tools and techniques.

9.6　WHY PROJECT RISK MANAGEMENT IS USED

There are many reasons for using project risk management, but the main reason is that it can provide significant benefits far in excess of the cost of performing it.

Turner and Simister (2000) believe benefits gained from using project risk management techniques serve not only the project but also other parties such as the organisation as a whole and its customers. Below is a list of the main benefits of project risk management:

- There is an increased understanding of the project, which in turn leads to the formulation of more realistic plans, in terms of cost estimates and timescales.

- It gives an increased understanding of the risks in a project and their possible impact, which can lead to the minimisation of risks for a party and/or the allocation of risks to the party best suited to handle them.
- There will be a better understanding of how risks in a project can lead to a more suitable type of contract.
- It will give an independent view of the project risks, which can help to justify decisions and enable more efficient and effective management of risks.
- It gives knowledge of the risks in projects which allow assessment of contingencies that actually reflect the risks and which also tend to discourage the acceptance of financially unsound projects.
- It assists in the distinction between good luck and good management and bad luck and bad management.

Beneficiaries from project risk management include the following:

- Corporate and SBU senior management, for whom a knowledge of the risks attached to proposed projects is important when considering the sanction of capital expenditure and capital budgets.
- The clients, as they are more likely to get what they want, when they want it and for a cost they can afford.
- The project management team, who want to improve the quality of their work. It will help meet project management objectives such as cost, time and performance.
- Stakeholders in the project or investment.

Project risk management should be a continuous process that can be started at any early stage of the life cycle of a project and can be continued until the costs of using it are greater than the potential benefits to be gained. The authors believe that it will be far more effective to begin project risk management at the start of a project because the effects of using it diminish as the project travels through its life cycle.

Norris *et al.* (2000) believe that there are five points in a project where particular benefits can be achieved by using project risk management:

1. *Feasibility study.* At this stage the project is most flexible enabling charges to be made which can reduce the risks at a relatively low cost. It can be helpful in deciding between various implementation options for the project.
2. *Sanction.* The client can make use of this to view the risk exposure associated with the project and can check that all possible steps to reduce or manage the risks have been taken. If quantitative analysis

has been undertaken then the client will be able to understand the 'chance' that it has of achieving the project objectives (cost, time and performance).

3. *Tendering.* The contractor can make use of this to ensure that all risks have been identified and to help it set its risk contingency or check risk exposure.

4. *Post-tender.* The client can make use of this to ensure that all risks have been identified by the contractor and to assess the likelihood of tendered programmes being achieved.

5. *At intervals during implementation.* This can help improve the likelihood of completing the project to cost and timescale if all risks are identified and are correctly managed as they occur.

Many project management procedures place considerable stress on the quantification of risk, although much evidence suggests that this is erroneous as many top executives ignore data in favour of intuition (Traynor 1990). The emphasis placed on the quantification processes fails to prompt a manager to take account of other areas more difficult or impossible to quantify, thus excluding a large element of risk.

9.7 RECOGNISING RISKS

It would be of great help if one could predict with certainty, at the start of a new project, how the performance, time and cost goals would be met. In some projects it is possible to generate reasonably accurate predictions; however, the larger the project, often the less accurate these predictions will be. There is considerable uncertainty about organisations' ability to meet project goals. Barnes (2007) states that risk management is intended to shrink the effect of uncertainty on the outcome of projects. All real projects are dominated by the need to add and to change the plans as reality replaces expectation. Barnes suggests that what actually happens is so likely to be different from what was expected that to achieve success, project teams must be masters of uncertainty, not victims.

Uncertainty decreases as the project moves towards completion. From the project start time, the band of uncertainty grows until it is quite wide by the estimated end of the project. As the project develops the degree of uncertainty about the final outcome is reduced. In any event, the more progress made on the project, the less uncertainty there is about achieving the final goal.

The project manager must have a good knowledge of the stakeholders in the project and their power. A consensus must be found with the majority of participants in the project. This is often not easy because stakeholders have conflicting interests. It is important that project managers continuously analyse the positions of the stakeholders, their expectations, their needs and foreseeable reactions. If the stakeholders think that they will only be collaborating once, then it is difficult to achieve creative co-operation (Simon *et al.* 1997).

9.7.1   Specific Risks at Project Level

A project manager must cope with different cultures and different environments. Different industries have different cultures and environments, as do different regions and countries. The word 'culture' refers to the entire way of life for a group of people. It encompasses every aspect of living and has four elements that are common to all cultures: technology, institutions, language and arts (Turner and Simister 2000).

The technology of a culture includes such things as tools used by people, the material things they produce and use, the way they prepare food, their skills and their attitude towards work. It embraces all aspects of their material life (Haynes 1990).

The institutions of a culture make up the structure of society (*The Economist* 2001). This category contains the organisation of the government, the nature of the family, the way in which religion is organised as well as the content of religious doctrine, the division of labour, the kind of economic system adopted, the system of education, and the way in which voluntary associations are formed and maintained.

Language is another ingredient of all cultures. The language of a culture is always unique because it is developed in ways that meet the express needs of the culture of which it is part. The translation of one language into another is rarely precise. Words carry connotative meanings as well as denotative meanings. The word 'apple' may denote a fruit, bribery, 'for the teacher', New York City, a colour, a computer, favouritism, 'of my eye', as well as several other things (Johnson and Scholes 1999).

Finally, the arts or aesthetic values of a culture are as important to communication as the culture's language. If communication is the glue that binds culture together, art is the most important way of communicating. Aesthetic values dictate what is found beautiful and satisfying.

If a society can be said to have style, it is from the culture's aesthetic values that style has its source (Jaafari 2001).

9.7.2   What Risks are Assessed at Project Level?

The project audit is a thorough examination of the management of a project, its methodology and procedures, its records, its properties, its budgets and expenditures, and its degree of completion. It may deal with the project as a whole, or only with a part of the project. The formal report should contain the following points:

- *Current status of the project.* Does the work actually meet the planned level of completion?
- *Future status.* Are significant schedule changes likely? If so, indicate the nature of these changes.
- *Status of crucial tasks.* What progress has been made on tasks that could decide the success or failure of the project?
- *Risk assessment.* What is the potential for project failure or monetary loss?
- *Information pertinent to other projects.* What lessons learned from the project being audited can be applied to other projects being undertaken by the organisation?
- *Limitations of the audit.* What assumptions or limitations affect the data in the audit?
- *Tools and techniques.* What tools and techniques were used at project level?

One must note that the project audit is not a financial audit. The project audit is much broader in scope and may deal with the project as a whole or any competent set of components of it. The audit may be concerned with any part of project management. One must also note that the project audit is not a traditional management audit. Management audits are primarily concerned that the organisation's management systems are in place and operative. The project audit goes beyond this. Amongst other things it is meant to ensure that the project is being appropriately managed. Some managerial systems apply fairly well to all projects, for example the techniques of planning, scheduling, budgeting and of course risk management (Turner and Simister 2000).

The present authors also believe that decommissioning risks play a fundamental part in risk management at project level. These are the risks associated with plant or machinery at the end of the project's life cycle.

For example, what will be done to a nuclear power station when it is decommissioned? What are the costs of decommissioning? What are the environmental effects? And which stakeholders are affected and how?

Cooper and Chapman (1987) suggest that the need for emphasising risk assessment is particularly apparent when projects involve:

- large capital outlays
- unbalanced cash flows requiring a large proportion of the total investment before any returns are obtained
- significant new technology
- unusual legal, insurance or contractual arrangements
- important political, economic or financial parameters
- sensitive environmental or safety issues
- stringent regulatory or licensing requirements.

The present authors consider that all or a combination of a number of the above parameters are fundamental to project strategies. The authors also suggest that each risk identified in the project must have a uniform basis of assessment which will inevitably involve cost and time.

Figure 9.3 shows the level of risk plotted against the stage of the project. As the diagram indicates greater risk at the earlier stages of the project cycle, it can be concluded that this is where the majority of risk management efforts should be concentrated as it offers greater yields (Merna and Owen 1998).

Precise quantitative data are unlikely to be available. Techniques such as Delphi, benchmarking and interviews can be used to get qualitative rankings and quantitative range estimates of both impact and probability. These tools are particularly useful, as the parties involved can be geographically disparate.

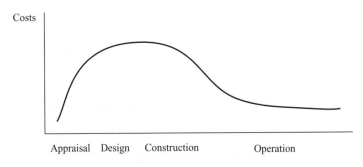

Figure 9.3   The project risk cycle

The greatest change comes at project level. The project strategy plan focuses on how all the macro-environmental factors and the micro-effect project success will be managed in order to meet the goals set by the business unit strategy.

During the feasibility stage of the project qualitative risk analysis and quantitative sensitivity analysis are appropriate. As the project progresses and a project network is defined, computer modelling such as Monte Carlo simulation can be performed. The major advantage is that it considers the effects of variables in combination, resulting in cumulative frequency predictions for the major strategic goals. This technique is particularly useful for selecting mitigating actions as their effect can be predicted by rerunning the modified model.

Khan (2006) suggests that identified risks such as bad weather, supplier unreliability and technical delays can be mitigated in a cost-effective way. Khan states that one solution has its roots in that most fundamental of project planning processes, the project schedule and the associated knowledge network. By incorporating risk and uncertainty parameters in respect of the individual activities within the schedule, and then applying simulation techniques to extrapolate potential outcomes, project managers can build up a precise picture of where mitigation will be most effective. Resources can be intelligently allocated to mitigate against risks where the probability of occurrence and consequence are clearly understood.

9.7.3   Project Managers and Their View of Risks

People vary in their approach to risk assessment and estimation; there is a tendency to shift the preferences of risk depending on budgets, resources and CEO characteristics. In the authors' opinion, the managers' previous experience in risk assessment and estimation will play an important role in how they respond to identified and quantified risk. Overconfidence about the estimation of risk is another factor in how individuals regard risk. Overall, individuals are poor assessors of risk. Experience, subjectivity and the way risk is framed play a major role in project managers' perceptions, to the detriment of project management.

Issues of risk that relate to people are often reclassified as management of 'human resources' and so are ignored as risk factors; consequently a large element of risk assessment is excluded from project risk management. The nature of the uncertainty which people contribute to the project can be divided into two principal areas: human resource management issues, concerned with effective management competencies and practices, and the perspectives of stakeholders concerning the project and its attendant risks (Oldfield and Ocock 1999).

The importance of effective management practices has often been highlighted, the main concerns being centred around poor leadership, lack of communication, lack of provision of necessary resources, insufficient use of resources, work overload, lack of knowledge, lack of decision-making authority, and inability to estimate accurately tasks and processes. Identification of these dimensions would aid the project manager's decision making and improve the quality and efficiency of the management process (Oldfield and Ocock 1999).

In many cases of project failure, the necessary information concerning risks and problems is available within project teams but often not sought out by management (Oldfield and Ocock 1999). A common problem in project risk management processes is the need to determine the relative significance of different sources of risk so as to guide subsequent risk management effort and ensure it remains cost effective. Chapman and Ward (1997) consider the use of probability impact grids to identify sources of risk which will receive most attention. In particular it is important to distinguish between the size of impacts and the probability of impacts occurring, the range of feasible responses and the time available to respond.

9.8   PROJECT RISK STRATEGY

Risk management is used throughout the full life cycle of the project from pre-tender through to after-market.

The risk management plan is the process of identifying and controlling the business, technical, financial and commercial risks throughout the project's life cycle by eliminating or reducing the likelihood of occurrence and the potential impact caused by any threat. For commercial undertakings, any impact on the project outcome is to be expressed in the terms of cost. Financial impact is therefore a baseline to measure risk. Risk that has a timescale is to be converted into cost. This will enable accounts to raise provisions early in the project if they are needed. It is important to remember that strategic project planning is the synergy between a best practice culture of project management and the effective implementation of corporate strategy, goals and objectives (Blanden 2002).

9.9   THE FUTURE OF PROJECT RISK MANAGEMENT

The project management profession is going through tremendous change – both evolutionary and revolutionary. Some of these changes are internally driven, while many are externally driven.

In discussing future issues in project management, Turner (1994) cited the study of risk management as an emerging area for academic study based on journal submissions. Whilst it may be said that the further development of technically specialist areas will certainly take place, the project manager's role will almost certainly move from that of a technical specialist, who has taken on the role of co-ordinator of a project, to that of a change agent. The function that these managers perform will be recognised as increasingly important for the survival of the organisation in all sectors, by management of all the stakeholders in projects. In addition there is the search for new management structures (Maylor 1996).

Barnes (2007) suggests that the way to make risk management work is to make it integrated, by taking steps to ensure that key players want to come and take part in the process because it benefits them all. Barnes suggests that there are two ways of moving in this direction:

- to give risk management meetings more importance than ordinary project progress meetings
- to make sure that any team member can bring a new risk to the table which the others will help to deal with.

9.10   SUMMARY

Projects are unique, novel and transient endeavours undertaken to deliver business development objectives. However, the authors believe that the long-term objective regardless of the project in question will always be profit.

This chapter outlined the history of project management and its functions. It also highlighted the importance of project management and its teams. Project risk, project managers as risks, and project risk strategy were also considered within this chapter.

10
Risk Management at Corporate, Strategic Business and Project Levels

10.1 INTRODUCTION

The previous chapters have discussed risk management tools and techniques, stakeholders' involvement and the structure of corporate organisations. This chapter presents a model illustrating the sequencing of risk assessment, risk management techniques and shareholder involvement at corporate, strategic business and project levels.

10.2 RISK MANAGEMENT

Figure 10.1 illustrates the levels of a typical organisational structure which allows risk management to be focused at each level. By classifying and categorising risk within these levels it is possible to drill down or roll up to any level of the organisational structure. This should establish which risks the project investment is most sensitive to so that appropriate risk response strategies may be devised and implemented to benefit all stakeholders.

Risk management is seen to be inherent to each level, although the flow of information from level to level is not necessarily on a top-down or bottom-up basis (Merna 2003). The risks identified at each level are dependent on the information available at the time of the investment and each risk may be covered in more detail as more information becomes available.

In many cases decisions will be made solely on qualitative assessments. In other cases decisions will be made after a quantitative assessment on the basis of computed metrics such as IRR and NPV.

10.3 THE RISK MANAGEMENT PROCESS

Figure 10.2 conceptualises the risk management process. Risk management looks at risk and the management of risk from each organisational

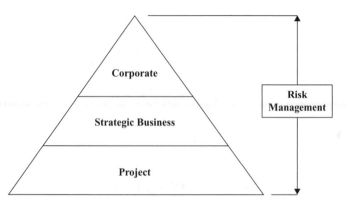

Figure 10.1   Levels within a typical corporate organisation

perspective, namely strategic, tactical and operational perspectives. The level within an organisation responsible for each organisational perspective can perform the necessary analysis.

Organisations have different levels with different objectives. Typically the risk management process separates the business processes into many levels which make up an organisation (typically the three levels previously identified). Risks specific to each level are identified using risk identification techniques (discussed in Chapter 4) and then logged on a risk register. Each level within the organisation will then analyse the identified risks and responses and contingencies can be made.

The risks identified at each level are consolidated and controlled by a single department within the organisation. Within this department the risk management analysis can be made either on a standalone basis or for bundles of projects (portfolios).

Risk management should be a continuous process over the whole life cycle of the investment.

Many project management procedures place considerable stress on the quantification of risk. However, at the strategic business and corporate levels a significant proportion of the risks are not quantifiable and thus favour less formal risk management. The emphasis placed on the quantification processes often leads to a failure at the corporate and strategic business levels to prompt a manager to take account of other types of risk more difficult or impossible to quantify.

All stakeholder requirements must be acknowledged and aligned and a consensus must be found. This is often not easy because stakeholders have conflicting interests. It is important that the positions of the

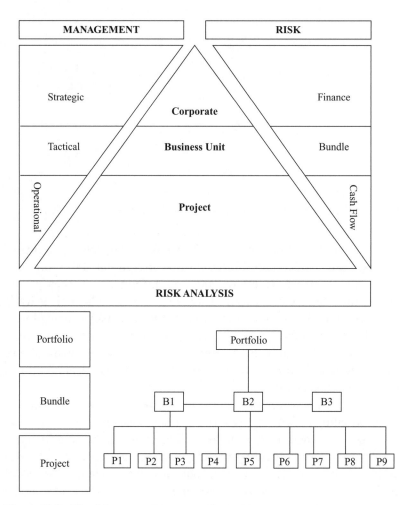

Figure 10.2   The risk management process/structure

stakeholders are continuously analysed and their expectations met as far as possible.

10.4   COMMON APPROACHES TO RISK MANAGEMENT BY ORGANISATIONS

Risk management may follow a top-down approach, originating at the corporate level, consolidated at the strategic business level and implemented at the project level as shown in Figure 10.3.

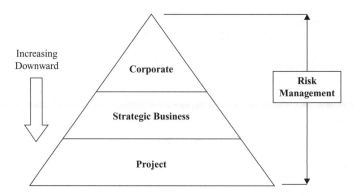

Figure 10.3   Downward approach to risk management (Merna 2003)

In the situation shown in Figure 10.3 risk management in terms of identification, analysis and response is first carried out at the corporate level. This is often a qualitative analysis. Information is then passed down to the strategic business level where a more detailed risk analysis takes place and information from the corporate level is further explored. This information is then passed on to the project level of the organisation. Again further information is gathered and analysed. This process allows a complete risk assessment to take place as information moves down through the organisation.

This process, however, does not allow the results of risk assessments and information to flow through to the strategic business and corporate levels. Disadvantages of this model include communication difficulties from level to level, difficulty knowing what risk assessment each level within the organisation is carrying out, difficulty updating the model because it is not a continuous process, and ambiguities found at strategic business and project levels are not passed to the corporate level because there is no procedure in place to do so.

Figure 10.4 illustrates an upward approach to risk management. In this situation the risk management begins at the project level, but here the assessment at the project level is much more detailed. This assessment is then passed to the strategic business level in the organisation, and then to the corporate level. As the assessment is passed up through the organisation a more detailed risk assessment specific to either the strategic business or corporate level is carried out.

Again this process does not allow the information and risk assessments to flow down through the organisation, causing the same disadvantages as the downward approach to risk management.

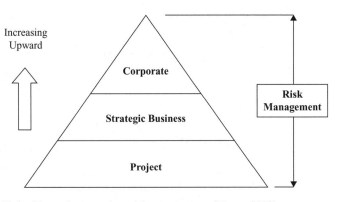

Figure 10.4   Upward approach to risk management (Merna 2003)

Both the increasing downward and increasing upward models may result in a risk register being developed at each level but do not provide an overall risk register to be managed at one level.

The authors believe that although less detailed risk assessment takes place at the corporate level, the influence at the corporate level in terms of risks is far more important than risk assessments at strategic business and project levels. Many of the risks identified at the corporate level are global or uncontrollable risks, often associated with political, legislative, regulatory, economic and environmental factors. If any of these risks are considered too great, then a project may not be sanctioned for further risk assessment at strategic business or project levels.

10.5   MODEL FOR RISK MANAGEMENT AT CORPORATE, STRATEGIC BUSINESS AND PROJECT LEVELS

Within any organisation performing risk management, tools and techniques must be used at each level. The use of these tools and techniques allows the identification and analysis of risks and forms the basis for investment appraisal. Stakeholders are also identified at each level, and are allowed to contribute to the risk management process. These stakeholders must be identified and their requirements recorded as well as their relative significance. In order to assess the risks at each level, various tools and techniques may be applied. These techniques may generally be applied at each level in the process, but some will be more applicable to a particular level than others. Figure 10.5 illustrates the levels and

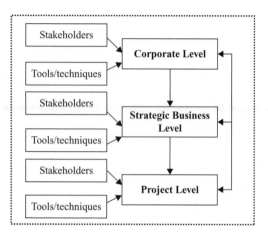

Figure 10.5   Risk management mechanism

required input at each level in the risk management mechanism. The tools and techniques used at each level will be determined by the risk analyst and related to the type of assessment undertaken at those levels.

Figure 10.5 divides the organisation into corporate, strategic business and project levels. At each level risk management tools and techniques are used and stakeholder requirements are taken into consideration. This process forms a basis for the risk management mechanism.

Figure 10.6 illustrates the risk management cycle, which includes the identification, analysis and control of risks to be applied at corporate, strategic business and project levels. The risk management cycle is dynamic and must be continuous over the project investment life cycle.

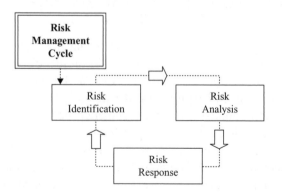

Figure 10.6   Risk management cycle

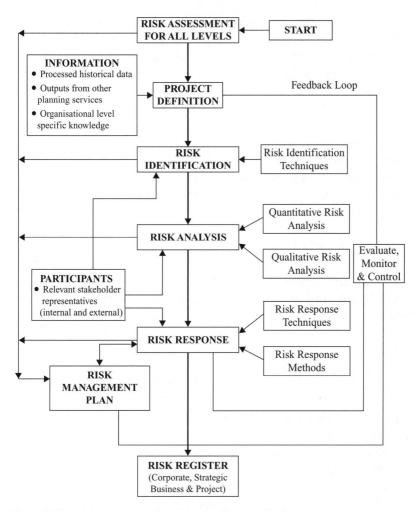

Figure 10.7   Risk assessment for all levels of an organisation

This risk management mechanism, proposed by the authors and illustrated in Figure 10.7 below, incorporates the risk management cycle shown in Figure 10.6 and is utilised at each organisational level with the purpose of identifying, analysing and responding to risks specific to that level within the organisation. The process illustrated in Figure 10.6 should be a dynamic process carried out in a continuous loop throughout the whole investment life cycle.

Figure 10.7 illustrates the processes that the authors suggest should be undertaken at each level of an organisation, the stakeholders and risk management tools and techniques being involved as and when appropriate.

The first step of risk management is investment appraisal at the corporate level where the overall investment objectives are determined. It is imperative that the investment and derived objectives are identified and clearly understood at the strategic business level and by the project team. At this stage each level of the organisation should define what the investment implications are at this level, for example business or project requirements, client specification, work breakdown structure, cost estimates, project programme, cost and type of finance, and project implementation plan. This is often performed through the use of historical data, organisational specific knowledge and from infor-mation specific to the project in hand and the organisation's overall goals.

The process of identifying risks is carried out through the use of a variety of techniques suited to the type of project and the resources available. The allocation of risk to owners is undertaken during this stage, which aims to place ownership of risk with the individual best placed to control and manage it. Identified risks and risk owners are recorded on the risk register, which later will become a database at the SBU level.

The information gathered at the identification stage is then analysed. Risk analysis tools and techniques, either qualitative or quantitative, are now employed to provide a thorough analysis of the risks specific to the project at each level within the organisation. Analysis may include defining the probabilities and impacts of risk and the sensitivity of the identified risks at each level.

After completion of the identification and analysis processes, the response to these risks can be carried out. This part of the process is exercised through the use of risk response methods and techniques. If the decision is to mitigate the risks the costs of mitigation must be assessed and budgeted for accordingly. Retained risks at each level will be identified in the risk register and be constantly reviewed.

Within this model stakeholders are of particular importance. Stakeholders are involved at each level and will have an input at each stage in the risk assessment process (identification, analysis and response). The model allows information from each stage to flow backwards and forwards through the organisation, where it can then be continually monitored, evaluated and controlled.

Once all the information has been processed through the model, a risk management plan is constructed and implemented. The plan should form an integral part of project execution and should give consideration to resources, roles and responsibilities, tools and techniques, and deliverables. This plan will include a review of the risk register, monitoring progress against risk actions and reporting. The final output of the model is a risk register at corporate, strategic business and project levels.

Feedback is a key vehicle used in this proposed model so that the organisation can learn from both its successes and mistakes, internally or externally. It provides continuous improvement at both SBU and project levels, and risk management itself. Feedback is a continual process of gathering data from known and unforeseen events. Information is held at the SBU level and disseminated throughout the organisation.

These risk assessments and risk registers at corporate, strategic business and project levels will be made available to each level within the organisation. These levels of an organisation are discussed in Chapters 7, 8 and 9 respectively. An overall risk register, incorporating the risk registers developed at corporate, strategic business and project levels, will be further developed at the strategic business level and continually updated as the project develops. It is important that the risk assessments carried out for the projects at the strategic business level are of the same format, thus providing a database for all projects. This will allow the database to be interrogated and inform future projects, strategic business and corporate decision making.

The authors suggest that risk assessments at corporate, strategic business and project levels should run concurrently. At any time during the assessments, risks can be flagged up from any level that may result in the project or investment being sanctioned or temporarily put on hold.

The proposed risk management assessment system will:

- identify and manage risks against defined objectives
- support decision making under uncertainty
- adjust strategy to respond to risk
- maximise chances through a proactive approach
- increase chances of project and business success
- enhance communication and team spirit
- focus management attention on the key drivers of change.

Figure 10.8 illustrates the risk management model and the interaction of each level within the organisation. Information regarding risk assessment and risk registers is passed freely through the organisation.

Within this model the strategic business level will act as a conduit between corporate and project levels. A risk officer will be designated

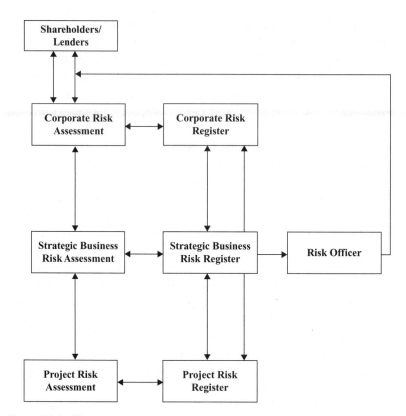

Figure 10.8   The risk management model

at the strategic business level with responsibility for ensuring that risks managed at corporate, strategic business and project levels are registered and that any further risks identified will be incorporated in the risk register held by the risk officer. All the information gathered from corporate, strategic business and project levels will be collated and passed on to the risk officer. The risk officer will be in direct contact with risk facilitators at both corporate and project levels. This model will ensure that all levels of the organisation will have an input into the overall risk register.

Managers and owners of risks retained and mitigated will be in the corporate, strategic business or project level within the organisation depending on where the risk originates. For example, a risk originating at the project level will be managed and owned by the project manager. The risk assessments and risk registers held by the project manager will be passed to the risk officer, at the strategic business level. The risk officer will review the overall register and inform both corporate and strategic levels of any changes in risk assessment as the project proceeds.

The advantages of the strategic business level of an organisation holding a risk register as a conduit from both corporate and project levels are as follows:

- The strategic business level is immediate to both corporate and project levels.
- One risk officer is responsible for the risk database.
- If any information is required about risk specific to a project, both project and corporate levels have access to this information.
- Both project and corporate levels will have access to all risk management systems and information.
- Stakeholders will have easy access as to how risks are managed at all levels of the organisation.
- Risk management throughout the organisation is co-ordinated and centralised.

However, in order for the model to work regular reviews and audits need to take place together with risk workshops at corporate, strategic business and project levels facilitated by the risk officer.

New risks, the cost of managing such risks and the status of all existing risks identified at each level will be addressed in the overall risk register database.

10.6 SUMMARY

This chapter identified the corporate, strategic business and project levels in a typical organisation. Each level is responsible for managing the risks identified and ensuring that information on such risks is available to the other levels.

In most cases risks are specific to each level. Corporate risks are typically difficult to quantify and manage. These risks include the political, legal, environmental and financial elements of an investment. Many of these risks can be assessed in greater detail at the strategic business level as more information becomes available.

Project risk management often entails risks being assessed in even greater detail as they become more specific to the project rather than higher level risk considered at strategic business and corporate levels. To ensure that all risks at all levels are managed it is paramount that an overall risk management system is implemented and risks identified at all levels are managed over the life cycle of the investment.

The risk register held by the risk officer at the strategic business level forms a database for all levels of the organisation. This risk register should be accessible to stakeholders, particularly shareholders investing in a project.

The continual cycle of risk management is fundamental to the risk management model illustrated in Figure 10.8.

11
Risk Management and Corporate Governance

11.1 INTRODUCTION

The concept of risk management was embedded in corporate governance in the late 1990s. Corporate governance guidance was issued and promoted based on reaction to scandals in the US and the UK over the last 20 years. The following is a presentation from the World Bank (2004):

- Internal fraud – Allied Irish Bank, Barings and Daiwa Bank Limited, $691 million, $1 billion, $1.4 billion respectively, fraudulent trading.
- External fraud – Republic New York Corp., $611 million, fraud committed by custodial client.
- Employment practices and workplace safety – Merril Lynch, $250 million, legal settlement regarding gender discrimination.
- Clients, products and business practices – Household International, $484 million, improper lending practices, Providian Financial Corp. $405 million, improper sales and billing practices.
- Execution, delivery and process management – Bank of America and Welles Fargo Bank, $225 million and $150 million respectively, systems integration failures, failed transaction processing.
- Damage to physical assets – Bank of New York, $140 million, damage to facilities related to September 11, 2001.
- Business disruption and system failures – Solomon Brothers, $303 million, change in computer technology resulted in 'un-reconciled balances'.

These scandals and losses have helped in a big way to shape the scope and depth of current regulation in operational risk management.

To understand more clearly how risk management came out of the corporate governance debate, it is necessary to look back into the development of 'corporate governance'.

---

* Reproduced by permission of A. Merna.

11.2   CORPORATE GOVERNANCE

Corporate governance can be defined as the:

system by which companies are directed and controlled.

(Cadbury Committee definition 1992)

While corporate governance has gained a lot of exposure in recent years, there is in fact nothing new about the concept. It has been in existence as long as the corporation itself, that is as long as there has been large-scale trade, reflecting the need for responsibility in the handling of money and the conduct of commercial activities. At the end of the nineteenth century, shareholders started to hand over the direct management of larger firms to hired professional managers. This was facilitated by the adaptation of British company law, which offered businesses the protection of limited liability by separating personal liability from that of corporate organisations. Personal liability could therefore be limited to the amount of the shareholding in an incorporated company, limited by shares. The concept of corporate governance truly appeared when the owners of a company were not also those who directed and managed the company. They then required some assurance that the directors and managers safeguarded their investments and reported to them the correct amount of profit from which they may have received their dividends.

The corporate governance debate in the UK focused most of the twentieth century on the relationship between management and shareholders and the shareholder's profit and wealth maximisation. Adam Smith who studied at length human motives once observed that the directors who are the fiduciary of other people's money cannot be expected to be as vigilant and careful with other people's money as they would with their own.

The nature of the debate on corporate governance changed radically in the late 1980s in the US and then in the UK. The 1970s and 1980s were marked by numerous financial failures, fraud and questionable business practices (the gin and tonic era). People started questioning the reasons for this happening, as these failures could not only be explained by senior management mistakes or misjudgements. This led to a number of initiatives in the US and Canada.

In 1985, the Tradeway Commission (formerlly the US National Commission on Fraudulent Reporting) investigated a number of large business failures and concluded that in more than 50% of the cases reviewed, failures were explained by breakdown in internal control. From that period the corporate governance debate broadened its scope, which became two-fold: still concerned with board management issues but also highly interested in the prevention of major business failures by implementing effective systems of internal control.

In the UK several committees were set up which issued recommendations (Cadbury 1992, Greenbury 1992, Rutterman 1994, Hampel 1995). In 1995, these were embodied in a code know as the Combined Code.

The code was not initially compulsory; however, every company listed on the London Stock Exchange has the obligation to report whether it complied with the code or not, and if not what were the provisions of the Combined Code which were not applied. In practice, as the Combined Code was viewed as a code of best practice, few companies departed from its guidance. It should be noted that health and safety, though not a central aspect of corporate governance, is nevertheless an issue on which directors are also asked to give some account. This relates to their own employees as well as suppliers and contractors working on their premises.

The provisions of the Combined Code relating to risk management are detailed in principle D2 and provisions D2.1 and D2.2 as follows:

Principle D2 — 'The board should maintain a sound system of internal control and safeguard the shareholder's investment and the company assets'

Provision D2.1 — 'The Directors should at least annually conduct a review of the effectiveness of the group system of internal control and should report to shareholders that they have done so. The review should cover all controls, including financial, operational and compliance controls and risk management.'

Provision D2.2 — 'Companies which do not have an internal audit function should from time to time review the need for one.'

The 12.43 London Stock Exchange Listing Rule stated that 'the annual report should explain how the principles set out in the Combined Code had been applied. Any departure from the Combined Code principles should be mentioned in the annual report.'

The first major appearance of the concept of risk management in corporate governance is quite ambiguous. It is mentioned as something that is distinct from the control review process. It is not clear whether risk management is actually another set of controls that should be reviewed. There is no definition of the concept of risk management within the Combined Code.

For this reason and because no practical guidelines were available, a new working party (Turnbull Committee) was set up to provide an explanation on the Combined Code. Guidance was issued which is now appended to the Combined Code, named the Turnbull guidance. Companies largely endorsed the Turnbull report recommendations even if they represented at the time both a real challenge for most companies and significant additional work to implement them. The Institute of Internal Auditors' guidance on Turnbull (2000) stated that three quarters of companies were still thinking in July 2000 that they would still require further work to comply with Turnbull guidance. The Financial Reporting Council (2005) undertook a review of the Turnbull report and stated 'the review found that the (Turnbull) Guidance had contributed to improvements in internal control in UK listed companies. It strongly endorses the principles-based approach of the Guidance, which allows companies to focus on the most significant risks facing them. It recommends only limited changes to the Guidance to bring it up to date.' However, the Institute of Internal Auditors issued a more reserved statement of effectiveness of Turnbull guidance.

The 47 notes of the Turnbull guidance brought some clarity about provision D2. However, with regards to the concept of risk management, the guidance still remained quite confusing by referring to the concept either in terms of governance structure or management objectives. For example, in article 10, risk management is defined as part of the system of internal control. However, in article 16, the system of internal control is said to be aiming at managing risk. Sarah Blackburn (1999) mentions the lack of 'clear concept of the relationship between internal controls and risk management'. She adds that the term of internal control when used in the Turnbull guidance is probably too narrow to pretend to embrace the concept of internal control. What is obvious at this stage is that neither the Combined Code provisions nor the Turnbull guidance and further professional guidance manuals from different institutions really approach the concept of risk management in a very easy to understand way.

In summary the Turnbull report is about managing the risks that are 'significant to the fulfilment of a company's business objectives'. Companies should not only create and maintain truly risk-facing internal control systems, but also ensure that the systems are embedded deep within the corporate anatomy. Ultimate responsibility for implementation falls on the board of directors and no distinction is made between executive and non-executive directors. Directors are required to review and report to shareholders, at least annually, on the effectiveness of all internal controls including financial, operational and compliance controls and risk management. This approach to risk management has been welcomed by a number of organisations as a means of enhancing performance and gaining competitive advantage. Investors (both lenders and shareholders) will regard the implementation of Turnbull not only as a safeguard against damaging mistakes but also as a measure of business success. With the scope of risk management now extending beyond financial, audiences with concerns about company values (product quality, health and safety, employee and customer loyalty etc.) or wider issues (environmental, ethical, social etc.) will be interested in disclosures made in these areas. Industry regulators and courts will regard the extent to which Turnbull has been implemented as a compliance indicator and pick up on deviations from its best practice standards when investigating companies.

Disasters catch out even the most vigilant organisations. When they occur, they can result in litigation against the company, criminal and civil actions against directors personally, negative publicity, damage to corporate reputation. The list goes on.

The companies which are likely to survive the consequences of a disaster will be those which:

- can demonstrate a good record of regulatory policy and compliance
- have crisis response systems in place which bring immediate effective relief, limit damage and negative exposure and work fast towards re-establishing business continuity and
- have insurance protection to minimise the financial impact on the business, its directors and officers.

In disaster situations, larger well-established companies are likely to derive additional support from their corporate reputation and stakeholder loyalty. For small to medium-sized companies and young companies, the satisfaction of the above criteria will probably determine whether or not they will weather the storm.

For all its upbeat and incentivising qualities, Turnbull should not be misunderstood. While proper implementation will bring benefits from business gains to a happier workforce, the critical test of benefit will come when the unavoidable disaster occurs. There is no doubt that in such situations, the extent of a company's compliance with Turnbull will be scrutinised. Proper risk management systems will prove to be the company's lifeline in such situations. They can be used to dissuade a regulator from prosecuting, or operate as powerful mitigation should the matter go to court. The implementation of a system of internal risk control requires an honest appraisal of the company's capabilities. What can it do in-house and what should be outsourced?

In fairness, despite the omission of risk management references, the Turnbull guidance still brings the following key clear directions with regards to the general concept of risks:

• A company should assess its risks on a regular basis and be capable of responding to risk.
• Procedures should exist in order to ensure that significant risk matters are reported to management.
• Companies should report on the process in place to manage risks.

The last aspect regarding the need for reporting information on risk in annual reports finally brought corporate advisers and auditors into the risk management debate. The prospect of advising boards on how to communicate on the subject in annual reports and how to implement the provisions of the Turnbull guidance provided a new solid stream of counselling income. Worldwide auditing firms and management consultants thus developed their own guidance on the guidance.

The Deloitte and Touch (2001) progress report on corporate governance lists key considerations on risk management:

• Link risk management to business improvement.
• Keep it simple and straight-forward.
• Build it into the decision-making process.
• Now is not the time to declare victory.

Risk management is not defined and general guidance does not stipulate the way risk management should be implemented. It only provides general principles for implementing the risk management as with any type of project.

Felton and Watson (2002) listed some general principles for effective risk management as part of a set of rules for strengthening corporate governance. These are summarised as:

• Companies should delineate the risks.
• The company should 'measure its risk exposure and update it risk profile routinely'.

- People who determine the company's risk policy, monitor and control its implementation should be different from those who manage the business.
- Any key decisions should include risk considerations.

The ICAEW published an Internal Control guidance (1999) which has taken into account its views that the guidance should be interpreted in a non-bureaucratic way and can be adapted to the particular circumstances of individual companies. In other words, companies have maximum flexibility to implement and report on risk management.

Barjon (2006) notes that the financial investment profession has also embraced the concept of risk management with title of chief risk officer first developed in financial institutions. In finance, risk is very much linked to reward. Risk is the concept used to appraise the profitability of the different investments depending on their risk profile, which is conceptualised into mathematical models, especially for quoted investments.

Barjon (2006) also states that risk management has been developed by different professions with relatively different perspectives and objectives:

- the minimisation of the financial impact of negative impact events (insurance)
- the assessments of likely rewards of financial investments (finance)
- the prevention of negative impact events with the view to safeguard assets and protect people (technical and engineering).

The profile of risk management over the last few years has become one of the core topics discussed by business and political leaders. Samuel DiPiazza Jr, the Global CEO of PricewaterhouseCoopers (PWC), made a presentation on risk management at the World Economic Forum at Davos in 2004. It is interesting to note the key elements of his presentation. DiPiazza stated: 'While there has never been a time when risk has been completely absent from our world, our businesses, and our lives, today risk comes in more flavours than ever before.' The flavours he refers to for justifying the rise of risk concerns are the threat of terrorism, the reality of wars, unpredictable economic gyrations, corporate scandals and tighter regulations.

DiPiazza also stated that risk management activities help organisations 'to achieve their objectives, reduce volatility of outcomes, and ensure effective reporting and compliance'. DiPiazzo also introduces the term enterprise risk management which is a term more frequently used in the US to talk about the global corporate perspective of risk management to avoid mixing it with insurance matters and sets very clearly the dilemmas of risk management. Firstly, 'reducing uncertainty about downside loss ... and upside gain entail a real cost'. In other words, risk management activities do represent a significant cost to companies. Preventing future unexpected losses comes at a premium cost. Secondly, 'reducing downside loss can reduce opportunities'. Companies need to find the right trade-off between risk and opportunities of rewards, and suggests risk management should not be treated as the 'be all and end all'. Companies should always be prepared 'to expect the unexpected and to act when the unexpected occurs, as it inevitably will'.

In the Anglo-Saxon world, risk management has become a high profile business management topic and it is almost anchored as an official management standard for managing large businesses.

11.3 CORPORATE GOVERNANCE APPROACH IN FRANCE

The interest of corporate governance and formal risk management theories has been more acute in countries, mainly Anglo-Saxon ones, where indirect ownership of quoted companies is widely spread and with English origin legal systems. Marc Goergen (2003) explains, for example, that German companies that are generally controlled by significant shareholders are less controlled than UK companies. In the UK and US, state and pension funds have invested large sums in quoted shares to meet the financial needs of their pensioners. However, pension funds are by nature adverse to risk and therefore they are very keen to influence the promotion of new initiatives in corporate governance. Pension funds represent a very large proportion of the shares quoted on the stock exchange in the USA, UK and Canada. In countries without such pension funds, the concept of corporate governance is more recent and less familiar. In France pensions are organised on a reallocation system (*repartition*) versus an Anglo-Saxon capitalisation system. In other words, those who work pay for those who are retired).

It is interesting to note that the trend is, however, changing due to international influences. More French companies are now quoted in London and New York and have to comply with the British or American regulations. The French society adapts slowly to the new world business environment. Disclosure of directors' remuneration in annual reports is now less a taboo, for example.

The main initiatives on corporate governance in France have been:

- Report Vienot I – June 1995, MEDEF
- Report Vienot II – July 1999, MEDEF
- Report Bouton – December 2002, MEDEF
- A proposal for Internal Control Procedures – December 2003, MEDEF
- Recommendations on the corporate governance – 1998, 2004, AFG-AGS.

The most relevant initiative was the French equivalent of the Turnbull report, the Vienot report. A committee was formed by chief executives of 14 of the largest French plcs to review the corporate governance matters. They included the need for separation of the functions of chairman and chief executive, the need to publish the executive directors' remunerations of quoted companies, and various questions relating to the administration of the board. The committee was sponsored by the powerful management private organisations MEDEF (*Mouvement des enterprises de France*) and the AFEP (*Association Française des Entreprises Privées*). A guidance, named Vienot, was produced in July 1999. The report has subsequently been updated by additional guidance from the MEDEF. A first reference to risk was made in a new report issued by the MEDEF and mentions that the objective of the system of internal control is to manage risk. The report, however, mainly focuses on suggesting that annual reports should detail the internal control procedures and responsibilities, and the key legislation and codes the companies comply with. It does not expand on the suggested action for managing risks.

Another report from the MEDEF, the Report Bouton (2002), only makes comments about risks which need to be better managed as a principle. The latest guidance issued by the French Asset Management Association only relates to the general principles of corporate governance.

It should be stressed that the main difference with the UK situation is that most of these recommendations have not been embedded in the law and are not enforceable. That kind of process takes years in France where the civil law type of system is very complex. There is an exception which relates to the compulsory information relating to internal control. The new law, *Loi de Sécurité Financière*, LSF (2003), imposes quoted companies to report on internal control in the annual report without saying what internal control is or without mentioning whether the report should be descriptive or should express an opinion on how controls are managed within the companies. In the absence of further guidance, companies have adopted a very low profile on these topics in the annual reports.

Overall, there is no official corporate governance guidance, in France, which in particular relates to risk management theories and recommended practices, which are equivalent to the Turnbull guidance that companies need to comply with.

11.4 CORPORATE GOVERNANCE APPROACH BY THE EUROPEAN COMMISSION

Internal Market Commissioner Fritz Bolkestein stated in 2003 that 'company law and corporate governance were at the heart of the political agenda' and that Europe had a 'unique opportunity to strengthen European Corporate Governance and to be a model for the rest of the world'. As a result the European Commission set out a plan of action which was presented in May 2003.

The position of the European Commission is well summarised by the European Commission (2003). 'The Commission does not believe that a Corporate Governance Code would offer significant added value but would simply add an additional layer between international principles and national codes.' The Commission suggests that 'The European Union should adopt a common approach covering a few essential rules.' The most urgent initiatives considered by the Commission being:

- introduction of an annual corporate governance statement
- shareholders' rights
- promotion of the role of non-executive directors
- directors' remuneration
- convergence of nations.

In response a European Corporate Governance Forum was set up in 2004, comprising representatives from member states, European regulators, issuers and investors and other market participants and academics. The Forum is chaired by the European Commission. It has not yet produced any relevant information regarding corporate governance and risk management.

11.5 CORPORATE GOVERNANCE AND INTERNAL CONTROL

Internal control is defined in the Combined Code as follows:

> *An internal control system encompasses the policies, processes, tasks, behaviours and other aspects of a company that, taken together:*

- *Facilitate its effective and efficient operation by enabling it to respond appropriately to significant business, operational, financial, compliance and other risk to achieving the company's objectives. This includes the safeguarding of assets from inappropriate use or from loss and fraud, and ensuring that liabilities are identified and managed.*
- *Ensure the quality of internal and external reporting. This requires the maintenance of proper records and processes that generate a flow of timely, relevant and reliable information from within and outside the organisation.*
- *Help ensure compliance with applicable laws and regulations, and also with internal policies with respect to the conduct of business.*

Internal control should not be confused with the simple definition of control often used as a response to a risk. In that sense, HM Treasury published a book called the *Orange Book* (2001) on risk in which a definition of control was presented as follows:

> *Control is any action, procedure or operation undertaken by management to increase the likelihood that activities and procedures achieve their objectives. Control is therefore a response to risk.*

Internal control is a concept that has been used by different governmental bodies and professional institutes to communicate best practices that companies should adopt to make their operations more reliant. Several models have been developed over time which have integrated the concept of risk gradually.

The first known model was the US model 'COSO' which inherited its name from the name of the organisation which developed it, known as the Commission of Sponsoring Organisation (COSO) of the Tradeway Commission. The Canadian Institute of Chartered Accountants developed their own model two years later in 1994 called 'Coco' (Canadian Criteria of Control). Private consulting companies also developed in the 1990s other internal control models such as the Cardmap system.

More recently the initial US model COSO was revisited and updated as COSO II. The model promotes the establishment of meaningful objectives for all activities of an organisation and the implementation of eight control elements supporting each objective. These elements relate to the following topics:

- internal environment
- objective setting
- event identification
- risk assessment
- control activities
- information
- communication
- monitoring.

This control model is now used by a large number of companies in the US and clearly places at its heart the basis of risk management. The promotion of control models has had the impact of making risk management more practical and discussed by staff at all levels of companies.

Finally corporate development in the US needs to be discussed. This incorporates powerful implied risk management strategic ideas and new guidance about internal control frameworks. It is known as the Sarbanes-Oxley Act of 2002 (SOX) or the Public Company Accounting Reform and Investor Protection Act of 2002. This US Act can be defined as 'wide ranging and establishes new or enhanced standards for all U.S. public company Boards, Management, and public accounting firms. The Act contains 11 titles, or sections, ranging from additional Corporate Board responsibilities to criminal penalties, and requires the Securities and Exchange Commission (SEC) to implement rulings on requirements to comply with the new law.' This Act was voted by the US Parliament following a deterioration of public confidence in company official information including financial results from the scandals relating to Enron, Tyco International and Worldcom. SOX goes much deeper than the accuracy of financial projections, it touches many areas affecting the management of every project within an organisation. Quoted companies in the US and their international subsidiaries must also comply with provisions of the Act.

Pavyer (2005) states that companies surveyed by AMR indicated that they expected to see business benefits from the work undertaken to comply with the above regulations, the business benefits being ranked as follows.

1. better alignment between business policies and related controls
2. improved capability to manage risks in the business

3. heightened importance of compliance related operations as part of every activity
4. improved governance of IT functions core to business operations
5. improved accountability across the entire organisation
6. improved financial decision making
7. better visibility into performance at business levels
8. improved ability to react to changes in market conditions.

The section most relevant to risk management, however, is section 404 of the Act 'Management Assessment of Internal Controls'. To fully present the impact of this section on businesses would require discussing the roles of external auditors and management in reporting financial performance of companies. In simple terms, within a risk management perspective, the Sarbanes-Oxley Act introduced the following principles:

- The risk of fraudulent, inaccurate, financial reporting must be reduced to a minimum.
- The effective financial reporting process is based on effective financial internal controls to ensure that financial transactions are accounted for effectively during the year and the control of financial statements by external auditors at year end.
- External auditors cannot audit fully internal control systems and senior management's responsibility should include making sure that a system of financial internal control is in place within the company.
- At year end external auditors should produce a report on the system of financial internal control in addition to their annual audit opinion on the accuracy of the accounts.

Section 409 requires public disclosure of material changes in financial condition or operation for those firms reporting under section 13(a) or 15(d) of the Securities Exchange Act of 1934.

It should be noted that the Sarbanes-Oxley Act's risk and the risk response (control) covers only the financial reporting process. Moxley (2003) points out that 'the rules drafted by the US regulator the Security and Exchange Commission (SEC) to implement the legislation talks only about a very narrow form of internal control . . . in relation to financial reporting and controls over information filed with the SEC'.

More globally the Act has re-established a more generic principle that management is ultimately responsible for anything that concerns the company they manage and thus that they should be aware of any risk that threatens their business and not only the risk of inaccurate financial reporting.

Major challenges to the Sarbanes-Oxley Act relate to the added cost burden that compliance has forced on to firms especially in increased auditor fees and additional human, time and financial resources that firms spend to comply. It is almost like mini external audits on top of the statutory yearly audits. Pavyer (2005) states that in a recent survey conducted by Fortune 1000, companies were spending, on average, US$4 million to comply with SOX and according to a *Financial Times* report, such companies will pay another US$2.9 million to ensure ongoing compliance. This covers spending across a range of business processes – financial, IT, operational – with an increasing amount expended on technology components.

Complying with SOX is an enormous challenge. With senior executives' personal liberty on the line it is inevitable that US companies will extend the spirit of the act beyond its graphic boundaries. It is, however, essential that with the returns from an investment of this magnitude, procedures go beyond tick-box compliance, particularly in terms of the risk management processes.

11.6 SUMMARY

Corporate governance provides a framework for all major organisations. Familiarity of one framework as opposed to another will often depend on the choice of framework and location of the organisation.

Corporate governance in itself is not new. The corporate governance frameworks in place now allow organisations to address the requirements to manage risk in a structured way.

Auditing and monitoring are inherent to corporate governance frameworks and these systems can be developed to aid in the management of risk.

12

Risk Management and Basel II

12.1 INTRODUCTION

Basel II is primarily a set of guidelines (framework) for the supervision of capital. Most banks use an internal rating-based (IRB) approach to determine credit risk based on borrowers' probability of default. During economic downturn losses on defaults are often greater than normal. Many banks seek to assess loss given default (LGD) on an exposure-by-exposure basis (risk on a loan-by-loan basis). Most banks do not as yet assess risks on a portfolio basis.

In the banking world, there is a variety of practice with respect to the risk rating process, ranging from systems almost purely driven by statistical models, like credit scoring, to those based almost exclusively upon judgement. Generally three broad process categories can be discerned, according to the degree to which the risk rating is a product of mathematical models or of decisions of judgement (Grupo Santander 2000):

- 'Statistical-based processes'
- 'Constrained expert-based judgement processes'
- 'Expert-based judgement processes'.

Credit risk is the risk of loss from the failure of a borrower to meet debt servicing and other payment obligations on a timely basis. Because there are many types of borrowers (individuals, small businesses, large businesses, sovereign governments and projects using project finance) and many types of facilities, credit risk takes many forms. However, there is a clear consensus that the credit risk associated with a loan depends on:

- credit exposure
- maturity
- default probability during that period and
- likely severity of loss if default occurs.

In order to measure the credit risk, financial institutions have to estimate adequately:

- the probability of default (PD) related to the borrower
- the loss given default (LGD) related to the facility.

It is considered by many practitioners that the most appropriate way to estimate PD and LGD is to start with external data and adapt it progressively to the financial institution's needs and environment.

For corporate lending, most rating systems are based on quantitative and qualitative evaluation. More and more financial institutions adopt a two-tier rating system. Firstly, a borrower risk rating linked to the probability of default concept. Secondly, a facility risk rating linked to the loss given default concept. Facility risk rating (FRR) depends on the seniority of the facility and the quality of the securities.

At this stage the links between risk rating, provisioning and capital charges are discussed.

The pricing is calculated as follow:

$$P = CM + O + CMR + S$$

where:

$P =$ Pricing
$CM =$ Cost of fund
$O =$ Overhead cost (generally includes all cost related to credit management but excludes specific overhead cost related to facilities and monitoring that are supported by fees)
$CMR =$ Cost of maintaining credit risk based on PD and LGD, and
$S =$ Desired net spread as determined by top management of the financial institution.

The cost of fund is the total of cost of debt and cost of capital. The cost of debt is the borrowing cost paid to acquire fund on the market, such as client's deposits or borrowing from other financial institutions. The cost of capital is the rate of return required by shareholders, which should be risk adjusted return on capital.

The cost of fund depends on reserve requirement, diversity and availability of funding channels, the base lending rate and the risk related to the financial institution. It needs to be assigned to lending activities.

In the financial world, to correctly price loans and other credit products is paramount to the lender's success. If a financial institution prices its loans too low in relation to the risk associated with the loans, its financial strength will deteriorate and this could affect its survival over time. At the opposite end, if the financial institution prices its loans too high, its competitiveness will deteriorate which would also affect its survival over time.

This chapter outlines the principles behind risk pricing and corporate lending. The concepts of probability of default, loss given default, provisioning, capital charges, pricing and cost of funds, the risk rating system and the methodology to apply the risk rating system are also discussed.

12.2   RISK RATING SYSTEM (RRS)

Hempel and Simonson (1999) state:

> *Most banks use a risk rating system to measure the risk of their loans because risk rating forces the loan personnel to quantify the risk perceived in their loans.*

RRSs are based on both quantitative and qualitative evaluation. The final decision is often based on an amalgam of many different items. The systems can be based on general considerations and on experience, but seldom on mathematical modelling. They also often rely on the judgement of the ratings evaluators.

Globally, more and more commercial banks and other financial institutions adopt a two-tier rating system as a requirement of the Basel Committee on Banking Supervision (2004). The system is composed of a borrower risk rating (BRR) linked to the probability of default concept and a facility risk rating linked to the loss given default concept. FRR depends on the seniority of the facility and the quality of the security.

Worldwide, the key issue for financial institutions is obtaining the right information and reliable data on borrowers or the borrowers' exposure. The credit analyst must assess the information available (data collection) in order to assess the risk. This is why analysts require experience and expertise to identify both reliable and unreliable data. Similarly it is difficult to rely on an automatic scoring system for larger borrowers.

12.2.1   Concept of Probability of Default

Credit risk exists in every credit engagement, and credit loss expenses must be expected as an inherent cost of doing business. Estimating PD is the first step in the process of calculating the probability of loss.

The key element in PD estimation is the definition of default. The Basel Committee on Banking Supervision defined (New Basle Accord, 2004, p. 80):

A default is considered to have occurred with regard to a particular obligor when either or both of the two following events have taken place:

- *The bank considers that the obligor is unlikely to pay its credit obligations to the banking group in full, without recourse by the bank to actions such as realising security (if held). The elements to be taken as indications of unlikeliness to pay include:*
  - o *The bank puts the credit obligation on non-accrued status.*
  - o *The bank makes a charge-off or account-specific provision resulting from a significant perceived decline in credit quality subsequent to the bank taking on the exposure.*
  - o *The bank sells the credit obligation at a material credit-related economic loss.*
  - o *The bank consents to a distressed restructuring of the credit obligation where this is likely to result in a diminished financial obligation caused by the material forgiveness, or postponement of principal, interest or (where relevant) fees.*
  - o *The bank has filed for the obligor's bankruptcy or a similar order in respect of the obligor's credit obligation to the banking group.*
  - o *The obligor has sought or has been placed in bankruptcy or similar protection where this would avoid or delay repayment of the credit obligation to the banking group.*
- *The obligor is past due more than 90 days on any material credit obligation to the banking group. Overdrafts will be considered as being past due once the customer has breached an advised limit or been advised of a smaller than current outsanding.*

The easiest method of PD estimation is based on historical data, where estimates are made for each rating grade. This data could be built internally and/or taken from external sources. However, for a specific internal RRS, it is preferable for a financial institution to build its own database that corresponds to its environment and specific market involvement. The PD does not include a loss component but only the number of defaults within a given time period. Basel II requires estimating one year PDs based on long maturity average (minimum five years).

The formula is:

$$PD\,(5\text{ years}) = \frac{\text{Number of borrowers with X that defaulted}}{\text{Number of borrowers with rating X}}$$

$$PD\,(1\text{ year}) = PD(5\text{ years})/5.$$

12.2.2   Concept of Loss Given Default (LGD)

LGD is usually defined (Basel Committee on Banking Supervision 2004) as the ratio of losses to exposure at default. Once a default event has occurred, loss given default shall normally include three types of losses:

- the loss of principle
- the carrying costs of non-performing loans, for example interest income foregone and
- workout expenses (collections, legal).

LGD is not attributed to the borrower but to the facility. The loss is linked to the maturity of the facility (seniority) and the security that supports the loan.

Most financial institutions adopt the dual method to estimate LGD. For acceptable (from very low to moderate) risk rates, they attribute to each security and to each maturity a LGD estimate based on historical data. Basel II requires estimating one year LGD based on long maturity average (minimum seven years).

For high and very high risks, LGD becomes specific and usually takes into consideration:

- realisation value of the security that supports the loan (RVG)
- workout expenses including legal fees and collections (W)
- outstanding balance of maturity loans or the approved amount of credit lines (OL) and
- carrying costs of non-performing loans such as interest income foregone (CC).

The formula can be expressed either in:

- in absolute terms: $LGD = (OL + W + CC) - RVG$ or
- in percentage terms: $LGD = ((OL + W + CC) - RVG)/OL^* 100\%$.

In order to keep LGD estimates up to date, financial institutions should monitor the value of the collateral on regular intervals, at minimum once a year. More frequent monitoring is suggested where the market is subject to significant changes in conditions or hysteresis in the currency markets. A qualified analyst could evaluate the collateral when market news indicates that the value of the collateral may decline materially relative to general market prices or when a credit event, such as default, occurs.

12.2.3 Database

It is important for a financial institution to start building a database in order to estimate PD and LGD adequately. This database should correspond to BRR (PD) and FRR (LGD). Except for major banks in the global market, most financial institutions do not have data categorised by risk rates. They usually rely on external data such as Moody's or Standard & Poor to estimate their PD and LGD. Most financial institutions build internal databases so as to be more precise with their future estimation. In general, the longer the period and the bigger the customer number the database covers, the better the estimation of PD and LGD. In particular, if the database records the evolution of at least one complete economy cycle including recession in a local market, it will provide representative information for the institution.

12.3 BORROWER RISK RATING SYSTEM AND PROBABILITY OF DEFAULT

Analysing a borrower's risk means estimating the likelihood that this borrower will default on its obligation over a specified period.

The rating process includes quantitative, qualitative and legal analyses. The quantitative analysis is mainly based on the client's financial report. The credit analyst should analyse the financial strength of the borrower in order to determine if cash flow is sufficient to cover its global debt. Then the asset's quality and the liquidity position of the borrower are analysed in order to determine whether or not the borrower's organisation could survive in an unexpected difficult situation such as economic recession (robust finance).

The qualitative analysis is mainly about the quality of management, the organisation's competitiveness within its own industry and its vulnerability to changes in technology, labour relations and regulatory changes. Regarding the industry, the analyst should take into account the environment and characteristics of the industry to which the borrower belongs, and the position of the borrower within this industry. The analyst should also consider the macro-economic situation and its eventual impact on the client. Finally, the analyst should identify the authenticity and legality of the establishment of the borrower through a legal analysis.

12.3.1   Facility Risk Rating and Loss Given Default

After identifying the borrower's risk, the analyst should assess the facility risk. The way the facility will be structured depends to a large extent on the borrower's risk. The facility risk rating depends on the maturity of the facility and the quality of the security to support the loan. In project financings by using project finance the facility risk rating will be determined by the strengths of the revenue generation streams since there will be no or limited recourse to the borrower's assets.

It should be borne in mind that a strong security (or collateral) does not improve the borrower rating since it has no (or very low) impact on the probability of default. Therefore, if the BRR is not acceptable as per the financial institution's policy, no security could deter a reject decision. The only exception to this rule is the cash collateral where the loan is fully secured by a cash deposit or equivalent. However, security serves only as a mitigating factor given the BRR is acceptable.

The maturity of the facility also contributes to the FRR, i.e. the longer the maturity the riskier it becomes.

12.3.2   Expected Loss

The expected loss (EL) is therefore:

$$EL = PD \times EAD \times LGD$$

PD = Probability of default
EAD = Exposure at default – the outstanding balance of maturity loans or the approved amount of line of credit (revolving)
LGD = Loss given default

The manner by which the EAD (exposure at default) is assessed is closely related to the nature of the loan facilities. For a term loan, a financial institution might calculate its EAD as the outstanding balance on the loan at the time of default. If the financial institution has extended a line of credit to a firm but none of the line has yet been drawn down, the immediate EAD is zero, but this doesn't reflect the fact that the firm has the right to draw on the line of credit. Indeed, if the firm gets into financial distress, it can be expected to draw down on the line of credit prior to any bankruptcy. A simple solution is for the bank to consider its EAD to be equal to the total line of credit.

12.4   RISK RATING AND PROVISIONING

Basel II requires total provisions to be equal to total expected losses. This means that provisions are made to cover expected losses (EL). For every FRR there is an EL attached to it. Therefore, financial institutions should make provisions corresponding to the EL attached to each FRR.

In the case of a lack of reliable data on expected losses, financial institutions normally take two types of provisioning: general and specific. Specific provisions are made for losses recognised at the balance sheet date. A loss is recognised when the financial institution considers that the creditworthiness of a borrower has undergone such deterioration that the financial institution no longer expects to recover the loan advance in full. Regarding general provisions, they should be for advances already impaired but not yet identified as such. In order to protect the financial institution's capital base from the damage of these losses, the financial institution shall pre-set proper provisioning proceeds as the 'buffer', which is usually from the interest income of each loan.

12.4.1   Risk Rating and Capital Charges

The management of a financial institution will usually take its capital as the financial resources available to absorb unexpected losses (UL). The increasing competition on the financial market exposes financial institutions to increasing risk. Thus, the capital becomes more important as a buffer against losses. The more risk a financial institution takes, the more capital it will need. This is described as risk-adjusted capital. For Basel I, the risk-adjusted capital ratio (RACR) is calculated as follows:

$$\text{RACR} = \text{Capital/Risk-adjusted assets} \geq 8\%$$

Risk-adjusted assets are calculated by applying risk-based weights to specific assets and summing the results.

Nowadays, Basel II (Basel Committee on Banking Supervision 2004) adopts more or less the same philosophy but introduces a new risk factor, the operational risk. The equation now becomes:

$$\text{RACR} = \text{Capital/(Operational risk} + \text{Market risk} + \text{Credit risk)} \geq 8\%$$

In both cases capital has to be adjusted to risk taken by the financial institution. This means that for each risk rate, a certain percentage of capital should be assigned as risk weight. For example, the capital required for BRR 1 is 20%, for BRR 2 is 25% and for BRR 10 is 90%.

This concept considerably affects the pricing. The cost of funds included in the pricing is defined as the total cost of debt and cost of capital. The cost of capital is the rate of return required by shareholders. The capital is a buffer against losses. Therefore the return on capital should be risk adjusted return on capital (RAROC).

$$RAROC = \frac{\text{Revenue} - \text{Expenses} - \begin{array}{c}\text{Expected} \\ \text{losses}\end{array} + \begin{array}{c}\text{Income from} \\ \text{capital (free of risk)}\end{array}}{\text{Capital}}$$

Expected losses represent expected losses from defaulting loans; capital is simply held as a buffer against losses and is presumably invested in some free risk instrument. Therefore we should reflect the extra income from that investment.

In project finance initiative (PFI) projects, for example, in a project scoring 3 on a 1 to 7 grading (which is usually the case) for every drawn pound, a pound has to be put away, and for every undrawn pound loaned 75 pence has to be put away. Previous to Basel II for every pound drawn, a pound had to be put away and for every undrawn pound loaned, 50 pence had to be put away. This was usually across the board irrespective of whether the loan was lending to junk or safer assets such as PFI projects. In effect PFI assets were discriminated against.

Although for Credit Grade 3, as cited in the above example, the undrawn is 25 pence more under Basel II, it is the corporate lending that suffers since the PD/LGD is much higher for corporate lending since you may only get back 12 pence in the pound under a default situation.

12.5   RISK RATING AND PRICING

After the risks have been identified and the decision to grant the credit has been made, it remains to integrate the credit decision to the pricing system. The pricing has to take into consideration the cost of maintaining credit risk (CMR). CMR represents the expected loss and the accompanying cost of carrying such losses for each type of borrower and facility. According to Hempel and Simonson (1999):

$$P = CM + O + CMR + S$$

where:

P = Pricing
CM = Cost of funds

O = Overhead costs (generally includes all cost related to credit management but excludes specific overhead cost related to facilities and monitoring that are supported by fees)

CMR = Cost of maintaining credit risk based on PD and LGD

S = Desired net spread as determined by top management of the financial institution

The cost of the fund is the total of cost of debt and the cost of capital. The cost of debt is the borrowing cost paid to acquire the fund on the market such as client's deposits or borrowings from other financial institutions. The cost of capital is the rate of return required by shareholders. Considering the capital is expected to work as the buffer against unexpected losses, the return on capital should be risk-adjusted return on capital.

The cost of the fund depends on reserve requirement, diversity and availability of funding channels, the base lending rate and finally the risk related to the financial institution itself. Northern Rock recently got into financial difficulties because interbank loans margins increased due to liquidity issues (uncertainty in the market). The cost of borrowing increased dramatically and the bank had to rely on the Bank of England to resolve the short-term cash flow issues. It is important to note that Northern Rock is a profitable organisation; further enhancing the importance of cash flow management.

12.5.1   Interest Rate and Fees

Generally, the income of a financial institution from a loan is composed of two parts: interest and commitment fees. Interest is the primary revenue source.

Commitment fees on loan facilities are usually the secondary income resource for a financial institution. They are supposed to cover specific overhead costs related to facilities and monitoring.

12.5.2   Managing Liabilities and the Cost of Funds

The cost to a financial institution to attract funds in the money market will be justified according to the risk profile of the financial institution's credit assets portfolio. Many banks attempt to measure their profitability by credit product lines; these being small business, large enterprises and consumers. Each credit product line will be deemed as a profit centre with its own balance sheet and income statement. Therefore, the financial institution's management shall assign a cost of fund to each of the credit product lines, which is called 'internal transfer price' including all costs in relation to raising funds on the money market such as interest and administrative costs, desired return on equity and overhead cost related to general credit management (senior management, risk management and portfolio management). The specific overhead cost related to facilities and monitoring is usually supported by fees, and therefore not included.

This internal transfer pricing is usually calculated by the treasury department in a bank. Hempel and Simonson (1999) summarised that most banks use a matched maturity framework that assigns rates by identifying the effective maturity of assets and assigning a rate obtained from a liability of the same maturity.

12.6   METHODOLOGY OF RRS AND RISK PRICING

A typical risk rating system (RRS) will assign both a BRR to each borrower or a group of borrowers and a FRR to each available facility. An RRS is designed to express the risk of loss in a credit facility and then to price this risk loss.

A good RRS should offer a carefully designed, structured and documented set of steps for the assessment of each rating. Therefore, an RRS should incorporate a comprehensive and standardised grid analysis. The goal is to generate accurate and consistent RRS, and also to integrate professional judgement to the rating process. Normally, a risk rating methodology (RRM) initiates a BRR that identifies the expected PD of that borrower (or group) in repaying its obligations in the normal course of business. Then, the RRS identifies the risk of loss by assigning an FRR to each credit facility granted to a borrower. RRS quantifies the quality of individual facilities, credits and portfolios. If an RRS is accurately and consistently applied, they provide a common understanding of risk levels and allow for active portfolio management. An RRS also provides the initial basis for capital charges used in various pricing models. It can also assist in establishing loan reserves. In order to keep the rating system consistent with the credit migration, the definition of every rating has to be reviewed at least once a year.

Table 12.1   BRR rating sheet

BRR	Description	Corresponding probable Moody's rating	Probability of default (Per Moody's)	Scoring	Risk quality
1	Excellent	A	0.4	80−100	Very low risk
2	Strong	Baa	0.6	70−79	Low risk
3	Good	Ba1	0.8	65−69	Moderate risk
4	Fair	Ba2	1.2	60−64	
5	Acceptable	B	1.6	55−59	High risk
6	Marginal	Caa	3	50−54	
7	Unsatisfactory	Ca	6	45−49	Very high risk
8	Substandard	C	10	40−44	
9	Doubtful	D	16	35−39	
10	Loss	D	20	0−35	

12.6.1   Example of a Risk Rating System

12.6.1.1   BRR – borrower Risk Rating

- A risk rate is assigned to each customer and should be reviewed at the frequency decided by the BRR rate (a higher rate implies more frequent reviews) (Table 12.1).
- It is based on a scoring system from 0 to 100. This scoring system is based on both qualitative and quantitative evaluation.
- New customers' loan requests should only be accepted with a BRR not worse than 5.

12.6.1.2   Review Process and Early Warning Signals

Like most of the rating systems, the above model adopts the point-in-time approach. It means that BRR is established according to borrower's current condition. This condition could change at any time. The review process is the adequate answer to update the BRR rating. The review frequency and review date are based on the RRS – the higher the risk (BRR), the more frequent the review.

In addition, a clear early warning signal process is incorporated in the model. The early warning signal process is the tool that helps the financial institution to track risk profile changes of the borrower between two reviews. Many studies have confirmed that a high percentage of avoidable losses might have been reduced or avoided had early warning signals been recognised and heeded, and remedial action been initiated in a timely manner.

12.6.1.3 Facility Risk Rating

PD is estimated on 5 year basis. That is why there is no adjustment to make for the medium term (MT). Rates should be upgraded by 1 for short term (ST), and degraded by 1 for long term (LT). Example: if the FRR is originally 5, with ST it becomes 4 and for LT it becomes 6 (Table 12.2).

In the case of multiple collaterals being provided for one facility, the credit analyst should score the higher rate if, at least, one collateral is within the percentage financing parameters. Otherwise it should score the lowest rate.

Table 12.2 FRR rating sheet

Collateral	FRR	Max % financing	LGD	Maturity adjustment	Comments
Cash 1 (with the lender's FI)	0	100 (face value)	0%	No adjustment	
Cash 2 (with other FI)	1	100 (face value)	10%	ST = +1 MT = 0 LT = −1	
Shares (blue Ship)	2	50 (market value)	20%	ST = +1 MT = 0 LT = −1	Market value should be followed on monthly basis
Residential mortgage	3	70 (market value)	30%	ST = +1 MT = 0 LT = −1	Market value has to be updated at least on yearly basis
Commercial mortgage	4	60 (market value)	40%	ST = +1 MT = 0 LT = −1	Same comment
Large enterprise corporate guarantee	5	60 (of tangible net worth)	50%	ST = +1 MT = 0 LT = −1	Same comment. TNW = Total tangible assets minus total liabilities

(continued)

Table 12.2 (*Continued*)

Equipment	5	50 (market value)	50%	ST = +1 MT = 0 LT = −1	Same comment
Other tangible assets	5	50 (market value)	50%	ST = +1 MT = 0 LT = −1	Same comment
Receivables	6	70 (total receivables minus 60 days past due and interrelated companies)	60%	ST = +1 MT = 0 LT = −1	Receivables have to be monitored at least on a monthly basis
Inventory	7	40 (finished product and raw material)	70%	ST = +1 MT = 0 LT = −1	Same comments for inventory
SME corporate guarantee	8	60 (tangible net worth)	80%	ST = +1 MT = 0 LT = −1	The value has to be verified on a yearly basis
Personal guarantee	9	60 (tangible net worth)	90%	ST = +1 MT = 0 LT = −1	Same comments
Other intangible assets	9	–	90%	ST = +10 MT = 00 LT = −1	
No collateral	10	–	100%	ST = +1 MT = 0 LT = No	

ST = Short maturity loan (less than 1 year), MT = Medium maturity loan (1 to 5 years), LT = Long maturity loan (more than 5 years).

12.7   GRID ANALYSIS OR STANDARDISING THE RISK ANALYSIS

Almost every bank has developed their own grid analysis tool as per their specific conditions. In this chapter, a very basic but clear analysis model 'CAMP' is discussed which is a very good analysis tool for banks in developing countries.

For every customer credit analysis, the financial institution needs to recognise the importance of the quality of the financial information initially provided. The information provided must always fully satisfy the quality, adequacy and reliability of the financial statement. The size and reputation of the accounting firm shall be inline with the size and complexities of the borrower and its financial statement.

Then, the credit analyst can analyse the borrower via the 'CAMP' model. CAMP refers to Cash (financial analysis), administration (management), market, and production. The analyst shall evaluate the borrower on these four aspects and compute a score. The resulting score will fall into a BRR rating range. The analysis should also be done according to the industry and current trend. The scoring can be distributed as follows:

- Cash counts for 60% of the scoring:
  o Liquidity position – 10%
  o Financial structure – 10%
  o Debt servicing capacity – 25%
  o Loan structure and covenants – 10%
  o Others – 5%

- Management for 15%:
- Market for 15%
- Production for 10%.

Based on the BRR rating, the analyst can estimate the LGD based on the facility structure, collateral arrangement and the tenor of the loan.

12.7.1 Risk Pricing Based on RRS – Sample Calculation

As seen previously the pricing (P) is calculated as follow:

$$P = CM + O + CMR + S$$

Examples:
Company X is rated BRR '4' and has three loans:

1. A short maturity loan of $10 millions collateralised by receivables estimated at $16 millions.
2. A medium maturity loan of $20 millions collateralised by commercial mortgage estimated at $45 millions.
3. A long maturity loan of $20 millions collateralised by equipments estimated at $40 millions.

BRR '4' = PD of 1.2%

1. Short maturity loan: Receivables = FRR '6'; adjustment for the maturity: FRR becomes '5'; % financing is 62.5% (within parameters); LGD = 50%.
   Pricing should be: P = CM + (1.2% ∗ 50%) + S = **CM + O +** **0.60% + S**
2. Medium maturity loan: Commercial mortgage = FRR '4'; no adjustment for the maturity; % financing 44% (within parameters); LGD = 40%.
   Pricing should be: P = CM + (1.2% ∗ 40%) + S = **CM + O +** **0.48% + S**
3. Medium maturity loan: Equipment = FRR '5'; adjustment for the long maturity: FRR becomes '6'; % financing is 50% (within parameters); LGD = 60%.
   Pricing should be: P = CM + (1.2% ∗ 60%) + S = **CM + O +** **0.72% + S**

As a condition to approve the above three facilities, the credit officer will require the relevant bank loan officer to add 0.6%, 0.48% and 0.72% respectively into the facility rate as the contribution to the bank's 'cushion' against the expected loss from its loan portfolio, or to deduct the risk margin from the bank's profits forecast over these facilities in order to have a risk-adjusted return rate.

12.8   REGULATION IN OPERATIONAL RISK MANAGEMENT

Managing risk and compliance has become an area of major spend in most financial institutions.

The two main regulations in operational risk management have been the Basel Accord which has evolved over time to the new Basel II and the Sarbanes-Oxley Act of 2002. Together they are dominating headlines and giving a lot of compliance headaches to financial institutions, especially US banks. Some critics have questioned whether the two are in conflict.

12.8.1   Basel II

The Basel Committee on banking supervision notes that management of specific operational risks is not a new practice; it has always been important for banks to try to prevent fraud, maintain the integrity of internal controls and reduce errors in transaction processing. However, what is relatively new is the view of operational risk management as a comprehensive practice comparable to the management of credit and market risk in principle, if not always in form.

The committee defines operational risk as the risk of direct or indirect loss resulting from inadequate or failed internal processes, people and systems or from external events. This includes legal risk but excludes strategic and reputation risks, although a significant operational loss can affect the reputation of an organisation.

In mid 2004, after a protracted period of consultations, the Basel Committee finally released its definitive proposals on capital charges for operational risk under Basel II. In its proposals it allows internationally active banks to calculate regulatory capital using their own internal models. It therefore has moved away from its original focus on quantitative techniques. It now concentrates on qualitative standards for operational risk management (ORM) systems.

Under Basel II, financial institutions must implement an operational risk management system with an independent operational risk management function responsible for developing and implementing 'strategies, methodologies and risk reporting systems to identify, measure, monitor and control/mitigate operational risk' (Basel Committee on Banking Supervision 2004). To comply with these requirements the ORM system must also be capable of being validated or reviewed regularly by internal and/or external auditors and be seen to 'have and maintain rigorous procedures'.

The Basel II Accord provides three methods for calculating operational risk capital charges:

- the basic indicator approach
- the standardised approach
- the advanced measurement approach (AMA).

Basel II prescribes two major criteria for assessing risks using AMA. For each business line/risk type, a bank will have to provide an exposure indicator (EI), probability of loss event (PE) and loss given event (LGE). Salcanda-Kachale (2007) states that one good thing about the AMA approach is that a bank can use its own internal loss data to show the regulators that – thanks to sound risk management – it should benefit from a further reduced charge. This reduction, though, will be subject to a floor for at least the first two years.

To qualify to use the AMA approach to calculate operational risk under Basel II, a bank must meet stringent 'qualitative standards' (Basel Committee on Banking Supervision 2004) those being:

- an independent operational risk management function
- an operational risk measurement system that is closely integrated into the day-to-day risk management processes of the bank
- regular reporting of operational risk exposures to business units, senior management and the board, with procedures for appropriate action
- The operational risk management system must be well documented
- regular reviews of the operational risk management processes/systems by internal and external auditors
- validation of the operational risk measurement system by external auditors and/or supervisory authorities, in particular, making sure that data flows and processes are transparent and accessible.

To qualify to use the AMA approach, Basel also states that a bank's measurement system must also be capable of supporting an allocation of economic capital for operational risk across business lines in a manner that creates incentives to improve business line operational risk management.

The accord also provides three methods of calculating reserve requirements:

- Firms may use what regulators enforce, that is: holding up to 12% of gross revenues in reserves – a burden on working capital efficiency.
- They can allocate a different percentage of reserves by segregating their lines of business based on the type of activity.
- They can use the Active Management Approach (AMA), which motivates them to proactively manage operational risk in return for reduced reserves.

Firms are required to analyse their historical losses and other key risk indicators on a regular basis, justify their level of controls, and develop a model for assessing the correct amount of reserves. Although compliance was expected to be by the end of 2006, the real deadline was before that date. Approval under AMA requires three years of historical-loss data and up to two years of running a parallel model to prove to regulators that effective risk management is tightly in place.

There are issues raised on the lack of clear direction in developing approaches to managing operational risk and for supervisors in standardising these approaches.

Patrick McConnell (2004) outlines some of the questions arising due to the lack of clarity, including:

- What would a conceptually sound ORM system look like?
- How can regulators compare one bank's ORM system with another and how can operational risk charges be compared?
- What can a bank use to allocate economic capital across its business units to satisfy the Basel qualitative standards for being integrated into the day to day risk management processes of the bank?

Spielman (2004) contends that Basel II faces many obstacles in the US, as well as other areas of the globe. Questions on the capital charges, and the methodology used to derive them, are growing more persistent. There is the 'home-host' issue over regulatory co-operation and trust that does not appear to be going away soon. In addition, he reports three specific concerns for US financial institutions:

- *Regulatory Clarity* – the main U.S. regulators have disagreed over Basel II's approach to capital charges and methodologies, which have made the waters murky. An agreement was reached which initially subjects only the top ten US internationally active banks to Basel II.
- *Cost* – cost estimates on implementing the Basel II AMA approach could be formidable. In addition, Sarbanes-Oxley has taken centre stage in the US. 'SOX', as it is affectionately known, is a US law and carries stiff legal consequences (fines and prison) for non-compliance. It is rooted in a widely accepted self-assessment methodology (COSO). Monies that previously were ear-marked for operational risk are in some cases going to ensure SOX compliance.
- *Focus* – Basel II has experienced delays, which has left some waiting for the final recommendations in order to fully comprehend the impact it will have on their institution. To the Basel Committee's credit, these delays have helped them obtain industry feedback, resulting in improved recommendations.

However, Spielman counterargues that regardless of the Basel II challenges, it has been monumental in energising operational risk management efforts around the globe, and that the issues, though formidable, will be worked out as more people develop practical methodologies that make sense to their businesses and regulators.

Spielman continues to argue that, whether financial institutions agree with Basel II or not, they would be hard pressed to dispute the benefits of some key components of the AMA, which improve how they manage their institutions. For example, self-assessment is a proven vehicle to building a better risk management culture that helps facilitate transparency from top to bottom. Most business managers will see the value of gaining a greater understanding of how their people, processes, technology and other risk may impede their business goals. Tracking losses and non-financial events that can impact business goals is a great indicator of control effectiveness, and can trigger questions about when trends start to shift in the wrong direction. Audit is essential to the process, and considering audit's input helps to present a balanced view of risk.

12.9 SUMMARY

This chapter has outlined the basic concepts in credit risk management and introduced the most commonly used risk evaluation tool, the risk rating system. Based on the application of the RRS, a simple loan pricing model was discussed. The need to address the requirements of Basel II in terms of PD/LGD to the risks associated with a loan are paramount to the banking industry.

13

Quality Related Risks

13.1 INTRODUCTION

Quality management is a philosophy that seeks to prevent defects in products or services rather than relying on inspection to sort out defects after they occur. Therefore, improper implementation of quality management or lack of it leads to many quality problems which then lead to quality risks. Many organisations use a quality management system (QMS) to mitigate risks, particularly risks inherent in the organisation. Many risks are in fact not risks but bad practice. Bad practice by definition is a risk in itself. A QMS helps create best practice and thus reduces many inherent risks and the risk of not meeting customer expectation.

13.2 DEFINING QUALITY RISKS

Risk refers to a lack of predictability about a problem structure, outcome or consequences in a decision or planning situation (Hertz and Thomas 1984). Quality risk has been defined as the potentiality that a product or service will not meet a consumer's minimum quality standards (Peterson and Wilson 1985).

Quality risks of products and services are often counted as operational risks. Operational risk is defined as the weakness or fallacies in the organisational processes and transactions (Ruin 2001). Managing operational risks not only ensures the comfort that the desired product or service is achieved, but also ensures that the required product or service is constantly of the quality that an organisation can boast of, for customer satisfaction and value for money.

Quality risks arise due to quality problems in products or services. Smith (2000) classified quality problems into performance problems and design problems. These were then categorised into five specific types of quality problems:

- *Conformance problems* – unsatisfactory performance by a well-specified system; users not happy with system outputs.

* Reproduced by permission of A. Merna.

- *Unstructured performance problems* – unsatisfactory performance by a poorly specified system.
- *Efficiency problems* – unsatisfactory performance from the standpoint of system owners and operators.
- *Product design problems* – devising new products that satisfy user needs.
- *Process design problems* – devising new processes or substantially revising existing processes.

Crosby (1985) states that 'there is no such a thing as a quality problem'; quality is seen as a series of managerial problems. He placed a heavy emphasis on top management's role in motivating quality improvement throughout the organisation in addition to targeting the problems to be eliminated.

Poor quality of goods and services can also lead to quality related risks which represents an impact on the survival of any economic unit. Figure 13.1 summarises the risks due to poor quality.

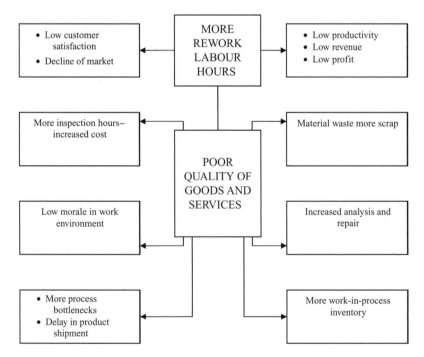

Figure 13.1   Risks encountered by poor quality (Edosomwan 1995)

BM Trade Certification Ltd (Ambrose 2005) stated that it is often found that organisations such as professional services are reluctant to admit that there is any risk of non-conformity in what they do. They are therefore reluctant to allocate resources to controlling something they believe could not exist in their organisation. Non-conformities can often be present but are continually corrected in the course of work, not recorded and therefore repeated.

Feigenbaum (1983) defined a non-conforming unit as 'a unit or service containing at least one departure of a quality characteristic from its intended level or state that occurs with a severity sufficient to cause an associated product or service to not meet a specification requirement'.

13.3   STANDARDISATION – ISO 9000 SERIES

One of the necessary conditions for entry and prestige on the international market is the possession of the ISO standard's certificate. If an enterprise endorses these standards, they maintain QMS, which will ensure that its products/services satisfy the needs and requests of the customers. The aim of this standard's implementation is to gain customer confidence through supplier reliability leading to a more efficient business.

ISO 9000 series was developed by the ISO Technical Committee (TC) 176. It was published in 1987 and is updated approximately every five years. The series consists of five documents whose focus is quality assurance systems: ISO 9000, ISO 9001, ISO 9002, ISO 9003 and ISO 9004 (Lamprecht 1993):

- ISO 9000: Quality Management and Quality Assurance Standards – Guidelines for Selection and Use
- ISO 9001: Quality Systems – Model for Quality Assurance in Design, Production, Installation, and Servicing
- ISO 9002: Quality Systems – Model for Quality Assurance in Production and Installation
- ISO 9003: Quality Systems – Model for Quality Assurance in Final Inspection and Test
- ISO 9004: Quality Management and Quality System Elements – Guidelines.

ISO standards developed in 1987 were revised in 1994 by the International Organisation for Standardisation and had a new version published in 2000. ISO 9000:2000 is far more process oriented than ISO 9000:1994 which was primarily based on procedures. ISO 9001:2000 sets new and different standards. It demands continuously assessing the processes and investigating how to improve them. In this case, it is important to differentiate between process and procedure, procedure is a number of processes.

ISO 9001:2000 identifies a set of outcomes to be achieved and is not specific about how the requirement is met, thus the fundamental responsibility for the design of the management system lies with the organisation creating it. Therefore for the quality system to be truly effective an organisation must consider all the influences on the system – including cultural – especially where this has a direct effect on the customers' experience (Lawson 2003).

Al-Khalifa (2000) stated that the benefits of ISO series certification are:

• creates a quality system and provides a base for a management system
• promotes trade through assurance of contract performance
• opens new markets
• meets EU business requirements
• provides a potential for less waste
• diminishes customer audits
• improves documentation and enhances creditability and
• promotes good working practices.

However, Ackers (2000) stated that in practice the benefits which have been obtained have been variable. He stated that 'the present drafting and audit controls allow scope for companies to comply with the letter of the standard but not its spirit, and companies which have chosen to do this have incurred the costs of implementation without gaining all of the benefits'. Therefore, while an enterprise will not resolve all of their problems upon receiving certification, it will aid the enterprise in winning over the clients and becoming more open (Kumburovic 2000).

Jacobs (2004) noted that optimists will argue that ISO 9001 certificated companies have a better survival rate than non-certificated ones. That may be a statistical fact but it is irrelevant to the fledging business just trying to survive in a relentless market with customers squeezing down prices and pushing up quality demands.

13.4 QUALITY RISKS IN MANUFACTURING PRODUCTS

Among the reasons offered for the failure of total quality management (TQM) initiatives is that firms do not measure quality effectively; they lack essential measures to monitor customer satisfaction, employee morale and management leadership (Sebastianelli and Tamimi 2002). But before quality is measured, organisations must understand the important dimensions they consider for competing on quality. Merna and Patel (2000) suggest that TQM has several facets, those being:

- identifying what (standards, performance, requirements) the customer rally wants
- defining the organisation's mission
- involving all personnel in identifying how the above can be better achieved
- designing ways in which performance can be improved
- measuring how well performance meets the required standard throughout the total production process and
- analysing continually how performance can be improved.

In their research Merna and Patel (2000) noted that of the 35 project management topics considered over the project life cycle risk management and quality management had been ranked 7th and 8th in terms of importance in the management of projects.

Garvin (1987) provides a well-known framework for thinking about product quality that is based on eight dimensions: performance, features, reliability, conformance, durability, serviceability, aesthetic, and perceived quality. Yet, product quality is a complex, multidimensional factor for which a global definition does not exist.

Building customer satisfaction is the next logical step in a chain that leads from product and process quality towards a complete, mutually beneficial relationship of loyalty and trust between customer and supplier (Hampshire 2003). The consequence of faulty products was that the level of customer satisfaction was low, profit margins were being eroded and administration staff spent a disproportionate amount of time and effort correcting these errors, in effect bad practice. Therefore, companies must contain potential quality problems before the product leaves the plant, while providing detailed product genealogy information to trading partners.

To be fair, even organisations with the highest quality reputation might be taken off guard by the emergence of a new quality problem; however, it is presupposed they will soon begin to search for the cause of the defects.

Juran (1988) defined defect as 'any state of unfitness for use, or non-conformance to specification, such as, oversize, low mean time between failures, illegible invoice'. Typical examples of defects are found in products constructed with materials of insufficient strength or durability. The consequence of design defect can be crippling: massive recalls, costly modifications, loss of reputation and sales, even going out of business.

The following deals with the consequences of product defect or non-conformance.

13.4.1   Product Recall

The most severe outcome of poor quality is product recall. Product recall is a term used to describe the actions taken due to non-conformity in products which have already been dispatched to consumers. The actions may consist of amendments made in the field. The actions may also consist of removing the product from the field. Recalled products are as diverse as automobiles, bicycles, chemical sprays, toys, food, and medical devices, to name but a few.

Companies which have the highest standards of quality in design and manufacturing may on occasions find it necessary to withdraw products from service for replacement, modification or refit (Dale and Plunkett 1990).

Recall is a costly and time-consuming event that should be avoided entirely, but without adequate quality programmes of process traceability, too many customers will receive defective products and too many products will be recalled for repair or replacement even though they are not defective. This has enormous implications for the quality-conscious manufacturer that gets rated on the number of recalls it performs, not to mention the risks associated with the direct and indirect costs.

The managing director of Aon's Crisis Management, Harrison (2005), mentioned that 'In addition to obvious food safety risks, many food manufacturers have begun to outsource the production and distribution of their products – lending recipes, production techniques and brand names to third parties. This high level of outsourcing has generated product recall and contamination exposures for third parties and their suppliers. Most suppliers are fully aware of general risks, but many fail to consider the damage their products could do to another company's reputation or its bottom line. The lack of awareness about this exposure means that many small companies are at risk for losses that could put them out of business altogether.' One of the supposed benefits of outsourcing is the risk transfer element. However, many organisations increase the risks associated with their product or service by outsourcing to suppliers. In some cases organisations outsourcing elements of work will mitigate their own risks by insisting on their own personnel being involved and their QMSs are adhered to by the supplier. This is evident in the manufacture of materials for pharmaceutical products.

To decide if a recall is necessary a firm must:

- gather all available information on the suspected defect (arrange testing, talk to consumers who have complained) and assess the reliability of that information (data risk)
- undertake a comprehensive risk analysis
- identify how the problem occurred – consider the possibility of tampering after the product left the firm's premises, or misuse or abuse of the product
- look at all possible ways of addressing the defect and decide whether the firm can repair or modify the product and
- decide what needs to be done.

Such trends underscore for producers the urgent need for quality programmes which not only will enhance the likelihood of turning out products of high initial quality but will provide the necessary records and logs and product-tracking mechanisms that are vitally important in the event of product recall (Feigenbaum 1983).

13.4.2 Re-work

Re-work represents all actions required to transform products which do not meet a pre-specified quality standard into such, fulfilling all requirements (Inderfurth *et al.* 2005). Re-work, in a broad sense, is wasted labour and if continued indicates the quality of work produced by one or more groups of people or departments (Moulis 1992). Re-work can be an expensive risk mitigation method.

Reasons for the existence of re-work include:

- unreliable production processes
- engineering/design defects

- improper interpretation of customer requirements
- inability of used tools or test equipment to meet the desired tolerance
- improper revision level in use and
- improper selection of people for desired operation.

Baker (2000) states that 're-work is a challenging business. There are still a large number of things that can go wrong (making bad things worse), and by the time you figure out that you need to re-work a production run, your deadlines are either very near or have already passed.'

Figures on the amount of re-work do not provide a signpost on how to reduce it. They do provide, however, a basis for understanding the magnitude of the problem. Moulis (1992) indicated that excessive and repetitive re-work usually results in the following:

- excessive and unauthorised use of man-hours reflected in a drain on profit
- excessive manufacturing flow time
- delays in schedule commitments – between departments as well as to customers
- unplanned use of fixed assets – test equipment, fixtures, special tooling, etc. and
- negative effect on morale; people just do not like to continuously go over their work or someone else's work without some indication that the cause is being corrected.

In many cases, defective items incorporate substantial value, such as those caused by expensive input materials, and hence there is an economical incentive to rework those products into 'as new' condition.

13.4.3   Scrap and Wastage

Scrap means scrapping the installed parts and those in stock. It involves the defective products that cannot be repaired, used or sold.

Scrap generation and defect origins are one of the major, basic concepts of evaluating manufacturing performance. They are the criteria and major contributors to the realisation of profit, productivity, quality, on time delivery, maximisation of capabilities, acceptable vendor performance, product redesign, scheduled preventive maintenance, and the list goes on. Since undue scrap losses may reflect poorly on individuals and groups, including supervisors responsible, a temptation to hide scrap losses may often presume to exist (Lester *et al.* 1985).

The major causes of scrap include:

- equipment failure, troubleshooting and waiting for repair
- a non-reported, or unscheduled for repair problem
- in-line production equipment installation and
- incorrect or lack of maintenance procedure (human factor).

Regardless of how a company handles scrap, everyone can agree that scrap is a bad thing. But companies vary as to what they actually do to reduce scrap. Companies should be willing to do more to minimise scrap if raw material is costly (Lynch 2002).

Wastage, on the other hand, is all the activities associated with doing unnecessary work or holding stocks as a result of errors, poor organization, the wrong materials, exceptional as well as generally accepted losses (Oakland and Porter 1995).

Generally speaking, waste is generated due to different types of causes. The following six types of waste are very common, according to Samaddar and Heiko (1993):

- waste due to overproduction
- waste of movement/transport and double handling
- processing waste
- waste due to waiting
- waste due to defects and
- waste due to lack of integration.

What we are concerned about here is wastage due to defects. Product defects themselves, such as scrap, may be a direct source of waste, but by a multiple effect can also bring about additional waste in production. First, rework costs may be incurred. Second, if defects are found in one station all other subsequent stations may have to stop and wait. The latter adds to the cost of the product and increases production lead time. While some defects may appear to be inevitable, the focus should be on designing the process to pre-empt such defects from occurring rather than finding them by inspection.

Waste costs companies money. The more waste that can be eliminated or reduced the greater the opportunity to create an effective and profitable manufacturing operation.

13.4.4   Consumer Complaints

Every organisation offering products to the public is likely to receive complaints at some time. Juran (1988) defined complaints about quality as an assertion of quality deficiency. The complaint may concern the product or it may concern other activities such as incorrect invoicing or shipment of incorrect goods.

Consumer complaints come from a wide variety of sources. Many are made by unsatisfied users of the product. However, many also come from consumers who are satisfied users of the product, non-users of the product, and even non-purchasers of the product (Jacoby and Jaccard 1981). The reason underlying complaints differ between each type of consumer; it thus becomes necessary to identify who is complaining and why, in order to determine if the complaints received are indicative of product defect.

There are a number of factors that influence whether the consumer complains:

- *The manufacturer's reputation* – if a firm has a strong image for quality and a well-known reputation for making adjustments, consumers are more likely to complain when they are unsatisfied (holistic risk).
- *The accessibility of the firm for lodging a complaint* – the consumer is more likely to make a complaint if it can be done at a conveniently located retail outlet.
- *Willingness of the firm to provide redress* – some consumers seek redress or complain only when they are reasonably confident of obtaining a favourable outcome.
- *Perception of organisation's intentions with respect to the problem* – consumers who believe that a firm intentionally deceived them or acted to dissatisfy them would be more likely to complain than those without this perception.

Product satisfaction is why clients buy the product. Product dissatisfaction has its origin in product failures. Customers buy products because of a positive attitude that they have toward the product. Complaints do shed some useful light on field performance but such data must be supplemented by market research to draw conclusions about customer satisfaction. Study of complaints is certainly necessary but it gives a biased picture of performance of a product or of a service (Deming 1986).

13.5   QUALITY RISKS IN SERVICES

Service quality perceptions often arise out of the service delivery process, that is, the interaction of service providers with customers, rather than from the production process (Zeithaml *et al*. 1988).

Unfortunately, interest and research in service quality seems to be running about 60 years behind interest in product quality (Gummesson 1988). One emerging view argues that service purchases are probably perceived as riskier than product purchases (Turley 1990). Since researchers have recognised that services tend to be less uniform than products, quality risk appears to be an issue that service managers need to be aware of when setting strategies.

Service quality perceptions are caused by: professionalism and skills, attitudes and behaviour, acceptability and flexibility, reliability and trustworthiness, recovery reputation, and control (Gronroos 1988). However, an understanding of how consumers evaluate quality is vitally important. It is, after all, the consumer's perception of quality that counts, not management's.

Turley (1990) reviewed a study in which it was concluded that the highest quality-risk service was savings and loans/banks. Therefore, managers of such services need to be particularly concerned with quality-risk perceptions.

Harrow (1997) indicated that public service managers know that, whatever attitude to managing and assessing risk they adopt, there is always the likelihood of public rejection, not only when decisions go disastrously wrong but also when outcomes are not quite as planned. From a competitive point of view, service firms that implement quality-risk reducing approaches should have an advantage over firms that do not.

Dr Joseph Juran, quoted by Hetland (2003), stated that if you continue to do the same thing you will get the same result. Improvement will require changes in the processes. The risks associated with changes, particularly in terms of quality, can result in loss of profit and loss of customers.

Hillier (2004), quoted in Elliott and Atkinson (2007), notes that price falls in recent years have not been what they seemed stating that a new phenomenon, 'stealth inflation', in which the quality of goods and services decline along with price is now prevalent in global markets. The authors suggest that the risks associated with this must be addressed by organisations in the same way as destructive technology. Customers will always seek value for money; however, most customers will have a minimum benchmark and should quality drop below that benchmark they seek alternatives. Similarly with destructive technology customers will seek more efficient ways of meeting specification by insisting on the latest technology available, usually at a more competitive price and with greater efficiency and reliability.

13.6 QUALITY CONTROL AND APPROACHES TO MINIMISE PRODUCT QUALITY RISKS

Productivity and profit improve if adequate quality control tools are applied in organisations. Deming (1986) states that quality to the production worker means that his performance satisfies him, provides him with pride of workmanship.

Improvement of quality shifts waste of man-hours and of machine time into the manufacture of good products. The result is lower costs, better competitive position, and hence better reputation as represented in Figure 13.2.

Early in the twentieth century, the term 'quality control' began to be used as a synonym for 'defect prevention' (Juran 1988). However, later on, the term included tools, skills and techniques through which quality is carried out. Quality control is defined as 'activities designed to minimise the incidence of non-conformance during and after production. Specifications and tolerances are established, process capabilities ascertained,

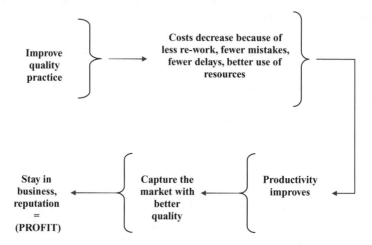

Figure 13.2 Schematic representation of the consequences of quality improvement (Al-Derham 2005)

and tests and inspections performed to compare actual against standard performance' (Enrick 1985).

The seven well-known tools of quality control are as follows (Mizuno 1988):

- *Cause and effect diagram* – a pictorial representation of the main inputs to a process, problem or goal, with detailed sub-features attached to each of the main inputs (also referred to as Ishikawa or fishbone diagrams).
- *Pareto chart* – a bar chart illustrating causes of defects, arranged in decreasing order. Superimposed is a line chart indicating the cumulative percentages of these defects.
- *Check Sheet* – generally in the form of a data sheet, used to display how often specific problems occur.
- *Histogram* – a diagram of the frequency distribution of a set of data observed in a process. The data are not plotted in sequence, but are placed in the appropriate cells to construct a bar chart.
- *Scatter diagram* – a collection of sets of data which attempts to relate a potential cause with an effect. Data are collected in pairs at random.
- *Control chart* – a graph of a process characteristic plotted in sequence, which includes the calculated processes mean and statistical control limits.
- *Flow chart* – a picture of a process, using engineering symbols, pictures, or block diagrams, which indicates the main steps of a process.

Smith (2000) introduced strategies and techniques for solving his classification of quality problems mentioned previously as shown in Table 13.1.

A quality aware company can eliminate most of the cost caused by a quality problem by directly and immediately focusing on quality improvement (Freiesleben 2004). Continuous improvement of processes and systems can be effectively achieved using statistical and associated techniques that help identify, predict and reduce process variation, and so improve consistency and quality (Grigg 2004).

Although we must accept the fact that variability does exist, there are methods to control it within satisfactory boundaries. Statistical tools are available to identify quality problems but must have support of management to improve quality. Deming has stated that 85% of the causes of quality problems are faults of the systems which will remain with the system until they are reduced by management. The following is a list of the more common statistical tools used in quality control application

Table 13.1   Types of quality problems and their problem solving techniques (Smith 2000)

Quality problem type	Solving strategies and techniques
1. Conformance problems	Use statistical process control to identify problems, cause and effect diagrams to diagnose causes.
2. Unstructured performance problems	Diagnostic methods; use incentives to inspire improvement; develop expertise; add structure appropriately.
3. Efficiency problems	Use employees to identify problems; eliminate unnecessary activities; reduce input costs, errors and variety.
4. Product design problems	Quality function deployment translates user needs into product characteristics. Value analysis and 'design for' methods support design activity.
5. Process design problems	Use flowcharts to represent processes, process analysis to improve existing processes, re-engineering to devise new processes and benchmarking to adapt processes from others.

(Hubbard 2003). These tools have specific applications in industry, and care should be taken to select proper one, as shown in Table 13.2.

Tassoglou (2006) identifies both qualitative and quantitative tools and techniques that are used to determine quality related issues. These include decision collecting tools, decision assessing tools and statistical process control tools which he concludes can be used in the data collection and data processing stages of a risk assessment.

Table 13.2   Common statistical tools used in quality control application (Hubbard 2003)

Statistical tool	Use
1. Acceptance sampling plans	Evaluate product attribute quality.
2. Analysis of variance	Establish significance of difference between two sets of data.
3. Cusum chart	Cumulative subgroup difference plot.
4. Design of experiments	Provide valid data with minimum test.
5. Process capability	Level of yield uniformity.
6. Statistical inference	Significance of data difference.
7. Taguchi method	Specification and tolerance technique.

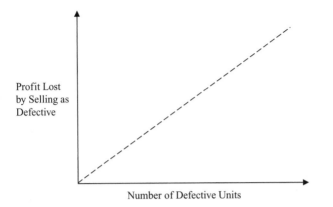

Profit Lost
by Selling as
Defective

Number of Defective Units

Figure 13.3 The financial loss incurred by the increase in the number of defective units (Al-Derham 2005)

Above all, the focus should be on eliminating core issues that cause problems, and taking steps to re-engineer processes and continuously monitoring and reviewing operational procedures. Management must accept any potential or known problem as a challenge and, more importantly, an opportunity to improve and control deficiencies.

Cost of poor quality measurement has proven to be a useful tool for focusing management attention on the profit impact of poor quality. Figures 13.3 and 13.4 illustrate a general representation of the relationship between defects and profit.

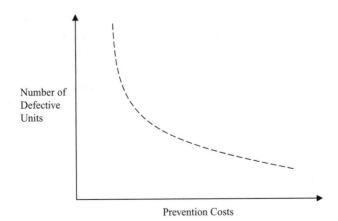

Number of
Defective
Units

Prevention Costs

Figure 13.4 A graph showing the decrease in the number of defective units as the prevention costs increase (Al-Derham 2005)

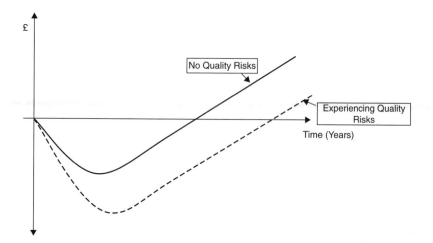

Figure 13.5   The effects of quality risks on the cash flow (Al-Derham 2005)

These defects lead to quality risks which consequently affect the cash flow negatively as illustrated in Figure 13.5.

Clearly, the costs associated with pure risk, that being negative effects, can have a major affect on a project's or investment's cash flow. The QMS helps to mitigate risks associated with quality and provides the first step to avoiding inherent risks in an organisation.

13.7   SUMMARY

Quality management systems and the tools and techniques used in assessing quality problems are used extensively to avoid bad practice. Bad practice alone is a major risk to any organisation. The risks associated with not meeting the required quality standards in terms of specification, delivery, quality and quantity can have serious financial implications.

All organisations require QMS. The ISO Standards form a framework for creating best practice and traceability. The processes associated with any service or product or project can not only be addressed in terms of conformance but also assessed in terms of the risks associated with each process.

14
CASE STUDY 1
Risks in Projects in the Pharmaceutical Industry

14.1 INTRODUCTION

Pharmaceutical companies spend billions of US dollars each year in the development of new products. On average, the development of a new drug costs between US$300 and US$800 million and takes between 8 and 12 years from conception of the initial idea for a drug design to production of a final product. The average success rate is about 1 in 12 ranging from 1 in 4 for 'me too' to 1 in 25 for 'blue-sky' products. Approximately 40% of the 'starting candidates' are not sanctioned for further development during the first 12 months of the drug development process (DDP).

Every drug discovered in the laboratory development stage is a potential candidate for further development. The decision to sanction further development is dependent on the results of tests at each stage of the DDP, the costs, time and risks associated with a particular candidate. The development of drugs is dynamic which results in numerous drugs being developed at any one time within the drug development industry. The development of drugs can be considered as a number of discrete phases, each having inherent risks at each stage of the DDP.

(A 'me too' drug can be defined as a drug product which may be typified by the commonly used antibiotic type drug following a composition that is already well established and not subject to a patent. An example of a 'blue-sky' product would be a drug which would be the first in its class, an example of this may be one which could cure cancer, or a drug such as Viagra which has recently been released to the market.)

Drug development often involves leading edge technology. This usually entails a long development period which is subject to extensive testing and regulation. However, the long-term effects of drugs are not always discovered in the DDP. In the case of Thalidomide, for example,

---

* Reproduced by permission of A. Merna.

which had a devastating effect on some children, the consequences were not apparent for many years after its production. The devastating effects of Thalidomide led to improved and stricter requirements for clinical testing. It should be noted that Thalidomide is currently being used in the treatment of Acquired Immune Deficiency Syndrome (AIDS) and as a painkiller and is still approved for use in Brazil and Mexico in its original form.

The development of Viagra, which began as a cure for angina, was found to have a side effect which reduced sexual dysfunction syndrome (SDS) predominantly in men and has, to date, proved to be a spectacular success. However, no data is yet available about the medium- to long-term effects of this drug.

Similarly the possible medium- to long-term effects from genetically modified crops such as soya, maize or potatoes are uncertain since a great deal of the gene technology is essentially new, and different from old methods of cross-breeding. The imposition of a global ban on available genetically modified crops or drugs, often the result of public outcry reflected in changes to regulatory procedure, could cause devastating commercial losses for the developers and producers. At the time of writing the British Medical Association (BMA) announced they were seeking a total ban on genetically modified crops subject to further monitoring to determine the effects on humans and the environment.

14.2   THE PHARMACEUTICAL INDUSTRY

Over 50% of worldwide pharmaceutical sales are developed by the top 20 international pharmaceutical companies. Most of these companies are based in the United States and Western Europe with bulk manufacturing facilities located in countries offering financial incentives, particularly Ireland, Singapore and Puerto Rico.

The 1990s have brought many changes to the pharmaceutical business, driven by a significant increase in mergers and acquisitions among major pharmaceutical companies. Most companies now focus on their core competencies of developing and marketing new drug products.

For example, a company might use a contract manufacturer to produce a bulk drug which is due to lose its patent, but would typically manufacture a new blockbuster product in house, to ensure total control of that drug over most of its patented life.

Another significant trend is the movement of traditional chemical companies away from commodity products towards high margin speciality products, particularly pharmaceutical and agricultural chemicals. Rhône-Poulenc, Monsanto, Pfizer Lambert, Hoechst and Zeneca are major international companies, which divested their commodity portfolios in order to concentrate on the high value healthcare industry.

The programme of drug design, development, production and finally marketing a drug product that is efficacious in the treatment of a human or animal condition is not highly innovative since the process is well known and understood and is also subject to regulation. However, the approach to the chemistry and the structure of the newly devised molecule may be innovative since the outcome cannot be stated with reasonable certainty at the start of the DDP.

There is generally very little historical data from which a basic starting block for the development of a new drug can be drawn. In the past companies tended to carry out intensive research into the cellular structure, nerve system or locations of the anatomical part of the human or animal. This development programme did not differentiate between beneficial whole body effects and any associated side effects.

In today's market, the efficacy (i.e. the ability of a drug to produce a desired clinical effect such as protection against infection at a prescribed dose rate) of a drug is more likely to be designed to combat disease and illnesses in a localised manner rather than the whole body. This involves much more in-depth research into the parts of the body requiring treatment and has resulted in improved drug design methods. The refining of the methods in which drugs are designed and developed has also impacted upon the way in which the chemicals are produced for the different stages of the DDP. The refining process has also resulted in an increase in the size of the chemical molecules as drug designs become increasingly complex.

The starting materials can be described as the basic building blocks to which the pharmaceutical company attaches further building blocks. The addition of these building blocks of molecules produces the active and effective drug to be employed in the treatment of specific human or animal conditions. Outsourcing the procurement of starting materials required for use in a candidate DDP is common practice.

During the development process the drug progresses through a number of major stages as shown in Figure 14.1.

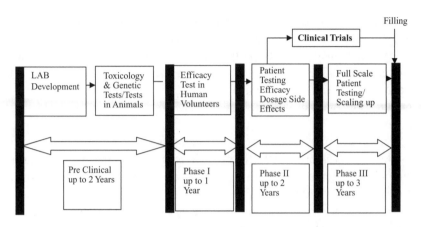

Figure 14.1   The major stages of a typical drug development process

During the DDP the following factors have to be taken into consideration and all data and information required by both internal and external authorities made available.

- *Quality assurance (QA)* – this factor requires that each step of the drug development process is adequately documented, recorded and traceable.
- *Quality control (QC)* – control methods are required as part of the development process to ensure all necessary tests which control such elements as impurity level tolerances and particle size are carried out.
- *Accepted good manufacturing practice* – all pharmaceutical facilities must meet current good manufacturing practice (cGMP) guidelines, the interpretation of which can vary from company to company and from supplier to supplier. The pharmaceutical company's quality control departments are usually looking for more stringent application of cGMP than those found in other manufacturing industries. Prevention of contaminants from operatives and cross-contamination is paramount. Dedicated equipment for testing and production is essential, often resulting in the need for comparmentisation during the DDP and subsequent manufacture. It is common for a candidate drug to be developed at more than one location as part of the DDP.
- *Toxicity* – this is the most important test carried out in the pre-clinical stage of a DDP. A drug can not proceed along a development path if it is found to be highly toxic.
- *Tests in animals* – these are important tests in the pre-clinical stage of a DDP; it is during this part of the development stage that carcinogens,

mutators and various other undesirable side effects are isolated. Animal testing is carried out prior to first-in-man tests to ensure that no serious harmful side effects are delivered to the subject patients.

- *First-in-man tests* – these are self-explanatory. It is during Phase 1 of the DDP that any uncertain harmful or unexpected side effects may be discovered. In 2006 the first-in-man tests for a drug, TGN 1412 manufactured by TeGenaro, as an antibody to cancer resulted in life threatening injuries to a number of the paid volunteers. At the time of writing this book the reasons for this have not yet been made public.
- *Stability tests* – these are performed to ascertain that the drug product will remain stable and efficacious over its stipulated storage shelf life. Testing is carried out throughout the three development phases.
- *Scaling up* – this is the manufacture of bulk quantities of the drug in the latter part of Phase 2 and all of Phase 3, so that clinical trials required for efficacy tests may proceed. The many factors that affect the scaling-up process include: stability, quality and unexpected reactions between substances not encountered during laboratory development.
- *Clinical trials* – a new drug is tested first in the test tube, then in animals and finally in humans. A clinical trial involving patients assesses the safety and efficacy of the therapy under highly controlled circumstances. These trials are carried out in three stages and take between two to four years to complete.

A clinical trial is based on a scientifically designed plan to develop new approaches for treating, diagnosing, or preventing specific diseases.

After clinical trials, regulatory authorities such as the Food and Drug Administration (FDA), European Medicines Evaluation Agency (EMEA) or the British Medical Control Agency (MCA) must approve the product for the marketplace. This normally takes two years.

14.3   FILING WITH THE REGULATORY AUTHORITY

Filing a drug is the act of an official request for permission to prescribe a drug. Approval to prescribe is required from regulatory authorities. The main aim of these authorities is the protection of the general public by enforcing public health laws.

Approximately 70% of the expenditure occurs in the last two to three years of the DDP. This is illustrated by the steepness of the curve in Figure 14.2. This is due to the scaling-up process of the drug in order to produce bulk material for clinical trials. The resourcing and allocation

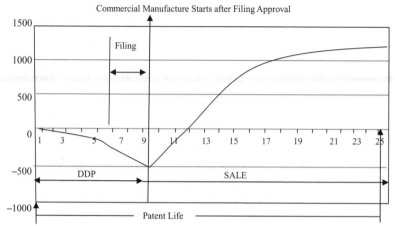

Figure 14.2 Typical cumulative cash flow over the patent life of 20 years. Over the first 6–7 years of the development process approximately 30% of the total development cost is expended

of essential personnel and equipment account for a large proportion of this expenditure.

During this period any small changes made to the constituents of the drug can have major time and cost implications and lead to rejection or substantial re-work. Any changes during this period can affect the acceptance of the drug since it is no longer identical to that originally filed.

Pharmaceutical companies work closely with regulatory authorities, especially in the last three months prior to filing approval. This relationship allows pharmaceutical companies to pre-empt the results and plan bulk manufacture. Once filing has been approved for sale of the drug, full scale manufacturing takes place.

Sales of the drug will determine the steepness of the curve and the commercial viability of the investment. Development costs must be recouped as soon as possible over the remaining patent life. During this period the dose form may be changed to suit customer requirements and efficacy. It should also be noted that during the sales phase of the drug long-term effects of the drug on users often become apparent. Vioxx manufactured by Merck as a treatment for osteoarthritis was withdrawn from sale in 2006, in the early sales period of its life. Litigation regarding this drug is now with the US courts. Thalidomide (Celgene) was originally developed to ease the pain of women in the early stages of pregnancy but resulted in the birth of deformed babies. The drug had been on sale for quite along period of time before the link between deformities and the drug were made. The drug is still sold as a treatment for leprosy.

The important factors associated with DDPs are:

- the product for which regulatory approval has been sought must be identical to that developed, tested and filed
- there is an increasing need to shorten development time and
- product capacity can be increased to meet demand in line with country by country regulatory authority approval.

14.4 IDENTIFICATION AND RESPONSE TO RISKS ENCOUNTERED IN DDPs

It is extremely important that the risks associated with each stage of DDPs are identified early in the development process. In this section the authors identify a number of typical risks which may affect the success of a candidate drug and appropriate risk response measures.

Risk – insufficient financial investment at the appropriate times

As the pharmaceutical industry becomes more competitive clinical trials are being expanded. Data required for filing by the regulatory authorities now needs to be achieved in a much shorter time period.

In order that clinical trials may proceed, adequate data are required by the pharmaceutical company to determine the amount of investment required. To provide the necessary materials for clinical trials, investment is required prior to the availability of confirmatory data proving the efficacy properties of the drug. A lack of financial investment may result in:

- increased development time
- the specified drug may not be produced in sufficient quantity for development to proceed and
- the quality of the drug may not meet the required specification should financial resources be relocated to more commercially viable candidates, resulting in unacceptable or varying tolerances. In DDPs candidate drugs are developed in parallel with a nominated drug considered most likely to achieve the desired results on a fast-track basis. In the event of the nominated drug not meeting the required specification the next most likely candidate is promoted to fast-track status.

The impact of these factors could delay the specified filing date and subsequent approval for marketing. This would in turn reduce the patent life of the drug and adversely affect revenue generation. If, however, a drug is found to be unviable in the early stages of the DDP, development can be stopped and no further investment sanctioned.

Response

The risk factors affecting investment may be reduced by carrying out an in-depth study of the technical and commercial factors affecting the project. The production of detailed documentary evidence that will support and endorse the application for adequate investment in technical, financial and resource requirements for each project is paramount. To ensure that the risk of exceeding clinical trial budgets is reduced the authors suggest that an integrated structured decision-making process is utilised concurrently by both scientific and commercial stakeholders. The decision-making process would be based on the data used, the stakeholders involved and the decision logic used and allow traceability of decisions made at each stage of the DDP. The aim of this being to determine which candidates should be fast-tracked on the basis of the actual/planned time and money allocated to each candidate and identify potential areas of risk at each stage of the drug life cycle.

Risk – unreliable test data

The risks in stability testing and data recording are often due to the omission of certain tests, poorly designed tests procedures, unexpected chemical reactions and particle size problems and human error often as a result of overconfidence due to familiarity of earlier tests. In order to understand the impact of stability on a drug, an understanding of a drug's final dose form is required. In the case of a tablet the size and dose rate are dependent upon the efficacy of the active drug. In a tablet dose form there are also additions of incipient (non-reactive) binding and filler materials required to produce an acceptable product. Stability test data is a mandatory requirement of the authorising bodies for approval and regulatory acceptance. Some of the risks associated with this part of the DDP include:

- a change in dose form which produces a change in the quantity of active drug constituent in the product

- a loss of part of the dose form due to ageing over the product shelf life which also causes loss of active drug constituent
- an unexpected reaction occurring between the active drug element and incipient materials during storage and
- Problems arising in the manufacturing process.

The possibilities of loss of an active drug constituent will be detrimental to the product attaining regulatory approval. This can result in delay in filing and affect the remaining patent life in terms of revenue generation and competitive lead. In some cases extra financial expenditure is required to re-engineer stability problems.

Response

Ensure that all testing has been carried out using best practice, and that any anomalous results have been thoroughly examined and recorded and any rectification work necessary carried out before proceeding to the next stage of development. Additional tests which may effect the drug stability at later development stages such as hygroscopy, shape and size should also be performed at this stage. This should reduce the risks associated with particle size, reactions between active drug elements and incipients and loss of dose form material in manufacture.

Risk – lack of quality assurance and quality control

The introduction of new materials and new suppliers of starting materials may result in the loss of QA/QC leading to a loss of time, money and revenue.

Response

Risks associated with QA or QC can be reduced by the introduction of a suitably designed quality management system (QMS) to monitor and record all stages of the development process including quality control techniques, inspections, specified tests and equipment especially for use with materials never manufactured. The QMS should be regularly audited both internally and externally and regularly updated. The QMS procedures must be developed and updated in parallel with the technical and commercial support available at each stage of the DDP. In some cases a new supplier may be required to adopt the pharmaceutical company's QMS and be supervised by the company's own quality manager, as described in Chapter 13. Although QMSs are common to most manufacturing industries it is surprising that in the pharmaceutical industry many disciplines prefer to retain information in their heads rather than commit it to paper.

Risk – difficulties arising through the outsourcing of starting materials

It is common practice within the pharmaceutical industry to outsource the starter materials for DDPs. This practice brings with it its own specific risks, those being:

- Employment of a new supplier can often result in delivery, quantity and quality problems which may have a serious impact on the production of the starting material.
- Uncertainties in the origins of the material to be synthesised may require specialist chemistry to be employed, such as explosive or cryogenic methods.

Response

A system of pre-qualification procedures and processes should be introduced to review potential suppliers to determine their technical, financial and managerial expertise, past experience, confidentiality and suitability of their own QMS. It is important to note that one of the main benefits of outsourcing is the risk transfer element. It is extremely important that supplier's are made aware of the specification required. New materials are based on specifications provided by the pharmaceutical company which must be strictly adhered to. Any changes made by the supplier to the specification can result in the risk of poor quality or low quantity or a complete loss of usable material. To alleviate this situation additional tests should be introduced by the supplier and witnessed by the pharmaceutical company's technical manager. The supplier should also ensure that his sub-contractors work in accordance with the pharmaceutical company's QMS requirements. The cost of additional tests will be offset against the occurrence of such risks. At manufacturing stage starting materials are often supplied by more than one supplier. It is essential that all suppliers adopt the same QMS and common lines of communication.

Risk – introduction of previously unseen effects due to the scaling-up process

The scaling-up process brings with it a number of risks, these include:

- Changes in the way the chemical's react to produce the active drug, resulting in an unsaleable product.
- Changes in the impurity levels in the active drug product which affects the stability test data results.
- Suitability of the quality management system employed
- Changes in the physical properties of the active drug compound that have a direct effect on both the manufacturing process and on the stability data.

Response

Risks in the scaling-up process may be reduced by:

- appointing experienced personnel in key functional roles
- ensuring that precise details of the production processes developed in the laboratory are recorded and incorporated into the scaled-up process
- ensuring that all necessary tests are completed before proceeding to the next stage of development and that any potential risks identified as a result of reducing risk in one area are analysed.

Risk – poor fit of the equipment to the chemical process

Ill-fitting equipment in the chemical process can result in a loss of valuable time, attaining the specified purity of the active drug element and numerous other related problems. Equipment is often dedicated to one candidate drug or one process in a DDP.

Response

Ensure that the equipment to be used fits the chemistry of the process as closely as possible and is regularly calibrated and maintained. Equipment should be clearly labelled to ensure it is used for its dedicated purpose and the dates and types of previous applications identified.

Risk – lack of suitable experience in key personnel at each stage of the DDP

DDP's typically involve many technical disciplines such as development chemists, biologists, pharmacists, process engineers and laboratory technicians. Commercial and production disciplines are typically drawn from accountants, project managers, IT specialists and technical support staff. The normally long development process often means that many disciplines are only involved with one specific stage of drug development and not the project as a whole. Many disciplines work in isolation, performing tests and recording results which are then passed to the next stage of development without actually being aware of how their results will be interpreted or used. Often the demands of each discipline are not understood throughout the DDP.

The experience of personnel involved in DDPs can be instrumental in causing serious problems on the project with regard to problem solving and critical decision making at each stage of development.

Response

The authors suggest that the project manager should keep all disciplines informed of any problems encountered at each stage of the DDP. The introduction of regular meetings and brainstorming sessions between representatives from each discipline would help bridge cultural and professional boundaries and form the basis for problem solving.

When choosing personnel for a candidate DDP, ensure that key members have adequate experience and are capable of making intuitive decisions when needed as part of a project and not one particular phase. Personnel with the basic skill level but lacking experience should always have a senior or skilled person to advise in situations where important decisions are to be made. Work instructions should form a major part of the QMS and not be seen, as at present, by many scientific disciplines as a barrier to innovation. These instructions should help to identify potential risks within the DDP whilst carrying out the identified processes.

A number of personnel involved in DDPs will have experience of a failed candidate drug who be aware of the reasons for its failure. There will also be personnel with experience of a successful candidate drug who be aware of the reasons for its success. The authors suggest that the choice of personnel for a DDP should include those with experience of success and failure. A combination of the two experiences would provide a more critical review of a DDP as it progresses through development.

Risk – inadequate testing and validation

Omission of certain tests during the processing of intermediate substances and final active drug substance may result in total loss of the product or a serious loss in product quality, quantity and time. This also has an impact on the stability test results.

Response

Ensure that specific intermediate and the final active drug substance tests are carried out and results are recorded prior to validation. This may be achieved by the introduction of a checklist to ensure all necessary tests are carried out and validated in sequential order and have been accepted by all disciplines. This checklist should be incorporated into the QMS. A survey of results found in the application of the drug should be analysed and their findings considered in all future DDPs.

14.5   SUMMARY

The conception, design and development of a drug form is a complex process. Although repetitive, the DDP process, which can involve 1000 activities, is laden with risk and uncertainty at each stage of development.

The drug development industry is in a dynamic environment. Typical risks identified by the authors encountered in DDPs include:

- insufficient financial investment at the appropriate times
- inadequate equipment and lack of suitable key personnel at each stage of the DDP
- the numerous quality functions required in a DDP
- the risk of time overruns at any stage of a DDP
- unreliable test data
- difficulties arising through the outsourcing of starting materials
- changes in regulatory approval.

The pharmaceutical industry has many characteristics of innovative manufacturing industries. The requirement of additional health and safety factors, in some cases longer testing and development times, uncertainty in starting materials and more complex drug designs, however, carry a greater uncertainty than those found in most manufacturing industries. There is also the uncertainty of the product being clinically suitable to all users prescribed the drug which can run into 10 of millions.

The defence and aeronautical industries are also often involved in the manufacture of innovative products. In most cases the funding of such projects is borne by the tax payer. In the pharmaceutical industry DDPs are funded by shareholders and commercial success depends on the volume of sales and selling price over the patent period. Drugs are also market led and do not have the comfort of contract led revenues and are often in competition with other styles of treatment. The funding of DDPs remains a high risk investment with the possibility of high returns or in some cases a total loss of investment.

Although uncertainty will exist over the drug's patent life the authors suggest that the risks identified in the DDP may be reduced, in most cases, by utilising best practice.

Best practice in this case would involve the development and implementation of a decision-making process and a comprehensive QMS to design out as many risks as possible during the DDP. Adoption of a comprehensive QMS would provide pharmaceutical companies with greater confidence that unexpected risks have been reduced during the DDP and subsequent life of the product. Reducing uncertainty will provide more confidence in the DDP investment.

The adoption of a comprehensive QMS may not be seen as a radical measure for reducing risk in DDPs. However, the authors believe that a QMS would not only help in the management of DDPs but also provide the first step to integrating the processes and disciplines involved. The QMS will provide a suitable risk management tool by ensuring that data feedback is analysed at each stage of the drug's life cycle and utilised in future decisions-making processes.

The authors wish to thank Dr Anthony Merna and Mr Edward Gould for allowing them to use this amended version of their paper.

15

CASE STUDY 2
Risk Modelling of Supply and Off-take Contracts in a Petroleum Refinery Procured through Project Finance

15.1 INTRODUCTION

For the last three decades, the oil industry has been burdened with surplus refining capacity, often resulting in low margins. Projects procured using project finance were developed primarily for cogeneration projects, typically undertaken by independent power producers. Compared to refining projects, the technology used in cogeneration projects is known and well proven, and project profitability is reasonably predictable (Jenkins 2005). By comparison, the hydrocarbon industry is far more uncertain. Apart from typical risks in a refinery, the different types of crude oil characteristics can significantly influence refinery cash flow.

The procurement of refinery projects is a high risk venture. Determining how to finance a refinery and manage typical risks in order to get sound economic returns is a major challenge. There are significant risks exposed in refinery business environment, for instance construction risk, demand risk, operation risk and especially price risk on both demand and supply sides. Availability and characteristics of types of crude oil supply and product derivatives can determine the choice of refinery types. Apart from buying crude oil in the spot market and selling its products on a similar basis it is necessary to create significant price certainty to ensure a robust cash flow is achieved. The supply contract and off-take contract can be used to create sufficient certainty of price, quantity and availability of both crude oil and sales of refined products, and thus ensure the financial viability of a refinery project. A mechanism for assessing the risks associated with procuring a refinery is presented

---

* Reproduced by permission of A. Merna.

and an evaluation of the economic parameters modelled in Visual Basic, Crystal Ball and Excel spreadsheet is illustrated.

15.2   FINANCING A REFINERY PROJECT

Financing a modern refinery is a risky business. In oil and gas projects risks can be identified in both upstream and downstream phases respectively. Typical risks faced by a refinery business are illustrated in Figure 15.1.

Project finance requires that the risks identified during the project life cycle are mitigated before sanction of a refinery and sufficient revenues can be generated to service the debt and make an acceptable

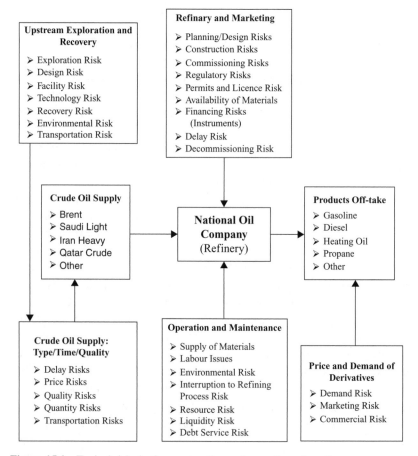

Figure 15.1   Typical risks in the construction and operation of a refinery

profit (Merna and Njiru 2002). Typically the financial instruments used in a project financing are debt, mezzanine (bonds) and equity. The higher-risk projects should normally take more equity to protect the interests of lenders and bond investors and lower-risk projects can accommodate more debt (Merna and Khu 2003).

A major risk in refinery operation is associated with the characteristics and quantities of the crude oil supply which can significantly influence refining margins. Refining low American Petroleum Institute (API) gravity crude oils requires more complex and expensive processing equipment, more processing stages and more energy, therefore costing more. The price difference between high-gravity and low-gravity crude oils reflects the refining cost difference. Investment in facilities to process heavier crude oils allows refiners to improve their profits by reducing the cost of their crude oils supply.

Each type of crude oil will produce different percentages of refined product. Buying cheaper heavy crude oil, for example, will have a high conversation cost to light products compared to buying expensive light crude oil which is cheaper to refine. Mixing a percentage of heavy crude with light crude oil is often used to refine at a lower cost. Therefore, the price difference between light and heavy crude oils and light and heavy products is among the most important variables affecting refinery margins. These differentials are incentives for installing expensive processing facilities in a refinery, including fluid catalytic cracking, hydrocracking, coking and other residual conversion facilities.

15.3   BUNDLING CRUDE OIL CONTRACTS

Bundling is the grouping of projects, products or services within one managed project structure in a manner which enables the group to be financed as a simple entity (Frank and Merna 2004). Similarly, bundling can be also used to bundle crude oil supply contracts to produce the optimum off-take contracts, in terms of refined products.

Modern petroleum refineries are designed to process a variety of indigenous and imported crude oils. Selecting supply contracts is crucial for companies as major costs are involved in purchasing raw materials (Bansal 2006). As the crude oil cost is about 90% of the refinery input cost, the selection of an optimum crude mix is extremely important to achieve higher margins. However, the number of options for buying crude oils under fluctuating prices and transporting them to refineries are huge, thus making evaluation of the crude oil mix extremely difficult.

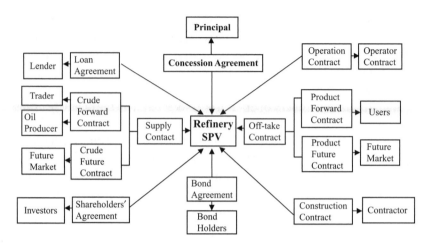

Figure 15.2   Contractual structure of a refinery procured through project finance

Refineries normally purchase crude oil and sell its products on term contracts from forward and future markets and by spot purchases from the spot market. If, for example, a refinery depends on the spot market for supply, then its profit margin could be seriously affected by movements in market prices. Apart from buying crude oil in the spot market and selling its products on a similar basis it is necessary to create significant price certainty to ensure a robust cash flow is achieved. Using a project finance strategy, the refiner would be required to enter into supply contracts to reduce spot market risk. A typical supply contract and off-take contract is arranged in a petroleum refinery project procured through project finance, as Figure 15.2 illustrates.

Long-term supply and off-take contracts (forward contracts) can be employed in the bundling of supply contracts to determine the cost and price structure of the off-take contracts as illustrated in Figure 15.3. The

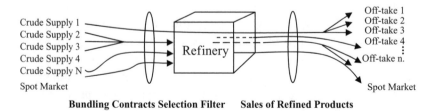

Bundling Contracts Selection Filter   Sales of Refined Products

Figure 15.3   Typical bundling of supply contracts and their product sales

principal aim of the supply and off-take contract is to create sufficient certainty of price, quantity and availability of both crude oil and sales of refined products, and thus ensure the financial viability of a refinery project.

Therefore, it is the supply contracts and off-take contracts for refined hydrocarbons that provide the guarantee on which a 'project finance' transaction is based (Elsey and Hurst 1996).

15.4   ASSESSING A CASE STUDY

The authors use a case study to assess the risks and financial viability of a refinery project procured utilising project finance. The refinery is designed to refine both heavy crude oil and light crude oil. The characteristics of the project are shown in Table 15.1.

The refinery can refine five crude oils from suppliers located near to the refinery. In this mechanism Crystal Ball is employed to assess the crude oil history data which can be obtained from the EIA database against probability distribution by using one of several standard goodness-of-fit tests. The distribution with the highest ranking fit is chosen to represent crude oil data. Figure 15.4 shows that lognormal distribution fits Iran H crude spot market price. However, if a crude oil supply is purchased on a long-term basis and its products sold on a contract led basis, the crude oil price and refined product price are bounded. Thus the triangular distribution is assigned to this supply–off-take agreement. This is illustrated in Figure 15.5

The risks identified have direct impact on the cost of each activity in the model, for instance the change in construction would increase or decrease the distillation plant cost between 99.6% and 103%

Table 15.1   Refinery project characteristics

Location Kalamayi XinJiang Province, China
Sponsors: SINOPEC and CNPC
Project Start: 01/01/2007
Construction Completion: 09/2012
Concession Period: 29 years
Estimated Construction Investment: (5 years) US$710 million
Estimated Operation and Maintenance Cost: (24 years) US$32 500 million
Expected Profits: US$1350 million per year
Key Players: SINOPEC and CNPC, Kelamayi Petroleum
Possible Crude Supplies:
Daqing, XinJiang, Saudi Light (Saudi L), Iran Light (Iran L), Iran Heavy (Iran H)

Assumption: Crude Cost
Lognormal distribution with parameters
Mean   29.85
Std. Dev.   15.69

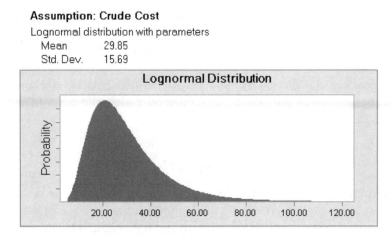

Figure 15.4   Iran H sport market price distribution

respectively as shown in Figure 15.6. The deterministic cost of each activity is calculated based on those ranges. However, the economic parameters with deterministic values do not reflect uncertainties in the refinery industry. Probabilistic analysis by means of Monte Carlo simulation can deal with this problem. Thus, both range and distribution can be assigned to those variables.

The same principle can be used in other variables such as refining cost and refining margins. A triangular distribution is commonly used

Assumption: Iran H expected price
Triangular distribution with parameters:
Minimum   22.00
Likeliest   25.00
Maximum   27.00

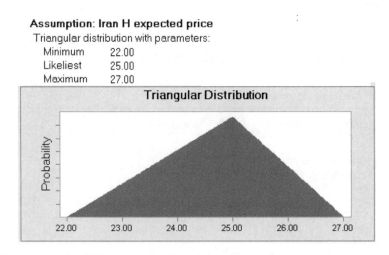

Figure 15.5   Iran H distribution with supply contract

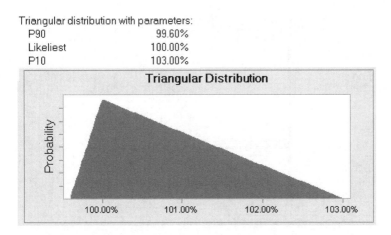

Figure 15.6   Change in construction cost on distillation plant

in the model where variable distributions are not well known but can be bounded, such as construction cost, transport costs, power and operating costs.

Computing refining margin varies from refinery to refinery. To simplify the computation gross product worth (GPW), crude oil prices and their GPW are imported directly from the EIA database into the model.

The bundle of crude oil supply contracts and respective off-take contracts can be determined by the analyst. Figure 15.7 illustrates examples of decision variables and corresponding constraints for lower and upper bounds.

15.4.1   Test 1

Figure 15.8 shows the probability analysis for the refinery with a 100% Daqing crude oil supply (with a combination of forward contracts, future contracts and spot market purchase) and six off-take products

Decision Variable: Daqing supply %   **Decision Variable: Iran Heavy supply %**

Variable bounds:
    Lower   20.00%
    Upper   80.00%
Variable type: Continuous

Variable bounds:
    Lower   30.00%
    Upper   70.00%
Variable type: Continuous

Figure 15.7   Decision variable examples

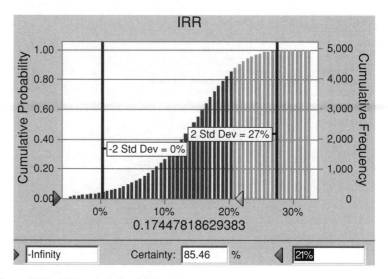

Figure 15.8   IRR cumulative frequency chart

over a 16-year operation period. The cumulative probability diagram shows there is 85% likelihood that the IRR will not exceed 21%, with 15% probability that the IRR would be less than 4%. This result shows that there is great financial uncertainty accompanying the project.

Figure 15.9 illustrates the results of a sensitivity analysis. Curves with steep slopes, positive or negative, indicate that those variables have

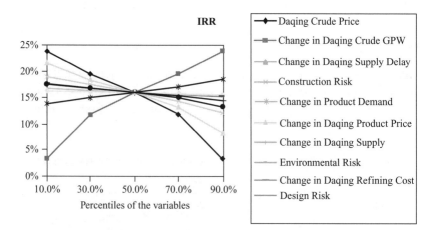

Figure 15.9   Sensitivity spider chart when taking Daqing crude oil supply

Table 15.2   Economic parameters of benchmark crude supply

Economics parameter	Base case	Best case	Worst case
NPV (million $)	1378.49	2933.45	88.87
IRR	16.7%	26%	4%
Payback period (year)	7.92	6.71	16.22
Discounted payback period	8.31	7.53	16.62
Cash lock-up (m$)	−713,66	−676.21	−897.06
Discounted cash lock-up (m$)	−699.50	−659.23	−872.22
Discount rate	3%	3%	3%

a large effect on the project's financial viability, whilst curves that are almost horizontal have little or no effect on the project's financial viability. Although the Daqing supply contracts and its off-take products contracts are in place it was found that the project is still very sensitive to the crude price risk, supply default risk, supply delay risk, construction risk and GPW risk and less sensitive to changes in refining the Daqing crude oil and design risk.

Table 15.2 and Figure 15.10 indicate the economic parameters and cumulative cash flow when assessed on a stochastic basis. The IRR for the base case is 16.7% and for the best case 26%; however, for the worst case it is only 4%. Clearly the project is risky with wide variation between the worst and best case cash flow in the operation period as illustrated in Figure 15.10, for a single Daqing crude oil supply.

A similar stochastic simulation process is also applied to four other possible crude oil supplies. Table 15.3 shows the economic parameters

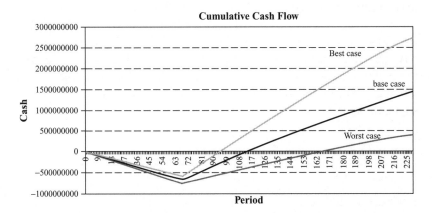

Figure 15.10   Cumulative cash flow of benchmark crude supply

Table 15.3   Summary of economic parameters of single crude supply (Note: The negative rate of return means that you cannot recover your initial investment by the end of concession period.)

Crude supplies	Payback period			IRR			NPV (million $)		
	Base	Best	Worst	Base	Best	Worst	Base	Best	Worst
Daqing	8.31	7.53	16.62	16.7%	26%	4%	1378.49	2933.45	88.87
Iran H	9.03	8.29	13.11	15%	17%	13.5%	1135.2	1806.44	645.5
Saudi L	12.93	7.98	Fail	9%	18%	1.9%	507.03	1978.03	39.00
XinJiang	8.35	7.38	13.29	17%	25%	11.5%	1387.62	2601.72	630.01
Iran L	7.42	7.13	17.2	26%	29%	2%	1420.50	3003.05	32.01

for each single supply. Xinjiang crude, for example, has competitive advantages such as low purchase price and low transport cost because of its location and availability to the refinery, resulting in less supply risk and price risk than other crude supply contracts.

Sensitivity analysis results show that most single crude oil supplies are sensitive to changes in supply, crude price, demand and GPW. The results of probability analyses of other single crude oil supplies are shown in Table 15.4. Clearly there is greater financial uncertainty accompanying the project if the refinery takes a single crude oil supply. Thus, apart from the single Xinjiang supply, the other crude oil supply would be unattractive to investors when such risks were taken into account.

The same testing process is employed to test two types of crude oil supplies (Test 2), three crude oil supplies (Test 3), four crude oil suppliers (Test 4) and five crude oil suppliers (Test 5). The decision in these tests is to determine the percentage of each crude oil the refinery should take to maximise the IRR and return whilst maintaining an acceptable level of risk. The constraint in those tests limits the total crude oil procured per day at no more than the refinery capacity of 220 000 b/d. Investors expect the maximum mean IRR for the minimum risk. Thus, the objective of a bundle of crude oil supplies is set to maximise the mean IRR with a standard deviation between 0.030 and 0.039.

Table 15.4   Summary of probability analysis results for crude oils

Probability/Supplies	Daqing	Iran H	Saudi L	Xinjiang	Iran L
85% likelihood IRR not exceed	21%	19%	15%	22%	21%
15% likelihood IRR less than	3.5%	1.9%	1.2%	7.1%	3.2%

Table 15.5   Solutions of mean return and standard deviation for combinations of five crude supply contracts

Solutions	Proportion Daqing	Proportion Saudi L	Proportion Xinjiang	Proportion Iran H	Proportion Iran L	Maximize IRR mean	Standard Deviation < = [0.03, 0.06]
1	0%	0%	100%	0%	0%	0.167	0.03
2	59%	0%	7.0%	34%	0%	0.19	0.033
3	75%	0%	25%	0%	0%	0.22	0.036
4	40%	0%	25%	30%	10%	0.24	0.037
5	10%	0%	50%	20%	25%	0.25	0.038

15.4.2   Summary of Results of Test 2, Test 3 and Test 4

It was found, after a number of simulations that a combination of 75% Daqing and 25% Xinjiang crude provides the highest mean IRR in Test 2. In Test 3 if the refinery took Saudi L supply it would significantly increase risk on both supply and off-take sides in the bundle.

In Test 4 when the fourth crude supply (Iran H) was then added to the bundle and tested in the model the bundle became more attractive than other solutions. This is because the risks associated with the fourth crude oil supply balanced the total risks on both supply and off-take sides and thus overall supply risk.

15.4.3   Test 5

The fifth test combines five crude oil supplies. Table 15.5 illustrates that a bundle of 10% Daqing, 25% Iran L, 50% Xinjiang, 20% Iran H, and 0% Saudi L provides the highest return with higher risk than previous tests.

15.4.4   Bundle Analysis

The analyses show that there is no perfect bundle solution. Some bundle solutions such as 100% Xinjiang have relatively lower return with a lower given risk, whereas some bundles have higher return with relatively higher risks. However, the best bundle of crude oil supply contracts and off-take contracts should be determined by the level of risk acceptable.

Efficient frontier analysis is then employed to consider the balance between return and risk in selecting the optimal crude supply contract bundle based on the risks identified.

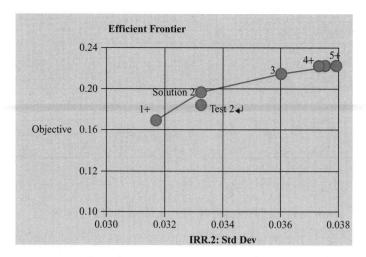

Figure 15.11   Efficient frontier

Table 15.5 illustrates mean return and standard deviation for combinations of crude supply contracts of a bundle of the five crude oil supplies tested. Under certain risk levels different bundles will generate different returns.

Figure 15.11 shows the efficient frontier for the bundle of five crude oil supplies. The efficient frontier is the intersection of the set of bundles with minimum variance (risk) and the set of bundles providing the maximum return. For example, a bundle of 59% Daqing, 0% Iran L, 0% Saudi L, 7.0% Xinjiang 34% Iran H crude oils is more efficient than the bundle of 61% Daqing/39% Iran H in Test 2 because it has a higher IRR and NPV although both of them are exposed to a similar risk level.

15.5   BUNDLE SOLUTIONS AFTER RISK MANAGEMENT

When the bundle forming the efficient frontier was simulated new economic parameters were generated, as shown in Table 15.6. The risks associated with this bundle were then assessed. The risks associated with supply contracts were analysed and it was found that crude supply risks in Solution 3, shown in Table 15.5, are more difficult to manage than Solution 4. Table 15.7 and Table 15.8 illustrate that after risk

Table 15.6 Summary of economic parameters of five crude supplies

	Payback period			IRR			NPV (million $)		
Crude supplies	Base	Best	Worst	Base	Best	Worst	Base	Best	Worst
100% Xinjiang	8.35	7.38	13.29	17%	25%	11.5%	1367.62	2601.72	630.01
59% Daqing, 0% Iran L, 34% Iran H, 0% Saudi L, 7.0% Xinjiang	8.2	7.9	14.96	19%	28%	11.02%	1388.08	2796.76	572.0
75% Daqing, 25% Xinjiang	8.3	7.5	15.23	21%	29%	10.5%	1422.0.0	2933.7	552.0
15% Daqing, 0% Saudi L, 35% Xinjiang, 30% Iran H, 20% Iran L	7.79	7.23	15.29	23%	31.5%	10.1%	1800.16	3328.78	546.0
10% Daqing, 25% Iran L, 50% Xinjiang, 20% Iran H, 0% Saudi L	7.5	7.0	16.21	25%	33%	9.95%	2500.25	3956.0	540.0

management, Solution 4 is more attractive to investors than Solution 3 because the risk level of Solution 4 can be reduced to the same risk level as Solution 3 but with high returns. Therefore Solution 3 is no longer on the efficient frontier after risk management.

The analyses show that the project is exposed to different levels of risks and different economic returns. After risk management, Solution 5 still has the highest return with highest risk; Solution 1 has lowest economic return but lowest risk. Investors choosing Solution 1 would seek a large amount of debt; whereas investors choosing Solution 5 wouldrequire more equity as risk finance.

Table 15.7 Mean return and standard deviation for combinations of crude supply contracts after risk management

Solutions	Proportion Daqing	Proportion Saudi	Proportion Xinjiang	Proportion Iran H	Proportion Iran L	Maximize IRR mean	Standard Deviation $< = [0.03, 0.06]$
1	0%	0%	100%	0%	0%	0.169	0.029
2	59%	0%	7.0%	34%	0%	0.20	0.031
3	75%	0%	25%	0%	0%	0.23	0.035
4	40%	0%	25%	30%	10%	0.24	0.035
5	10%	0%	50%	20%	25%	0.26	0.037

Table 15.8   Economic parameters after risk management

Crude supplies	Payback Period (years)			IRR			NPV (Million $)		
	Base	Best	Worst	Base	Best	Worst	Base	Best	Worst
XinJiang 100%	8.26	7.28	13	17%	25.5%	12%	1367.62	2791.72	640.0
59% Daqing, 0% Iran L, 34% Iran H, 0% Saudi L, 7.0% Xinjiang	8.2	7.7	13.9	19%	29.5%	12.5%	1588.08	2996.76	869.0
75% Daqing, 25% Xinjiang	8.3	7.2	14.03	22%	31%	12.9%	1622.0	3433.7	899.0
15% Daqing, 0% Saudi L, 35% Xinjiang, 30% Iran H, 20% Iran L	7.5	7.23	15.19	24%	31.5%	11.1%	1800.16	3528.78	765.0
10% Daqing, 25% Iran L, 50% Xinjiang, 20% Iran H, 0% Saudi L	7.5	6.9	15.21	25%	34%	10%	2500.25	4256.0	656.9

15.6   SUMMARY

The authors simulated a bundle of supply and off-take contracts and compared different economic outputs from each bundle.

The assessment clearly illustrates the bundles' best, worst and base case economic parameters with impact of both supply risk and typical refinery risks.

The assessment offers a detailed method for determining the crude oils to be purchased and their percentage within a bundle of crude oil supply contracts.

The assessment can aid stakeholders in the decision-making process regarding the type and quantity of crude oil supply contracts based on identified risks.

Investors in refinery projects can assess specific risks affecting crude oil supply in relation to the overall project economic parameters.

There are numerous combinations of crude oil supply bundles. The risks associated with supply and off-take are extremely complex. From the tests shown in the analyses the refinery economic viability is very sensitive to the crude oil supply and off-take. The choice of a bundle of crude oil supplies is paramount to the commercial viability of a refinery thus making risk management an integral part of refinery procurement and operation.

The authors wish to thank Dr Anthony Merna and Mr Yang Chu for allowing them to use this amended version of their paper.

16

CASE STUDY 3
Development of Risk Registers at Corporate, Strategic Business Unit and Project Levels and a Risk Statement

16.1 INTRODUCTION

The following provides a description of a generic risk management process for the identification of risks within a typical hierarchical organisational structure of corporate, strategic business unit and project/functional levels, along with preliminary risk assessment necessary for the initial sanctioning of a project.

A project opportunity scenario is presented along with fictitious company profile and products/projects to satisfy the requirement.

Risk registers are provided, identifying project related risks to the fictitious scenario, along with cumulative cash flow diagram and other supporting information.

Finally, a risk statement is demonstrated, in a format suitable for the high-level decisions related to the sanctioning of a project by corporate, shareholder and financiers, including a tornado diagram to provide a visual overview of the project's risks and associated cost.

16.2 LEVELS OF RISK ASSESSMENT

Risk assessments are carried out at each level in an organisation. Typically the 'big picture' risks are identified at corporate level and more detailed assessment at SBU level associated with the characteristics of the relevant market. At project level more data are usually available to allow a more detailed assessment and to consider project specific activities and their associated risks.

---

* Reproduced by permission of A. Merna.

16.2.1 Corporate Risk Assessment

At the corporate level, issues related to each of the below areas would be identified and recorded for further assessment and processing by the specific SBU responsible for the undertaking:

- reputation (brand image)
- ethical risk (animal testing, green, military)
- market/demand
- health and safety (directors' liability insurance may be sought)
- creating/maintaining competitive advantage
- alignment of SBU undertakings with corporate strategy plan (CSP)
- SBU's ability to finance the undertaking and gain returns on capital employed
- synergy with and potential involvement for other SBUs
- compliance with legal and regulatory issues
- country risk (tax, political, war, currency)
- political and environmental issues
- contract strategy.

Table 16.1 illustrates the identification techniques used at each level.

16.2.2 Strategic Business Unit Risk Assessment

The strategic business unit ultimately responsible for the undertaking identified the following risks to be considered at this level. In some cases risks initially identified at corporate level will be assessed in greater detail and be more specific to the SBU market.

- stakeholder satisfaction
- long-term goals
- demands of customers and end-users

Table 16.1 Risk management technique at each level

Brainstorming	C, SBU, P	Interviews	C, SBU, P	Checklists	C, SBU, P	Risk mapping	SBU, P
Assumptions analysis	SBU, P	HAZOP	P	Prompt lists	SBU, P	Probability impact tables	SBU, P
Delphi	SBU, P	FMECA	P	Risk registers	C, SBU, P	Risk matrix chart	C, SBU, P

- market conditions/trends
- product specific issues (design, production)
- customer's ability to pay
- ability to finance the undertaking and gain returns on capital employed
- compliance with legal and regulatory issues
- customer satisfaction
- availability of resources (human, raw, technical)
- future opportunities
- contract strategy
- maintaining/increasing market share
- compliance with corporate strategy and business strategy
- synergy with current and future commitments
- synergy with other strategic business undertakings
- knock-on effects from other SBU risks
- country risk (contract law, political conditions, climate, telecommunication, infrastructure)

16.2.3   Project Level Risk Assessment

Project level risk assessment will normally be the remit of the project manager ultimately responsible for the undertaking and may be governed by the risk management plan (RMP) resulting from the corporate and SBU risk strategy.

Here initial focus would tend to be at the lowest level of project delivery, with concerns for typical project management constraints of cost, time and quality being the most prevalent along with anxiety with regards to adequate resources for the specific project (time, materials, labour/technical skills etc.).

Other main areas of uncertainty may be:

- requirements
- solution: such as fit for purpose, bespoke, off-the-shelf
- raw materials
- key human resources: desired versus available, location, culture, skill-sets
- time/schedule: desired versus achievable, conflicts for implementation periods such as holidays or working restrictions
- customer organisation: environment, culture, working hours, synergy
- end-users: involvement in project, acceptance, level of education, language, culture

- implementation environment/location: accommodation, access, language, security, weather, working conditions (site, ground conditions, water level), travel, labour, safety, logistics
- technical concerns: interfaces, communication medium, known issues with existing technology or unknown technology.

16.3 AMALGAMATION AND ANALYSIS OF RISKS IDENTIFIED

Upon completion of initial risk identification activities by each organisational level and subsequent documentation, specifically risk registers, SBU resources (or appointed risk manager) would then be responsible for further processing and amalgamation of results, such as:

- assessment of true impact–probability weighting in line with corporate and strategic policy
- further analysis (qualitative and/or quantitative) of time and cost variations to the project
- determination of possible responses (avoidance, reduction, transfer or retention)
- identification of appropriate risks owner.

An appropriate technique for gauging the intensity of individual risk is the probability–impact grid depicted in Figure 16.3.

To facilitate this, within each of the risk registers utilised in the previous stages, fields are provided for the scoring of both probability and impact as perceived by the document authors. This not only provides a starting point for the analysis tasks of the risk manager, but also gives insight into the deemed sensitivity of the project, the specific risk (in contrast with other risks identified) and also possibly an idea of the risk tolerance of the group which authored the register. This is shown in Figure 16.1.

This score or criticality value relates to the weighting factors described in the associated key displayed in Figure 16.2.

Risk Value	
Probability	60%
Impact	9
Score = P * I	**5.4**

Figure 16.1 Risk register criticality value

KEY:

VL	$<\approx$	1
L	$\approx$	2
M	$\approx$	4
H	$\approx$	5
VH	$>\approx$	6.5

Figure 16.2   Impact weighting factors for PIG analysis

An appropriate technique for gauging of intensity of individual risk is the probability–impact grid depicted in Figure 16.3.

Kerzner (2003) provides a set of risk definitions which are appropriate for use in risk analysis using the PIG as depicted in Figure 16.3.

- *High risk* – substantial impact on cost, schedule, or technical. Substantial action required to alleviate issue. High priority management attention is required.
- *Moderate risk* – some impact on cost, schedule, or technical. Special action may be required to alleviate issue. Additional management attention may be needed.
- *Low risk* – minimal impact on cost, schedule, or technical. Normal management oversight is sufficient.

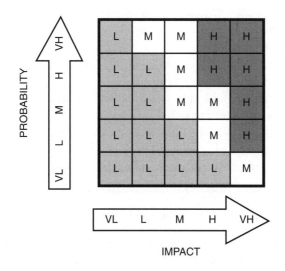

Figure 16.3   Probability – impact grid

Kerzner also advises of the importance of using agreed-upon definitions (such as the definitions above) and procedures for estimating risk levels, rather than subjectively assigning them.

Those risks deemed as high or very high by the risk manager would be candidates for further analysis, in order to determine time and/or cost variations to the project.

Results of all risks would at this stage be amalgamated into a separate database, spreadsheet or other facility and made available within the organisation for all stakeholders to access. Additionally, those risks deemed critical during this process would be extracted for project sanctioning purposes and inclusion within a risk statement for the attention of lenders and shareholders.

The risk statement is expected to be an executive summary of high-level content, with the intention of providing a non-subjective description of visible risks for a proposal to the corporate board, stakeholder and lender representatives, approval of which would need to be obtained before commitment of further resources for any subsequential risk analysis or possibly the initiation of the project undertaking.

The following points should be considered when the undertaking is sanctioned.

- Initially it is expected that further risk analysis would be performed on the more critical of risks (both qualitative and quantitative).
- Risk registers would be published such that all stakeholders have controlled access and may assist with the address of any risks.
- Stakeholder feedback would be encouraged throughout all project and risk management phases via brainstorming, interviews and access to risk registers.
- Risk registers would be continuously updated throughout all further stages of the project undertakings.
- Budget for risk would in most cases be allocated to the project for contingency of identified risks.
- Purpose of the project and benefits of the outcome also need to be kept in mind throughout all stages of a project, as scope creep due to change of requirements is all too often ignored upon project sanctioning.

16.4   THE PROJECT: BAGGAGE HANDLING FACILITY

The following risk registers are developed at each level of the organisation for the baggage handling project. It is intended that this project will be undertaken in a developing country.

16.4.1 Corporate Level

Corporate- Risk Matrix

Risk ID	Date the risk is identified	Activity programme overview activity	Stage/Phase expected occurrence	Risk Type Internal, External	Risk Description and Impact — Brief description of the risk and its impact on the project	Owner of the risk	Probability High, Medium, Low	Impact High, Medium, Low	Most likely Expected outcome	Mitigation — Describe what you do to minimise the impact of the risk	Status Open, Close
C01	2007-2-23	N/A	ALL	I	Health & Safety: Damage to health or loss of life to member of staff on company premises.	CORP	Low	High		All parties to be aware of and agree to H&S policies within Employment contracts. All visitors to be provided adequate H&S instruction, safety equipment where necessary and signed-in by visiting dept upon arrival.	Open
C02	2007-2-23	N/A	ALL	I	Health & Safety: Damage to health or loss of life to member of staff on-site.	CORP	Low	High		H&S policy for site to be provided to all employees before work commences. Same to be formally signed-for by employee, as per H&S Policy.	Open
C03	2007-2-22	N/A	Pre-contract	E	Project Sponsor is removed after commissioning which effects investment for future projects/ programmes in region.	SBU	Medium	Medium		Need to prevent losses for this initial implementation.	Open
C04	2007-2-23	N/A	Post	E	Clients unable/unwilling to pay.	Legal	Low	High		Ensure contracts provide adequate coverage for English Law (not sharia law). If necessary have contract signed outside of host country (i.e. in UK).	Open
C05	2007-2-24	N/A	All	E	Natural disaster in project host country.	Corp	Low	High	$250,000	On-site Engineers to be register with British Embassy upon arrival. Adequate contract clauses must be in place to ensure that all equipment delivered to site is to be moth-balled disasteris normalised. Losses to be shared equally amongst parties all project parties.	Open
C06	2007-2-25	N/A	All	E	War in project host country.	Corp	Low	High	$250,000	On-site Engineers to register with British Embassy upon arrival. Ensure adequate clause in Contract that all activities to be moth-balled until peace is declared. Losses to be shared equally between all contract parties.	Open
C07	2007-2-26	N/A	All	I/E	Employee requiring medical treatment in project host country. This could result in poor quality of healthcare for employee and/or expenses detrimental to the project/business.	Corp/SBU /HR	High	High	$300,000	All parties to abide by Corporate policy with regard to immunisation, medical health insurance and registration with native Embassy in host country.	Open

Figure 16.4 Risk register output at corporate level

C08	2007-2-26	60, 64	N/A	I	Technical disaster. Loss of critical data. This has potential to cripple the organisation and must be given top-priority by IT Dept until contingency in place for full recovery.	IT	Low	High	$100,000	Corporate IT Policy to updated and agreed by all employees upon employment or employment contract renewal. All Laptop users to be provided with current Anti-virus applications and all hardware to be replaced after max. 3 years - as per policy. All USB and Floppy drives to be locked for internal workstations.	Open
C09	2007-2-27	1	All	I	Loss to reputation due to employee corruption or losses as a result of issues with installed systems or products.	SBU	Medium	Low		All employees to agree to abide by Rules of Conduct/Ethics. Corruption and bribery by 3rd parties to be highlighted in all induction courses.	Open
C10	2007-3-1		All	E	Loss or Death of critical board member.	Corp	Medium	High		All board members to ensure 1 other Board Member is advised of any passwords etc. for access to Laptops, PC's and other Databases for company data.	Open
C11	2007-2-27		Implementation	E	Environmental concerns (host country and home base).	Finance	Medium	High		How doEco concerns effect theorganisation?SBU to provide feedback on this matter.	Open
C12	2007-2-28	1 - 12	Pre-contract whole life costs	E	Interest Rate Risk	Finance	Medium	High		Finance to advise further on possibilities for Caps, Floors and hedgingfor reduction ofthis risk	Open
C13	2007-3-1	1 - 12	Pre-contract		Country Tax rises	Finance Contracts	Medium	High		Possibilities for Tax breaks should be discussed with sponsor. Maybe the sponsor can advise further on the matter. Finance toadviceon sensitivity. Provisions for Tax to be calculatedseparately in contract payment agreement.	Open
C14	2007-3-2	All	Pre-contract		Exchange rate risk (FOREX)	Finance	Medium	High		Currently all payments from and fees and to be in USD. This is also same for global agreements with Hardware vendors. Negligible FOREX Risk for local (host country) purchases- contracts with these vendors to be drawn up forUSD payments else risk reduced by future purchase of local currency.	

Figure 16.4 (*Continued*)

16.4.2 Strategic Business Unit Level

SBU – Risk Matrix

Risk ID	Date Date the risk is identified	Activity programme overview activity	Stage/Phase expected occurrence	Risk Type Internal External	Risk Description and Impact Brief description of the risk and its impact on the project	Owner of the risk	Probability High, Medium, Low	Impact High, Medium, Low	Most likely Expected outcome	Mitigation Describe what you do to minimise the impact of the risk	Status Open, Close
S01	2007-2-22	1	ALL	E	Necessary licenses.	Board/PM	Low	High	Cost $2,000 per month	PM to maintain vigilance on these issues. PM to provide details on this within monthly report for Board attention. Contract to be amended to include clause to allocate any fees in this regard (without acception). Can the Board assist with this risk?	Open
S02	2007-2-23	N/A	ALL	E	War/Embargo in country cancels contract.	PM	Low	High	$600,000	Watch international affairs esp. www.cia.org (https://www.cia.gov/cia/publications/factbook/geos/pk.html) for signs. Emergency Meeting to be called in even of any issues and Shipment of all hardware to be postponed.	Open
S03	2007-2-24	N/A	Pre-contract	E	Natural disaster in area. Recent Tsunami wiped-out all major telecommunications in region; this would render all system unusable.	PM	Medium	Low	$400,000	Ensure adequate clause in Contract to cover for coincidental losses doe to theft/damage of Hardware.	Open
S04	2007-2-25	16	Pre-contract	I	Issues with Global Purchasing agreement with Hardware vendors.	Procurement	Medium	Medium	$120,000	Procurement to follow up immediately. Software Dept to give advice on possible use of other Operating Systems for future implementations.	Open
S05	2007-2-26	1	Post	E	Finance difficulties for foreign project.	Finance/ Contracts	Low	High	$50,000	Finance to double check all outstanding details and where possible identify back-up financier	Open
S06	2007-2-27	91	All	E	Insufficiently skilled/educated staff for use of systems.	PM/Training	Low	Medium	$28,000	PM to identify Training requirements ASAP and report back in case End-user need to employ new team members before cut-over date.	Open
S07	2007-3-3	91	All	E	Customer cannot keep-up payments for services.	SBU/Finance	Medium	High	$70,000	Contract to be under UK Law and not Sharia law. Signed in UK if necessary.	Open
S08	2007-3-3	N/A	All	I	Server Vendor Global Support agreement due to expire November 07. Price increases above 3% year-on-year are unacceptable.	PM	Low	High	$450 per month	Procurement to address this issue immediately. Software Dept to advise if Applications can be compiled to run on other Operating Systems without issue.	Open
S09	2007-3-3	34	Implementation	I	Telecom connectivity and quality issues.	PM	Medium	High	$5,000 per month	Back-to-back SLA contract with Telcom to mitigate any downtime fines from Client.	Open

Figure 16.5 Risk register at strategic business level

16.4.3 Project Level

Project- Risk Matrix

Risk ID	Date Date the risk is identified	Activity programme overview activity	Stage/Phase Expected occurrence	Risk Type Internal, External	Risk Description and Impact Brief description of the risk and its impact on the project	Owner of the risk	Probability High, Medium, Low	Impact High, Medium, Low	Most likely Expected outcome	Mitigation Describe what you do to minimise the impact of the risk	Status Open, Close
P01	2007-2-22	11	PRE	E	License fee Introduced for company.	IM/PM	Low	High	Cost $2,000 per month	Must be included in contract the any License fees are outside the remit of contract.	Open
P02	2007-2-23	29	INST	E	Changes to any Immigration Laws - forbidding key members of the installation team from accessing country.	IM/PM	Low	Medium	$19,000 Training, remote support	Keep informed of all political issues with region. Identify host country natives within contract to train-up.	Open
P03	2007-2-24	52	INST	E	Gate Passes - Delays (AND/OR) Changes to the Gate Pass procedure has the potential to delay the project.	IM/PM	Medium	Low	$15,000 fines	Obtain and keep up to date - Full Gate Pass procedure. (Local Eng. Has confirmed he will advise of any changed immediately).	Open
P04	2007-2-25	88	CUT	E	Inability to obtain Project Cut-Off signature.	IM/PM	Medium	Medium	$22,000 additional 3 weeks effort	Identify Sign-Off Personal at earliest opportunity and work closely with them, regarding perceptions of all deliverables, functionalities etc.	Open
P05	2007-2-26	86	TRAIN	E	Unable to get Training resources into country (Work-VISA).	IM/PM	Low	High	$8,000 Training and remote support	Attempt to use native Training resource from implementations in Dubai UAE else train other native for training purposes.	Open
P06	2007-2-27	87	TRAIN, FINAL, CUT, OPS	E	Insufficiently skilled and educated handlers to use systems. This could lead to 2/3 weeks additional on-site hand-holding after cut-over date. And bad relations with other project opportunities if not handled correctly in advance of cut-over.	PM	High	High	Best case is $15,000 3 weeks for additional on-site support. Loss of future contracts at worst.	i) Include basic levels of education and literacy in Project Documentation package. ii) Include that training to be provided only one time; additional to be extra cost to client. iii) Identify native speaking engineer to provide translation during training activities to prevent issues.	Open
P07	2007-3-3	33	INST	I	Network issues where it is deemed necessary to use existing infrastructure.	PM	Medium	High	Cost for contract amendment $4,000-difficult & lengthy negotiations.	Ensure new/separate Network Infrastructure is installed.	Open
P08	2007-3-3	17, 19, 20	PROC/INST	I	Desks will not fit new equipment properly. This would delay use of check-in facilities until resolve.	PM	High	High	4/5 weeks lost revenue of $28,000 + same delays in installation and cut-over $25,000.	Source from proven manufacturer. Hardware vendor to agree to contract terms upon purchase and confirm 100% Hardware dimensions and Model's before any firm dimensions provided to Desk Manufacturer.	Open
P09	2007-3-3	17, 19, 20	INST	E	Hardware suppliers change Printer or Workstation Model and Dimensions.	PM	Medium	High	$16,000 new desks + 4 wks lost revenue $14,000	Suppliers for PC/Workstations, Printers and Document Feeders must agree to terms for the supply this equipment.	Open
P10	2007-3-3	24, 62, 88	INST	E	Telecom connectivity and quality issues.	PM	Medium	High	$3,000 contract negotiations + possible $96,000 per annum lost revenues.	- Ensure issue is identified in contract with 3rd Party supplier and adequately accounted for in contracts.	Open
P11	2007-3-4	51	LOG	E	Customs clearance issues with servers.	PM	Medium	Medium	$1,000 for meals and meetings	Seek assistance from client and sponsor for expediting clearances. Ensure Procurement have latest information for paperwork requirements.	Open

Figure 16.6 Risk register at project level

16.5   RISK STATEMENT

A risk statement is a document that identifies all those risks identified at each level of the organisation which can be examined by the lenders and shareholders. In most cases the risks identified in the risk statement will be those risks identified as high in each risk register and those that must be retained by the organisation, typically those that cannot be mitigated.

A risk statement, as described above, associated with every potential project or investment considered by the organisation provides a simple yet useful tool to lenders and shareholders when considering which projects or investments should be sanctioned in relation to the risk and uncertainty surrounding them.

Figures 16.4, 16.5 and 16.6 illustrate the risks and their probability/impact for each level. Figure 16.7 illustrates the risk classified as high due to their probability and impact which will form the basis of the risk statement.

16.6   SUMMARY

Risk management is not an exact science and each undertaking will have different risks to previous and following opportunities. Risks are also individual to the organisation performing the task; hence risk management also needs to be subjective to the organisation. However, contrary to implying that risk management is undertaken in an ad-hoc manner, this stresses the importance of proactive risk identification and the management thereof, which must be planned for and ingrained within the establishment.

Processes and procedures for risk management need to be established and continually revised as lessons are learnt and standards and regulations change. Risk management efforts without control and guidance will be patchy and inconsistent throughout the undertaking as different stakeholders (and differing hierarchical levels of involvement) attempt to address different risks and opportunities. Furthermore, this may lead to the creation of additional risks brought about through ignorance and assumption that risks are under control.

Risk management which occurs as an afterthought, upon initiation of a project, may be too late to prevent negative implications. Risk management processes and procedures must be initiated before sanctioning of a project, such that identification of external and inherent risks can be

Risk Manager- Whole Project Risk Matrix

Risk ID	Date the risk is identified	Activity programme overview activity	Stage/Phase expected occurrence	Risk Type Internal, External	Risk Description and Impact Brief description of the risk and its impact on the project	Owner of the risk	Probability High, Medium, Low	Impact High, Medium, Low	Most likely Expected outcome	Mitigation Describe what you do to minimise the impact of the risk	Status Open, Close
P06	2007-2-27	87	TRAIN, FINAL, CUT, OPS	E	Insufficiently skilled and educated handlers to use systems. This could lead to 2/3 weeks additional on-site hand-holding after cutover date. And bad relations with other project opportunitiesif not handled correctly in advance of cutover.	PM	High	High	$15,000 $1,000	i) Include basic levels ofeducation and literacy in Project Documentation package. ii) Include that training to be provided only one time; additional to be extra cost to client. iii) Identify native speaking engineer to providetranslation during training activities to prevent issues. May be sufficiently skilled already and only basic training required. Savingnegligible	Open
P09	2007-3-3	17, 19, 20	PROC/INST	I	Desks will not fit newequipment properly. This would delay use of facilities until resolve.	PM	High	High	$53,000 $1,000	Source from proven manufacturer. Hardware vendor to agree toterms upon purchase and confirm 100% Hardware dimensions andModel'sbefore any firm dimensions provided to Desk Manufacturer. Desks may fit perfectly and install easier that expected. Saving negligible	Open
C08	2007-2-26		All	I	Employee requiring medical treatment in project host country. This could result in poor quality of Healthcare for employee and/or expenses detrimental to the project/ business.	Corp/SBU/HR	High	High	$300,000 $144,000	All parties to abide by Corprate policy with regard to immunisation medical health insurance and registration with native Embassy in host country. Illnesses may not occur. Blanket Medical Insurance for all Project staff may cost less than expected.	Open
S09	2007-3-3	41, 51	N/A	I	Only 1 database expert after 30-Aug-2007.	HR Technical Manager	High	High	$39,000 $50,000	Employ of 2 Oracle Database Admins (31-05-07) Both to shadow existing Engineer until skills have been passedn. New recruits may have superior skill set and greater abilities with database. Asset to the company with intangible know-how.	Open
S11	2007-3-3	20	All	I	Sister business has reneged on payments to desk manufacturer. This could have major delays on all current undertakings which would create a backlog for future contract furniture.	Board	High	High	$22,800 $12,600	Issue to be escalated to Board. Issues between vendor and sister business to be resolved ASAP! Cost of same desks from other acceptable vendor is $1,200 more that current vendor. Keep lookout for acceptable replacement vendor and order books are full till October 07 Opportunity to bring Manufacture in-house. Estimate that these could be made for a 50% reduction.	Open

Figure 16.7 Risk register for risk statement

identified, addressed and recorded for the attention of all stakeholders, so that proactive mitigation can occur.

Risk management must be balanced, controlled, consistent and most importantly cyclical.

Risk registers and risk statements should be seen as simple methods of illustrating the potential risk at individual level and a tool for decision making respectively.

The authors wish to thank Mr Darren Burnside and Dr Anthony Merna for allowing them to use this amended version of their paper.

17

CASE STUDY 4
Development of a Typical Risk
Statement to Shareholders

17.1 INTRODUCTION

The theoretical model for performing risk management, as described here, consists of risk identification, analysis, and response and the application of this model in the construction of a risk register for UUU. As this is a largely qualitative analysis due to lack of project level information, there will be more risks listed at the corporate level and fewer at the project level. A risk statement to shareholders is developed based on a summary of typical risks at each level of the corporation.

17.2 UUU OVERVIEW AND RISK REGISTER

UUU is a corporation which deals with heating and air conditioning systems, aerospace and industrial systems, elevators and escalators, aircraft engines, helicopters, fire and security protection services, and power systems. It has over 3000 locations in 52 countries and conducts business in 120 countries. Figure 17.1 gives a brief overview of the organization levels.

17.3 CORPORATE RISK REGISTER

The corporate risk register deals with the macro-level risks that have the largest impacts on the organization. Although these risks may not be prominent for each individual project, they are risks because of the cumulative effects they can have on the corporation.

17.3.1 Foreign Exchange Risk

UUU's involvement in the world economy has grown tremendously as its share of domestic revenues has declined relative to its European and East

* Reproduced by permission of A. Merna.

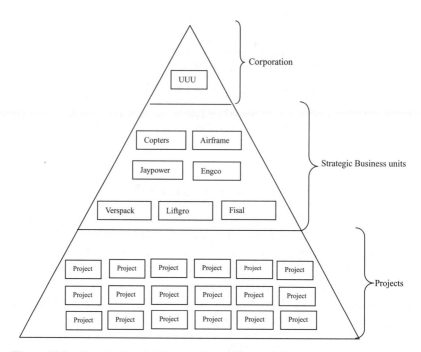

Figure 17.1   Organisational structure of UUU Corporation

Asian revenues. UUU has a large volume of foreign currency exposures that result from international sales, purchases, investments, borrowings, and other international transactions. As a result, the strengthening of foreign currencies actually contributes to additional revenue for UUU but a sudden depreciation could result in a loss of revenues. Therefore, it is best to retain this risk and in areas of weak exposure use currency hedging.

17.3.2   Political/Country Risk

UUU has physical infrastructure throughout its worldwide locations and is therefore subject to a high degree of political or country risk. Countries in emerging markets like Russia, China, and Argentina bring with them a higher level of political risk. In addition, risk in one emerging market can lead to contagion in other markets. As a precautionary measure, UUU's investment in any particular country does not 'exceed 2.5% of consolidated shareowners' equity'.

17.3.3   Market Performance Risk (Demand Risk)

UUU's overall performance is driven by general economic conditions. There is significant fluctuation across international markets over time. Some of these fluctuations spill over into important determinants of demand like residential and commercial construction activity, labour costs, and customer attrition. However, this risk is not unique and impacts the competition across the market. The only means to manage it is to continually improve productivity despite market conditions.

17.3.4   Commodity Prices (Supply Risk)

UUU is subject to fluctuations in the international commodities market. One of the commodities with volatile prices is oil. In addition, titanium and copper, which are important commodities for UUU's commercial and aerospace projects, also experience price fluctuations. Although there is the opportunity to gain on purchasing raw materials as the price declines, this is a high impact risk on cash flow variability and can be managed by means of forward contracts. However, forward contracts will not be used in every circumstance and sometimes part of the risk will be held.

17.3.5   Interest Rates

Interest rates can have a significant impact on both short-term and long-term debt. For example, in 2005 UUU had higher interest costs due to higher average rates for commercial paper and short-term borrowings In addition UUU carries a significant amount of long-term debt that is mostly at a fixed rate. Therefore, a means to manage this risk is fixed-for-floating interest rate swaps for a portion of the long-term debt portfolio. This is an effective tool particularly when interest rates can experience significant fluctuation.

17.3.6   Government Contract Risk (Demand Risk)

Defence spending provides a sizeable portion of demand for UUU products. In fact, in 2004 UUU was responsible for nearly $6 billion in sales to the US Government. Although this carries risk based on Department of Defence needs, there has been a recent increase in military expenditures due to the global war on terrorism, particularly for aviation procurement.

In addition, contracts with the government are subject to frequent contract audits that may have legal implications. This contract risk can be tolerated because of the recent increase in defence spending and is reduced by the fact that UUU is diversified among multiple industries.

17.3.7 Legislative Risk

There is another kind of risk associated with the government known as legislative risk. This occurs when there is a change in corporate tax laws or accounting procedures. For instance, the Bush administration tax cuts have led to higher operating profits for many corporations. In contrast, the Sarbanes-Oxley Act (2002) was an accounting 'tax' on corporations for the additional reporting procedures necessary. This risk is ultimately retained because no corporation has a means to avoid or transfer it.

17.3.8 EH and Safety Risk

Like every corporation, UUU is subject to environmental regulation by federal, state, and local authorities in the US and abroad. In terms of health and safety, UUU must ensure a safe work environment for its employees and mistakes in this area can lead to litigation with high costs. This risk can be reduced in some areas by ensuring workers are protected against potential hazards in terms of protective clothing and working areas and transferred in other areas through accident insurance for employees.

17.3.9 Information Technology Risk

Since UUU deals with government contracts, there is the increased propensity for hackers to try to infiltrate its network. The company also faces legal risks associated with the theft or release of personnel data such as an employee's social security number or bank account number. Part of this risk can be reduced by firewall software and addition access codes, but part of it must be retained as technology is constantly changing.

17.3.10 Leadership Risk

Leadership decisions pose one of the most significant risks to UUU. Whilst there are potential downsides, this risk can be viewed mainly in a positive light in that strong leadership will enhance the productivity of UUU. UUU has consistently outperformed the market and has an experienced board of directors which makes this a manageable risk. Leadership in an ever-changing market is a core function of UUU.

17.3.11   Reputation/Product Quality Control Risk

Reputation poses a large risk for UUU because of the quality associated with its product line. Therefore product quality control is an important challenge for management. It is particularly difficult from the legal perspective because of the product use such as helicopters and jet engines. This is a risk that cannot be transferred away entirely; instead it can only be reduced through good management.

17.3.12   Compliance Risk

Given the size and scale of UUU, there is the chance of compliance risk. This includes non-conformance with laws, rules, regulations or prescribed practices, internal policies, or ethical rules. This can result in a diminished reputation for UUU or a loss of business opportunities, as well as other legal implications. UUU's primary method to reduce this risk is its Code of Ethics which is mandatory for all employees to read, sign, and comply.

17.3.13   Audit Risk

The number of government contracts associated with the sale of UUU's products makes it subject to intense scrutiny and more frequent audits. There is also significant liability if UUU is audited and is not compliant with the current tax structure. However, this risk can be transferred by hiring an external auditor.

17.3.14   Legal Risk

In addition to the legal risks associated with EH and Safety discussed above, UUU has to deal with government litigation as well as defend its intellectual property. UUU is also exposed to legal risks in many of its contracts which if not properly dealt with could result in a significant loss in revenues. However, this risk can be reduced by hiring experienced corporate lawyers.

17.3.15   Terrorism/Security Risk

UUU's worldwide locations could create potential targets for a terrorist attack, particularly in a smaller country where radicals might view UUU buildings as 'Western imperialism'. In addition, security is also a general risk with regards to designs, product shipment, product tampering, and physical infrastructure. This risk can be reduced through UUU's own security products as well as taking further security precautions.

17.3.16   Human Capital Risk

UUU, by nature of its technical products, demands highly skilled labour. UUU could suffer a loss of skilled labour in either domestic or foreign markets. Other human capital risks include labour rate fluctuations, unionisation of labour with a hostile position towards company operations, rising labour costs, such as healthcare and pensions, and labour strikes. One way UUU can reduce this high risk is the Employee Scholar Program which pays the tuition of additional education for employees, gives them paid leave to finish their education, and then awards company stock for completion of the accredited programme.

17.3.17   Merger and Acquisitions Risk

UUU is constantly expanding operations by purchasing or merging with smaller companies in an effort to increase its competitiveness and market share. However, mergers and acquisitions have many risks such as firm integration, which can pose challenges for UUU. This can best be reduced by hiring advisers and a strong legal team.

Table 17.1 provides a summary of each corporate risk defined by its probability and impact and the appropriate response. Notice the majority of risks are reduced or managed instead of transferred to avoid unnecessary premiums. Figure 17.2 provides a visual summary of the probability impact distribution of the risks UUU faces.

17.4   STRATEGIC BUSINESS UNITS RISK REGISTER

Moving one step down the organisational structure, strategic business units also generate their own risks. Whilst some are linked to corporate risks, many are unique to the business unit or operating market. The

Table 17.1 Corporate risk register for UUU

Risk	Category	Response	Probability	Impact
Foreign exchange	Yellow	Transfer/Retain	Medium	Medium
Political/Country	Yellow	Reduce	Medium	Medium
Market performance	Yellow	Retain	Medium	Medium
Commodities	Red	Transfer/Retain	High	Medium
Interest rate	Green	Transfer/Retain	Low	Medium
Government contract	Red	Reduce	Medium	High
Legislative	Green	Retain	Low	Low
EH and Safety	Red	Reduce/Transfer	Medium	High
Information technology	Green	Reduce/Retain	Low	Medium
Leadership	Yellow	Retain	Low	High
Reputation/Quality control	Yellow	Reduced	Low	High
Compliance	Yellow	Retain	Low	Medium
Audit	Green	Transfer	Medium	Low
Legal	Yellow	Reduce	High	Low
Terrorism/Security	Green	Reduce	Low	Medium
Human capital	Red	Reduce	Medium	High
Merger and acquisition	Green	Reduce	Medium	Low

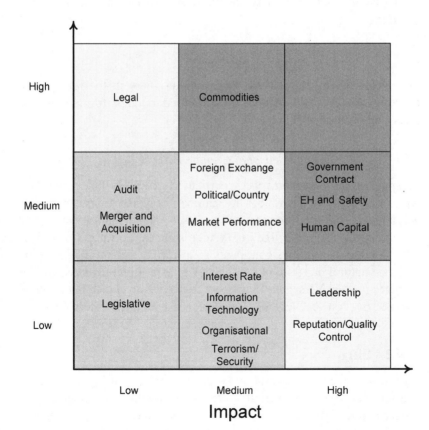

Impact

Figure 17.2 Probability impact grid for risks at corporate level

following section looks at some of the specific risks faced by each of the strategic business units.

17.4.1 Verspack

Verspack is an SBU of UUU and is a manufacturer and distributor of heating, ventilating and air conditioning (HVAC) systems. It also produces food service equipment and HVAC and refrigeration related controls for residential, commercial, industrial and transportation applications.

17.4.1.1 Residential Housing Construction Demand

A large portion of Verspack HVAC systems are installed in new houses which poses a market risk in the construction market. In 2005 a strong level of construction activity in North America contributed to high revenues.

17.4.1.2 Trucking Industry Performance

Verspack systems also have a large market share in the refrigerated trucking industry. Its demand is therefore tied to the performance of the truck and trailer business.

17.4.1.3 Weather and Seasonal Climate Patterns

Verspack systems perform well, particularly in areas that experience warm summers. For example, a hot summer for North American in 2005 was a favourable condition that had to offset a cooler summer in Europe which experienced a decline in HVAC resources. Fortunately, UUU is diversified across various continents so a warmer season in one region acts as a natural hedge to other areas. A general trend towards warmer climates favours Verspack, suggesting they have no choice but to retain the risk. In addition, weather derivatives are a high risk alternative.

17.4.2 Liftgro

Liftgro is engaged in elevator and escalator manufacturing, installation and services. It designs, manufactures, sells and installs a range of passenger and freight elevators for low, medium, and high speed applications, as well as a line of escalators and moving walkways.

17.4.2.1   International Urbanization Levels

As one of the most international of the strategic business units, Liftgro is heavily influenced by global urbanisation. Commercial industry construction is the main demand for its products and services. Particularly large markets like China or India are key players in driving demand.

17.4.2.2   Foreign Exchange/Foreign Currency

Foreign exchange risk exists because of Liftgro's global footprint. 2004 proved to be a favourable year for exchange as 6% of the 13% revenue growth was due to foreign currency translation.

17.4.3   Fisal

Fisal provides security and fire safety products and services. Its products and services are used by governments, financial institutions, architects, building owners and developers, security and fire consultants, and other end-users requiring a high level of security and fire protection for their businesses and residences.

17.4.3.1   Foreign Exchange/Foreign Currency

Fisal operates in a large number of countries and faces a similar foreign exchange risk as Liftgro.

17.4.3.2   Information Technology

Fisal faces the constant challenge of integration of its various security systems, particularly systems that may be outdated in emerging economies. Also, there is the risk of hacking into the security network.

17.4.4   Jaypower

Jaypower manufactures fuel cell systems for on-site, transportation, space and defence applications. In addition it produces combined cooling, heating, and power systems for commercial and industrial applications.

17.4.4.1   Government Contract Risk

Many of Jaypower's projects are procured through government contracts. If the government decides to allocate fewer resources toward efficient energy systems there would be a corresponding fall in Jaypower revenues.

17.4.4.2   Falling Energy Costs

One of the major incentives for companies to switch to Jaypower is its ability to lower energy costs associated with oil. If oil should become significantly cheaper, companies may have less incentive to shift to energy saving systems from Jaypower.

17.4.4.3   World Transportation Demand

Many of Jaypower's projects are associated with fuel cells for transportation systems.

17.4.5   Aerobustec

The three strategic business units of Engco, Airframe, and Copter are grouped together under the Aerobustec businesses because their risks are very similar. Their collective performance is tied directly to the economic conditions of the commercial aerospace and defence industries.

17.4.5.1   Airline Industry Performance

Corporate profits for the aerospace industries are linked to airline profits and global aircraft demand. Historical data on the airline industry suggests that the demand for flights is generally increasing.

17.4.5.2   Global Defence Spending

Many of the aircraft and systems manufactured by these industries are dependent on the level of global defence spending.

17.4.5.3   Defence Contract Risk

The largest market for helicopters is from the US Department of Defence. Although the demand for US defence spending, particularly for aviation acquisitions, has risen steadily, Copters can be constrained to demand by government contracts.

Table 17.2   Strategic business unit risk register

Risk	Category	Response	Probability	Impact
Verspack				
Climate change	Yellow	Reduce	Medium	Medium
Housing demand	Yellow	Reduce	Medium	Medium
Trucking industry	Green	Retain	Low	Low
Liftgro				
International urbanisation	Red	Retain	Medium	High
Foreign exchange	Yellow	Transfer/Retain	Medium	Medium
Fisal				
Foreign exchange	Yellow	Transfer/Retain	Medium	Medium
Information technology	Yellow	Retain	Low	High
Jaypower				
Government contract	Green	Retain	Low	Medium
Falling energy costs	Green	Retain	Low	Medium
World transport demand	Green	Retain	Low	Medium
Aerobustec				
Airline industry	Green	Retain	Low	Medium
Global defence spending	Yellow	Retain	Low	High
Defence contract	Red	Retain	Medium	High
Political risk	Green	Reduce	Low	Medium

17.4.5.4   Political Risk

There is the risk that changing regimes will place a lower priority on military imports.

Table 17.2 and Figure 17.3 provide a summary of the risks UUU faces at the strategic business unit level.

17.5   PROJECT LEVEL RISK REGISTER

Although there is a great diversity in projects that UUU undertakes with its seven strategic business units, there are common risks across the majority of its projects. Because there is no detailed information for these projects there will be fewer risks for this register as only the most common ones will be covered.

17.5.1   Cultural/Language Risk

As a global company that conducts business worldwide, projects must overcome cultural and language barriers. For instance, projects in the

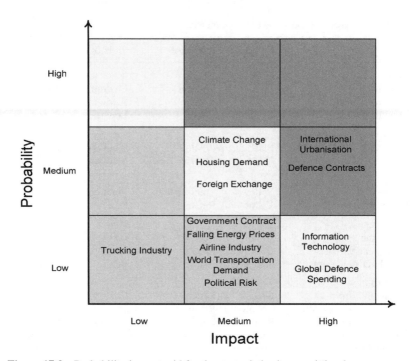

Figure 17.3   Probability impact grid for the strategic business unit level

Middle East will require prayer tents and some countries have limited working hours per week. It may also be difficult to recruit highly skilled foreign labour who can also speak the necessary project languages.

17.5.2   Purchasing Risk

For the aerospace projects, purchasing new commercial engines carries risk due to the size of investment required and some of the issues surrounding engine development. This can put a large strain on liquidity and cash flows. One means to transfer this risk to sell partner shares for some projects. By allowing other companies to finance portions of the commercial projects, UUU can reduce its initial costs by sacrificing a percentage of revenues from future revenues which are redistributed to partner companies.

17.5.3   Design Risk

Design risk, particularly for the aerospace projects, is very high due to the costs associated with the design process. Design is especially stringent when trying to meet government specifications and most contracts require submitting multiple design proposals. Some Federal Aviation Administration certifications take 3–5 years to attain making design an expensive investment. Also, mistakes in the early stages of the design process can lead to costly mistakes throughout the project's life cycle.

17.5.4   Cash Flow/Liquidity Risk

Many of UUU's commercial projects have cash flows which may not be positive for 7–10 years and profitability may not occur until 15–20 years. Additional warranty and engineering costs in the initial stages of product purchase also contribute to negative cash flows. Already narrow profit margins can be reduced by economic fluctuations, changing manufacturing costs, and demand for spare parts. For UUU's government contracts this risk is naturally reduced but remains high in private sector purchases.

17.5.5   Regulatory/Environmental Risk

UUU has numerous regulatory and environmental constraints which can be even more stringent for government contracts. Strong management and regulatory enforcement are needed to minimise these risks.

17.5.6   Maintenance Risk

Many of the products sold by UUU are covered by warranty and therefore UUU holds the majority of the maintenance risk. High upfront maintenance costs will add to a project's negative cash flows. However, maintenance risk can be positive if not covered under warranty as spare parts are one of the most profitable aspects of any UUU project.

17.5.7   Counter-party Risk

Many of the contracts UUU enters depend on the strength of its counter-party. For instance, contracts in countries that are politically weak or suffer high budget deficits may pose a counter-party risk. In addition,

Table 17.3 Project level risk register

Risk	Category	Response	Probability	Impact
Cultural/Language	Yellow	Reduce/Retain	Medium	Medium
Purchasing	Red	Transfer	High	High
Design	Red	Reduce/Retain	Medium	High
Cash flow/Liquidity	Red	Transfer/Retain	Medium	High
Regulatory/Environmental	Green	Retain	Low	Medium
Maintenance	Yellow	Retain	Medium	Medium
Counter-party	Yellow	Reduce	Low	High
Delay	Green	Retain	Low	Medium
Technology/Integration	Yellow	Reduce	Medium	Medium

cancellation of a particular programme or product by the government is a large threat to project profitability.

17.5.8   Delay Risk

Some of UUU's contracts have penalties associated with project delay. Delay risk can also have costs in the design phase of a product when there are competitors who can offer a better bid earlier than UUU.

17.5.9   Technology/System's Integration Risk

For projects lasting decades there is the risk of dealing with technological and engineering innovations which make earlier designs outdated. Integrating newer technology systems may be costly or impossible.

Table 17.3 and Figure 17.4 provides a summary of the risks UUU faces at the strategic business unit level.

17.6   RISK STATEMENT TO SHAREHOLDERS

After identifying the risks at all three levels of a corporation, it is necessary to summarise and transmit this information to shareholders and lenders. When purchasing stock, most shareholders look at the most recent annual report of a corporation as well as historical annual reports. This provides the best information on what risks a company faces and by looking at former reports it also acts as a condensed historical risk register. Thus, a short risk statement included in the annual report is acceptable for shareholders and the majority of lenders. However, lenders

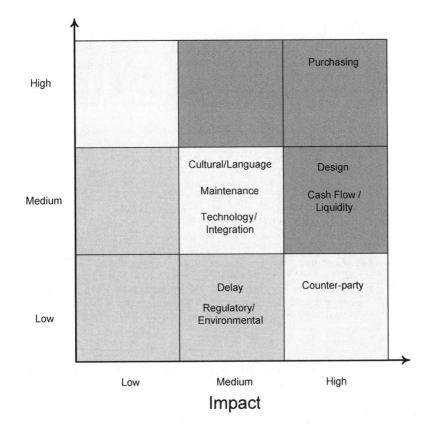

Figure 17.4   Probability impact grid for the project level

may be involved in lending for a specific risky project. In the event that UUU was borrowing for such a project it would need to provide a separate risk statement for that project which would include far more detailed information than shown here.

Thus, a typical risk statement to shareholders and most lenders could be presented as follows:

To UUU Shareholders,

UUU is a diversified company whose products include Verspack, Liftgro, Fisal, Jaypower and Aerobustec. As one of the world's largest privately held manufacturers, we seek to provide shareholders with the best information about their investment. The following is an assessment of the risks and opportunities in the global market we manage on a daily basis.

(a) **Corporate risks**

- Global economic conditions *UUUs operates on a worldwide basis. Thus, we are subject to general world economic conditions and demand for our projects. However, our global footprint acts as natural diversification among the different geographical regions. UUU also seeks to capture growth from emerging market economies like China, India, Russia, and Argentina. As a precautionary measure, UUU's investment in any particular country does not 'exceed 2.5% of consolidated shareowners' equity'.*

- Commodities risk *As one of the United States' largest manufacturers, we use large volumes of certain commodities which have volatile prices. The impact is significant; in 2005 the increase in commodity and energy costs decreased operating results by $120 million. However, we seek to manage some of the fluctuations in oil, copper, and titanium prices through the use of forward contracts. These will not be used in every instance as we strive for opportunities to capture commodity prices when they decline.*

- Human capital risk *UUUs product line calls for a highly skilled labour force, both domestic and abroad. As one of the largest employers in the world, we strive to maintain a hedge on recruiting the most talented employees. Our Employee Scholar Programme offers unmatched educational incentives, including full tuition, expenses, and paid study time for accredited degree programmes. We also reward graduates with stock compensation. In return we know our employees will respond with new abilities, knowledge, and motivation to continue to make UUU a leading global company.*

- Leadership risk *At UUU we pride ourselves on our executive and management leadership. We believe leadership is the most important factor in remaining a global competitor. However, decisions made by our leadership and management carry risk due to imperfect information and a continuously changing marketplace.*

- Government contract risk *At UUU a significant portion of our revenues, particularly in the aerospace businesses, are derived from government contracts. The contract process itself carries risk through the tendering and design phases, as well as uncertainty about the cancellation of certain programmes. However, our corporation is diversified in international governments as well as between public and private sector sales. In addition, rising global defence expenditures have raised revenues.*

- Foreign currency risk *Operating in a global market carries the risk of foreign currency translation. Fortunately, the last few years saw appreciation in particular currencies which added to UUU revenues. For example, in 2003 and 2004 there was a favourable impact from foreign currency of $0.11 and $0.14 per share. One of UUU's strengths in managing this risk is our natural geographic diversification. In the event there is a high level of foreign currency exposure we will use limited amounts of derivatives to mitigate the risk.*

(b) **Strategic business units**

- Information technology risk *Fisal relies on cutting-edge technology to develop products which meet the demand for security needs. In addition, other business units, particularly those with government contracts, face network infiltration from computer hackers. UUU makes every effort to ensure security of its information, particularly employee personal information like social security numbers and bank account information.*

- International urbanisation levels *Liftgro elevators and escalators rely on increasing urbanisation as the main demand for its products. Urbanisation is also a key source of revenues for Jaypower which develops alternative fuel options for public transportation systems.*
- Regional construction markets *Verspack heating and air conditioning systems are reliant on regional housing markets. For instance, slowing demand in the US housing market has been replaced by growth in European nobreak markets.*
- Airline industry performance *Many of UUU's products are sold to aerospace businesses. The recent rise in air transport demand has been favourable to UUU's performance.*

As a global leader, we see all these risks as opportunities for success. Confident in our leadership and employees, we expect continued growth for UUU throughout uncertain economic forecasts.

17.7 SUMMARY

Typical risks affecting each level can be addressed through a risk register. The detail of information provided in the above risk registers is relatively low compared with the case study in Chapter 16. The risk register shown in this case study reflects only the category or risk, response and the probability/impact of identified risks.

An amalgam of the information derived from these risk registers can be used to create a risk statement for shareholders on which they can determine their willingness to invest in the business based on the risks associated with each SBU and the characteristics of the project they may enter into.

The authors wish to thank Dr Anthony Merna and Mr Jacob Sheehan for allowing them to use this amended version of their paper.

References

Abell, D. (1980). *Defining the Business – The Strategic Point of Strategic Planning.* Prentice Hall, Englewood Cliffs, NJ.

Ackers, K. (2000) *ISO 9001:2000 (DIS),* Highgrade Resources Limited.

Alabastro, M.A., Beckmann, G., Gifford, G., Massey, A.P. and Wallace, W.A. (1995). The Use of Visual Modelling in the Design and Manufacturing Process for Advanced Composite Structures. *IEEE Transactions of Engineering Management,* Vol. 42, No. 3, pp. 233–242.

Al-Bahar, J.F. and Crandell, K.C. (1990). Strategic Risk Management Approach for Construction Projects. *ASCE Journal of Construction Engineering and Management,* Vol. 16, No. 3, September.

Al-Derham, N. (2005). The Effects of Quality Risks on Profitability in GCC Countries, Unpublished MSc Dissertation, School of MACE, University of Manchester,

Al-Khalifa, K (2000). Understanding the Cultural Constraints of TQM Implementation in Qatar Industries, Unpublished PhD thesis, University of Birmingham.

Allen, D. (1995). *Risk Management in Business.* Cambridge University Press, Cambridge.

Ambrose, B. (2005). Question Time. *Quality World,* Vol. 31, No. 1, pp. 48–50.

Andrews, K.A. (1998). The Strategist: The Concept of Corporate Strategy. *The Strategy Process,* 3rd Edition, Edited by Mintzberg, H. *et al.* Prentice Hall, Englewood Cliffs, NJ.

Ansell, J. and Wharton, F. (1995). *Risk: Analysis Assessment and Management,* John Wiley & Sons, Chichester.

Archibald, R.D. and Lichtenberg, S. (1992). Experiences Using Next Generation Management Practices. *Proceedings of the INTERNET World Congress on Project Management, Florence, Italy,* Vol. 1, pp. 83–97.

Ariani (2001). Country Risk in Infrastructure Finance. MSc Thesis, UMIST, Manchester.

Artto, K.A. (1997). *Fifteen Years of Risk Management Applications: Where are we going in managing risks?.* Edited by Kahkonen, K. and Artto, K.A. E&FN Spon, London, pp. 3–14.

Association française sur le gestion financière (AFG) (1998, 2001, 2004). *Recommandations sur le gouvernement d'entreprise.*

Baker, H. (2000). Fixing Problems. *Global Cosmetic Industry,* Vol. 164, No. 4, pp. 50–51.

Barjon, F. (2006). Introducing Elements of Risk Management and Risk Portfolio Management Systems to a Business, Can they Bring Value? Unpublished MBA dissertation, Manchester Business School, University of Manchester.

Barnes, M. (2007). Masters of Uncertainty. *Project*, Vol. 19, Issue 7, February 2007.

Bartlett, C.A. and Ghoshal, S. (1994). Changing the Role of Top Management: Beyond Strategy to Purpose. *Harvard Business Review,* November–December, pp. 79–88.

Basel Committee on Banking Supervision (2003). *Trends in Risk Integration and Aggregation from Basel Committee on Banking Supervision*, The Joint Forum.

Basel Committee on Banking Supervision (2004). *The New Basel Capital Accord.* Basel, Bank for International Settlements.

Bennett, R. (1996). *Corporate Strategy and Business Planning.* Pitman Publishing, London.

Benoit, P. (1996). Project Finance at the World Bank – An Overview of Policies and Instruments. *Technical Paper No. 312.* World Bank, Washington, DC.

Bernes, B. (1996). Managing Change: A Strategic Approach to Organisational Dynamics. *Strategic Management,* 2nd Edition, Ch. 5. FT Prentice Hall, Harlow.

Bessis, J. (2000). *Risk Management in Banking.* John Wiley & Sons, Chichester.

Birchall, J. and Morris, G. (1992). *Business Studies: What is Business?* Nelson, Cheltenham.

Blackburn, S. (1999). *Managing Risk and Achieving Turnbull Compliance.* ICAEW.

Blanden, R. (2002). What is Strategy? *Project,* Vol. 15, Issue 2.

Blank, S. (1980). *Assessing the Political Environment: An Emerging Function in International Companies, The Conference Board.* New York: Haggard.

Blythe, J. (1998). *Essentials of Marketing.* Pitman, London.

Borge, D. (2001). *The Book of Risk: Risk Taking.* John Wiley & Sons, Chichester.

Bouton, D. (2002). *Report Bouton: For a better corporate governance.* MEDEF.

Bower, D. and Merna, A. (2002). Finding the Optimal Contractual Arrangement for Projects on Process Job Cites. *Journal of Management in Engineering,* Vol. 18, No. 1, pp. 17–20.

Bowman, C. and Ash, D. (1987). *Strategic Management.* Macmillan, London.

Brealey, R. A. and Myers, S.C. (2000). *Principles of Corporate Finance,* 7th Edition. McGraw-Hill, New York.

British Standard (1996). *BS 8444: Risk management, Part 3 Guide to analysis of technological systems – application guide.* British Standards Institution, London.

Burnside, D. (2007). An investigation of risk management assessment tools and techniques and the application of Caspar software. Unpublished MSc dissertation, School of MACE, University of Manchester.

Bussey, L.E. (1978). *The Economic Analysis of Industrial Projects.* Prentice Hall, Englewood Cliffs, NJ.

Cadbury Report on Corporate Governance (1992). Prepared by Sir John Cadbury. Gee (Professional Publishing), London.

Central Computer and Telecommunication Agency (CCTA) (1994). *Guide to Programme Management.* The Stationery Office, London.

Chambers, I. and Wallace, D. (1993). *Collins Gem. Business Studies: Basic Facts.* Harper Collins, Glasgow.

Chapman, R. (1998). The Effectiveness of Working Group Risk Identification and Assessment Techniques. *International Journal of Project Management,* Vol. 16, No. 6, pp. 337, Surrey.

Chapman, C.B. and Ward, S.C. (1997). *Project Risk Management: Processes, Techniques and Insights.* John Wiley & Sons, Chichester.

Clarke, K. (1993). Survival Skills for a New Breed. *Management Today,* December, p. 5.

Cole, M. (2002). Measure of Success. *New Civil Engineer,* 14 March, p. 14.

Collins English Dictionary (1995). Harper Collins, Glasgow.

Collins, J.C. and Porras, J. (1996). Building Your Company's Vision. *Harvard Business Review,* September–October, pp. 65–77.

Conklin, D. and Tapp, L. (2000). The Creative Web. *Ivey Business Journal,* May.

Connaughton, J.N. and Green, S.D. (1996). *Value Management in Construction: A client's guide.* CIRIA, London.

Cooper, D. and Chapman, C. (1987). *Risk Analysis for Large Projects: Models, Methods and Cases.* John Wiley & Sons, Chichester.

Cooper, R.G., Edgett, S.J. and Klienschmidt, E.J. (1998). *Portfolio Management for New Products.* Perseus, New York.

Cornell, B. (1999). *The Equity Risk Premium: The Long-Run Future of the Stock Market.* John Wiley & Sons, Chichester.

Coyle, B. (2001). *Interest Rate Options.* Financial World Publishing, Canterbury.

Crosby, P. (1985). *Quality is Free.* McGraw-Hill Book Company.

Cuthbertson, K. and Nitzsche, D. (2001). *Financial Engineering: Derivatives and Risk Management.* John Wiley & Sons, Chichester.

Dale, B. and Plunkett, J. (1990). Managing Quality. *Philip Allan.*

Damodran, A. (1997). *Corporate Finance. Theory and Practice.* John Wiley & Sons, New York.

David, F.R. (1989). How Companies Define their Mission. *Long Range Planning,* Vol. 22, No. 1, pp. 90–97.

Davies, D. (2000). Holistic Risk Management. *Project Today,* pp. 10–11.

Dawson, P.J., Mawdesley, M.J. and Askew, W.H. (1995). A Risk Perspective Approach to Risk Management. *A Construction Organisation: First International Conference on Construction Project Management, Singapore.*

Deloitte and Touche, (2001). *Corporate Governance: 2001 Progress Report.* Deloitte & Touche.

Deming, W. (1986). *Out of Crisis.* Cambridge, MA: MIT Centre for Advanced Engineering.

Department of Trade and Industry (1996). *Protecting Business Information:* 1 *(Understanding the Risks)* and *11 (Keeping it Confidential).* DTI, London.

Derivatives and Risk Management in the Petroleum, Natural Gas, and Electricity Industries (2007). EIA. (date accessed 01.2007), http://www.eia.doe.gov/

Desta, A. (1985). Assessing Political Risk in Less Developed Countries. *Journal of Business Strategy,* Vol. 5, No. 4, pp. 40–53.

De Wit, B. and Meyer, R. (1994). *Strategy – Process, Content: Context, An International Perspective.* West, New York.

Diekmann, J.E., Sewester, E.F. and Taher, K. (1988). *Risk Management in Capital Projects.* The Construction Industry Institute. Austin, TX.

DiPiazza, S.A. Jr. (2002). *Enterprise Risk Management: Managing and Benefiting from Risk.* World Economic Forum.

Dobins, R. *et al.* (1994). *Portfolio Theory and Investment Management: An Introduction to Modern Portfolio Theory,* Blackwell Science, Oxford.

Dybvig, P.H. (1988). Distributional Analysis of Portfolio of Choice. *Journal of Business,* Vol. 61, Issue 3 (July), pp. 369–393.

Edosomwan, J. (1995). *Integrating Productivity and Quality Management,* 2nd Edition. Marcel Dekker Inc., Industrial Press Inc.

Elbing, C. (2000). Management of Large Projects in City Centres: A case study. MSc Dissertation, Weimar University.

Ellafi J. and Merna, T. (2005). *Investigating the Finance Strategies for Gas Projects in Developing Countries.* PhD thesis, Supervisor Merna, T., Faculty of Engineering and Physical Science, School of MACE, University of Manchester.

Elliott, L. and Atkinson, D. (2007). *Fantasy Island*. Constable, London.

Ellis, J. and Williams, D. (1995). *International Business Strategy – Strategy, Performance and Process*. Pitman, London.

Ellis, T.S., Jiang, J.J. and Klein, G. (2002). A Measure of Software Development Risk. *Project Management Journal*, Vol. 33, No. 3, pp. 30–41.

Eloff, J.H. *et al.* (1995). Information Security – the next decade, *11th International Conference on Information Security, Athens*

Elsey, M. and Hurst, P. (1996). *Projects Procured by Privately Financed Concession Contracts*. Hong Kong, Asia Law and Practice Ltd.

Energy Information Administration (2001). Financial Performance. September. Online: http://www.fedstats.gov/key_stats/EIAkey.html.

Enrick, N. (1985). *Quality, Reliability, and Process Improvement*, 8th Edition. Industrial Press Inc., New York.

Esty, B.C. (2004). *Modern Project Finance: A Case Book*. John Wiley & Sons, New York.

Europa (2005). European Coporate Governance Forum.

European Commission (2003). *Modernising Company Law and Enhancing Corporate Governance in the European Union: A Plan to Move Forward*.

European Corporate Governance Institute, (2006). *Modernising Company Law and Enhancing Corporate Governance*.

Fabozzi, F.J. (2002). *The Handbook of Financial Instruments*. John Wiley & Sons, New York.

Fabozzi, F.J. and Markowitz, H.M. (2002). *The Theory and Practice of Investment Management*. John Wiley & Sons, New York.

Fachtagung Projektmanagement (1998). *Bundesprojekte Deutsche Einheit*. Deutscher Verband Projektsteuerer, Berlin.

Falsey, T. A. (1989). *Corporate Philosophies & Mission Statements*. Quorum, New York.

Feigenbaum, A. (1983). *Total Quality Control*, 3rd Edition. McGraw-Hill Book Company.

Felton, R.F. and Watson, M. (2002). Getting Governance Right. *McKinsey Quarterly report*, issue number 4, McKinsey and Company.

Field, M. and Keller, J. (1999). *Project Management*. Thompson Business Press, London.

Financial Reporting Council (2005). *Review Endorses the Turnbull Guidance*. IIA, 2000, *Turnbull: An Opportunity for Internal Audit*.

Financial Times (2004). Loan deal paves way for liquid PDI market. FT Companies and Markets, 27 September.

Finkel, A.M. (1990). Confronting Uncertainty in Risk Management: A Guide for Decision-Makers. *Resources for the Future*. Center for Risk Management, Washington, DC.

Fischhoff, B., Lichenstein, S., Slovic, P., Derby, S. and Keeney, R. (1983). *Acceptable Risk*. Cambridge University Press, New York.

Flanagan, R. and Norman, G. (1993). *Risk Management and Construction*, Blackwell, Oxford.

Foster, C. (2002). Time is on the side of PPP as partnerships grows up. *Sunday Herald, Glasgow,* 21 July.

Frank, M. and Merna, T. (2003). Portfolio Analysis for a Bundle of Projects. *Journal of Structured and Project Finance,* Vol. 9, No. 3, Fall, pp. 80–87.

Fraser, B.W. (2003). Managing Risk Proactively. *Strategic Finance,* Vol. 84, No. 10. pp. 36–40.

Fraser, D.R., Gup, B.E. and Kolari, J.W. (1995). *Commercial Banking: The Management of Risk*. West, Minneapolis.

Freiesleben, J. (2004). Quality Problems and their Real Costs, *Quality Progress*, Vol. 37, No. 12, pp. 49–55.

French, D. and Saward, H. (1983). *A Dictionary of Management*. Pan, London.

Frosdick, S. (1997). The Techniques of Risk Analysis Are Insufficient in Themselves. *Disaster Prevention and Management*, Vol. 6, No. 3.

Galitz, L. (1995). *Financial Engineering: Tools and Techniques to Manage Financial Risks*. Pitman, London.

Ganas, M. (1997). Value-Based Feasibility Studies. MSc Dissertation, UMIST, Manchester.

Gareis, R. (1998). The New Project Management Paradigm. *14th World Congress on Project Management, Ljubljana, Slovenia*.

Garvin, D. (1987). Competing on the Eight Dimensions of Quality. *Harvard Business Review*, Vol. 65, No. 6, pp. 101–109.

Ghasemzadeh, F. and Archer, N.P. (2000). Portfolio Selection Through Decision Support. *Decision Support Systems*, Vol. 29, pp. 73–88.

Glen, J.D. (1993). How Firms in Developing Countries Manage Risk. *Discussion Paper No. 17*. International Finance Corporation (IFC), Washington, DC.

Goergen, M. (2003). *Why are the Levels of Controls so Different in German and UK Companies?* The University of Sheffield Management School, European Corporate Governance Institute finance working paper No. 07/2003.

Goodman, S.H. (1978). *Financing and Risk in Developed Countries*. Praeger, New York.

Goold, M. and Campbell, A. (1989). Good 'corporate parents' can see off 'unblunders'. *Financial Times*, Letter, 6 November.

Gorog, M. (1998). Pre-requisites and Tools for Strategy Orientated Project Management. *14th World Congress on Project Management, Ljubljana, Slovenia*.

Gratt, L.B. (1987). Risk Analysis or Risk Assessment: A proposal for consistent definitions. *Uncertainty in Risk Management, Risk Asses-sment, Risk Management and Decision Making*. Plenum Press, New York, pp. 241–249.

Gregory, G. (1997). Decision Analysis. Pitman, London.

Grigg, N. (2004). Food Stats. *Quality World*, Vol. 30, No. 12, pp. 34–39.

Gronroos, C. (1988). Service Quality: The Six Criteria of Good Perceived Service Quality. *Review of Business*, Vol. 9, pp. 10–13.

Grundy, T. (1998). Strategy Implementation and Project Management. *International Journal of Project Management*, Vol. 16, No. 1, pp. 43–50.

Grundy, T. (2000). Strategic Project Management and Strategy Behaviour. *International Journal of Project Management*, Vol. 18, No. 1. pp. 93–103.

Grupo Santander (2000). *Financial Risk Management – A Practical Approach for emerging markets*. Inter-American Development Bank.

Gummesson, E. (1988). Service Quality and Product Quality Combined, *Review of Business*, Vol. 9, pp. 14–19.

Gutmann, P. (1980). Assessing Country Risk. *NatWest Bank Quarterly Review*, May, pp. 58–68.

Haendel, D. (1979). *Foreign Investment and The Management of Political Risk*. Westview Press, Boulder, CO.

Hamphire, S. (2003). Satisfaction's What You Need, *Quality World*, Vol. 29, No. 5, pp. 10–13.

Handy, C. (1999). *Beyond Certainty: The changing worlds of organisation*. Harvard Business School Press, Boston, MA.

Harley, M. (1999). Integrated risk management – the complete guide to a new way of looking at risk and its management. Financial Times Information Management Report.

Harrison, B. (2005). Product Recall Risk is Becoming a Supplier Problem, *Business Insurance* magazine. http://www.aon.com/focus, date accessed 02/07/2005.

Harrow, J. (1997). Managing Risks and Delivering Quality Services: A Case Study Perspective. *International Journal of Public Sector Management*, Vol. 10, No. 5, pp. 331–352.

Haynes, M.E. (1990). *Project Management: From idea to implementation.* Kogan, London.

Heald, D. (2003). PFI accounting treatment and value for money. *Accounting, Audit and Accountability Journal,* Vol. 16.

Health and Safety Executive Guidance. Note GS23 (1993). Health and Safety Executive, UK.

Hefferman, S. (1986). *Sovereign Risk Analysis.* Unwin Hyman, London.

Hempel, G.H. and Simonson, D.G. (1999). *Bank Management – Text and Case.* John Wiley & Sons, Inc., USA.

Hertz, D.B. and Thomas, H. (1983). *Risk Analysis and its Applications.* John Wiley & Sons, Chichester.

Hertz, D. and Thomas, H. (1984). Practical Risk Analysis: An Approach through Case Histories. John Wiley & Sons, Chichester.

Hetland, P.W. (2003). Uncertainty Management. *Appraisal, Risk and Uncertainty,* Edited by Smith, N.J. Thomas Telford, London.

Higgins, R.C. (1995). *Analysis for Financial Management,* 4th Edition. Irwin, New York.

Hillson, D. (1998). Project Risk Management: Future Developments. *International Journal of Project and Business Risk Management,* Vol. 2, Issue 2, Summer.

Hillson, D. and Murray-Webster, R. (2006). Understanding Risk Attitude, Association of Project Management, *Yearbook* 2006/07

HM Treasury (2001). *Management of Risk, a Strategic Review.*

Houlden, B. (1990). *Understanding Company Strategy: An Introduction to Thinking and Acting Strategically.* Blackwell, Oxford.

Hugenholtz, K. (1992). Ethic, not efficiency first, decision makers will need new skills: project managers are the last to know. Project Management without Boundaries. Internet, Florence, Italy.

Hussain, A. (2005). Development of risk envelopes and testing for the formulated envelope on a case study. Unpublished MSc. University of Manchester.

Hussey, D.E. (1991). The corporate planning process. *Introducing corporate planning – guide to strategic management.* Butterworths, London.

Hwee, N.G. and Tiong, R.L.K. (2001). Model on Cash Flow Forecasting and Risk Analysis for Contracting Firms. *International Journal of Project Management,* Vol. 20, pp. 351–363.

ICE design and practice guide (1996). *Creating Value in Engineering.* Thomas Telford, London.

Inderfurth, K., Linder, G. and Rachaniotis, N. (2005). Lot Sizing in Production System with Rework and Product Deterioration. *International Journal of Production Research*, Vol. 43, No. 7, pp. 1355–1374.

Institute of Charted Accountants in England and Wales (ICAEW) (1999). *Internal Control: Guidance for Directors on the Combined Code.*

Institute of Internal Auditors (2005). *Response to Evidence Gathering Phase of Review of Turnbull Guidance on Internal Control.*

International Journal of Project and Business Risk Management (1998). Embedded Operational Risk Management and Key Competencies in the Modern Adaptive Organisation, Vol. 2, Issue 1, Spring.

Jaafari, A. (2001). Management of Risks, Uncertainties and Opportunities on Projects: Time for a fundamental shift. *International Journal of Project Management,* Vol. 19, pp. 89–101.

Jacob, M. (1997). Corporate Risk Management and the Use of Derivatives. MSc Thesis. UMIST, Manchester.

Jacobs, G. (2004). Think Before You Leap. *Quality World,* Vol. 30, No. 8, pp. 20–22.

Jacoby, J. and Jaccard, J. (1981). The Sources, Meaning and Validity of Consumer Complaint Behaviour: A Psychological Analysis, *Journal of Retailing,* Vol. 57, No. 3, pp. 4–22.

Jenkins, J.H. (2005). *Off-Balance-Sheet Financing to the Refinery Industry,* Jacobs Consultancy.

Jia, F. and Jobbling, P. (1998). Expenditure and Cash Flow Forecasting Using an Integrated Risk, Time and Cost Model. *International Journal of Project and Business Risk Management,* Vol. 2, Issue 4, Winter.

Jiang, J.J. and Klein, G. (2001). Software Project Risks and Development Focus. *Project Management Journal,* Vol. 32, No. 1, pp. 4–9.

Johnson, G. and Scholes, K. (1999). *Exploring Corporate Strategy,* 4th Edition. Prentice Hall Europe, Harlow.

Jong, Jian Yang (1995). The Re-engineering of Design Office – A case study of applying modelling techniques. MSc Thesis, UMIST, Manchester.

Juran, J. (1988). *Juran's Quality Control Handbook,* 4th Edition. McGraw-Hill.

Kahkonen, K. and Artto, K.A. (1997). *Managing Risks in Projects: Institutional risk management.* E&FN Spon, London.

Kaplan, L. and Gerrick, G. (1981). On the Quantitative Definition of Risk. *Risk Analysis.*

Kaplan, R.S. and Norton, D.P. (1996). *The Balanced Scorecard – Translating Strategy into Action.* Harvard Business School Press, Boston, MA.

Keasey, K., Thompson, S. and Wright, M. (1997). *Corporate Governance: Economic, Management and Financial Issues.* Oxford University Press, Oxford.

Kedar, B.Z. (1970). Again: Arabic Risq, Medieval Latin Riscum. *Studi Medievali.* Centro Italiano Di Studi Sull Alto Medioevo, Spoleto.

Kerzner, H. (2003). *Project Management: A Systems Approach to Planning, Scheduling, and Controlling.* John Wiley & Sons, Inc, Hoboken.

Khan, S. (2006). Intelligent Thinking. Project. Vol. 19, Issue 6, Dec/Jan 06/07.

Khu, S. (2002). An Investigation to Determine the Allocation of Financial Instruments Associated with the Risks Identified in Project Activities. PhD Thesis, UMIST, Manchester.

Kolluru, R., Bartelli, S., Pitblado, R. and Stricoff, S. (1996). *Risk Assessment and Management Handbook: For Environmental, Health and Safety Professionals.* McGraw-Hill, New York.

Kumburovic, A. (2004). Quality Management System and ISO Standards – Global Phenomenon of Today, Center for Entrepreneurship and Economic Development CEED, pp. 52–57.

Lamb, D. and Merna, A. (2004a). *A Guide to the Procurement of Privately Financed Projects.* Thomas Telford, London.

Lamb, D. and Merna, A. (2004b). Development and Maintenance of a Robust Public Sector Comparator. *Journal of Structured and Project Finance,* Vol. 10, No. 1, p. 162.

Lamprecht, J. (1993). Quality and Reliability – Implementing the ISO 9000 Series. Marcel Dekker Inc.

Lane, K. (1993). A Project Culture Permeates the TSB. *Project Manager Today,* February, pp. 24–25.

Langford, D. and Male, S. (2001). *Strategic Management in Construction.* Blackwell Science, Oxford.

Lawson, D. (2003). Is ISO your System. Quality World, Vol. 29, No. 9, pp. 34–36.

Leavy, B. (1984). Country Risk for Foreign Investment Decision. *Long Range Planning,* Vol. 17, No. 3, pp. 141–150.

Leftly, M. (2003). Big Three to Bid for PFI Hospital Bid. *Building Magazine,* May.

Leiringer, R. (2003). Technological Innovations in the Context of Public Private Partnership Projects. Doctoral Thesis, KTH Industrial Economics and Management, Stockholm.

Lester, R., Enrick, N. and Mottley, H. (1985). *Quality Control for Profit,* 2nd Edition, Margel Dekker Inc.

Lifson, M.W. and Shaifer, E.F. (1982). *Decision and Risk Analysis for Construction Management.* John Wiley & Sons, Chichester.

Lockitt, W.G. (2000). *Practical Project Management for Education and Training.* FEDA, London.

Logan, Twila Mae (2003). Combining Real Options and Decision Tree: An Integrated Approach for Project Investment Decisions and Risk Management. *Journal of Structured and Project Finance.* Vol. 9, No. 3, Fall.

London Stock Exchange (2002). Online: http://www.londonstockexchange. com.

Loose, P. (1990). *The Company Director: His functions, powers and duties,* 6th Edition. Jordan, Bristol.

LSF (2003). French Law No. 2003-706 *Loi de Sécurité Financière*, 1 August 2003.

Lynch, M. (2002). Implementing a Scrap Reduction Program. *Modern Machine Shop,* Vol. 74, No. 12, pp. 154–155.

MacCrimmon, K.R. and Wehrung, D.A. (1986). *Taking Risks.* Free Press, New York, pp. 36–37.

Mandelson, P. and Liddle, R. (1996). Can Britain survive? *Observer,* 2 August 1998.

March, J.G. and Shapira, Z. (1987). Managerial Perspectives on Risk and Risk Taking. *Management Science,* Vol. 33, pp. 1404–1418.

March, J.G. and Shapira, Z. (1992). Variable Risk Preferences and Focuses of Attention. *Psychological Review,* Vol. 99, No. 1, pp. 172–183.

Marshell, C. (2000). *Measuring and Managing Operational Risks in Financial Institutions: Tools, techniques and other resources.* John Wiley & Sons, Chichester.

Maylor, H. (1996). *Project Management: The nature and context of project management.* Pitman, London.

McConnell, P. (2004). Measuring Operational Risk Management Systems Under Basel II, Available at: http://www.continuitycentral.com/measuringORMsystems.pdf

McCoy, C.S. (1985). *Management of Values.* Ballinger, Cambridge.

McDowall, E. (2001). Bundling School PFI Contracts. *Facilities Management,* March, pp. 8–9.

McNamee, P.B. (1985). *Tools and Techniques for Strategic Management.* Pergamon Press, Oxford.

Merna, T. (2007). Quality Management Seminar Notes – Seminar 9. Management of Projects MSc Programme, University of Manchester.

Merna, A. and Dubey, R. (1998). *Financial Engineering in the Procurement of Projects.* Asia Law & Practice, Hong Kong.

Merna, A. and Khu, F.L.S. (2003). The Allocation of Financial Instruments to Project Activity Risks. *Journal of Project Finance,* Vol. 8, No. 4, pp. 21–33.

Merna, A. and Merna, T. (2004). Development of a Model for Risk Management at Corporate, Strategic Business and Project Levels. *Journal of Structured and Project Finance,* Vol. 10, No. 1, pp. 79–85.

Merna, A. and Njiru, C. (1998). *Financing and Managing Infrastructure Projects.* Asia Law & Practice, Hong Kong.

Merna, A. and Njiru, C. (2002). *Financing Infrastructure Projects.* Thomas Telford, London.

Merna, A. and Owen, G. (1998). *Understanding the Private Finance Initiative – The New Dynamics of Project Finance.* Asia Law & Practice, Hong Kong.

Merna, A. and Smith, N.J. (1996). *Projects Procured by Privately Financed Concession Contracts,* Vols. 1 and 2. Asia Law & Practice, Hong Kong.

Merna, A. and Smith, N.J. (1999). Privately financed infrastructure for the 21st century. *Proceedings of the Institution of Civil Engineers. Civil Engineering,* Vol. 132, November, pp. 166–173.

Merna, T. (2002). Risk Management at Corporate, Strategic Business and Project Level. MPhil Thesis, UMIST, Manchester.

Merna, T. (2003). Management and Corporate Risk. *Appraisal, Risk and Uncertainty,* Edited by Smith, N.J. Thomas Telford, London.

Merna, A. and Patel, M. (2000). Quality and the Management of Projects, Technical Paper, *Quality World,* Vol. 20, Issue 12, December.

Merna, T. and Young, R. (2005). Portfolio Analysis for a Bundle of Investments. BT Conference Paper, Manchester.

Merrett, A.J. and Sykes, A. (1983). *The finance and analysis of capital projects,* 2nd edition. Longman, London.

Meta Group (2002). The Business of Portfolio Management: Balancing Risk, Innovation and ROI. January, Stamford.

Meulbroek, L. (2002). *Integrated Risk Management for the Firm: A Senior Manager's Guide.* Harvard Business School Press, Boston, MA.

Mills, R. and Turner, R. (1995). Project for Shareholders' Value. *The Commercial Project Manager,* Edited by Turner, J.R. McGraw-Hill, New York.

Mintzberg, H. (1984). Who Should Control the Corporation? *California Management Review,* Vol. 27, Fall, pp. 90–115.

Mizuno, A. (1998). *Management for Quality Improvement – The 7 New QC Tools.* Productivity Press Inc.

Mokhiber, R. and Weissman, R. (2001). Corporate Manslaughter? Common Dreams News Center, 17th March.

Monbiot, G. (2000). *Captive State: The Corporate Takeover of Britain,* Pan, London.

Morris, P.W.G. and Hough, G. (1987). *The Anatomy of Major Projects.* John Wiley & Sons, Chichester.

Moulis, P. (1992). Is Hidden Rework Draining Company Profits? *Quality* Vol. 31, No. 5, pp. 15–19.

Mouvement des Entreprises de France (MEDEF) (2003). *Proposal for Internal Control Procedure.*

Moxley, P. (2003). Let's Talk about Risk, *Internal Audit and Business Risk Magazine.*

Munro, E. (2001). The world of project bundling: a dream or a nightmare? *PFI Intelligence Bulletin,* January.

Nagy, P.J. (1979). *Country Risk: Quantify and Monitor it.* Euromoney, London.

Nevitt, P.K. (1983). *Project Finance,* 4th Edition. Bank of America Financial Services, New York.

Newland, K.E. (1992). On behalf of the APM SIG for Risk Management Benefits of Risk Analysis and Management, Project, November.

Newland, K.E. (1997). Benefits of Project Risk Management to an Organisation. *International Journal of Project and Business Risk Management*, Vol. 1, Issue 1, Spring.

Norris, C. (1992). The Management of Risk in Engineering Projects. MPhil Dissertation, UMIST, Manchester.

Norris, C. *et al.* (2000). *Project Risk Analysis and Management. A Guide by the APM.* Association for Project Management, Norwich.

Norton, B.R. and McElligott, W.C. (1995). *Value Management in Construction.* Macmillan, London.

Oakland, J. and Porter, L. (1995). *Total Quality Management: Text with Cases.* Butterworth-Heinemann Ltd.

Office of Government Commerce (2002). OGC Guide on Certain Financing Issues in PFI Contracts. Private Finance Unit, 31 July, London.

Oldfield, A. and Ocock, M. (1999). 3rd Annual. *Risk Symposium Proceedings, Risk Assessment for Strategic Planning. Project Manager Today,* October, p. 358.

Ould, M.A. (1995). *Business Process – Modeling and analysis for re-engineering and improvement.* John Wiley & Sons, New York.

Oxford English Dictionary (1989). 2nd Edition. Clarendon Press, Oxford.

Parker, H. (1978). Letters to a New Chairman. *Director,* April–December, p. 265.

Parkinson, J.E. (1993). *Corporate Power and Responsibility.* Oxford University Press, Oxford.

Pavyer, E. (2005). SOX: A Foot in the Door. *Project,* Vol. 17, Issue 7, February.

Pearce, J.A. (1982). The Company Mission as a Strategic Tool. *Sloan Management Review,* Spring, pp. 15–24.

Peterson, R. and Wilson, W. (1985). Perceived Quality: How Consumers View Stores and Merchandise. Lexington Books.

PFI Fact Sheet (2003). Sheet 5: Bundling. Online: www.scotland.gov.uk/pfi/documents/fs5.pdf (April).

Pidgion, N.M.L., Hood, C., Jones, D., Turner, B. and Gibson, R. (1992). Risk: Analysis, Perception and Management. Report of a Royal Society Study Group, London.

Pinkley, R. and Northcroft, G.B. (1994). Conflict Frames of Reference: Implications for dispute processes and outcomes. *Academy of Management Journal,* Vol. 37, No. 1, pp. 193–205.

PMBOK (1996). *A Guide to the Project Management Body of Knowledge.* Project Management Institute (PMI), USA.

Pollio, G. (1999). *International Project Analysis and Financing.* Macmillan, London.

Porter, M.E. (1987). From Competitive Advantage to Corporate Strategy. *Harvard Business Review,* May/June, pp. 43–59.

Prahalad, C.K. and Hamel, G. (1998). The Core Competence of a Corporation: Strategy Formulation. *The Strategy Process,* 3rd Edition, Edited by Mintzberg, H. *et al.* Prentice Hall, Englewood Cliffs, NJ.

Pressinger, C. (2005). Project Portfolio Risk Management – Managing Business Risk Across a Full Portfolio of Strategic Change Programmes within Companies. Unpublished MSc dissertation, University of Manchester, Manchester.

Public Private Partnership-Initiative NRW (2003). Finanzministerium des Landes Nordrhein-Westfalen. Online: http://www.ppp.nrw.de.

Pye, A. (2001). Corporate Boards, Investors and their Relationships: Accounts of accountability and corporate governing in action. *Corporate Governance,* Vol. 19, No. 3 July.

Rafferty, J. (1994). *Risk Analysis in Project Management.* E&FN Spon, London.

Rahman, T. (1997). Property Portfolio Construction in the UK Property Market. MSc Dissertation, UMIST, Manchester.

Reichmann, P. (1999). Profile Business. *Sunday Times,* 7 March, Section 3, p. 6.

Reiss, G. (2000). Information Systems for Programme Management. *The Handbook of Project Management,* Edited by Lock, D. Gower, Aldershot.

Rescher, N. (1983). *Risk: A Philosophical Introduction to the Theory of Risk Evaluation and Management.* University Press of America, Lanham, MD.

Rowe, W.D. (1977). *An Anatomy of Risk.* John Wiley & Sons, New York.

Ruin, J. (2001). Managing Risk Ensures Quality, *New Straits Times* 2.

Ruster, J. (1996). Mitigating Commercial Risks in Project Finance. *Public Policy for the Private Sector, Note 69.* World Bank, Washington, DC.

Rutterford, J. and Carter, D. (1988). *Handbook of UK Corporate Finance.* Butterworths, London.

Sakanda-Kachale, C. (2007). Implementing an Integrated Control Framework at the AfDB, Weighing and Analysing the Importance of a Strong Control Environment in Operational Risk Management. Unpublished MBA Dissertation, University of Manchester.

Samaddar, S. and Heiko, L. (1993). Waste Elimination: the Common Denominator for Improving Operations, *Industrial Management,* Vol. 93, No. 8, pp. 13–19.

Sandvold, O. (1998). Programme Management: Added Value or Increased Overhead? *14th World Congress on Project Management, Ljubljana, Sloveria, 10–14 June.*

Sarbanes-Oxley Act. (2002). Combined Code, original document can be found on the site of the Financial Service Authority.

Sawacha, E. and Langford, D.A. (1984). Project Management and the Public Sector Client: Case studies. *Draft Paper CIB-W-65,* Bruneil University.

Sealy, T.S. (2001). *International Country Risk,* May, Vol. XXI, No. 5. The Political Risk Services (IBC USA) Group Inc., New York.

Sebastianelli, R. and Tamimi, N. (2002). How Product Quality Dimensions Relate to Defining Quality. *The International Journal of Quality and Reliability Management,* Vol. 19, No. 4, pp. 442–453.

Select Committee on Environment, Transport and Regional Affairs, (1999). Memorandum by the Centre for Corporate Accountability, *HSE 20.*

Sengupta, C. (2004). *Financial Modelling Using Excel and VBA.* John Wiley and Sons, Hoboken.

Silk, M., Tse, J. and Lui, R. (2002). Portfolio project financing: The Asian perspective. *Project Finance International,* July, London.

Simister, S.J. (1994). The Usage and Benefits of Project Risk Analysis and Management. *International Journal of Project Management,* Vol. 12, part 1.

Simon, P. *et al.* (1997). *Project Risk Analysis and Management Guide: PRAM.* APM, Norwich.

Sitkin, S.B. and Pablo, A.L. (1992). Re-conceptualising the determinants of risk behaviour. *Academy of Management Review,* Vol. 17, pp. 9–39.

Skoulaxenou, E. (1994). The Use of Risk Analysis in Project Appraisal. MSc Dissertation, UMIST, Manchester.

Slapper, G. (1999). *Blood in the Bank: Social and Legal Aspects of Death at Work.* Ashgate, Dartmouth.

Slovic, P. (1967). The Relative Influence of Probabilities and Payoffs upon Perceived Risk of a Gamble. *Psychometric Science,* pp. 223–224.

Smith, G. (2000). Too Many Types of Quality Problems: Categorizing Your Problems in Solution Relevant Ways. *Quality Progress,* Vol. 33, No.4, pp. 43–49.

Smith, J.E. (1975). *Cash Flow Management.* Woodhead-Faulkner, Cambridge.

Smith, N. (1995). *Engineering Project Management.* Blackwell Science, Oxford.

Smith, N.J. (1999). *Managing Risk in Construction Projects.* Blackwell Science, Oxford.

Smith, N.J. (2002). *Managing Risk in Construction Projects,* 2nd Edition. Blackwell, Oxford.

Smith, N.J., Merna, T. and Jobling, P. (2006). *Managing Risk in Construction Projects.* Blackwell Publishing, Oxford.

Smithson, C.W. (1998). *Managing Financial Risk: A guide to derivative products, financial engineering, and value maximization.* McGraw-Hill. New York.

Spackman, M. (2002). *Public-private partnerships: lessons from the British approach.* Economic Systems, London.

Spencer, A. (1983). *On the Edge of the Organisation: The role of the outside director.* John Wiley & Sons, New York.

Spielman, C. (2004). Basel II for Operational Risk and Sarbanes-Oxley (SOX): Do they Conflict? Available at: http://www.gtnews.com/article/5487.cfm

Sullivan, W.G., Wicks, E.M. and Luxhoj, J.T. (2003). *Engineering Economy,* 12th Edition. Pearson Education, Englewood Cliffs, NJ.

Sunday Times (2001). Brainstorming the Markets. Business Section, 23 September.

Tassoglou, S. (2006). An Investigation of the Qualitative and Quantitative Tools and Techniques for the Management of Quality Related Issues. Unpublished MSc dissertation, School of MACE, University of Manchester.

Taylor, B. and Hawkins, K. (1972). *A Handbook of Strategic Planning.* Longman, Harlow.

The Economist (1998). Finance and Economics: Meet the Risk Mongers: Risk Management Moves In-house. 18 July.

The Economist (2001). Risk New Dimension. 29 September.

Thompson, P.A. and Perry, J.G. (1992). Engineering Project Risks – A guide to project risk analysis and assessment. *SERC Project Report,* Vol. 15, No 1, London.

Thunell, L.H. (1977). *Political Risks in International Business: Investment and Behaviour of Multinational Corporations.* Praeger, New York.

Tinsley, R. (2000). *Advanced Structured Financing: Structured Risk.* Euromoney Books, London.

Toffler, A. (1985). *The Adaptive Corporation.* Gower, Aldershot.

Traynor, V.T. (1990). Project Risk Analysis. MSc Thesis. UMIST, Manchester.

Tricked, R.I. (1994). *International Corporate Governance: Text, Reading and Cases.* Prentice Hall, Singapore, p. 9.

Turley, L. (1990). Strategies for Reducing Perceptions of Quality Risk in Services. *The Journal of Service Marketing,* Vol. 4, No. 3, pp. 5–12.

Turnbull Report (1999). *Internal Control: Guide for Directors on the Combined Code.* Institute of Chartered Accountants, London, September.

Turner, J.R. (1994). Project Management: Future Development for the Short and Medium Term. *International Journal of Project Management,* Vol. 12, No. 1, pp. 3–4.

Turner, R. and Simister, J. (2000). *The Handbook of Project Management,* Edited by D. Lock. Gower, Aldershot.

Tversky, A. and Kahneman, D. (1974). Judgement Under Uncertainty: Heuristics and Biases. *Science,* pp. 1124–1131.

Vernon, J.D. (1981). *An Introduction to Risk Management in Property Development.* The Urban Land Institute, Washington, DC.

Verway, A. and Comninos, D. (2002). Management Services: Business Focused Project Management. *Journal of the Institute of Management Resources,* January, p. 305.

Vienot, M. (July 1999). *Rapport sur le Gouvernement d'Entreprise.* AFEP, MEDEF.

Wearne, S. and Wright, D. (1998). Organisational Risks of Joint Ventures, Consortia and Alliance Partnerships. *International Journal of Project and Business Risk Management*, Vol. 2, Issue 1, p. 137.

Werner, F.M. and Stoner, J.A.F. (2002). Mathematical Limitations of the IRR Technique. *Fundamentals of Financial Managing*. Academic Press, Corvallis, OR.

Wharton, F. (1992). *Risk: Analysis, assessment, and management*. John Wiley & Sons, Chichester.

Wightman, D. (1998). Justifying Risk Management. *International Journal of Project and Business Risk Management*, Vol. 2, Issue 1, Spring, pp. 37–44.

Winch, G.M. (2002). *Managing Construction Projects: An Information Processing Approach*. Blackwell, Oxford.

Witt, E. (1999). Commercial Risk in a Portfolio of Projects. MSc Thesis, UMIST, Manchester.

World Bank (2004). A Regulatory Perspective on Operational Risk. World Bank presentation, 20 May 2004.

Ye, Sun (2006). Risk Pricing for LCC Bank. Unpublished MBA Dissertation, University of Manchester.

Ye, S. and Tiong, R.L.K. (2000). NPV-at-Risk in Infrastructure Project Evaluation. *Journal of Construction Engineering and Management*, May/June, pp. 227–233.

Yoshimori, M. (1995). Whose Company is it? The Concept of the Corporation in Japan and in the West. *Long Range Planning*, Vol. 28, pp. 33–45.

Zahra, S.A. and Pearce, J.A. (1989). Board of Directors & Corporate Financial Performance: A Review and Integrative Model. *Journal of Management*, Vol. 15, pp. 291–334.

Zeithaml, V., Berry, L. and Parasuraman, A. (1988). Communication and Control Process in the Delivery of Service Quality. *Journal of Marketing*, Vol. 52, pp. 35–48

Ziegler, L., Harrison, I.R. and Nozewick, A. (1996). Anomalies in Prospect Theory: Risk Perception in Strategic Decision Behaviour. *International Seminar on Risk in Human Judgement and Decision Making, Leeds*.

Index

Index compiled by Terry Halliday